AIRCRAFT CARRIERS
of the World, 1914 to the Present
An Illustrated Encyclopedia

Preceding spread: By the end of the First World War the concept of the through-deck carrier had gained general acceptance and the major navies were all engaged in the design of such ships. More typical of carriers during the 1914-18 period were seaplanes stowed aft, housed in a hangar and deployed by crane, and bow take-off ramps. *Pegasus*, here launching a Beardmore W.B.III (a modified Sopwith Pup), shows both these features. (Fleet Air Arm Museum)

Below: A somewhat battered *Hermes* returns from her duties in the South Atlantic, 19 October 1982. Sea Harriers, Sea Kings and Wessexes line the flight deck; note, too, the landing craft, in drab camouflage, abaft the island. Ironically, the bow ramp made a reappearance in the late 1970s, albeit in a rather different form, to assist heavily laden STOVL aircraft get airborne. (Fleet Photographic Unit, HMS *Excellent*)

ROGER CHESNEAU

AIRCRAFT CARRIERS
of the World, 1914 to the Present
An Illustrated Encyclopedia

*To the memory of Norman Sharpen
– a special friend*

First Published in 1984 by Arms and Armour Press, Lionel Leventhal Limited.
New revised edition published 1992 by Arms and Armour Press, Wellington House, 125 Strand, London WC2R 0BB.

© Arms and Armour Press 1992.

This edition published 1998 by Brockhampton Press, a member of The Caxton Publishing Group
Reprint 2000

ISBN 1 86019 87 5 9

British Library Cataloguing in Publication Data:
Chesneau, Roger
Aircraft carriers of the world, 1914 to the present
1. Aircraft carriers – History I. Title
623.8'225'09 V874
ISBN 0-85368-636-X

Designed by David Gibbons. Edited by Michael Boxall. Ship line drawings by Ray Burt. Diagrams by A. A. Evans. Production: Beryl Gibbons and Tessa Rose. Typeset by Typesetters (Birmingham) Limited, Smethwick. Camerawork by Wyvern Typesetting Limited, Bristol.
Printed at APP Printing Pte Ltd

LIST OF BUILDERS

American American Shipbuilding Corp, Lorain, Ohio, USA

Ansaldo Ansaldo, Genoa, Italy

Armstrong Whitworth Sir W. G. Armstrong, Whitworth & Co, Newcastle-upon-Tyne, England

Asano Asano Shipbuilding Co, Tsurumi, Japan

Bazan EN Bazan, El Ferrol, Spain

Beardmore William Beardmore & Co Ltd, Dalmuir, Scotland

Bethlehem Bethlehem Steel Co, Quincy, Mass, USA

Blyth Blyth Shipbuilding & Dry Docks Co, Blyth, Northumberland, England

Blythswood Blythswood, Scotstoun, Scotland

Brest Arsenal de Brest, France

Burntisland Burntisland Shipping Co, Burntisland, Fifeshire, Scotland

Caledon Caledon Shipbuilding Co Ltd, Dundee, Scotland

Cammell Laird Cammell Laird & Co Ltd, Birkenhead, England

Ch de la Gironde Chantiers de la Gironde, Bordeaux, France

Ch de l'Atlantique Chantiers de l'Atlantique (Penhoët-Loire), France

Cockatoo Cockatoo Dockyard, Sydney, Australia

CRDA CRDA, Trieste, Italy

Denny William Denny & Bros Ltd, Dumbarton, Scotland

Deschimag Deschimag Werke AG, Bremen, Germany

Detroit Detroit Shipbuilding Corp, Wyandotte, Mich, USA

Deutschewerke Deutschewerke, Kiel, Germany

Devonport Devonport Dockyard, England

Duncan R. Duncan & Co Ltd, Port Glasgow, Scotland

Fairfield Fairfield Shipbuilding & Engineering Co Ltd, Govan, Glasgow, Scotland

F Ch de la Gironde Forges et Chantiers de la Gironde, Bordeaux, France

F Ch de la Med Forges et Chantiers de la Méditerranée, La Seyne, France

Federal Federal Shipbuilding & Dry Dock Co, Kearny, NJ, USA

Harima Harima Co, Harima, Japan

Harland & Wolff (Belfast) Harland & Wolff Ltd, Belfast, Northern Ireland

Harland & Wolff (Govan) Harland & Wolff Ltd, Govan, Glasgow, Scotland

Hawthorne Leslie R&W Hawthorne Leslie & Co Ltd, Hebburn-on-Tyne, England

Hitachi Hitachi Co, Innoshima, Japan

Howaldtswerke Howaldtswerke, Kiel, Germany

Ingalls Ingalls Shipbuilding Corp, Pascagoula, Miss, USA

John Brown John Brown & Co Ltd, Clydebank, Scotland

Kaiser Henry J. Kaiser Co Inc, Vancouver, Wash, USA

Kawasaki Kawasaki Co, Kobe, Japan

Kure Kure Navy Yard, Japan

Lithgow Lithgow, Port Glasgow, Scotland

Mare Island Mare Island Navy Yard, Vallejo, Ca, USA

Mitsubishi Mitsubishi Co, Nagasaki, Japan

Nederlandse Dok Netherlands Dock & Shipbuilding Co, Amsterdam, Netherlands

Newport News Newport News Shipbuilding & Dry Dock Co, Newport News, Va, USA

New York New York Navy Yard, New York, NY, USA

New York SB New York Shipbuilding Corp, Camden, NJ, USA

Nicolayev Nicolayev Dockyard, Russia

Nicolayev (S) Nicolayev (South) Dockyard, USSR

Norfolk Norfolk Navy Yard, Portsmouth, Va, USA

Osaka Osaka Iron Works, Osaka, Japan

Philadelphia Philadelphia Navy Yard, Philadelphia, Pa, USA

Puget Sound Puget Sound Navy Yard, Seattle, Wash, USA

Seattle-Tacoma Seattle-Tacoma Shipbuilding Corp, Seattle, Wash, USA*

Stephen Alexander Stephen & Sons Ltd, Govan, Glasgow, Scotland

Sun Sun Shipbuilding Corp, Chester, Pa, USA

Swan Hunter Swan, Hunter & Wigham Richardson Ltd, Wallsend-on-Tyne, England

Todd-Pacific Todd-Pacific Shipbuilding Corp, Seattle, Wash, USA

Vickers-Armstrong (Barrow) Vickers-Armstrong Ltd, Barrow-in-Furness, England

Vickers-Armstrong (Newcastle) Vickers-Armstrong Ltd, Newcastle-upon-Tyne, England

Vickers (Barrow) Vickers (Shipbuilding) Ltd, Barrow-in-Furness, England

Vulkan (Bremen) Bremer Vulkan, Bremen, Germany

Vulkan (Vegesack) Bremer Vulkan, Vegesack, Germany

Western Pipe Western Pipe & Steel Corp, San Francisco, Ca, USA

Workman Clark Workman Clark Ltd, Belfast, Northern Ireland

Wilton-Feyenoord Wilton-Feyenoord, Schiedam, Netherlands

Yokohama Yokohama Co, Yokohama, Japan

Yokohama Dock Yokohama Dock Co, Yokohama, Japan

Yokosuka Yokosuka Navy Yard, Japan

*Later became Todd-Pacific (qv)

Contents

Preface

This book represents an attempt to catalogue all the aircraft carriers that have seen service in the world's navies, together with the designs that, whilst not realised, have had a significant influence on the technical evolution of the type or on the design of subsequent vessels within a particular navy. With such broad terms of reference, some qualifications are naturally called for. Thus, for the purposes of this work, an aircraft carrier has been defined as a sea-going warship, the primary responsibility of which is the direct operation of heavier-than-air craft in an offensive or a defensive role and the provision for these aircraft of such facilities as are required for their sustained operation. Ships such as seaplane tenders, whose principal roles have generally been support and maintenance, have therefore been excluded, as have 'hybrid' carriers – for example, the battleship-carriers that served with the Japanese Navy during the Second World War, where the air element was subordinated to other naval considerations (in their case, heavy guns). Similarly, ships equipped with auxiliary take-off facilities, such as catapult-armed merchant (CAM) ships and, for that matter, modern cruisers and frigates, have been omitted.

The inclusion of so many individual vessels, several the sole representative of their class, has inevitably restricted discussion; however, in order to supply something other than a mere list of statistics, which can mean very little if taken in isolation, each class is provided with background information explaining why a particular design was adopted and why certain characteristics were highlighted. Brief career notes for each commissioned carrier, together with details of important modifications made and of its fate, are also given.

The data tables in each case relate to the carrier in question as originally completed, any in-service alterations being outlined in the accompanying notes. Where several ships in one class were completed to slightly different designs, for example the Japanese *Soryu*s and the US Improved *Forrestal*s, the data apply to the first completed ship in that class, deviations from these in subsequent vessels again being noted in the text. The statistics for classes or individual carriers not completed generally give information for the final design.

In the tables, it should be noted that flight-deck dimensions are approximate and relate to usable flight-deck area; for example, round-downs are not for these purposes included. Moreover, flight-deck width varies along the length of the carrier, most particularly where an angled deck is incorporated. 'Beam' is maximum waterline beam, or below-water maximum beam where bulges are fitted. The figures for aircraft complement give only a general picture of a carrier's aviation capacity: much would, of course, depend on aircraft type and whether a permanent deck park was employed – the wartime *Illustrious*, for example, had a nominal capacity of 36 machines, but in practice operated over fifty on many occasions. Crew complement figures combine that of the ship and that of the air group.

The main part of the book is prefaced by some introductory chapters in which the evolution of the carrier as a ship type has been traced, together with the development of those design features that differentiate the carrier from all other warships. In this context, particular emphasis has been given to early air operations, since these provided the foundations upon which modern carrier-borne aviation has been built. A historical survey of carrier building and wartime exploits has consciously been avoided; such information is readily available elsewhere. Thus it is hoped that the present work will complement, rather than attempt to repeat, what has already been published on the subject of aircraft carriers.

Compiling a book such as this has of course been a time-consuming task, and I owe my wife Joananne a debt of gratitude for her patience and support and her tolerance of many silent hours. In a more tangible sense, the book would have been very much the poorer – indeed, it could hardly have been completed – had it not been for the generous assistance of many friends and acquaintances. I am therefore very grateful to Ray Burt for his diligent work in producing the line drawings that appear throughout the following pages and for placing his impressive photograph collection at my disposal. Norman Friedman read through the US section of the book (and also lent many photographs), and David Lyon checked the British entries and also arranged for me to study official British documents at the National Maritime Museum; both offered sound advice and pointed to modifications in the text that needed to be incorporated, and I am grateful to them for their expert comment. Ray Rimell's assistance, especially his knowledge of early aviation, was sought and unhesitatingly given, whilst Antony Preston kindly clarified some perplexing points; both also lent valuable photographs from their collections. I am particularly grateful, too, to A. D. Baker III for the help he gave in obtaining photographs, to Len Lovell of the Fleet Air Arm Museum, Yeovilton, for his assistance with illustrations, and to Pierre Hervieux, who arranged for the provision of photographs both from his own library and from those of colleagues. Special mention must be made of Robert Carlisle of the US Navy Still

Photo Branch in Washington, whose sympathetic response to my appeal for assistance made nonsense of the fact that his resources were 4,000 miles away from the author's study. Norman Sherry, editor of *British Fleet News*. Shell Tankers (UK) Ltd, was most help in providing background details of British ex-tanker escort carrier conversions, together with numerous illustrations. Assistance, frequently in the form of photographs, was also kindy provided by Ted Barlow; British Aerospace; Leanett Browning of Newport News Shipbuilding; Barbara Burger of the US National Archives; Jean-Pierre Busson of the Service Historique de la Marine; Frank Collins; James W. Croslin of the Vought Corporation; Captain Antonio Flamigni of the Italian Navy; Capitaine de Frégate Gaucherand of the Marine Nationale; Captain M Gómez Diez-Miranda of the Spanish Navy; Charles R Haberlien and H. A. Vadnais Jr, of the US Naval Historical Center; John Halstead; Toshio Imachi; R. R. Mitchell of MacTaggart, Scott & Co Ltd; the Musée de la Marine, Paris; Commander F. C. van Oosten of the Ministerie van Defensie (Royal Netherlands Navy); Marilyn Phipps of the Boeing Company; Michael Piggot of the Australian War Memorial; John Roberts; Lieutenant-Commander A. W. Rowse of the Royal Canadian Navy; Chris Schildz of McDonnell Douglas; A Segura of Avions Marcel Dassault-Breguet Aviation; Eric Speakman of the Ministry of Defense (Navy); Ian Sturton; Lieutenant-Colonel M. F. Taylor of the Australian Department of Defence; Capitaine de Vaisseau Thireaut of the Service d'Information et de Relations Publiques des Armées, Ministère de la Defence; John Tilley; Vickers plc and Harry Woodman. I am of course also grateful to my publishers, in particular David Gibbons, for help both of an advisory and of a material nature. Any errors or oversights that occur in the following pages are, naturally my own responsibility.

Roger Chesneau, Bobbingworth, Essex, August 1983

UPDATED INFORMATION

It is almost eight years since the text for this book was first prepared, and in that time a number of important developments have come to pass. Not the least of these is the perceptible lessening of political tension between the world's two great military powers, the United States and the Soviet Union – a détente that in the eyes of many is so momentous as to proclaim the end of the 'Cold War'. Whether this optimism about future international relationships is justified only time will tell, but the Western governments with an interest in these matters appear to be so certain of future events that they have been cutting defence budgets with gusto. Thus, estimates of the future strengths of navies, including aircraft carriers, have been continually revised over the last few years, and building programmes, refit schedules and decommissioning dates have been thrown into some confusion. The information that follows is based on the best available data but the reader should be aware that the whole subject of defence expenditure is at the moment in a state of flux – at least that concerning Western Navies.

The one major conflict since 1983 has been the 1991 'Gulf War', in which US fleet carriers stationed both in the Persian Gulf and the Red Sea played a significant active role, their aircraft flying attack and fighter missions on a scale not seen since the days of the Vietnam War.

ARGENTINA

25 de Mayo

The ship, having seen very little in the way of flying operations since the end of the Falklands War, completed a major refit in 1988 and now operates as a fully capable aircraft carrier once again. There has been some speculation that her ancient steam turbine machinery may be replaced with diesel engines at some time during the 1990s.

BRAZIL

Minas Gerais

This carrier is now expected to be finally decommissioned in the early 1990s. There has been little information concerning a possible replacement carrier.

FRANCE

The PA88 vessels are now 'live' projects, as follows:

Ship	Builder	Laid down	Launched	Commissioned
Charles de Gaulle	Brest	April 1989	Mid-1992?	1996?
Clemenceau?	Brest?	1991-2?	?	?

Displacement: 34,000 tons / 36,000 tons.
Machinery: Two Type K15 nuclear reactors; 2 shafts.
Performance: 82,000shp; 28kts.

GREAT BRITAIN
CENTAUR CLASS
Hermes has been sold to India and renamed *Viraat* (qv).

INVINCIBLE CLASS
Ark Royal commissioned on 1 November 1985. *Invincible* underwent a major refit from 1986 in which her 'ski jump' was redesigned and had its angle increased to 12°, three Goalkeeper systems were added and her facilities were enlarged, enabling her to accommodate up to 21 aircraft. *Illustrious* was due to start a similar refit in 1991. All three ships are scheduled to be equipped with the Seawolf missile system.

INDIA
Vikrant

This ship underwent a major refit in 1987-89 to enable her to continue in service until about 1996 in which a 6° 'ski jump' was added to the bows and her catapults were removed. As a result she can now operate only STOVL aircraft and helicopters and her usual complement is 6 Sea Harriers and 9 Sea Kings.

Viraat (ex-Hermes)

Purchased from Great Britain in the spring of 1986 for a reported £50 million and, following a refit at Devonport, commissioned into the Indian Navy on 20 May 1989. It is thought that some Soviet CIWS have since been fitted. The aircraft complement is believed to remain at a nominal 6 Sea Harriers and 12 Sea Kings.

ITALY
Giuseppe Garibaldi

This carrier was commissioned on 9 August 1987. The fixed-wing aircraft complement is now expected to comprise radar-equipped AV-8B Harrier-Plus fighter-bombers. There has been some discussion about the possibility of a second, slightly larger carrier being built for the Italian Navy in the mid-1990s. It will, if built, replace the cruiser *Vittorio Veneto* and may be named *Giuseppe Mazzini*.

JAPAN
Since 1983 there has been much written about the possibility of the Japanese Navy acquiring light aircraft carriers similar in general design to those operated by Great Britain, Italy and Spain. However, no firm decision appears to have been taken yet to proceed with procurement.

SOVIET UNION
KIEV CLASS
The fourth ship of the class commissioned in January 1987 as *Baku*, not *Kharkov*, having been launched on 17 April 1982. She differs in major respects from her three predecessors, most notably in that she is equipped with 3-D planar radar. She has no torpedo tubes and her missile fit includes twelve SSMs and 24 SN-N-9s. Two 100mm guns are carried.

TIBILISI CLASS

Ship	Builder	Laid down	Launched	Commissioned
Tibilisi (ex-*Leonid Brezhnev*)	Nikolayev (S)	Jan 1983	5 Dec 1985	1991?
?	Nikolayev (S)	Dec 1985	10 Dec 1988	1993?

Displacement: 60,000 tons.
Length: 984ft / 300m (oa); 922ft / 281m (wl).
Beam: 239ft 6in / 73m (oa); 125ft / 38.1m (wl).
Draught: 36ft / 11m.
Machinery: Gas turbines.
Aircraft: 42.

The first Soviet carriers capable of operating fixed-wing CTOL combat aircraft, which will probably comprise 12 Su-27s; in addition, 12 Yak-41 VTOL aircraft and 15 to 18 Ka-27 helicopters may be embarked. The hangar dimensions are reportedly 610ft × 98ft × 25ft (186m × 30m × 7.6m).

SPAIN
Principe de Asturias

This ship commissioned on 30 May 1988. AV-8B Harrier aircraft are embarked.

UNITED STATES
The training carrier *Lexington* (AVT-16) is, after all, due to be replaced in service by *Coral Sea* (CV-43) – in 1992. *Theodore Roosevelt* (CVN-71) was launched on 27 October 1984 and entered service on 25 October 1986. Further carriers in this class are planned as follows (all building at Newport News):

Ship	Laid down	Launched	Commissioned
Abraham Lincoln (CVN-72)	3 Nov 1984	13 Feb 1988	1990
George Washington (CVN-73)	25 Aug 1986	1989	1992?
John C Stennis (CVN-74)	1991?	?	?
? (CVN-75)	1993?	?	?

Roger Chesneau 1992

Evolution of the Aircraft Carrier

At the beginning of the twentieth century, the advent of controlled flight began slowly to be perceived in its potential to enhance the capabilities of navies. The motive was, originally, exclusively intelligence. As battleship ranges increased, it became more and more problematic to estimate an enemy's position and, as importantly, to assess the accuracy of one's own shooting. At first, this was not so much a matter of mere physical distance *per se* as one of the extent to which intervening factors such as local sea state, relative wind direction (with its effect on smoke drift) and natural atmospheric visibility influenced range, not only battle range but also the range at which flag signals hoisted by units of detached scouting screens could be positively interpreted. A partial solution was observation from height, generally by means of spotters installed on masthead platforms ('spotting tops'), but later, and experimentally, by means of observation balloons and towed kites; the Royal Navy, for example, was evaluating such equipment from 1903.

Further impetus was provided by the growing efficacy of wireless transmission. For the first time, there seemed to be the opportunity for independent reconnaissance, both aloft and outside effective visual range on the surface. Nor would there be a delay in the reception of such information – 'real-time' long-distance intelligence was now attainable.

By the end of the first decade of the twentieth century, one promising line of development was the observation airship; however, in order to endow the craft with a useful speed and range, the weight of engines and fuel would require so large a volume of gas as to make it impracticably large and unwieldy for deployment on board ship. To be flexible, machines dispatched on intelligence-gathering missions, physically detached from the Fleet, would, in tactical situations, need to be carried on board, sent off from and, ideally, recoverable by the ships themselves: the integration of sea-borne offensive capability and land-based reconnaissance was too uncertain, other than in a strategic sense. Airships would, for sure, exercise the minds of naval planners in the years ahead, though not quite in this direction.

AIRCRAFT AT SEA

More might reasonably be expected of heavier-than-air craft. Far more compact than airships, they were, at least theoretically, capable of carriage on board ship. The problems, initial and long-term, would be associated with their safe launch and recovery.

One possibility was the equipping of aircraft with the means to take off from the sea: Henri Fabre accomplished such a take-off in March 1910, and a pontoon-equipped Avro Biplane successfully rose from the water at Barrow-in-Furness in November 1911. With sustained manned flight in heavier-than-air machines still in its infancy (the practicability of such flight having only been demonstrated in Great Britain two years previously), this was indeed a considerable achievement. Not only were weight penalties imposed upon the airframe by pilot and powerplant, but the aircraft had also to be capable of lifting the heavy float undercarriage and, furthermore, of overcoming the increased drag involved in travelling through the water. In some senses, however, the 'hydroaeroplane' was not the ideal fleet reconnaissance vehicle: for example, relatively placid waters such as those experienced by Commander Schwann at Barrow in November 1911 did not typify the kinds of conditions that could be anticipated by aircraft working at sea. Moreover, the preparation necessary for the launch of such machines would require the parent vessel to heave-to and perhaps manoeuvre, thereby laying herself open to enemy attack and, in effect, imposing a speed limit on any accompanying vessels.

The better solution, and the one that would prove the more delicate to fulfil, was spawned in the United States: the operation of aircraft directly from on board ship. Prompted by rumours of mail flights from German merchant ships, it was arranged that a platform be erected over the forecastle of the light cruiser *Birmingham*, and in November 1910 a successful take-off, albeit a somewhat damp one, was achieved by a US aviator, Eugene Ely, flying an early Curtiss Pusher. Similar demonstrations were to take place aboard battleships of the Royal Navy within a year or so, Lieutenant Samson giving demonstration flights from *Africa*, *Hibernia* and *London*.

In order to give these early shipboard aircraft the speed necessary to produce sufficient lift for take-off, a runway, generally downward-sloping, was fitted to the parent vessel; length dictated that this could only be installed over the forecastle deck. As a peacetime experiment this arrangement was acceptable, but in conditions of war it would render a fair percentage of the warship's main battery inoperable. Such launches were also strictly one-shot operations. Although flotation bags might be fitted to aircraft as an insurance (more for the benefit of the pilot than for the machine itself), aircraft recovery remained a seemingly intractable problem.

One objection at least had been partially overcome, however. Lieutenant R. Gregory, operating from HMS *Hibernia* in May 1912, showed that take-offs from moving warships were feasible. Indeed, one of the principles of successful flight was readily understood, that relative

Left: Another view of *Hibernia*, circa 1912; an S.27 sits atop the forecastle ramp and a Short T.5 is being hoisted. (Fleet Air Arm Museum)

Centre: Short Folder Seaplane No. 119, which served aboard *Hermes* in 1914. This type was one of the earliest carrier aircraft and pioneered techniques such as wing-folding and torpedo-dropping — and indeed strike operations, two such aircraft taking part in the abortive RNAS raid on Cuxhaven in December 1914. (Fleet Air Arm Museum)

Bottom: The first fleet carriers were very basic conversions of fast cross-Channel packets. These two photographs of *Engadine* show the extent of the modifications: canvas hangars forward and aft, a raised bridge and minor adjustments to the paint scheme. (Fleet Air Arm Museum)

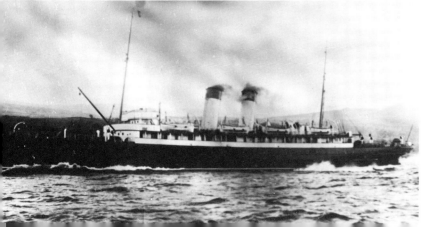

wind speed over an aircraft's wing, not the speed achieved by the machine alone, is what counts. Thus an aircraft requiring 45 knots in order to achieve lift need make 30 itself if being launched into a 15 knot breeze, but only 20 if launched in the same conditions from a ship making 10. Hence, it proved possible to operate early aircraft from quite short flight platforms. Late in the First World War, for example, aircraft were routinely dispatched from turret-top platforms little more than three times their overall length.

Even at this early date, the suitability of mechanical launching devices was being investigated. Such a device – an accelerator, or catapult – would confer several advantages. It would shorten the distance required for an aircraft to take off, thus reducing the 'inconvenience' caused by aircraft facilities to the fighting abilities of the parent ship, whose primary purpose was generally something quite different; it would enable an aircraft to achieve its take-off speed more quickly and, perhaps, more surely; moreover, if the launcher were capable of rotation, either on a turret, for example, or independently, ship course and speed (and hence fleet course and speed) might be maintained throughout launching operations. The US Navy was the early champion of the shipboard catapult, pioneered by Lieutenant Ellyson with a largely unsuccessful wire and counterweight system in 1911 and then with a satisfactory compressed-air mechanism the following year. These trials were conducted on land; shipboard deployment was carried out before the end of 1915.

The question of recovery was more vexing, at least where wheeled aircraft (landplanes) were required to return to the parent ship. Seaplane recovery was pioneered by Glenn Curtiss, who in February 1911 alighted near USS *Pennsylvania* and was hoisted back on board, and by Lieutenant Longmore, whose airbag-equipped Short S.27 landed on the River Medway in November of that year. This operation imposed penalties similar to those at launch, but at least it more or less guaranteed the safety of pilot and machine, given agreeable sea states. This was not the case with landplane recovery directly on board ship, despite the intrepid Ely's demonstration of its feasibility in January 1911. Flying-off decks did not make ideal landing-on platforms: they were too short for safety, even with a sandbag-and-wire arrester system such as that utilized by Ely; to a returning airman, their upward slope would be virtually impossible to negotiate; and the approach from ahead would, with the ship under way, invite disaster. The alternative, a separate landing deck as installed for Ely in January 1911, consumed far too much space and rendered too great a percentage of the ship's armament inoperable to be worthy of serious consideration, certainly for the time being.

Seaplane carriage was espoused by the Admiralty. Such modifications as were required to enable ships to undertake this role were minimal: a space to stow the aircraft on board ship and a derrick to hoist it from the water. The quarterdeck was the obvious location, being relatively free from spray and green seas and providing sufficient space, while not impeding the conning of the vessel. Additional protection for the ship's frail cargo could be afforded by the erection of canvas screens. Greater flexibility could be brought about by ramp-launching over the bows, the aircraft being mounted on recoverable wheeled trolleys.

Modifications to the aircraft, other than equipping them with floats, were also minimal, although one early naval concession was the provision of wing folding. Seaplanes, owing to the difficulty of getting them airborne from the water, required particularly large wing areas in order to generate sufficient lift, and thus presented special difficulties for stowage on board ship. With reconnaissance their declared role, aircraft otherwise differed little from contemporary landplanes, yet already their potential was being explored. For example, Samson had taken a dummy bomb aloft and ejected it in 1912; a 1½pdr gun was fixed to and successfully test-fired from an aircraft in 1914; and Longmore demonstrated the viability of the airborne torpedo that same year by launching a 14-inch missile from a Short Folder. The successful deployment of aircraft on board the protected cruiser *Hermes* during the Royal Navy's 1913 Naval Manoeuvres bore witness to the fact that virtually all the basic ingredients of carrier-borne operations and equipment, albeit in embryonic form, had been identified before the outbreak of the First World War.

THE PARENT SHIP

'The power of air-craft may be easily exaggerated. From the way in which some writers expound the subject it might be imagined that air-craft in the future must be omnipotent.' *The Naval Annual* of 1913 reflected opinions that were held by a large number of people at the time and, indeed, would persist for the next quarter-century or so in the minds of many. With 'Dreadnought Fever' at its peak, there was no doubt which type of warship was ultimately responsible for national security. Nevertheless, *Hermes* having shown such promise, the Royal Navy considered that the aircraft carrier was worthy of development. Within four years, by the time the First World War had been brought to a close, it had evolved into a purpose-designed naval vessel entirely recognizable in configuration by comparison with its present-day descendants.

Although reconnaissance in its varied forms provided the impetus to shipboard aircraft deployment, there was an inherent conflict in determining the type of ship best suited to foster it. The outbreak of war clearly militated against the wholesale conversion of front-line warships to carriers, nor was this seen as being necessary. *Hermes* was recommissioned as such, but she was the sole representative for some time. The alternative, a mercantile design, brought its own problems. Ideal characteristics called for high speed and high endurance to enable the ship to operate with the scouting screen, and high capacity to enable a reasonable complement of aircraft to be accommodated. Moreover, in order to expedite delivery to the Fleet, existing hulls would have to be adapted, and these would have to be surplus ships that were not vital to the war effort.

Demands for space were best met by bulk cargo vessels, whose holds were fairly readily adaptable to the carriage of aircraft. However, such ships tended to be slow, incapable of keeping station with the Fleet, and were therefore best suited to independent operations – spotting and reconnaissance during naval bombardment of land targets, for example. It was primarily for this reason that *Ark Royal* was dispatched to the Dardanelles in 1915, shortly after she commissioned. Other seaplane carriers of her generation (for example, the Japanese *Wakamiya*) performed similar duties in different theatres. The speed requirement was fulfilled by the acquisition of fast packets, which were given a limited conversion along the lines of *Hermes*, soon after the outbreak of war, enabling them to handle up to three seaplanes. These ships, however, did not entirely satisfy the need for high endurance, and this particular difficulty was first eased by the acquisition of longer-range steamers and ultimately by the purchase and modification of the liner *Campania*.

Ark Royal, although originally designed as a bulk carrier, at least had the advantage of being converted at a very early stage in her construction, and her internal arrangements were modified to suit the requirements of naval air operations on the high seas as they were then assessed. In fact, she was virtually a purpose-designed aircraft carrier, certainly to the extent of having her internal accommodation completely reorganised in the interests of her role. The packets, by contrast, were extempore affairs, little altered except for the addition of ramps, screens and handling arrangements.

As the First World War progressed and as carrier experience accumulated, the outline requirements of a purpose-built ship began to be filled in. A particular stimulant was provided by German Zeppelin airship activity over the North Sea, both in a fleet reconnaissance role and en route to the UK mainland on bombing missions. March 1916 proposals by Rear-Admiral Vaughn-Lee, Director of Air Services, envisaged floatplane-equipped vessels forming an early-warning/interception screen out from the British East Coast, but it quickly became apparent that once the airships were sighted seaplanes would not only lose time being readied for flight, they also lacked the speed (in particular the climb rate) necessary to close with the enemy craft. Bow ramps went some considerable way towards solving the first difficulty, but a successful interception demanded aircraft of higher performance − aircraft not encumbered with drag-

producing floats. Recovery would thus be out of the question − the best a pilot could hope for was a nearby landfall or, failing that, ditching close to friendly shipping if not the parent ship itself. Nevertheless, so seriously was the airship threat regarded that this was considered an acceptable penalty. A Bristol Scout flown off *Vindex* by Flight Sub-Lieutenant Towler in early November 1915 paved the way for further shipboard take-offs by wheeled aircraft, although in the event sea conditions and the unwillingness of commanders to commit themselves to single-mission sorties unless they had a good chance of success kept the number of such operations relatively small.

Only by extending flight-deck area dramatically could these problems be seriously tackled. An effective aircraft carrier would have to reproduce as exactly as its sea-going demands would permit the configuration of an on-shore airstrip, and this would require a very large hull. Fortunately the enormous forecastle of the high-speed large light cruiser *Furious* beckoned: the ship was fitting out in early 1917 and authority was quickly given for her to complete as an anti-Zeppelin carrier. However, she could not land-on her aircraft successfully, despite Squadron Commander E. H. Dunning's brave (and initially fruitful) efforts to demonstrate otherwise, and despite her subsequently receiving a half-length landing-on deck aft. By the end of 1917 it was clear that only a full-length flight deck would provide carriers with the flexibility for trouble-free air operations.

Far left: Landplanes based aboard carriers enjoyed significant performance advantages over seaplanes but, at first, could not be recovered satisfactorily; seaplanes *could* be recovered, however, and were capable of being launched from platforms using a wheeled trolley. Here a Fairey Campania departs *Furious*, 1917. (Fleet Air Arm Museum)

Centre top: Seaplane trolleys were halted at the end of the take-off deck by 'buffers', as seen in this view of *Furious*. Note, too, the longitudinal guide slot. (Fleet Air Arm Museum)

Below far left: The first flush-decked carrier was the Royal Navy's *Argus*, converted from a liner hull; her uptakes were led aft so that no structure encumbered the flight deck. Seaplanes could still be operated, recovered over the stern by lattice-type cranes. (Fleet Air Arm Museum)

Left: Even after the flight-deck island had become an accepted feature of carrier design, many pilots, especially in the USA, advocated a return to the fully-flushed deck. *Ranger* almost emerged as one, and her uptakes were led along each side of the flight deck (note the six rectangles, indicating the positions of the funnels) with this in mind. As completed, however, she had a small island fitted. (US Navy)

FLIGHT DECKS

Flight-deck design evolved with extreme rapidity during the course of the First World War. Most obviously, the dimensions were steadily enlarged in order to cope with the larger and heavier aircraft demanded by increased range and greater load-carrying capability: it was one thing to launch a 15cwt Sopwith Schneider from a flying-off deck, but quite another to dispatch a two-ton Fairey Campania. Indeed, foreshadowing the problems that would afflict carrier designers in the immediate post-Second World War years, the carrier *Campania* herself, very quickly after entering service, had to have her flight deck (a forecastle platform) virtually doubled in length to 200 feet to cope with the demand for larger and more capable aircraft. This reconstruction brought to light another taxing problem, that of organising a carrier's superstructure, in particular her funnels, in such a way that flight operations would not be impeded.

In many instances, some compensation for the restricted lengths of flying-off decks could still be received by sloping them downwards towards the bows; flying speed could be achieved by an aircraft somewhat more rapidly if the machine were assisted, as it were, by gravity. But there was a limit. A balance had to be struck between the need to achieve air speed and the risk of the aircraft not rising sufficiently after take-off. Moreover, different aircraft had different take-off characteristics, and an ideal angle for one might be unsuited to another – an important reason for the adoption

of downward-sloping ramps was that they raised the tails of aircraft in an approximation of the take-off attitude.

A further problem was the shape of the take-off surface. Hull form, with its fining towards the stem, was not conducive to the operation of aircraft inasmuch as the latter's acceleration tended to produce yaw (most markedly, of course, in adverse wind conditions) and its turning propeller produced torque, both of which resulted in a take-off run that was liable to follow something other than a straight line. A flight platform ideally needed to be considerably wider at the point of departure than it was at the beginning of the roll. Early ramps, recognizing this problem, were in effect a pair of shallow channels, though varying undercarriage tracks had difficulty countenancing the restrictions such a system imposed. Trolley-assisted take-offs by seaplanes were more predictable in character, which provided further encouragement for their use. This predictability was enhanced by arranging for a trailing arm fitted to the trolley's axle to engage a slot running along the fore-and-aft axis of the deck; stops at the extremity of the deck prevented the trolley from being carried over into the water.

For a time, owing to the shortage of carriers (as in later conflicts, there would never be enough) and the need to defeat the Zeppelin menace, there was no alternative to the short-run take-off. Light cruisers, for example, were hastily fitted with forecastle platforms and Grand Fleet battleships with turret-top platforms so that fighters could rise at short notice to intercept the airships. A somewhat bizarre scheme saw lighters towed to sea by destroyers, each with a Sopwith Camel aboard: the 'flight decks', only some 30 feet long, sloped downwards and broadened towards the 'bows'. These strange craft did claim some success – Lieutenant Culley shot down *L53* in August 1918.

Sanction for the fitting of carriers with landing-on decks (*Argus* was the first so designed, although *Furious* and *Vindictive* preceded her into service) was a recognition of the superiority of landplanes over floatplanes in the interceptor role, an appreciation of the risks and waste involved in having such aircraft ditch in the sea rather than recovering them intact, and a product of the availability for the first time of hulls of sufficient dimensions to make safe shipboard recovery practicable. Unforeseen were the difficulties pilots would experience in attempting to carry out landings. The same light weight and frailty necessary to enable small aircraft to respond to short, relatively low-speed flight-deck runs led to their instability in swirling air currents; such were encountered in trials aboard *Furious* after her second conversion (1918), where the amidships superstructure generated cross-currents and eddies, compounded by down draughts and smoke drift abaft the funnel. Still longer landing decks, with the touchdown point yet further removed from sources of turbulence, appeared to be the answer, but these were clearly out of the question for the moment: no hull longer than that of *Furious* was available. The alternative was a 'through' deck, a flight deck occupying the entire length of the ship. The forward portion might be used for launch and the after part for recovery. *Furious*, despite her evident shortcomings, was considered too valuable an asset to be spared for a further – and more protracted – period away from the Fleet, but *Argus*, building in 1917 with a similar fore-and-aft arrangement, could be modified and a new, purpose-built ship (*Hermes*) designed.

The fully flush deck brought problems of its own. In *Campania* smoke discharge arrangements had already needed to be rethought, as her lengthened take-off platform and the facilities necessary for manhandling her aircraft onto it began to impinge on the ship's superstructure, and her fore funnel had been split, port and starboard, to enable folded aircraft to pass between. A completely flush deck implied no visible superstructure at all. Alternative sites would have to be sought for navigating positions and the fixed battery, especially for the growing number of anti-aircraft guns that were being installed aboard warships and which called for clear sky arcs. Other fittings requiring lofty positions, such as lookout platforms and W/T aerials, would need to be reassessed. These rearrangements would probably not entail major re-engineering; but the re-siting of funnels, involved not only problems of turbulence but also of simple visibility owing to smoke drift.

In fact, the discharge of funnel gases has been a consistent aggravation in carrier design throughout the years, more especially concerning ships converted to carriers from other configurations. It has only finally been solved with the adoption of nuclear propulsion, which requires no such amenities. Externally, an early solution was to divert the boiler gases so that they ran via trunking to discharge towards the stern of the ship, ensuring that at least the major proportion of the flight deck would be unobscured while the vessel was making way. *Argus*, for example, incorporated this arrangement, and was even fitted with a system whereby port or starboard vents could be closed off for two minutes and the fumes accumulated in an enclosed bay, according to the wind conditions prevailing during landing operations. Other ships, such as the US *Langley* and the Japanese *Hosho*, had hinged stacks installed which could be lowered while the flight deck was being used, to minimise drift over the landing area. Heat adjacent to funnel trunking was also a problem, and some carriers carried water-spraying equipment in an effort to cool the temperature.

The navigation problem was initially overcome by fitting wing platforms to port and starboard of the forward flight deck, in some instances complemented by a retractable charthouse which, unfortunately, could not be used while aircraft were flying off. A return to some form of superstructure seemed inevitable, and preliminary studies for both the British *Eagle* and the US *Lexington*s envisaged radical solutions whereby slim superstructures would be mounted on either side of the flight deck, the through flight track running between. The question of turbulence was addressed, in particular, by Britain's National Physical Laboratory at Teddington, and in 1920 *Argus* was fitted experimentally with a dummy structure on the starboard side of her flight deck. This was of canvas but more or less aerodynamic in configuration, and it was found to be readily

negotiable by incoming aircraft. However, doubts persisted, as a June 1924 memo from the British Air Ministry to the Admiralty concerning the reconstruction of *Courageous* and *Glorious* showed:

'. . . Considered in relation to the question of whether an "island" structure should be situated on one side of the flying deck so as to form an escape for the funnel gases combined with a navigating position, it becomes apparent that the following are the chief points against such a proposal:—
(a) The wind is not always steady in direction and however well streamlined the structure may be, it must deflect and disturb the air flow . . .
(b) A structure at the side of the deck is a hindrance to the freedom of the aeroplane. It is a formidable obstacle to a hurried escape over the side of the ship, so as to avoid an accident in the case of emergency, eg sudden switching on of engine after an attempted landing . . .
(c) It lessens the width of the deck at an important part . . .
(d) The funnel gases coming from so forward a position must flow over the landing area of the deck, whereas if they are released at the stern, the disturbances they create are not harmful.
(e) The presence of an obstruction on one side of the deck will be adversely felt by landing aircraft when the ship is rolling . . .
'. . . The advantages of the vertical funnel structure . . . would appear to be as follows:—
(a) It is of considerable advantage from a naval constructional point of view.
(b) In comparing "Furious", "Glorious" and "Courageous", it allows the size of the hangars to be increased so that in a vertical funnel carrier, 44% more aircraft (large) can be carried than in a flush deck carrier.
(c) It is understood to allow of greater width at the after end of the hangars (approximately 50ft instead of 25ft).
(d) Some pilots have stated that it assists them in estimating their position and height.'

The 'naval constructional point of view' prevailed, but the decision to site the island on the starboard side rather than on the port was taken much earlier. This arrangement was to find favour in other navies, all of whose early carriers were designed with considerable British assistance, direct in the cases of the Japanese and French navies, perhaps less so in the case of the US Navy. In March 1918, the British Director of Naval Construction, Sir Eustace Tennyson d'Eyncourt, was quite convinced:

'The island [of *Eagle*] has been shown on the starboard side as this was the expressed view of Captain Nicholson and Wing Captain Clark Hall as aeroplanes prefer to come in from port and generally prefer turning to port. This point is raised as one would naturally expect the island on port side for navigating purposes. . . .

'The tripod mast is shown as it is considered that it will not disturb the air appreciably by eddymaking and from [an] aircraft point of view may be of great assistance in judging heights while it has considerable advantages for the fighting of the ship. If the wind is slightly off port bow the smoke, funnel gases and all eddies due to funnels and masts will be carried well clear of the ship.'

In retrospect it is difficult to determine whether a desire for the most convenient system of smoke discharge or the need for a high-sited navigating platform was the main reason why islands were adopted. However, it is quite clear that they could provide both and might even be advantageous to pilots as well.

There was less enthusiasm in other navies. The big Japanese fleet carrier *Kaga* of the 1920s, for example, featured long, trunked casings along her sides, discharging at the stern; the contemporary *Akagi* had funnels amidships and to starboard, but, in a prototype system that was to become characteristic of Japanese carriers, these were curved down in an arc to divert the fumes away from and below the flight deck. US aviators, through the Bureau of Aeronautics, also pressed for flush decks, and nearly got them on a number of occasions. The prewar *Ranger* (CV-4), for example, experienced some design problems with her uptakes, which eventually took the form of six hinged cylinders disposed three each to port and starboard to provide a completely unobstructed flight deck for air operations, but at the last moment she was given an island, primarily for gun control. The abortive postwar *United States* would have emerged as a fully flush-decked carrier because, in Admiral Mitscher's words, an island would result in 'a definite restriction on the size of aircraft which may be operated', which might in the 'foreseeable future' be 'unacceptable'. Aircraft dimensions did indeed on occasions influence the decision as to whether or not an island would be necessary, as in some of the early makeshift escort carriers of the Second World War where flight-deck size was so marginal that the island had to be dispensed with. However, within a matter of two or three years the absolute necessity for radar made some sort of above-deck structure inevitable, even though, as envisaged for *United States*, such systems might effectively be dispersed among escorting ships.

Below: A late 1920s photograph of *Furious*, showing typical British flight-deck features of the day: the aerodynamic forward edge to the main flight deck; the auxiliary flying-off deck below (with Fairey Flycatcher parked); wind-breaks; and, far right, cruciform forward lift. Note, too, the unobtrusive navigating position (starboard) and flying control (port) set into the flight deck; *Furious* was a flush-decked carrier at this time. Also visible is one of the carrier's 5.5in anti-surface guns, intended for defence against cruisers but fast becoming outdated. (Fleet Air Arm Museum)

FLIGHT-DECK GEOMETRY

Some consideration was also given to the aerodynamics of the flight decks themselves, especially in the Royal Navy. Wind tunnel tests at the National Physical Laboratory in 1921, for example, were particularly exhaustive, and resulted in rounded-off noses to upper flight decks, although it was reported to be 'rather curious that the conditions at the after end are somewhat improved by the flat deck instead of the round down, but as this round down is considered essential for the morale [?] point of view of pilots, it is thought that this should be adhered to'. Some carriers, for example the French *Béarn* and, initially, the British *Argus*, retained the downward slope of the forward flying-off deck after the manner of the early seaplane carriers.

Auxiliary flying-off decks were a concern of the 1920s in particular. With the launch of aircraft likely to require greater alacrity than their recovery (which could, it was presumed, be conducted in more leisurely fashion), two flying-off decks would enable twice the number of aircraft to be sent off in any given period. Alternatively, aircraft might thereby be simultaneously launched and recovered, an exercise fraught with hazard on a single flight deck. The early British fast fleet carriers showed such an arrangement, a secondary forecastle-mounted deck from which short-roll aircraft such as lightweight fleet fighters could be flown directly from the hangar. The Japanese went one better, literally: *Akagi*, for example, featured two such auxiliary platforms. But with the advent of faster and heavier aircraft, requiring longer take-off runs, these forecastle decks fell into disuse. They disappeared completely from the Japanese carriers when the latter were reconstructed during the 1930s; however, although *Courageous* and *Glorious* kept theirs, since 'the extension forward of the flying deck [ie, extending the flying deck] is absolutely out of the question either now or in the future as it would entail complete rebulging of the ship [in] order to obtain stability'.

Simultaneous launch and recovery has been an attractive theme throughout the decades of carrier development. Briefly embraced by the US Navy before the Second World War, when the *Yorktown*s and *Essex*es were given an athwartships launch capability permitting scout floatplanes to be dispatched from beneath the flight deck, it only became practicable with the general use of the shipboard catapult (see below) and the introduction of the angled deck postwar. The angled deck, characteristic of all modern carriers that operate conventional take-off and landing aircraft, was itself a radical response to the problems engendered by the advent of jet propulsion. The seductive attraction of high-speed flight unfortunately required high-speed landings and called for prodigious lengths of runway both for take-off and landing. Launch could be achieved satisfactorily by catapult, and ever-stronger arresting systems could handle the increased shocks they were required to absorb, but there remained, more starkly than before, the spectre of wreckage-strewn flight decks should incoming aircraft fail to 'hook' – the experiences of the Second World War left an indelible impression. Diverting landing aircraft away from the longitudinal axis of the flight deck provided them with a completely unobstructed touchdown path. Not only was the possibility of collision removed but the opportunity for making a second attempt at landing should the first prove problematic was also presented. Ironically, too, the apprehension expressed by many over the inclusion of an island in early carrier studies was finally extinguished, since the landing area now led incoming aircraft away from the superstructure and, in US carriers, the increased size of

flight decks made it virtually irrelevant, certainly as a source of turbulence.

Flight-deck geometry has remained essentially unchanged for large fleet carriers since the mid 1950s, but there have been other postwar design developments, some of which have proved to be of considerable importance. Angled decks effectively produced three distinct flight-deck zones: the angled landing area; the take-off area forward (later supplemented by the forward section of the landing area when that was not being used for recovery); and the 'triangle' between for deck parking. However, hull length still exerted a considerable influence on the dimensions of the landing deck which, with still faster and heavier aircraft entering service or in prospect, would need to be maximised. Clearly, the angle of the landing deck is limited by ship beam, in turn a product of efficient hull form and thus intimately dependent on hull length; if the angle is too great, the sponson necessary to support it on the port side becomes unmanageably large. Lessening the angle, but still aligning the landing strip well outboard of the centreline, at once gives extra length and, provided beam is adequate for the purpose, smaller overhang; the deck park is also preserved, although it becomes more nearly a rectangle in shape. This was the

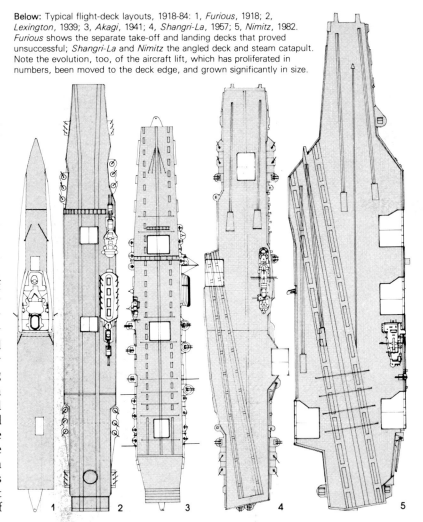

Below: Typical flight-deck layouts, 1918-84: 1, *Furious*, 1918; 2, *Lexington*, 1939; 3, *Akagi*, 1941; 4, *Shangri-La*, 1957; 5, *Nimitz*, 1982. *Furious* shows the separate take-off and landing decks that proved unsuccessful; *Shangri-La* and *Nimitz* the angled deck and steam catapult. Note the evolution, too, of the aircraft lift, which has proliferated in numbers, been moved to the deck edge, and grown significantly in size.

1   2   3   4   5

essence of the ill-fated 1960s British CVA-01 layout, where the angle of the landing deck was barely discernible yet still provided an unobstructed flight path parallel to a taxi-lane / deck-park area further to starboard (see page 147).

This carrier design showed a further development – an 'Alaskan highway', providing passage for aircraft movement *outboard* of the island and a progression from the narrow strip installed on some earlier British carriers for moving deck vehicles. The 'parallel deck' concept has re-emerged in modified form aboard the current *Invincible*-class light carriers, although these ships have no separate take-off and landing areas and deck parking is severely restricted. They do, however, show one other innovation: like the angled deck, the idea is startlingly simple. As a response to fixed-wing V / STOL operation, and in particular the requirement to launch Harrier aircraft with increased payloads, the forward end of the flight deck terminates in an upswept platform – the so-called 'ski-jump' – which enables the aircraft's wing to generate greater lift at the point of departure. The invention has been taken up by the Spanish and Indian navies, which operate similar machines, but it might be pointed out that the benefits of ramp launch are by no means confined to V / STOL air-

craft. Tests have shown that conventional aircraft can also lift heavier pay-loads over a given take-off run in this way (or, alternatively, take off over shorter distances with smaller loads) using the system, although rolls (unassisted take-off runs) are still considerably longer than equivalent cata-pult tracks, and these would presumably be precluded in ships fitted with ramps.

Below left: The arrival of the fast jet posed considerable problems of recovery, its high landing speeds increasing dramatically the possibility of overshooting and consequent collision with aircraft parked forward. The angled deck removed the dangers and, incidentally, reduced the number of arrester wires needed. This is *Bennington*, February 1960, with Furies sitting on her forward catapults and ranged along the deck edge, and Skyraiders parked aft. The large twin-engined aircraft are AJ Savages, former nuclear bombers now converted to tankers. (US Navy)

Below: Flight-deck capacity could be increased considerably by parking aircraft with their tailwheels mounted on outriggers. Here a Boeing F4B-4 demonstrates the technique. (The Boeing Company)

Bottom right: Perhaps the most important flight-deck innovation since the angled deck has been the so-called 'ski jump', an angled ramp at the forward end of the deck which enables STOL take-offs to be made by V/STOL aircraft carrying greater payloads than would otherwise be possible. A Sea Harrier is shown leaving *Invincible*, about 1980. (British Aerospace)

The other major influence on flight-deck physiognomy has been the helicopter. In a sense, this influence was at first negative, since axial-deck carriers, whose dimensions were too restricted to support the operation of fast, heavy jets or whose reconstruction for such operation was rejected on other grounds (for example, finance), could, and did, embark helicopters with minimal alteration. Purpose-built helicopter carriers have in general either been through-deck assault ships with an exclusively air capability (*Iwo Jima* class) or an air and surface capability (*Tarawa*), or else multi-role vessels with the after half of the hull given over to air operations (*Moskva* class, *Jeanne d'Arc*). In either case, the flight deck has been built to the maximum size permissible given the relative importance of other (frequently ASW) features: the larger the flight deck, the larger is the number of individual helicopters that can be spotted (ranged on deck) for take-off. Through-deck helicopter carriers obviously also have a fixed-wing V / STOL capability, as has been shown with *Invincible*.

Above: The advent of the helicopter has had a significant effect on warship design, and has been responsible for a return to small flight decks on mixed-capability (but primarily ASW) ships. Here, five Ka-25 ASW helicopters dot the flight deck in an autumn 1980 view of the Soviet *Moskva*. (US Navy)

Right: The Italian *Vittorio Veneto* is able to handle nine small helicopters but is generally classed as an ASW escort rather than a carrier. (Italian Navy)

Below: The other major role of the helicopter-carrying ship is amphibious assault; two classes of ships, their through flight decks giving them the appearance of aircraft carriers, have been purpose-built by the US Navy, following earlier operations with converted ex-fleet and escort carriers. This is *Okinawa*, August 1965, with CH-46s and a pair of VH-1s on board. (US Navy)

THE CATAPULT

One continuing theme of aircraft carrier evolution has been the effort always to provide the largest possible flight deck in order not only to enable the maximum number of aircraft to be operated from the ship but also to enable groups of machines to become airborne (or to be recovered) in the shortest possible time. Moreover, since the introduction of jet aircraft in particular, deck rolls have in general exceeded the lengths of available flight decks. Despite such expediences as flight-deck overhang (longitudinal, as with the British *Ark Royal* of the late 1930s, or lateral, as with current angled-deck carriers), flight-deck dimensions were ultimately governed by hull length and beam (with, in turn, the influence of such considerations as docking facilities, speed requirements and ship stability) instead of by aviation demands. Hence there was always a design conflict between the needs of the aircraft and the physical limits within which a carrier constructor was forced to work.

Ways had therefore to be sought of reconciling two opposing ideals, most obviously by providing the means to shorten the extent of deck needed to fly off and recover aircraft. One method of cutting take-off roll commonly adopted by first-generation carriers was, as we have seen, to slope the launching platform downwards in an attempt to increase forward acceleration, but more especially to arrange the aircraft in a tail-up flying attitude. Official documents relating to *Furious* for the year 1925 reveal that this particular posture was beneficial for other reasons:

'Trials with a Dart [the Fleet Air Arm's torpedo-bomber of the day] have shown that machines can be flown off using an overhead rail to support the tail, and it is considered that sufficient experience has been obtained to justify the installation of permanent fittings to enable other types of machines to be flown off from this position in rapid succession.' One of the most bizarre episodes involving attempts to shorten take-off runs occurred during the trials for launching fighters from towed lighters (see above), when the tail of an aircraft was reportedly raised by a supine RNAS officer, who placed his feet beneath the rear fuselage and pushed. Another expedient, for helping seaplanes, reportedly involved the greasing of flight decks, as undertaken with *Ark Royal* during the First World War.

The most successful and enduring means of shortening take-off rolls has, however, been the aircraft catapult, developed extremely quickly as a safe, effective means of launch by the US Navy during the First World War. With very few exceptions, all US carriers were fitted with such equipment; the Royal Navy did not adopt them wholesale until the Second World War, although it did adopt catapult devices ('accelerators') during the 1930s. Japan, in contrast, eschewed them altogether, although some interest was beginning to be shown during the second half of the Second World War. Catapults had an additional advantage: they could enable aircraft to be launched without the need for the carrier to generate wind over the deck – indeed, it was theoretically possible for aircraft to be sent away from a stationary ship – and this carried with it considerable tactical advantages.

Early catapults proved to be the descendants of the First World War seaplane trolleys, since it was seaplanes that they principally launched. The Royal Navy's accelerator was closely related to this: the equipment did not launch the aircraft *per se*, but drove a car atop of which the floatplane was perched. The first carrier catapults embarked by the US Fleet were compressed air types (developed from the experimental Santee Dock installation pioneered by Ellyson and fitted during the First World War aboard US cruisers and subsequently aboard battleships) and powder (explosive) types. *Langley*, the first US carrier, was originally fitted with one of the former, but powder catapults were never employed on board carriers although *Ranger* had one designed for her, as did the postwar *Forrestal*. The *Lexington*s were equipped with flywheel catapults, but hydraulic devices were adopted for all subsequent carriers up to *United States*. The Royal Navy did not consider catapults necessary, at least prior to the Second World War. Quick-release gear was adopted for First World War turret-top fighters, but this was more in the nature of a wire braking system controlled by the pilot which enabled the aircraft's engine to be

Left: Heavy seas have always been a major hazard to carrier operations, and the comparative robustness of postwar aircraft and the higher freeboards of modern carriers cannot guarantee immunity. The take-off ramp of *Ben-My-Chree* (top), of the First World War, is here contrasted with a Sea Hawk catapult launch aboard *Eagle* in 1957. (Fleet Air Arm Museum/By courtesy of John Halstead)

run up to full power before being unleashed – the effect to an observer was that of a catapult launch, but the device was considerably less complex.

Jet aircraft demanded something more potent than a hydraulic catapult. Their relatively slow acceleration and high minimum flying speeds required very much more power than hitherto could be supplied. The solution – adopted worldwide – was the steam (slotted cylinder) catapult, which took up less space and was lighter in relation to its power output. More and more, however, the steam catapult has come to have a considerable degree of influence over carrier size, and hence operating capacity and ultimately cost. In contrast to prewar carriers, aviation features now dominate. Tasked with a particular role, a carrier needs to embark a particular aircraft type, which has to be of a certain size (and, by implication, weight) to enable it to fulfil its function; these aircraft in turn require a catapult of the power, and hence length, needed to launch them, and there is thus a minimum portion of the flight deck that the catapult must occupy, quite apart from the size necessary for other activities. With 30-ton aircraft (for example, F-14s) unable to operate from tracks less than 250–300ft long, it is easy to see why 'super carriers' are the size they are; one might also be able to appreciate why Britain's CVA-01 could not be built below a certain size, and hence cost.

Below: A view of *Saratoga*, showing the early flywheel-type catapult fitted to the carrier. An F4B-4 departs; another wheels away to port. (The Boeing Company)

Far left: Shipboard aircraft have not of course been confined to specialised carriers: from the First World War until the present day some sort of air capability has been worked out for larger warships. Here, a Fairey IIIF spotter is readied for launch aboard a Royal Navy capital ship (almost certainly *Hood*), c.1931. (MacTaggart, Scott & Co. Ltd.)

Left: Cordite catapults in production for Royal Navy cruisers, about 1930. (MacTaggart, Scott & Co. Ltd.)

Right: Hydraulic catapults were unable to cope with the demands of heavy, high-performance jet aircraft; the steam catapult could, and it was universally adopted. Here an Étendard of the *Aéronavale* awaits launch, steam rising from the slot, aboard *Foch*. (ECP Armées)

LANDING SYSTEMS

The functional complement of a catapult is an arrester system, the means by which a landing aircraft's forward momentum can be artificially absorbed, thereby reducing the distance the machine has to cover after touchdown. Again, the requirement for such equipment was appreciated very early on, and modern systems do not differ in fundamental principles from that laid across *Pennsylvania*'s platform for Ely's epic landing of early 1911. Even with the low landing speeds of early carrier aircraft – the Sopwith Pup, for example, stalled at about 35 knots, not greatly in excess of *Furious*'s top speed – some form of ship-induced braking mechanism was considered essential. Initially, it took a variety of forms, from the spontaneity of grasping hands on wing toggles during Samson's bold venture, through sandbag-weighted cross-wires and hurdles to be respectively caught and knocked over by incoming aircraft, to the ultimate safety precaution, an athwartships rope barrier rigged at the far end of the landing area.

The Royal Navy was at first enthusiastic; as early as 1918 it was championing the cause, considering that 'The success of landing on a ship's deck at sea appears to depend very largely on the provision of efficient arresting devices, and it may become necessary to specially design the landing parts of the aeroplanes for ship use with this in view.' However, by 1925 opinion was rather more cautious: 'Throughout the [*Furious*] trials the arresting gear was hardly used and it appears to be

established that the improved airflow over the deck . . . together with the high speed of wind [over deck] render the use of arresting gear unnecessary, except possibly in very high natural winds or the rolling or pitching motion on the ship. Since, however, the arresting gear undoubtedly gives confidence to pilots, it is considered that arresting gear should not be omitted until some alternative such as power operated palisades at the deck edges has been fitted in lieu.'

The 'arresting gear' in use with the Royal Navy at this time consisted of a series of longitudinally aligned wires designed as much to keep an aircraft within the confines of the flight deck as to slow its progress. In early systems, at least, the wires were so arranged that they converged towards amidships, braking being achieved both by friction and by pressure as hooks attached to the undercarriage axles engaged the wires on touchdown. Before long, however, arrester wires had been abandoned completely and were only reintroduced after trials with friction-type gear (Mk I) in September 1931 and two further experimental sets, an improved friction-brake type (Mk II) and a hydraulic system (Mk III), 'with a view to installation in *Courageous* during the November–December 1932 refit'. The DNC commented in September 1932 that 'The fitting of arresting gear in Carriers should enable flying operations to be carried out in circumstances in which deck landing is not practicable without it, and it is understood may have advantages of a military character in reducing loss of position of the Carrier through the wind being in an unfavourable quarter

during flying on. There should also be a reduction in the wear and tear of machinery and a saving in fuel consumption. . . .' This was a reversal of the general opinion held six or seven years previously, when the gear was abandoned, partly because it caused damage to aircraft, and ran counter to thinking in the US and French navies, where such equipment was deemed essential. The lack of arresting gear on Royal Navy carriers (and, at first, Japanese carriers) was also a product of, and at the same time a reason for, contemporary landing procedures, where the only shipboard concession to the need to slow down incoming aircraft was the gradient of the flight deck, from the stern to amidships in the case of the Japanese and in the form of a ramp abaft the forward lift in the case of the British. Possibly because of the analogy with airfield practice (the RAF manned the Navy's aircraft during the 1920s and 1930s), the carrier flight deck was regarded purely as a runway: aircraft not concerned in landing or taking off had to be removed from the flight line as quickly as possible, just as on a land-based aerodrome. In a carrier, this meant they would be struck below.

With aircraft merely rolling forward to be parked at the bows after recovery, US carriers plainly could not tolerate the absence of some sort of arresting system. After some years of using both longitudinal and transverse wires, they relinquished the former in favour of the latter in about 1930. Early transverse gear was of the friction-brake type (the *Lexington*s were originally so fitted), but at just about the time that fore-and-aft wires were abandoned, more powerful, hydraulically-operated arresting gear was

Top far left: Early arrester systems consisted of a series of converging, longitudinal wires intended both to slow the landing aircraft and keep it in the centre of the deck. This photograph was taken aboard *Furious* at the end of the First World War, and also shows the ultimate safety barrier immediately abaft the funnel. (Fleet Air Arm Museum)

Below far left: A development of the longitudinal wire system incorporated a series of raised flaps which, falling flat as a landing aircraft made contact, absorbed some of its momentum. They were not entirely welcomed, because of their tendency to damage undercarriages. The aircraft seen is a Blackburn Dart and the carrier is *Eagle*, about 1923. (Fleet Air Arm Museum)

Top centre: The US Navy utilised longitudinal arrester wires for a time: these Boeing F2Bs aboard *Saratoga* in 1928 clearly show the hooks fitted along the axles for engaging the wires. (The Boeing Company)

Below centre: A Grumman Martlet catches the wire and veers to port aboard an *Illustrious*-class carrier. (MacTaggart, Scott & Co. Ltd.)

Above: Transverse wires were adopted prewar and continue in use today; indeed, a modern fleet carrier is incapable of operating her aircraft without them. Here a Westland Wyvern catches the wire aboard *Eagle*, about 1955. (British Aerospace)

introduced and has continued in service, modified to cope with heavier aircraft, up to the present day. One peculiarity of systems adopted for the *Yorktown*s and *Essex*es was the provision of additional wires forward. This was a response to a requirement for over-the-bows landings – these ships were able to steam astern at considerable speeds, which facilitated such practice. It would also be an asset in the event of the after half of the flight deck being damaged.

88mph **Short 184 Seaplane** 1915. British-built torpedo-bomber/
reconnaissance aircraft; one 260hp Sunbeam engine; range c.150
miles; 63ft 6¼in wingspan; 40ft 7½in long; 13ft 6in high; weight
5,363lb (loaded); one machine-gun plus one 14in torpedo or 520lb
bomb load.

176mph **Boeing F4B-1** 1929. US-built fighter; one 450hp P&W
R-1340-8 engine; range 370 miles; 30ft wingspan; 20ft 1in long;
9ft 4in high; weight 2,750lb (loaded); two machine-guns.

139mph **Fairey Swordfish I** 1934. British-built torpedo-spotter-
reconnaissance aircraft; one 690hp Bristol Pegasus engine; range
c.550 miles; 45ft 6in wingspan; 36ft 4in long; 12ft 10in high; weight
9,250lb (loaded); two machine-guns plus one 18in torpedo or up to
1,500lb bomb load.

235mph **Nakajima B5N2 (Kate)** 1940. Japanese-built torpedo-bomber;
one 1,000hp NK1B Sakae 11 engine; range 600 miles; 50ft 11in
wingspan; 33ft 9½in long; 12ft 1¾in high; weight 8,375lb (loaded);
one machine-gun plus one 1,600lb torpedo or 1,600lb bomb load.

240mph **Aichi D3A1 (Val)** 1940. Japanese-built dive-bomber; one
1,000hp Kinsei engine; range 915 miles; 47ft 2in wingspan;
33ft 5½in long; 12ft 7½in high; weight 8,047lb (loaded); three
machine-guns plus 810lb bomb load.

330mph **Mitsubishi A6M2 (Zero)** 1940. Japanese-built fighter; one
940hp NK1C Sakae 12 engine; range 1,160 miles; 39ft 4½in
wingspan; 29ft 8¾in long; 10ft high; weight 5,310lb (loaded); two
machine-guns; two 20mm cannon.

415mph **Vought F4U-1** 1942. US-built fighter; one 2,000hp P&W
R-2800-8 engine; range 1,015 miles; 41ft wingspan; 33ft 4in long;
16ft 1in high; weight 14,000lb (loaded); six machine-guns.

460mph **Hawker Sea Fury FB.11** 1948. British-built fighter-bomber;
one 2,480hp Bristol Centaurus 18 engine; range 700 miles;
38ft 4¾in wingspan; 34ft 8in long; 15ft 10½in high; weight 12,500lb
(loaded); four 20mm cannon plus twelve 60lb RP or two 1,000lb
bombs.

166mph **Sikorsky SH-3D Sea King** 1961. US-built
ASW/transport helicopter; two 1,400hp GE T58-GE-10
turboshafts; range 625 miles; rotor diameter 62ft;
72ft 8in long; 16ft 10in high; weight 21,000lb (loaded); up
to 840lb ordnance (torpedoes, depth charges, etc.)

720mph **British Aerospace Sea Harrier FRS.1** 1979. British-built fighter/strike/reconnaissance aircraft; one Rolls Royce
Pegasus 104 engine (output 21,500lbst); range c.800 miles; 47ft 7in wingspan; 25ft 3in long; 12ft 2in high; weight
26,200lb (loaded); two 30mm cannon plus AIM-9s, bombs or ASMs up to c.5,000lb total.

0   100mph   200mph   300mph   400mph   500mph   600mph   700mph

Carrier aircraft development

The explosive growth in carrier dimensions can be explained
partly by advances in the performance of aircraft. Particularly
in the years following the Second World War, the advent of
turbojet propulsion and relatively high stalling speeds have
necessitated longer take-off and landing runs. This diagram
illustrates the top speeds of twelve significant carrier-based
aircraft, plus one helicopter for comparison. It should,
however, be noted that maximum speeds and normal
operating speeds are quite different, especially with regard to
fast, afterburning jets. Similarly, roles and load-carrying
capabilities may compromise individual performances: for
example, attack aircraft have traditionally sacrificed
performance in the interests of weight (ie, ordnance, fuel and
crew capacity). Nevertheless, the trends are strikingly clear.
The coming of an effective STOVL aircraft has provided the
first real break in the rising graph of carrier dimensions; a
supersonic STOVL machine, however, remains merely a
project at the moment.

Note: the figure quoted for the range of each aircraft is for an aircraft
without external fuel tanks. The silhouettes are drawn to a constant
scale.

There still remained the problem of overshooting, which was only solved with the changeover to the angled landing deck. It was quite possible (and in wartime it frequently happened) that incoming aircraft would miss catching the wires altogether. The ultimate defence against such a contingency was the safety barrier. First installed on board First World War carriers (*Furious* and *Vindictive*), it took the form of a 'goal post' type structure rigged with ropework that stretched across the forward edge of the landing-on deck, with the objective not so much of stopping the aircraft – structures were generally too frail to offer much resistance – as of fouling its propeller. With the introduction of through-deck carriers, the barrier had to be capable of being lowered, although in the Royal Navy it was abandoned for a time, along with arrester gear. The nature of the US Navy's flight-deck operating procedure demanded that the safety barrier be mandatory in that service, taking the shape of a low-slung, steel tripwire or wires; again, it was expected that only an aircraft's propeller, or its undercarriage, would be caught. Jet aircraft once more demanded something novel, and the result was a nylon safety 'net' of vertically aligned strips, rather taller than the old steel barrier it replaced, that would absorb the entire oncoming airframe.

Arresting gear and safety barriers did not entirely solve the problem of wayward landings: for example, aircraft frequently 'bounced' both the transverse wires and the barrier, burying themselves in other machines parked forward, particularly if the carrier was pitching heavily. A further safety measure in early carriers was the provision of hinged palisades along the edges of the flight deck, which could be raised to act as a 'fence' to prevent aircraft from running over the side. High winds were an additional difficulty, particularly for lightly-built aircraft parked on deck, and retractable athwartships palisades were a general carrier feature, aided by lash-down of the aircraft themselves, to meet it.

Carrier approach could be monitored by a Deck Landing Control Officer (DLCO) stationed near the point of touchdown, who might indicate to an approaching pilot whether he was too high or too low for a successful 'hook' and, in the case of the US Navy LSO (Landing Signal Officer), when the pilot might cut his engine. As aircraft approaches grew faster, reaction time shrank and the DLCO found his task ever more taxing; he was ultimately replaced by a mechanical sight (initially a movable mirror, later a mirror and reflecting sight, now a system of gyro-stabilized lenses and coloured lights) that could be viewed at a considerable distance by an incoming pilot. The aviator could thus judge for himself whether his approach attitude was correct.

Top: The athwartships safety barrier was a very necessary feature of all axial-deck carriers with aircraft parked forward. A Firebrand is shown demonstrating its efficacy aboard *Eagle*. (Fleet Air Arm Museum)

Above: Further safety measures were necessary along flight-deck edges, in order to prevent aircraft from careering over the side after an imperfect landing. A Nimrod with a damaged undercarriage has stopped just short of the palisades in this 1930s photograph. (Royal Air Force, by courtesy of Ray Rimell)

690mph **Grumman F9F-6** 1952. US-built fighter; one P&W J48-P-8 engine (output 7,250lbst); range 1,000 miles; 36ft 5in wingspan; 41ft 7in long; 15ft high; weight 20,000lb (loaded); four 20mm cannon; 2,000lb ordnance.

1,485mph **McDonnell F-4B** 1961. US-built fighter/strike aircraft; two GE J79-GE-8B engines (output 34,000lbst with reheat); range 1,800 miles; 38ft 4¾in wingspan; 58ft 3¾in long; 16ft 3in high; weight 54,500lb (loaded); AIM-7, AIM-9 or bombs, etc., up to 16,000lb total.

Over 1,500mph **Grumman F-14A** 1972. US-built fighter; two P&W TF30-P-412A engines (output 41,800lbst with reheat); range c.1,500 miles; 64ft 1½in wingspan; 61ft 11¾in long; 16ft high; weight 72,000lb (loaded); AIM-7, AIM-9 or AIM-54 or bomb up to 14,500lb.

00mph   900mph   1,000mph   1,100mph   1,200mph   1,300mph   1,400mph   1,500mph

THE HANGAR

The effectiveness of a carrier is, of course, measured not only by naval concerns such as speed, range and seakeeping properties, nor only by her competence to launch and recover aircraft; a central issue is the number of aircraft she can handle – not necessarily total capacity, but rather the size of air group she can effectively operate.

Aircraft were, and still are to a large degree, more vulnerable than the ship herself: they are prone to damage from spray, subject to corrosion from funnel gases and salt water, and needful of servicing, fuelling, arming and repair. This was particularly the case with the frail structures taken to sea before and during the First World War. Very early on (in fact with the 1913 *Hermes* conversion) some sort of protection for aircraft carried on board ship was deemed essential, and canvas screens, frequently roofed, were erected around stowage areas. The introduction of wing folding facilitated the easing of aircraft into their protective shelters, and perhaps allowed additional machines to be taken aboard. By 1915 the canvas hangar, a considerable help but itself liable to damage during bad weather and heavy seas, was being replaced by a more rigid structure. Ensuring adequate protection for aircraft requiring a take-off run forced designers to abandon above-decks hangars however, since such superstructure could only be provided at the expense of flight-deck area, which itself was

Above: Sopwith Cuckoo torpedo-bombers stowed in *Argus*'s hangar; the machine at left is sitting on one of the carrier's two lifts. Hangar width was restricted by the ducted uptakes on each side. (Fleet Air Arm Museum)

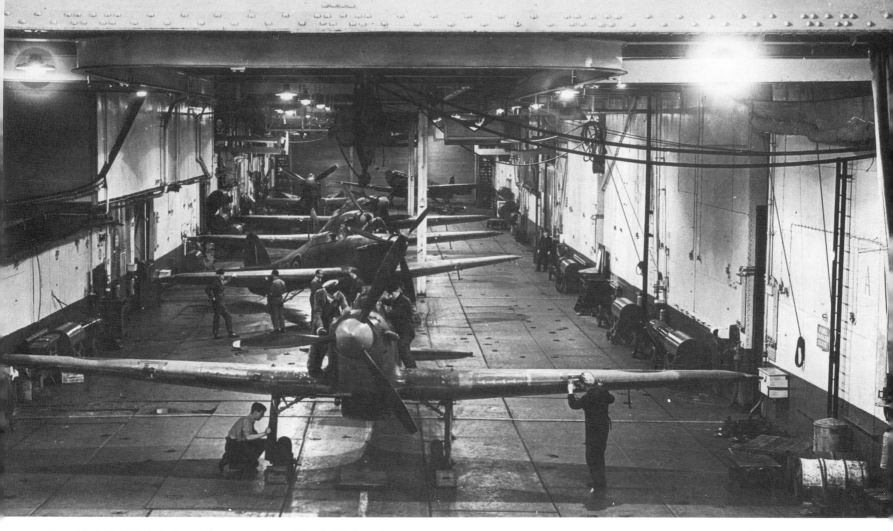

Above left: Boeing F3Bs in *Lexington*'s hangar, seen from a lift well; O2U observation floatplanes are stowed aft. The capaciousness of both this ship and her sister *Saratoga* was to prove valuable during the Second World War, when considerably larger naval aircraft were in service. (US Navy)

Above: Five Sea Hurricanes and a Seafire demonstrate the drawbacks of non-folding wings aboard *Argus* in 1942. (MacTaggart, Scott & Co. Ltd.)

proving difficult to embark in the acreage that seemed necessary. *Ark Royal* had demonstrated the feasibility of stowing aircraft in holds, and indeed of providing repair and maintenance facilities for them, the only impediments to completely clear take-off platforms being handling derricks or cranes and hatches to provide access.

The carrier's now characteristic hangar – the spacious vault immediately below the flight deck – developed from such early beginnings. However, this hangar, although evidently a place for aircraft not engaged in flying operations, has meant subtly different things to different navies at different times. Until the Second World War, for example, the Royal Navy looked upon it not only as a servicing, re-arming and repair bay but, more fundamentally, as a sort of refuge, capable of accommodating the entire complement of aircraft. For a navy operating for much of its time in heavy seas or within range of potentially hostile land-based bomber forces, this made a good deal of sense, but unfortun-

ately it restricted the total number of aircraft that could be carried, since, unlike US Navy practice, none could be embarked permanently on deck. Early British carriers did allow for disassembled aircraft to be accommodated, but again these tended to occupy hangar space; some US carriers had *additional* holds for such purposes, the *Lexington*s for example having the capacity for numerous extra aircraft thus stowed.

The 'enclosed box' concept was carried a stage further with the design of the Royal Navy's 1936 aircraft carrier (*Illustrious* class) which, as a result of pressure brought by Admiral Henderson, then Controller, was given a fully armoured hangar. The latter was thus accorded the status of a magazine, which of course in effect it was. The restrictions on aircraft capacity were alleviated to some degree by the adoption of two-storey hangars, both British and Japanese constructors resorting to this design feature; it enabled *Akagi*, for example, to be fitted with her two auxiliary flying-off decks. However, the double hangar also posed problems of top-weight, with the result that boiler trunking distribution, etc., had to be rethought; indirectly, it contributed to the loss of *Ark Royal* during the Second World War (page 103). US design practice contrasted sharply. Apart from *Saratoga* and *Lexington*, all US fleet carrier hangars were not only unarmoured but open along the sides, capable of being closed off by means of shutters but in no sense enclosed spaces. This arrangement was

Above left: One of *Clémenceau*'s lifts, with an F-8E(FN) Crusader on board. Note the catapult strops stowed along the side of the well. (ECP Armées)

Left: Inside the hangar of the French carrier *Foch*; a Super Étendard and an Alizé ASW aircraft can be seen. Note the partly closed fire screen in the background. (ECP Armées)

Above right: In early carriers, readying aircraft for take off was both time-consuming and tricky: strong winds could cause problems when hoisting aircraft out, and choppy seas would hinder, indeed perhaps prevent, take off. Thus pure seaplane carriers were not ideally suited to fleet work and tended to be employed in isolation. This photograph shows *Ark Royal* handling a Short Type 166 in early British insignia; note the crewman guiding the tail of the aircraft. (By courtesy of Ray Burt)

Right: Fairey Swordfish aboard a Second World War escort carrier. These seemingly anachronistic aircraft gained a legendary reputation for their wartime exploits in the Atlantic and did much to promote airborne ASW, a major concern of modern carriers. (MacTaggart, Scott & Co. Ltd.)

possible because the longitudinal strength member of the carrier hull was the hangar deck, in effect the hangar floor, the hangar itself being a lightweight structure built out on top of the hull but, along with the flight deck, contributing little to the ship's overall structural rigidity. It made for a comparatively small displacement on a large hull, and for a high aircraft capacity. Unfortunately, although it proved capable of venting off hangar-deck explosions and the consequent pressure waves (in contrast to Japanese experience, where hangars were enclosed but unprotected), the unarmoured flight deck associated with it was not bomb-resistant. As a result, US vessels were to be put out of action and, in the early stages of the Second World War, lost altogether.

The movement of aircraft from flight deck to hangar, or vice versa, requires specialised equipment unique to air-capable ships. At first it was achieved with a crane, together with manhandling, and it was merely an extension of the task involved in hoisting a seaplane out of the water to move it through a hatch into the hangar. However, such cranes consumed valuable flight-deck space, as indeed did the hatch covers necessary to keep out the weather. It was possible to dispense with the latter by providing a movable platform that would alternate between being part of the hangar floor and part of the flight deck as circumstances required — in other words, a lift or 'elevator'. Pioneered by Britain's First World War carriers *Pegasus* and *Nairana*, it quickly became an established feature of aircraft carrier design.

The siting of aircraft lifts aboard a carrier is partly dependent upon flight-deck operating procedure, but their positions — and to a degree their

dimensions − are also a function of ship construction. For example, since they serve the hangar, it is desirable to place them where they offer the least inconvenience below, which usually means that they should be placed at the ends. If lifts are necessary amidships, where perhaps the hangar is divided into two bays, they obviously need to be considerably narrower than the hangar deck in order to facilitate movement around the hangar wells should the platforms be raised. This requirement is echoed topside, where aircraft may need to be wheeled the length of the flight deck: US carriers had their flight decks widened out to port for just this reason. Moreover, they must be kept clear of catapults and arresting gear. In British carriers, any piercing of the flight deck might have consequences for the structural strength of the entire ship. Meanwhile, deck-edge lifts, generally adopted by postwar carriers, inevitably introduced questions concerning hangar enclosure, ingestion of water in heavy seas, passage through confined channels such as canal locks (very important for the US Navy in particular, whose warships regularly had to transit the Panama isthmus) and siting (for example, the flare of the bows would appear to exclude deck-edge lifts from that area). However, they might not encroach on hangar-deck space, nor for that matter on flight-deck space, advantages that in the end proved irresistible.

FUEL AND ORDNANCE

Internally, the aircraft carrier must also house other vital resources for her aircraft; for example, ordnance and aviation fuel. She must also have sufficient room to accommodate a much enlarged crew: pilots and other aircrew, flight-deck hands and mechanics. All demand space and, in the case of the volatile materials, specialized protection as well. A particular problem, eased with the arrival of jet carrier aircraft, was petrol stowage. The Royal Navy, mindful of the dangers of fire and explosion aboard ship, at first stowed aviation fuel in commercial two-gallon tins; refuelling was a slow process, but invariably a safe one. Experiments aboard *Furious* in 1918 with the Bywater (direct transfer) system were inconclusive, and the close of the First World War saw a return to individual containers, finally abandoned only two decades later as the tempo of flying operations increased. The US Navy fostered the use of fuel lines right from the start. Vapour could be dispersed readily enough via the unshuttered hangar sides or into open air on the flight deck, but there still remained the danger of explosion as bunkers were gradually emptied. The resultant spaces were therefore filled with compressed nitrogen, and the bunkers themselves were surrounded by sea water for protection. British carrier designers subsequently incorporated a sea water replacement system direct into the tanks, as well as surrounding them with sea water. Jet fuel is not nearly so hazardous (since it burns rather than explodes), and design constraints were certainly eased with the phasing out of piston-engined aircraft.

Aircraft ordnance is a separate question, although its explosive nature places it in the same category as inflammable fuel – bulk-stowed, one mishap might entail the loss of the entire ship. It is therefore accorded similar status to machinery and placed behind as much protection and as far away from the impact of enemy projectiles as possible, generally (at least until comparatively recently) behind armour. However, not only does aircraft ordnance have to be carefully protected from potential hazards, it also has to be physically moved around the ship in order to arm the aircraft. It requires lifts or hoists, trolleys and, in the case of heavy weapons, jacks in order to transfer it from the magazines to the machines that will take it aloft. It both affects displacement and consumes volume, to some extent competing with more traditional warship concerns such as boilers, machinery, oil fuel, crew accommodation and perhaps armour. More immediately, it may compete with aviation fuel and even hangar space, and ultimately it affects to some degree flight-deck area. Air

capability in wartime is certainly influenced by ordnance since, like aviation fuel, a given quantity will only enable so many aircraft to carry out so many sorties.

A carrier is thus a uniquely complex weapon system, embracing conventional naval construction dilemmas but further affected by a new set of problems concerning its primary role of operating aircraft. Its aircraft are its main armament – its instruments of offence and, to a considerable degree, defence; also its eyes and ears. Carriers represent nothing startlingly new in basic warship functions, but they extend the reach and firepower of the warship to a prodigious degree. They are uniquely flexible, and this flexibility has seen particular roles and tactics emphasized throughout their development history – to which we might now turn.

The Role of the Aircraft Carrier

EARLY DOCTRINES

From the time the first carrier went to sea in 1913, shipboard aviation developed with astonishing rapidity. Within five years – by the end of the First World War – it had established itself in the Royal Navy as an indispensable asset. However, early carriers were not an independent force: the big naval gun, aboard ships of the battle fleet, remained the dominant weapon, the final arbiter in disputes concerning sea power, and the carrier function was always subordinated to that doctrine. Shipboard aircraft, flying ahead of the battle line, would gather intelligence about the strength and disposition of the enemy, and would aid gunnery officers by 'spotting' the fall of their shot and advising correction by wireless.

To be sure, other opportunities for demonstrating the effectiveness of carrier air power presented themselves during the First World War: for example, as early as December 1914 the Cuxhaven raid by RNAS carrier-based seaplanes showed that it was possible to strike against land targets, even if that particular sortie was plagued with problems (mostly caused by the weather) and as a consequence its objectives were not realised. Later, carrier-based landplanes were on several occasions sent against enemy aircraft and airships, the success of a number of these missions showing that an interceptor function was not beyond the means of the sea-going RNAS, given the right aircraft. At the end of the war, moreover, a plan was being developed by Admiral Beatty (C-in-C, Grand Fleet) for attacking the High Seas Fleet with Cuckoo torpedo-bombers. Independent missions though these were, all were pursued with the aim of reducing the threat posed to the Royal Navy's battle fleet. The attack on Cuxhaven (and later the more successful Tondern raid) was undertaken in order to neutralise part of the German maritime reconnaissance force by destroying Zeppelins, while by sending torpedo aircraft against German battleships the type of decisive action sought, but not realized, at Jutland in 1916 could perhaps have been achieved by alternative methods.

By 1920, with the experience of the First World War digested, thoughts about the role of the carrier were beginning to crystallize further. In February of that year, for example, Wilmot Nicholson, the Controller, considered that the function of an aircraft carrier was to provide:

'(a) An aerial reconnaisance [sic] screen.
(b) Airplane [sic] spotting for capital ships.'

The attack role was not ignored, but there were problems. Nicholson continued:

'For the next few years it will not be possible to obtain sufficient carriers to develop any form of attack by aircraft, i.e. by torpedo or bomb, and it is considered that the two functions of aircraft as stated [above] are of primary importance.

'In the case of a carrier used for reconnaissance duties an efficient armament is of great importance and it is preferred to class this type as a "reconnaissance cruiser". Such a ship must work ahead of the fleet, generally ahead of the cruiser line and is therefore exposed to attack by hostile light cruisers. . . .

'Owing to the high speed this type should possess (at least 30 knots) in order to maintain position in the fleet when flying on and off, an effective torpedo armament might also be provided.

'Having flown off their aircraft, it is possible that with the speed at their command these ships would find themselves able to take up a position of torpedo advantage and attack the enemy's van. An ideal type exists in the Furious, Courageous and Glorious.

'These two latter ships could be converted . . .
'The Hawkins class of cruiser is also worthy of consideration . . .'

The priorities were again clearly stated in 1921 by the DNC: *Furious* was being redesigned 'to carry Artillery Observation Machines for two Divisions of Battle Cruisers, and also as many Torpedo Machines and Fighters as possible', 'artillery observation' implying a general tactical reconnaissance role as well.

This policy – reconnaissance first and strike second – dominated Fleet Air Arm tactics for two decades, and was to have important consequences. It has often been criticised for an excessive emphasis on battle-line spotting and reconnaissance rather than on anti-carrier tactics (as practised by the US and Japanese navies), but it should be remembered that the policy was formulated at a time when the British battle fleet was by a large margin numerically superior to that of any potential enemy (which included, at that time, the United States) and when potentially hostile carriers simply did not exist, except on paper. Moreover, US and Japanese carrier roles also emphasized integration with the battle fleet at first, and it was not until the early 1930s – two-thirds of the way through the inter-war period – that the anti-carrier function came to dominate.

Clearly, it would not be long before carriers were brought into service by other major navies. Prior to a fleet action, circumstances would probably arise in which opposing carrier aircraft made contact, perhaps before surface scouting screens were within sight of each other. The

Right: The role of the carrier was first seen as supporting the battle fleet, providing reconnaissance, spotting and attack functions against the enemy fleet. Here *Langley* trails US capital ships, June 1927. (US National Archives)

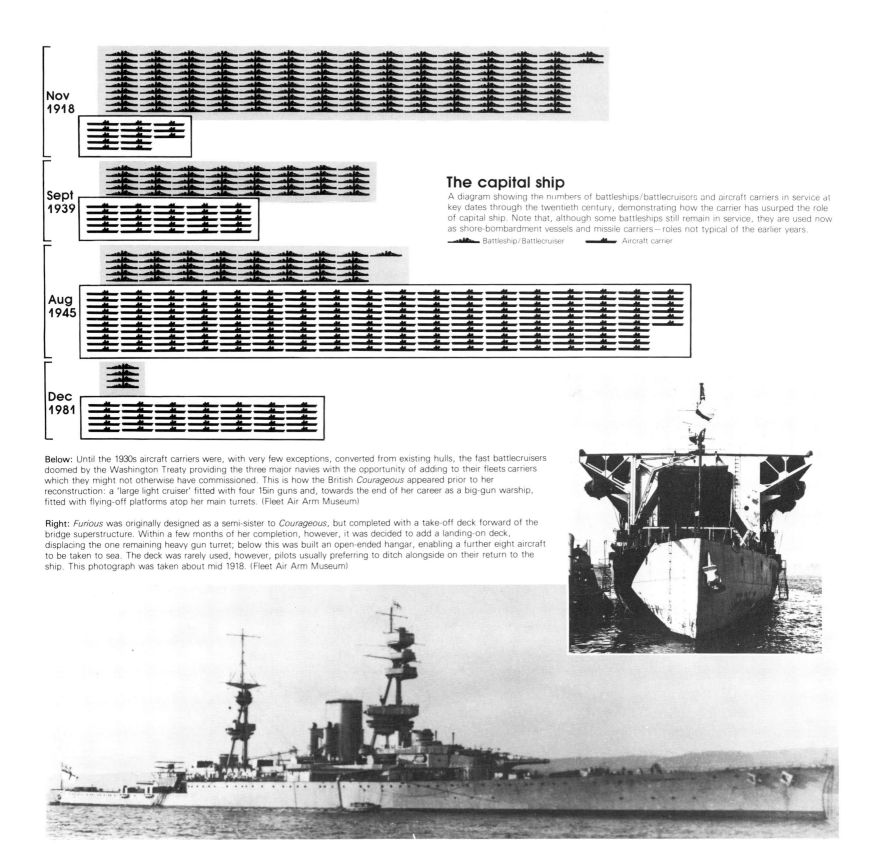

Nov 1918

Sept 1939

Aug 1945

Dec 1981

The capital ship

A diagram showing the numbers of battleships/battlecruisers and aircraft carriers in service at key dates through the twentieth century, demonstrating how the carrier has usurped the role of capital ship. Note that, although some battleships still remain in service, they are used now as shore-bombardment vessels and missile carriers — roles not typical of the earlier years.

Battleship/Battlecruiser   Aircraft carrier

Below: Until the 1930s aircraft carriers were, with very few exceptions, converted from existing hulls, the fast battlecruisers doomed by the Washington Treaty providing the three major navies with the opportunity of adding to their fleets carriers which they might not otherwise have commissioned. This is how the British *Courageous* appeared prior to her reconstruction: a 'large light cruiser' fitted with four 15in guns and, towards the end of her career as a big-gun warship, fitted with flying-off platforms atop her main turrets. (Fleet Air Arm Museum)

Right: *Furious* was originally designed as a semi-sister to *Courageous*, but completed with a take-off deck forward of the bridge superstructure. Within a few months of her completion, however, it was decided to add a landing-on deck, displacing the one remaining heavy gun turret; below this was built an open-ended hangar, enabling a further eight aircraft to be taken to sea. The deck was rarely used, however, pilots usually preferring to ditch alongside on their return to the ship. This photograph was taken about mid 1918. (Fleet Air Arm Museum)

commander who could deny his opposite number reconnaissance would gain a considerable tactical advantage. Thus there developed the concept of the fleet fighter, a nimble single-seater that would engage enemy reconnaissance aircraft and protect friendly ones from attack. They would not be used for escorting the expected follow-up torpedo strike: as single-seaters, they could not be permitted to fly too far from the parent ship owing to problems of navigation; indeed, more frequently than not they operated within visual range of the carrier. It was probably this limitation, as well as a desire to combine the functions of two aircraft into a multi-role airframe and thus buy greater flexibility, that persuaded the Fleet Air Arm to court the fighter-reconnaissance aircraft as a dual-role type.

Through the 1920s the US Navy saw the carrier as performing much the same sort of role. However, one important difference began to emerge during the latter years of the decade: a shift in emphasis away from using carriers to attack the enemy battle line in favour of concentrating on the destruction of opposing carriers. This had considerable implications, for it fostered the use of carriers as independent units not tied to the fleet; in its turn, this encouraged the development of specialised anti-carrier tactics. For example, it led to a move away from torpedo aircraft and towards bombers – a carrier's flight deck was a large and obvious target, and one accurately placed missile could render the flight deck unusable and, hence, the ship inoperable (at least for the purposes of launching and recovering aircraft), something that was unlikely to be the case with a single hit on a battleship. Successful bombing demanded much greater precision than could possibly be achieved, except by chance, with level bombing, which had to be conducted at relatively high altitudes, out of range of anti-aircraft fire. Thus developed the concept of dive-bombing. Provided an adequate bomb-sight could be furnished, considerably greater accuracy could be achieved with this type of attack, and an aircraft so approaching, even at low level, would present a much smaller target to defending gunners. It was fortunate for the US Navy that these types of tactics were already part of their established doctrine, for after the Japanese attacked Pearl Harbor in December 1941, there was virtually no battle fleet into which carriers might be integrated, and independent carrier operations were the only means available of projecting sea power in an effective way.

POLITICAL LEGACIES IN THE 1920s

Carrier tactics were also, to some extent, a product of the political legacies of the First World War. With the removal of Germany, there arose a new alignment of power blocs and the threat of a new naval 'race' similar to that which had followed the appearance of *Dreadnought* in 1906. The progress of naval rearmament was checked by the Washington Treaty of 1922, which decreed the scrapping of battleships and incomplete capital ship hulls on a major scale but also permitted the construction of aircraft carriers within individual ship displacement limitations and within aggregate tonnages for each of the signatory powers. Coinciding as it did with the emergence of flush-decked carriers and the decision of the major navies to adopt them, Washington therefore actually promoted these ships: costs could be eased by converting some of the surplus hulls. Only Great Britain, in *Argus*, had enjoyed any real opportunity to evaluate through-deck carriers by the time of the Treaty, but it was clear that the larger the carrier the longer might be the flight deck and the greater the air group that could be embarked – and Washington imposed no limitations on the number of aircraft such a ship might operate.

America's two *Lexington*s thus emerged as extremely large vessels; the Japanese *Kaga* and *Akagi* rather smaller; and the single French *Béarn* as a fairly limited and, being an ex-battleship not an ex-battlecruiser, rather slow carrier. Great Britain had no capital ship hulls at so advanced a stage of construction as to make conversions possible, although the large light cruisers *Glorious* and *Courageous*, half-sisters to *Furious*, were being considered for complete reconstruction. Moreover, she already had *Eagle*, *Hermes* and *Furious* as front-line carriers, and so had already consumed a considerable proportion of her allocated tonnage. However, the pioneering adoption of carriers by the Royal Navy had resulted in ships whose characteristics were now seen to be somewhat less than ideal for their tasks. Commenting on the effects of the Washington Treaty on 16 February 1922, the DNC wrote to the Controller:

'It is desired to call attention to the fact that, with the exception of H.M.S. ''HERMES'', all these [existing ships] are converted vessels so that the number of tons in their present displacement is not a proper criterion of their value as Aircraft Carriers.

'It is further to be noted that the exercises carried out in 1921 by H.M.S. ''ARGUS'' have emphasised the necessity of very high speed, apart from all other considerations and it would appear from these exercises that the ''FURIOUS'' is the only carrier . . . which has a really acceptable speed for fleet use.

'As regards displacement it may be stated that if a new design were prepared for an Aircraft Carrier of the ''FURIOUS'' type, possibly 4,000 tons less displacement would suffice, while in the case of ''EAGLE'', probably 8,000 tons could be saved, and the remaining vessels as shown on [*sic*] the following table.

'Name of Ship	Speed (knots)	Present disp. (tons)	Tons req. for a new design
Furious	30	22,000	18,000
Eagle	24	23,000	15,000
Hermes	25	11,000	11,000
Argus	19	14,500	12,000
Pegasus	20	3,000	3,000
Ark Royal	11	7,080	4,000'

Replacement carriers for the older flush-decked vessels (the slow sea-plane carriers having been quickly discarded) were certainly planned: paying off *Argus*, *Hermes* and *Eagle* would, with the conversion and commissioning of *Furious*, *Glorious* and *Courageous*, make some 68,000 tons available for new construction, and new carriers each of 17,000 tons were to be laid down at three-yearly intervals from 1926. However, they were never built. Economic problems and the comforting feeling that Washington had swept away all prospect of conflict in the foreseeable future combined to cause continual postponement and, finally, their complete abandonment. The Royal Navy was destined not to get a new carrier until 1938.

The *Lexington*s furnished the US Navy, by contrast, with two extremely fast and very capacious carriers. With so many more aircraft embarked, the desire to use them to the maximum effect brought about the concept of the mass strike and, with it, flight-deck procedures rather different from those practised in the Royal Navy, which fostered the policy of operating aircraft in small groups. Fleet Air Arm torpedo-bombers of

the early 1930s typically had an endurance of about four hours. It would take, perhaps, two minutes to launch each aircraft, and by the time a strike force of, say, twelve machines had been assembled in the air above the carrier half an hour would have elapsed since the first propellers were turned. Landing, with each aircraft required to roll forward to the lift and be struck down, and the lift then being reset for the next aircraft, might consume five minutes per machine; one hour to recover the whole force would not provide any margin for error, for example a flight-deck accident. Hence as much as half an aircraft's endurance might need to be reserved for unproductive manoeuvring on and around the parent ship, assuming the target to be at extreme range (say 100 miles). Larger strikes would enable only less distant targets to be attacked; and a force of 24 aircraft would, plainly, be very difficult if not impossible to handle under any circumstances, even if the target were within visual range.

US practice was to assemble the strike force, fly it off as rapidly as possible, and recover the machines after the mission by landing them on and simply rolling them forward to the bows. Hence the deck park, first aft and subsequently forward, became a standard feature of the flight deck, and obliged the Navy to install efficient arrester and safety barrier systems. By avoiding striking individual machines below as they landed, touchdown intervals were short and more aircraft could be brought aboard in a given time.

GUNS

The particular role envisaged for the carrier, then, did not at this time dictate the latter's essential form; rather was it to a large extent the other way round. With the exception of the second *Hermes*, and perhaps the Japanese *Hosho*, all such ships until the appearance of the Japanese *Ryujo* in 1933 were conversions of existing hulls or more dramatic reconstructions of existing ships, so that features such as flight-deck area and hangar capacity were to some extent imposed on designers. The same could not be said for the ships' fixed batteries, which from 1922 were restricted only by the terms of the Washington Treaty. These would not permit the installation of guns larger than 8in in calibre, nor the fitting of more than ten guns over 6in in calibre; there were no limits on the number of smaller guns, nor on the number of high-angle guns (which, it was presumed, would not exceed 6in in calibre anyway). The fixed armament selected for a carrier gave a clue to the sort of opposition she was expected to face and hence to the sort of environment in which she was to operate. When the designs for the British *Courageous* were being prepared in mid 1922, DNC Department considered the options:

'It is certain that the carriers will be special objects of attack, but the two forms which it is specially desired to emphasise . . . are:
(a) Air attack
(b) Attack by Light Cruisers

'*Air Attack*
'. . . It is considered that we must be prepared for air attacks preliminary to a fleet action, to begin long before the main fleets are in contact, viz., when they are 70, 80 or even 100 miles apart. Such attacks, being the first to materialise, may perhaps be regarded as the most important.
'. . . The positions at present allotted in Atlantic Fleet Cruising formations are:—
(i) Fast flying squadron 4 miles in rear of the A.K. line* and
(ii) Divisional aircraft carriers about 4–5 miles on the bow of the main fleet.
'In general, it may be said that the carriers require considerable sea room to exercise their functions, which means that they will be in a comparatively isolated position and will be forced to rely largely on themselves for defence against attacks from hostile aircraft.
'. . . Assuming that the H A armament will be engaged with aircraft at high angles of elevation, it is very desirable that the main armament should be able to assist in breaking up more distant formations. A high angle of elevation for the main armament is therefore considered a matter of extreme importance.
'*Attack by Enemy Light Cruisers*
'. . . The position of the fast flying squadron makes it possible that an enemy light cruiser might break through the A.K. line, and attack our carriers immediately contact was made between the advanced forces. Later in the action the carriers might lose position (due to flying off and on) to such an extent that they would be liable to attack from single enemy light cruisers, without being supported quickly by any of our own ships. In these circumstances, it seems essential that a carrier should be able to render a good account of herself against a contemporary light cruiser, whilst working up her speed to rejoin her own forces. Alternatively, the CinC will be forced to detach a defensive escort for the carriers to the detriment of his offensive powers.
'. . . Consideration of these forms of attack points to the desirability of 8-inch guns for the main armament.
'. . . The possibility of a carrier being able to defend herself against a hostile light cruiser by means of her own aircraft has been investigated . . . [but] the conclusion [of C-in-C Atlantic Fleet] is that aircraft carriers cannot rely on protecting themselves at present from the attack of even a single light cruiser by means of torpedo planes, and need either a very high speed to escape attack or an adequate escort.'

By the time *Courageous* completed, however, surface guns had been abandoned altogether: she and her sister ship *Glorious* commissioned with an all-AA battery of 4.7in weapons, suggesting that as early as the late 1920s the cruiser threat was held to be less serious than previously and emphasising, in the Royal Navy, the threat to the carrier from the air. The heavy 8in and 6in guns installed on earlier carriers of other navies were similarly discarded as carrier operations detached from the battle fleet evolved. In any case, the decision to devote tonnage available under Washington to carriers smaller in size then the first generation discouraged the fitting of such mountings, since they took up weight and space that might more profitably be given over to aviation facilities. The heavy anti-aircraft gun was retained for medium-range defence, supplemented by new dual-purpose weapons of medium calibre and large

*The line-abreast cruiser scouting screen which preceded the main battle fleet.

numbers of small-calibre weapons for close-in work. More and more, long-range defence by means of the carrier's own fighters was emphasized in the US and Japanese navies, in contrast to British practice, wherein right up until the Second World War carriers continued to strike down aircraft on board a threatened carrier, relying on the fixed battery for self-preservation.

AIRCRAFT BETWEEN THE WARS

US carrier complements reflected both the larger ships available to the Navy and the different priorities of their tasks. As the anti-carrier mission came to assume greater importance at the expense of fleet work, for example, the Navy became less reliant on torpedo-bombers, which were probably the only effective means of stopping heavily armoured ships. Spotters were quickly abandoned as carrier-borne aircraft: instead, the task was transferred directly to the heavy units themselves, floatplanes being launched by catapult and recovered in the way seaplanes were retrieved by First World War carriers. Reconnaissance was still a vital carrier function, and specialist aircraft ('scouts') were embarked for the purpose. However, multi-role functions became attractive to the US Navy too, and the scout gradually merged with the dive-bomber, to give the type an offensive rather than a purely passive role. Finally, there were the fighter squadrons, whose tasks evolved from providing air cover for offensive strikes and carrier self-defence through to multi-mission capabilities that included light attack and reconnaissance.

Fleet Air Arm strength throughout the 1920s barely rose above 100 machines, and even with the commissioning of *Glorious* and *Courageous* it advanced only to about 150. Whilst these figures may seem luxurious in comparison with the Royal Navy's fixed-wing inventory of the 1980s, they represented about half the contemporary US Navy's carrier-borne strength yet were taken to sea aboard twice the number of carriers. Indeed, the entire Fleet Air Arm of 1930 could probably have been accommodated aboard either *Lexington* or *Saratoga*, instead of being dispersed, as it was, among six vessels. The Royal Navy, with its reluctance to abandon the priority accorded to the battle fleet, the unwillingness or inability of politicians to invest more money in the service, and the unfortunate effects of allocating to the Air Ministry (rather than to the Admiralty) the responsibility of procuring its aircraft and to the Royal Air Force that of operating them, was obliged to wring as much as possible out of its resources. The temptation for them to adopt the multi-role aircraft, with its reputation (not always justified) of being able to undertake two or more diverse tasks reasonably well but no single task outstandingly well, could not be shunned. Thus the spotter-reconnaissance function was combined with that of torpedo strike (the classic TSR aircraft being, of course, the Fairey Swordfish) and the fighter was developed into the fighter-

reconnaissance machine, the first representative of which was the Hawker Osprey. Later, the first fleet dive-bomber, the Blackburn Skua, was considered suitable for use also as a fighter.

Much has been made of the alleged deficiencies of the Fleet Air Arm's aircraft during the years leading up to the Second World War compared with their US and, indeed, Japanese contemporaries. There is no doubt that, viewed against development in land-based RAF aircraft during the mid 1930s, which saw the introduction of high-speed monoplane fighters and fighter-bombers such as the Spitfire and Blenheim, Navy machines had less satisfactory capabilities. The reasons for this unfortunate state of affairs were myriad. Undeniably, a significant factor was the doctrine that has been so aptly termed the 'indivisibility of the air': from the time of the formation of the Royal Air Force in 1918 and the consequent transfer of thousands of RNAS officers and men to the control of a service whose loyalties were directed towards land-based military aviation, the view prevailed that the Admiralty's concerns were more properly those of ships and the sea, and not what might take place in the skies. As a result, not only were the tactics, roles and relative strength of the Fleet Air Arm dictated in large part by the perceived requirements of the land-based air force, but the development of machines to be deployed on board carriers was generally accorded a much lower priority. When, in the mid 1930s, the need for the expansion of the naval air element was accepted, the defence of the mainland assumed, in the face of political changes evident in Continental Europe, even greater relative importance. A further factor was the Navy's reluctance to dispense with the multi-seater aircraft: providing greater flexibility to carrier air operations, from ships whose air groups were limited by the individual capacities of the carriers themselves, this preference was also a product of the desire to carry an observer / navigator as well as a pilot on each mission, which at once enabled aircraft to range farther from the ship in the safe knowledge that they could find their way back, and ensured that one naval officer at least was aboard each aircraft. But multi-seaters had to sacrifice range, speed or payload in order to accommodate the additional crew member, and also needed to be considerably larger, with all the problems of stowage aboard already cramped ships that that implied. Folding wings, necessary to strike down large aircraft, in their turn imposed additional weight penalties affecting performance, and consumed time during landing operations, thus limiting the number of aircraft that could be flown together in a single sortie.

The British lack of a modern, capable fleet fighter was particularly apparent. Combining the fighter and reconnaissance roles in one airframe again produced aircraft of relatively low performance, and the practice of consigning aircraft to the protection of the hangar and relying on anti-aircraft fire to deter attacking enemy aircraft discouraged the development of short-range, lightweight, high-performance interceptors for carrier self-

Aircraft carriers extant, 1914-1983

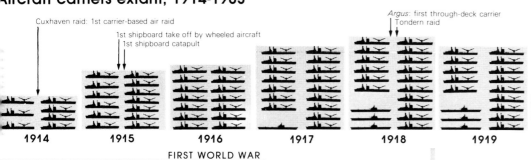

Cuxhaven raid: 1st carrier-based air raid

1st shipboard take off by wheeled aircraft
1st shipboard catapult

Argus: first through-deck carrier
Tondern raid

From tentative experiments prior to the First World War, the through-deck carrier became an accepted (albeit grudgingly in some circles) asset by the mid 1920s. By the Second World War — which witnessed massive carrier building programmes in the United States — the seaplane carrier had been virtually displaced. Carrier numbers remained high throughout the 1950s, although large numbers were in reserve fleets; by the 1970s, the high unit costs of such vessels dramatically decreased the numbers of ships that could be afforded.

| 1914 | 1915 | 1916 | 1917 | 1918 | 1919 | 1920 | 1921 | 1922 | 1923 |

FIRST WORLD WAR

Aug: Great Britain 2, France 1, Japan 1, Russia 1.

Nov: Great Britain 12, France 4, Japan 1, Russia 1+?.

Washington Treaty

Top: One of the many problems facing the Fleet Air Arm at the outbreak of war in 1939 was the lack of a high-performance fighter capable of dealing with German and Italian land-based bombers; to meet this need, US aircraft were ordered, but ex-RAF aircraft were acquired as a stop-gap measure. They had failings: for example navalised Hurricanes, shown here, could not fold their wings and thus could not be struck below on board armoured fleet carriers. (Fleet Air Arm Museum)

Above: The US Navy, in contrast, produced several outstanding naval fighters, none better than the F4U Corsair (a cannon-armed -4B is shown, in postwar colours); quality and numbers swept the Japanese from the Pacific skies. (Vought Corporation)

defence. When the value of such aircraft became self-evident in the very early stages of the Second World War, none was immediately available. The adaptation of obsolescent land-based types, such as the Gladiator, and the acceptance of modern ex-RAF aircraft whose characteristics were not entirely suited to carrier operations (for example the Hurricane, the wings of which could not fold and which thus posed problems of hangar stowage, and the Spitfire, the narrow-track undercarriage of which was to result in serious landing-on difficulties) was the only alternative pending the arrival of aircraft acquired from the United States.

THE SECOND WORLD WAR

Despite the difficulties and shortcomings that beset the Fleet Air Arm during the inter-war years, several aspects of established carrier aviation doctrine proved to be fully vindicated when the Royal Navy went to war. For example, the value of fleet spotting was underlined when a Swordfish aircraft, albeit not operating from a carrier, played a decisive role in the successful advance of the battleship *Warspite* and her attendant destroyers up Ofotfjord during the Norwegian campaign of April 1940; when in November of that year a torpedo strike by Swordfish bombers crippled the Italian battle fleet at Taranto; and when the same aircraft 'fixed' the German battleship *Bismarck* at large in the Atlantic and slowed her sufficiently for capital ships of the Home Fleet to move in and finish her off. The value of armoured hangars was proven both in the Mediterranean, where *Formidable* and *Illustrious* were both able to survive heavy bomb hits, and in the Far East, where kamikaze hits proved more of an inconvenience to British armoured carriers operating there than a menace which might disable them.

However, deficiencies in fighter protection, and indeed in air cover itself were ultimately responsible for the loss of two carriers. First *Glorious*, with no air patrol up scouting for enemy ships and with a deck load of RAF machines recently evacuated from Norway, was caught unprepared by German battlecruisers; then, off Ceylon, *Hermes*, fleeing harbour to escape an expected Japanese air raid and with no machines on board, was sunk by Japanese carrier aircraft. Three fleet carriers were lost to submarine attack, emphasising the requirement for comprehensive surface escort and, given the advances in detection made possible by radar and the growing effectiveness of ASW weapons such as air-dropped depth-charges and air-to-surface rockets, specialist anti-submarine carriers.

By 1944 the role of the Royal Navy carrier had developed along three distinct paths. The large fleet carrier was to be used mainly as a strike weapon, but embarking a growing proportion of fighters in relation to attack aircraft both to escort strikes and to provide an aerial defence for the carrier herself. The trade protection carrier was most useful in the Atlantic, first as a pure convoy escort developed from catapult-armed

Key to symbols

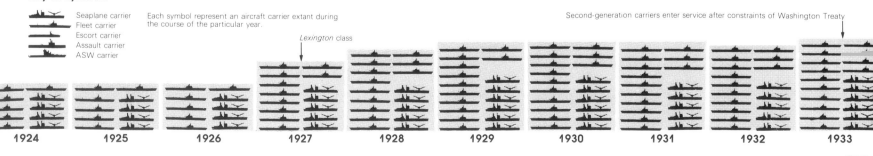

Seaplane carrier
Fleet carrier
Escort carrier
Assault carrier
ASW carrier

Each symbol represent an aircraft carrier extant during the course of the particular year.

Lexington class

Second-generation carriers enter service after constraints of Washington Treaty

1924 1925 1926 1927 1928 1929 1930 1931 1932 1933

Continu

June: Great Britain 7, Japan 7, USA 3, France 2, Italy 1.

merchant (CAM) ships, but soon, with the introduction of HF / DF, as a semi-independent unit that could carry the war to the enemy submarine by pinpointing its location at a considerable range and then follow up with an attack. Finally, a transport was particularly valuable for moving reinforcement landplanes to threatened areas. Older carriers proved useful for this last task, but the convoy escort carrier could only be made available by the rapid conversion of merchant ships, at first from such British hulls as were available in extremely limited numbers, but subsequently when US-built escort carriers were made over in large quantities.

The Pacific War saw the US carrier force develop along somewhat similar lines, although with very different priorities. The strike carrier was the principal weapon, ASW was rather less pressing in the Pacific than in the Atlantic and there was much less emphasis on convoy protection, but transports assumed growing importance as the westward advance of the US Pacific offensive came to mean longer and longer resupply routes. A

Top: Typifying the US-built CVE (escort carrier) is *Slinger*, which served with the Royal Navy and is seen here in October 1943. (US National Archives)

Above: The Pacific War of 1942–45 was fought and won largely on the basis of carrier operations: it proved the ascendancy of the carrier-borne aircraft and relegated the battleship to a subsidiary, often supporting role. The *Essex* class typified the fast US fleet carriers which gained that victory: this is *Yorktown* (CV-10), in 1943.

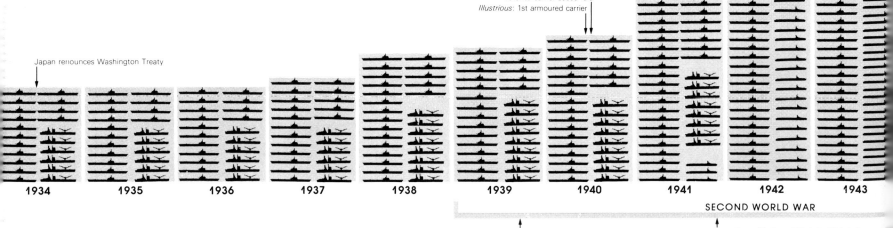

Japan renounces Washington Treaty

Taranto carrier-based raid
Illustrious: 1st armoured carrier

Bismarck disabled by carrier-borne aircraft

Audacity and *Long Island*: 1st escort carriers

Pearl Harbor carrier-based raid

Carrier battles: Coral Sea, Midway and Santa Cruz

| 1934 | 1935 | 1936 | 1937 | 1938 | 1939 | 1940 | 1941 | 1942 | 1943 |

SECOND WORLD WAR

Sept: Japan 11, Great Britain 9, USA 5, France 2, Australia 1, Italy 1.

Dec: Japan 16, Great Britain 9, USA 9, France 1

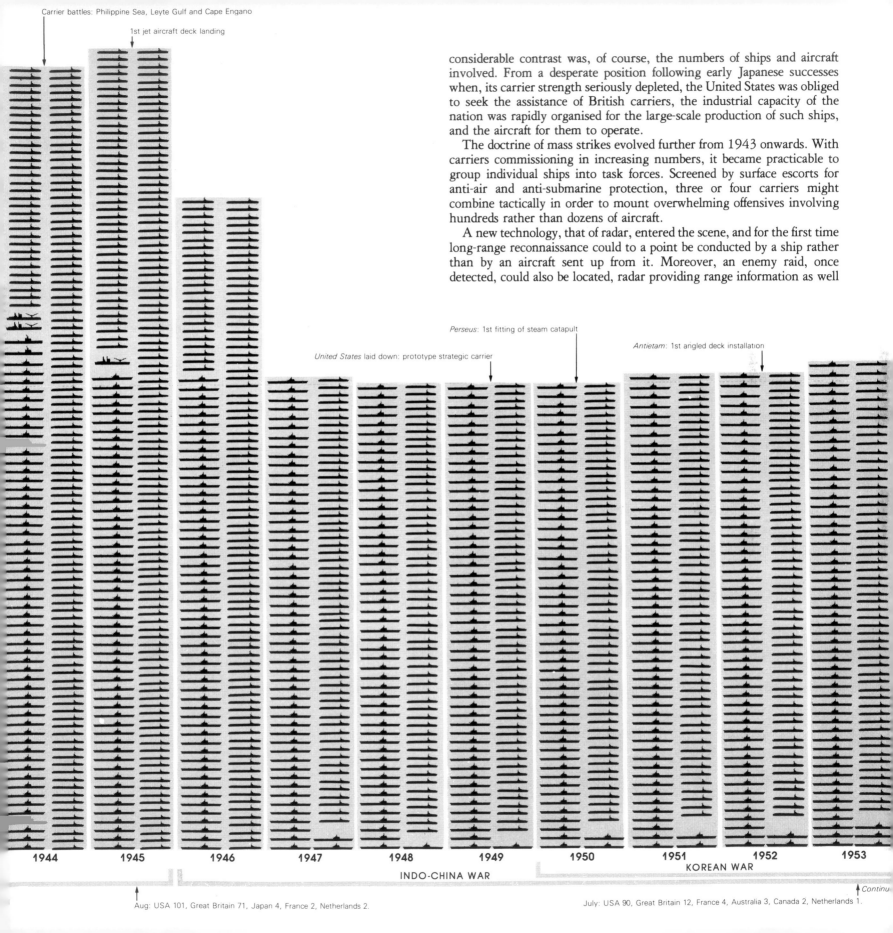

Carrier battles: Philippine Sea, Leyte Gulf and Cape Engano

1st jet aircraft deck landing

considerable contrast was, of course, the numbers of ships and aircraft involved. From a desperate position following early Japanese successes when, its carrier strength seriously depleted, the United States was obliged to seek the assistance of British carriers, the industrial capacity of the nation was rapidly organised for the large-scale production of such ships, and the aircraft for them to operate.

The doctrine of mass strikes evolved further from 1943 onwards. With carriers commissioning in increasing numbers, it became practicable to group individual ships into task forces. Screened by surface escorts for anti-air and anti-submarine protection, three or four carriers might combine tactically in order to mount overwhelming offensives involving hundreds rather than dozens of aircraft.

A new technology, that of radar, entered the scene, and for the first time long-range reconnaissance could to a point be conducted by a ship rather than by an aircraft sent up from it. Moreover, an enemy raid, once detected, could also be located, radar providing range information as well

Perseus: 1st fitting of steam catapult

United States laid down: prototype strategic carrier

Antietam: 1st angled deck installation

| 1944 | 1945 | 1946 | 1947 | 1948 | 1949 | 1950 | 1951 | 1952 | 1953 |

INDO-CHINA WAR

KOREAN WAR

↑Continu

Aug: USA 101, Great Britain 71, Japan 4, France 2, Netherlands 2.

July: USA 90, Great Britain 12, France 4, Australia 3, Canada 2, Netherlands 1.

as bearing. Thus aircraft could be directed to deal with the imminent threat, more capably and more quickly if they were already aloft. The Combat Air Patrol (CAP) was a feature of US carrier operations well before the Pacific War broke out, but radar enabled it to be used more effectively, and at greater range. It was less of an asset if several simultaneous raids were approaching a carrier, each one comprising relatively few aircraft, since there was the inherent problem of ranking the threats according to the degree of danger they presented. Plotting the path of an approaching attack and vectoring defending fighters to it was an operation that demanded time: aircraft closing at 300mph – five miles a minute – from different directions might present too great and too complex a problem for a manual plot to handle.

Carrier radar became more effective with the development of the Combat Information Centre (CIC), by means of which it was possible to gather radar data from a spread of different sources (ie, from accompanying ships) and build up a complete picture of the activity within the airspace surrounding the force. IFF (Identification Friend or Foe) solved the problem of engaging the wrong targets. These only became fully effective, however, with the postwar introduction of automated (computerised) CICs for only then could data be processed with sufficient speed, especially as raids might be expected to arrive from half a dozen or more directions.

There remained a further problem: saturation. However many defending aircraft might be available for interception (and however large an air group, only a few would be assigned such a task, and not all of these would be simultaneously committed to CAP), there was always a chance, indeed a probability, that some of the attackers would evade them. The advent of the kamikaze, piloted by determined airmen whose machines, even if fatally damaged, might still strike home, caused particular concern to commanders aboard carriers whose flight decks were unprotected and whose hangars were open at the sides. Hence, shipboard anti-aircraft weapons were not merely retained but proliferated.

Japanese practice to some extent parallelled that of the United States, although there was a greater emphasis on torpedo strike and level (as opposed to dive-) bombing; in each case, the attacking aircraft were pro-

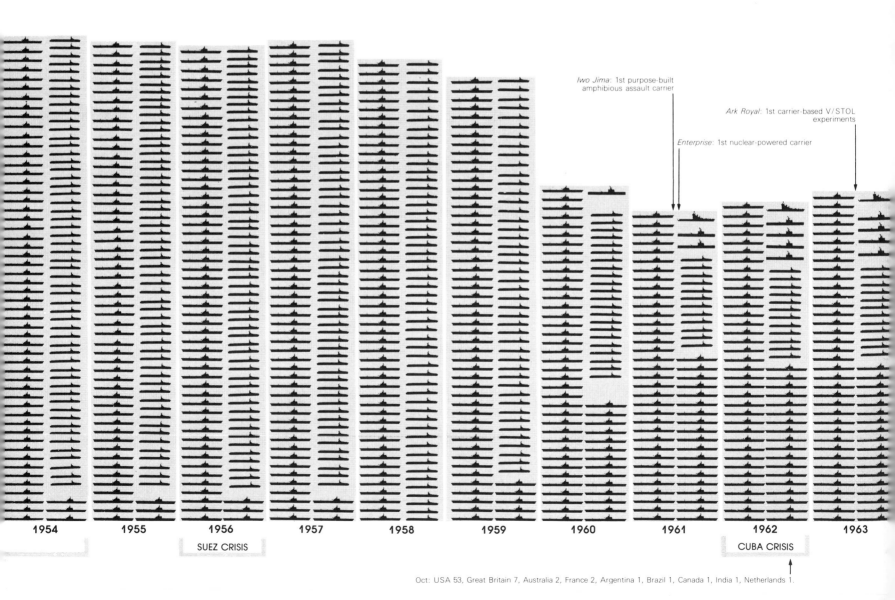

Iwo Jima: 1st purpose-built amphibious assault carrier

Ark Royal: 1st carrier-based V/STOL experiments

Enterprise: 1st nuclear-powered carrier

1954   1955   1956   1957   1958   1959   1960   1961   1962   1963

SUEZ CRISIS

CUBA CRISIS

Oct: USA 53, Great Britain 7, Australia 2, France 2, Argentina 1, Brazil 1, Canada 1, India 1, Netherlands 1.

tected by a heavy fighter escort. As in the US Navy, the advantages of combining carriers to form task groups were appreciated, although, faced with overwhelming numbers of enemy aircraft, the Japanese later tended towards dispersal in order to reduce the chances of several carriers succumbing simultaneously. Interest in the dive-bomber (Judy) and fighter-bomber (modified Zero) was awakened as a result of carrier-versus-carrier operations, but the great handicap to all technological advance, and for that matter to increased numbers of ships and aircraft, was the gradual erosion of Japan's already limited industrial capacity, and, from 1944, the simple unavailability of both carriers and (more importantly) trained aircrew.

One particular Japanese phenomenon (but not an exclusively Japanese one) was the concept of the hybrid carrier. The problem of commissioning additional flight decks for operation at sea was common to all three major navies during the Second World War, and was met in large part on the Allied side by the mass production of US-built escort carriers and, in the US Navy, by light cruiser hulls. Although numerous full-deck carriers were also realised by the Japanese from 1942 onwards, a number of ships, notably the two *Ise*-class battleships, were fitted with large flight decks aft in order to operate dive-bombers. Such hybrids were not new in concept: they recalled, in a sense, the configuration of *Furious* in 1917. Flight-deck cruisers had been the object of serious US interest in the inter-war period and in 1938 the Soviet Union evinced interest in acquiring a battleship with a 400-foot flight deck amidships derived from a private design supplied by the US company Gibbs & Cox. The Italians during the Second

World War contemplated modifying the cruiser *Bolzano* and ranging aircraft the length of the forecastle deck. More practicable was the widespread use of seaplane carriers in an offensive role: Japan's island empire made such a vessel attractive, and her espousal of floatplane fighters like the Rufe was founded on a belief that such aircraft could be successfully operated from these ships.

Above: The need for more and more flight decks during the Second World War sometimes led to desperate measures; the Japanese battleship *Ise*, for example, sacrificed a third of her main battery in order to operate a handful of aircraft via a limited flight deck aft. Apparently Judy dive-bombers were envisaged as the air group, but neither machines nor pilots were available in sufficient quantity when the ship was ready, and only floatplanes were ever embarked. (By courtesy of A. D. Baker III)

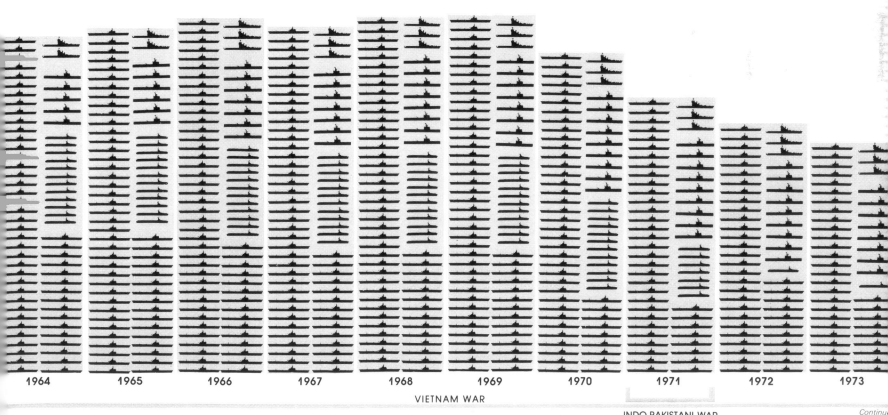

1964   1965   1966   1967   1968   1969   1970   1971   1972   1973

VIETNAM WAR

INDO-PAKISTANI WAR

Continued

A ROLE FOR THE NUCLEAR AGE

Postwar carrier development has seen a large number of radical changes, both in terms of the roles to which the ships have been assigned and in terms of technological evolution. With the end of the war in 1945, the huge US carrier force suddenly found itself with no obvious purpose, at least not in the sense of combating an aggressive navy as had been necessary during the previous four years. There was no new potential enemy equipped to fight a carrier war; indeed, there was only one other carrier power, Great Britain, and so closely had these two countries aligned themselves (and so unequal had become their relative strengths) that hostilities between the two seemed beyond sober contemplation. The one potential adversary was the Soviet Union, a land power with little in the way of a surface navy although possessing a significant submarine force. Hence, postwar US carrier policy revolved around two central themes: anti-submarine warfare and seaborne strike against land targets. The latter, in view of the events of August 1945, might well embrace strategic strike and, hence, the carriage of nuclear weapons.

The question of a strategic nuclear strike role for the US Navy, today a familiar and accepted part of its task, achieved through the submarine-launched ballistic missile (SLBM) deterrent, was raised early in the post-war years and threatened at one point to cause considerable inter-service acrimony – as serious in relative terms as the 'indivisibility of the air' doctrine that was a feature of prewar British carrier policy. The argument was, as it were, the indivisibility of the air over land masses. The source of the argument was the newly-acquired atomic bomb, the horrific power of which had so recently been demonstrated. The Navy was anxious to participate, but early atomic weapons were exceptionally heavy, and it would take a carrier-based aircraft of unprecedented size and weight to lift them; such aircraft would require, in turn, a carrier of huge dimensions and radical design. A ship capable of operating these aircraft, *United States*, was laid down in April 1949, but the Air Force viewed the Navy's ambition with considerable distaste, interpreting the building of the ship as a threat not merely to its monopoly of atomic weapons but to its strategic role. The USAF view prevailed, and CVA-58 was summarily cancelled in favour of additional land-based bombers. Indeed, at that time there was

some question concerning the wisdom of retaining a large attack carrier force at all, especially since it consumed considerable defence funding.

Several factors combined to cause a switch of opinion. The first was the detonation, in 1949, of an atomic bomb by the Soviet Union and the consequent realisation by the United States that its pre-eminent military position would within a few years be challenged; as a corollary, carriers would thus offer additional bases for mounting nuclear strikes and at the same time mobile ones, more difficult to eliminate in the event of hostilities. A second factor was the outbreak of the Korean War, seen by many as a first move in a possible global conflict. In support of the South Koreans, carriers were the only means of launching an air offensive of any credibility. Hence, the tactical value of carriers in a land war, particularly one where offshore enemy activity was likely to be minimal and where carriers could thus operate more or less unmolested, was promoted; this role would be exploited much more fully two decades later during the Vietnam conflict.

The strategic carrier inevitably meant a large one, not only to support the heavy aircraft required to lift the nuclear payload, but also to provide adequate fuel capacity for the long-range operations that such a role demanded. A ship with the dimensions necessary to support the A3D Skywarrior, the successor to the abortive 45-ton ADR-42 bomber that was to have been developed for carriage on board *United States*, would also embark a considerable number of smaller conventional attack aircraft and, moreover, equip them to conduct a large number of strikes. Time would also prove the choice of large dimensions to be particularly fortunate: although atomic weapons, and by extension the aircraft necessary to carry them, began to decrease considerably in weight from the late 1950s on, the fighter aircraft has grown in dimensions beyond anything remotely conceivable at the time of Korea, so that the ship capable of operating the 32-ton A3D is also able to handle the current F-14, which weighs about the same. With the introduction of the Navy's submarine-based strategic missile, carriers relinquished their strategic role and returned to the promotion of air power at a tactical level.

The anti-submarine requirement was met initially by the adoption of surplus escort carriers. Such ships did not immediately need to be fast; the

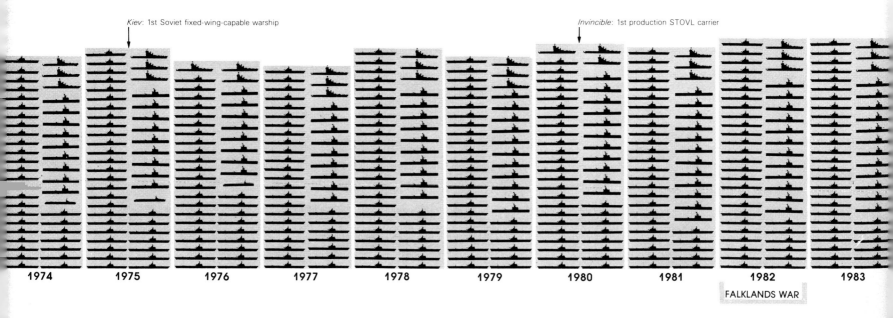

Kiev: 1st Soviet fixed-wing-capable warship

Invincible: 1st production STOVL carrier

| 1974 | 1975 | 1976 | 1977 | 1978 | 1979 | 1980 | 1981 | 1982 | 1983 |

FALKLANDS WAR

Dec: USA 32, Soviet Union 5, Great Britain 3, France 3, Argentina 1, Brazil 1, India

prime consideration was that of endurance, since ASW calls for search and detection preliminary to any prosecution. Two factors, however, suggested that ex-CVEs would soon be unsuitable: the increasing speeds attainable by submarines, and the larger, specialized ASW aircraft that would be required to lift both the airborne detection equipment essential for pinpointing hostile craft and the weapons to destroy it. Indeed, first-generation postwar ASW aircraft (AF) had to split the detection and attack functions between two machines in order to move the necessary equipment to the target. *Independence*-class CVLs were sufficiently fast, but could not operate the new twin-engined S2F anti-submarine aircraft then in prospect; only the *Essex*-class fleet carriers among existing designs could satisfy all the immediate demands of ASW. Conveniently, the modernization plans imposed by the introduction of fast jet aircraft on board attack carriers left a batch of axial-deck *Essex*es available for use as anti-submarine carriers (CVS), and early reconstructed *Essex*es followed them into service. As these ships neared the end of their useful life during the late 1960s and early 1970s however, and as new ASW technology demanded still heavier equipment, the anti-submarine element was transferred to the large attack carriers, which now operate long-range S-3 turbofan aircraft (whose fuel is compatible with that of the rest of the air group, and indeed of the carriers themselves) for the task. Helicopters have since the 1950s been employed for close-in ASW, localising and dealing with threats in the immediate vicinity of the carrier or her task force.

One other line of development in the postwar US carrier story has been amphibious assault. Originally purely helicopter carriers were employed for the purpose – the prototype was a converted CVE and the next batch converted *Essex*es – but amphibious operations demand a ship rather different in concept from the true aircraft carrier, despite its superficial resemblance to the type. Amphibious assault carriers arose from a desire for increased beachhead flexibility: the need to remove the tempting nuclear target of vast numbers of small craft streaming together towards a shoreline. The converted fleet carriers quickly demonstrated how unsuited to the task they were: a considerable internal volume, for example, was devoted to machinery (which might be better used for low-power propulsion units and considerably greater accommodation for troops and equipment), and *Essex*-class carriers were expensive to maintain. Much increased volume might be offered in a new design, and the *Iwo Jima* LPHs were developed as a result. A return to more traditional forms of assault has been encompassed in current ships (LHA), which carry landing craft but retain the through flight deck for airborne operations.

Below: Carrier-based ASW is a primary postwar concern, and the United States pioneered the use of specialist fast ASW carriers. Angled-deck *Essex*es proved suitable in this role; overtaken by strike carrier technology by the late 1950s, they were nevertheless able to operate the large S2F ASW aircraft. This is *Yorktown*, redesignated CVS-10, in June 1962, with S2F Trackers, AD-5W Skyraiders and Seabat helicopters on deck. (US Navy)

THE MODERN CARRIER

If the strategic role envisaged by the US Navy for its carriers in the early 1950s dictated a certain minimum size of hull and flight deck, the changing nature of carrier-borne aircraft exerted an equally powerful influence. The new generation of jet aircraft promised at the close of the Second World War posed a whole range of problems to existing carriers. One was the fundamental issue of launch and recovery: jets easily outpaced propeller-driven aircraft in flight, or showed obvious signs of being able to do so, but were considerably less sympathetic to the low-speed near-carrier environment. For example, the combination of high stalling speed and poor acceleration characteristic of jet aircraft meant that unassisted take-offs were more or less out of the question, even given empty flight decks and high WODs; landing required stronger arresting systems to absorb the more powerful forces generated by higher-speed approaches. Perhaps even more important, jets are voracious consumers of fuel. Assuming comparable dimensions to a piston-engined predecessor, jet fighter airborne endurance might be cut by half; increasing endurance by providing more fuel could reduce performance (if carried externally), might require a larger aircraft and affect air group capacity, and in either case would call for a still longer, and perhaps stronger, flight deck (or a more powerful catapult). In addition, much greater bunkerage within the carrier would be needed if the capacity to launch a comparable number of sorties over a given distance were not to be seriously compromised. Catapult launch itself slowed the task of assembling a strike force: each aircraft needed individual attention to manoeuvre it on to the equipment, thereby setting an interval between two successive take-offs, which suggested the advantages of multiple catapults – in their turn needing enlarged flight decks.

Other postwar pressures have forced up the size of carriers. For example, even during the Second World War detachments of specialist aircraft types — night-fighters and photo reconnaissance machines — were considered important enough to displace more conventional types aboard carriers. Since then, electronic countermeasures (ECM), early warning (AEW), tanker, strategic attack (for a time) and most recently ASW aircraft have entered, all affecting the capacity for the carrier to embark aircraft for her primary role (although, of course, all essential to the effectiveness of those aircraft). More significantly, however, the multiplicity of different aircraft types places great strain on maintenance facilities and internal volume. Costs and the pressure for space aboard carriers, large as the latter currently are, have promoted the development of multi-mission aircraft such as the F-4 Phantom and now the F / A-18 Hornet; the tanker / ECM / medium attack role is conducted by what is essentially a single airframe; and the reconnaissance role is being assigned to existing aircraft (F-14 TARPS and, perhaps, the RF-18).

The decision to opt for nuclear power for US front-line carriers conferred great range and the capability to operate ships at continuously high speeds. It also released space taken up by carrier oil fuel for other purposes; for example, escort replenishment. But the provision of nuclear power created a demand for *additional* internal volume, since a ship with an endurance of hundreds of thousands of miles is of limited advantage if she cannot accommodate additional ordnance for the sustenance of repeated air sorties; this is why a small nuclear carrier is somewhat anomalous. Sophisticated electronic equipment also eats up internal volume, again setting certain limits, while the proliferation of radar implies a certain level of above-decks structure, which might in a small carrier seriously compromise flight-deck area.

Top: Multi-role aircraft have always been an attractive proposition, since they reduce maintenance loads, may ease space aboard carriers, and theoretically lessen costs. The most recent US Navy acquisition has been the F/A-18 Hornet, seen here deployed aboard *Constellation*, October 1982. Aircraft designed from the start for two or more different roles often meet unforeseen difficulties: the Hornet, for example, is now reportedly as expensive as the F-14, the aircraft for which it was designed to be, in part, a cheaper alternative. (McDonnell Douglas)

Above and left: Only the 'super carrier', typified by *Kitty Hawk* (above) and the nuclear-powered *Nimitz* (left) seen here, can operate aircraft of sufficient individual size, adequate numbers and the required varying roles for the effective projection of sea power in distant waters — and only the US Navy is at present willing to afford them. (US Navy)

Carrier fixed armament has seen considerable changes in emphasis over the last 40 years. There has been a general downgrading of medium (long-range) gun batteries, first, because of the high manpower levels they require; second, because of the topweight they create (especially problematic in reconstructions that introduced, for example, catapults, lifts and radars that were much heavier than the ships were designed to accommodate); third, in early postwar carriers, because of the seakeeping problems they posed; and, fourth, because of increased ranges from which enemy aircraft might attack, with the advent of the stand-off missile. For a time, these considerations and the fact that carrier AA defence could conveniently be offloaded on to escort ships, led to US fleet carriers (for example, *Enterprise*) being commissioned without any fixed battery, gun or missile. The question of saturation, wherein the sheer numbers of aircraft or missiles attacking a carrier meant that some would very likely penetrate outer defence layers (ie, defending fighters), and the lightweight nature of recent defence systems such as Sea Sparrow and the Phalanx CIWS has seen their reintroduction on a limited scale.

The spectacular growth in carrier dimensions, and the consequent cost of producing, maintaining and operating these ships, has left the United States as the only naval power capable of supporting a realistic attack carrier fleet, although there is strong evidence to suggest that the Soviet Union may within a decade or so be in a position to challenge that monopoly. Sheer economics has forced Great Britain, despite her postwar (and continuing) technological influence on carrier design, particularly in the sphere of flight-deck equipment, to give up conventional carriers, and only France among the other Western navies continues to operate such a force, albeit it with comparatively limited numbers of ships.

There has, however, been a continuing interest, recently enhanced, in light carriers. The Royal Navy operated light fleet carriers with considerable success during the early 1950s, for example during the Korean War, and a number of other navies were offered such vessels as were surplus to British requirements. With some reconstruction, especially involving the fitting of a partially angled landing deck, they proved capable of operating light jets such as Sea Hawks and Skyhawks, and also helicopters. Additionally, they made suitable ASW platforms. Some continue in service to the present day.

The helicopter carrier, an attractive ASW or amphibious assault possibility using redundant fleet carrier hulls, has ironically ushered in a return to fixed-wing operations, made viable with the introduction of the V / STOL aircraft. V / STOL, epitomised by the Harrier family, buys not so much flight-deck space as a reduction in the complex technology required to launch and recover conventional aircraft: no catapults or

Top: The large nuclear-powered carrier has not been without its critics in the United States, and on several occasions attempts have been made to introduce a smaller, cheaper alternative. This is an artist's impression of the CVV, a 50,000-ton, two-shaft, two-lift, two-catapult vessel proposed during the 1970s. Its low capability and low speed in relation to existing ships finally discouraged its adoption. (US Navy)

Centre: An artist's impression of how the Spanish Navy's new carrier *Principe de Asturias* will appear upon completion. The ship is scheduled to receive AV-8B V/STOL aircraft as part of her air complement. (Spanish Navy)

Bottom: V/STOL aircraft have proved to be the key to effective naval air power from smaller platforms, requiring considerably less flight-deck area although hardly much less internal volume. Moreover, thrust-to-weight ratios of present-generation powerplants tend to keep airframes relatively small and capabilities therefore limited. These Yak-36 Forgers are deployed aboard *Minsk*, autumn 1982. (US Navy)

arrester gear are required, no complex recovery procedures, and, provided fuel and / or payload penalties and time-consuming take-off and landing cycles are accepted, no full-length flight deck. Indeed, recent British studies involving crane-launched V / STOL aircraft ('Skyhook') imply no flight deck at all. There are distant echoes here of Second World War emergency carrier programmes. Conversions of merchant ships to 'instant' carriers by the addition of flight decks perhaps require nothing further than the fitting of a small, heat-resistant platform, as has been shown on numerous occasions during peacetime sales demonstrations, and as was in fact carried out during the British mobilization for the South Atlantic during the spring of 1982. A multi-mission V / STOL aircraft can indeed provide a significant air capability for smaller navies, although sustained operations still call for on-board stowage, maintenance, fuelling and rearming facilities, even for a single-aircraft ship; moreover, the necessary dispersion rather than concentration of such forces implies a

defensive, not offensive, role, for example for the purposes of trade protection and ASW instead of land attack.

In US eyes, however, the case for the 'super carrier', despite encountering much opposition (mainly on grounds of cost), has stood up. Smaller carriers such as STO-ships, embarking limited air groups operating conventional aircraft off ramped flight decks, may well be built, but so long as the fleet attack carrier is embraced, any reduction in the size of individual units seems unlikely to be countenanced. Coincidentally, it appears that some upper limit in carrier dimensions may also have been reached: in an era of electronics and miniaturisation, unit size and weight are not necessarily the only criteria for potency, even though numbers still have obvious advantages. However, history suggests that warship types, having reached a certain level of dimensions, do not generally shrink in size; they disappear when they are rendered obsolete by some new technology. That eventuality appears to be some way off.

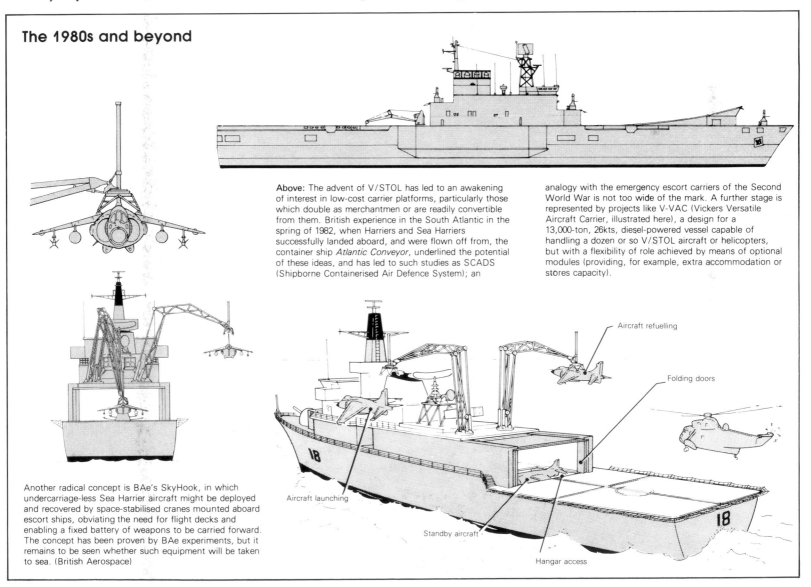

The 1980s and beyond

Above: The advent of V/STOL has led to an awakening of interest in low-cost carrier platforms, particularly those which double as merchantmen or are readily convertible from them. British experience in the South Atlantic in the spring of 1982, when Harriers and Sea Harriers successfully landed aboard, and were flown off from, the container ship *Atlantic Conveyor*, underlined the potential of these ideas, and has led to such studies as SCADS (Shipborne Containerised Air Defence System); an

analogy with the emergency escort carriers of the Second World War is not too wide of the mark. A further stage is represented by projects like V-VAC (Vickers Versatile Aircraft Carrier, illustrated here), a design for a 13,000-ton, 26kts, diesel-powered vessel capable of handling a dozen or so V/STOL aircraft or helicopters, but with a flexibility of role achieved by means of optional modules (providing, for example, extra accommodation or stores capacity).

Another radical concept is BAe's SkyHook, in which undercarriage-less Sea Harrier aircraft might be deployed and recovered by space-stabilised cranes mounted aboard escort ships, obviating the need for flight decks and enabling a fixed battery of weapons to be carried forward. The concept has been proven by BAe experiments, but it remains to be seen whether such equipment will be taken to sea. (British Aerospace)

Aircraft refuelling

Folding doors

Aircraft launching

Standby aircraft

Hangar access

Argentina

The Argentine Navy has operated two ex-British light fleet carriers during different periods postwar. The second, *25 de Mayo*, is currently in service.

INDEPENDENCIA

Builder	Laid down	Launched	Commissioned
Harland & Wolff	12 Dec 42	20 May 44	26 Jan 59

Displacement: 14,000 tons / 14,224 tonnes (standard); 19,540 tons / 19,853 tonnes (deep load).
Length: 630ft / 192.02m (pp); 650ft / 198.12m (wl); 695ft / 211.84m (oa); 680ft / 207.26m (fd).
Beam: 80ft / 24.38m (hull); 75ft / 22.86m (fd).
Draught: 23ft 6in / 7.16m (deep load).
Machinery: Parsons geared turbines; 4 Admiralty 3-drum boilers; 2 shafts.
Performance: 40,000shp; 24.25kts.
Bunkerage: 3,000 tons / 3,048 tonnes.
Aircraft: 21.
Guns: 22 × 40mm.
Complement: 1,075.

Design The former *Colossus*-class carrier HMS *Warrior* (qv), sold to Argentina in the summer of 1958 and transferred in December of that year.
Modifications Displacement was listed as 18,400 tons normal in 1962. *Independencia* flew piston-engined F4U and AT-6 aircraft for some years after commissioning into the Argentine Navy.
Service Notes Stricken in 1971.

25 DE MAYO

Builder	Laid down	Launched	Commissioned
Cammell Laird	3 Dec 42	30 Dec 43	12 Mar 69

Displacement: 15,900 tons / 16,154 tonnes (standard); 19,900 tons / 20,218 tonnes (deep load).
Length: 630ft / 192.02m (pp); 650ft / 198.12m (wl); 693ft 2in / 211.28m (oa); 685ft / 208.79m (fd).
Beam: 80ft / 24.38m (hull); 105ft / 32m (fd).
Draught: 21ft 6in / 6.55m (mean); 24ft 6in / 7.47m (deep load).
Machinery: Parsons geared turbines; 4 Admiralty 3-drum boilers; 2 shafts.
Performance: 40,000shp; 24kts.
Bunkerage: 3,000 tons / 3,048 tonnes.
Range: 12,000nm at 14kts.
Aircraft: 21.
Guns: 12 × 40mm.
Complement: 1,500.

Design The former *Colossus*-class light fleet carrier *Karel Doorman* (qv) of the Royal Netherlands Navy. Damaged by fire in April 1968, the ship was sold to Argentina some six months later and refitted and repaired by N V Dok en Werf Mij Wilton Fijenoord, replacement boilers being taken from the laid-up *Majestic*-class carrier *Leviathan*. DA-02 and LW-02 radar was installed, and the refit was completed in August 1969 subsequent to the ship commissioning in the Argentine Navy.

Modifications By 1975 the armament had been reduced to ten and by 1980 to nine 40mm / 70. The air group then consisted of S-2As and SH-3 helicopters (usually four of the latter) for the ASW role, plus a detachment of A-4Q Skyhawks, the latter currently (1983) being replaced by French-built Super Etendard fighter-bombers. The ship has been fitted with data links to enable her to operate with the Type 42 missile destroyers of the Argentine Navy.

Service Notes Believed to have been employed in covering the Argentine invasion of the Falkland Islands, spring 1982, and to have been at sea during the early period of the conflict, but following the sinking of the cruiser *General Belgrano* was not apparently deployed, officially because of mechanical defects.

Below: The second *Colossus*-class carrier to see service with the Argentine Navy was the much-modified *25 de Mayo*. This 1980 photograph shows well the large bridle catcher at the forward round-down, part of the steam catapult system that enables her to operate fast jets. (Dr Robert Scheina, by courtesy of A. D. Baker III)

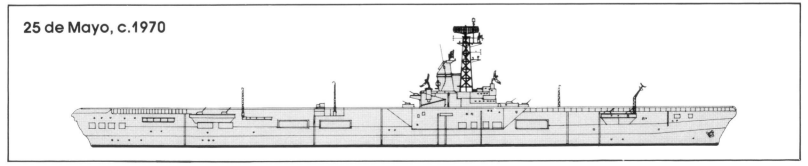

25 de Mayo, c.1970

Australia

The earliest involvement of the Royal Australian Navy in ship-based naval aviation of any specialist nature was the construction and commissioning of the seaplane carrier *Albatross*, similar in concept to (though more developed than) the early British *Ark Royal*. Postwar policy saw the purchase of the modernised light fleet carrier *Melbourne*, preceded by an unconverted sister-ship, *Sydney*, and, briefly, the closely similar *Vengeance*. Up to 1983 plans for replacing *Melbourne* were still very much under consideration, but a change in government has cast doubt over whether the Royal Australian Navy will ever again operate fixed-wing aircraft at sea.

ALBATROSS

Builder	Laid down	Launched	Commissioned
Cockatoo	5 May 26	23 Feb 28	Jan 29

Displacement: 4,800 tons / 4,877 tonnes (standard); 6,000 tons / 6,096 tonnes (deep load).
Length: 422ft / 128.63m (pp); 443ft 9in / 135.26m (oa).
Beam: 60ft 10in / 18.54m (hull).
Draught: 13ft 9in / 4.19m (mean); 16ft 3in / 4.95m (deep load).
Machinery: Parsons geared turbines; 4 Yarrow small-tube boilers; 2 shafts.
Performance: 12,000shp; 22kts.
Bunkerage: 1,000 tons / 1,016 tonnes.
Aircraft: 9.
Guns: 4 × 4.7in; 4 × 2pdr.
Complement: 450.

Design One of Australia's largest indigenous ship-building projects in the pre-war years, the seaplane carrier *Albatross* was authorised as a vessel that could provide the Navy with a trade protection and seaboard defence capability. Not dissimilar in concept to the Royal Navy's *Ark Royal*, the ship possessed a long, flat forecastle equipped with a compressed air catapult; below was a hangar which could accommodate nine aircraft, handling being by means of three lattice-type cranes: one well forward on the starboard side serving the catapult and a pair abreast the hangar hatch further aft, just forward of the bridge which was situated at the forecastle break. The hull was bulged to provide increased stability, but there was no armour protection. The single 4.7in were open mountings and disposed half-way along and each side of the forecastle and in superfiring positions on

the centreline aft. Petrol capacity was 8,300 gallons and the ship reportedly embarked Fairey IIID floatplanes before equipping with Seagull amphibians in the early 1930s.
Modifications Believed none in RAN service.
Service Notes Served with the Royal Australian Navy until September 1938 when she was transferred to the Royal Navy (qv).

Sydney, 1950

SYDNEY

Builder	Laid down	Launched	Commissioned
Devonport	19 Apr 43	30 Sept 44	5 Feb 49

Displacement: 14,512 tons / 14,744 tonnes (standard); 19,550 tons / 19,863 tonnes (deep load).
Length: 630ft / 192.02m (pp); 650ft / 198.12m (wl); 698ft / 212.75m (oa); 685ft / 208.79m (fd).
Beam: 80ft / 24.38m (hull); 75ft / 22.86m (fd).
Draught: 19ft 9in / 6.02m (mean); 24ft 6in / 7.47m (deep load).
Machinery: Parsons geared turbines; 4 Admiralty 3-drum boilers; 2 shafts.
Performance: 40,000shp; 25kts.
Bunkerage: 3,480 tons / 3,536 tonnes.
Range: 9,320nm at 12kts.

Aircraft: 37.
Guns: 30 × 40mm.
Complement: 1,200.

Design The ex-British *Majestic*-class carrier *Terrible* (qv), transferred to the Royal Australian Navy on 16 February 1948 and little altered from the original *Majestic* design. As completed she was equipped to operate 12 Sea Furies, 24 Fireflies and a Sea Otter amphibian, petrol bunkerage amounting to 80,000 gallons. The ordnance lists include 35 × 2,000lb AP, 54 × 1,000lb MC, 72 × 500lb SAP and 73 × 500lb MC bombs as typical stowage, plus 438 × 60lb shells, 732 × 3in air-to-air rockets and 108 depth-charges. The radar fit included the Types 277Q/293Q search/height-finder/air direction system.

Modifications Converted to a fast transport in 1962, with a reduced armament, for operations in South-East Asia.

Service Notes *Sydney* was employed as an operational carrier during the Korean conflict in 1951–52, remaining on patrol in that region until 1953. From 1957 she was used principally as a training carrier, but saw active service as a transport from 1962 supporting Australian involvement in Malaya and subsequently in Vietnam. She was stricken in 1973 and sold for scrapping in 1975, being broken up the following year.

Below: *Sydney* transports 'cocooned' Fireflies and Sea Furies, probably on passage from the UK to Australia. (Australian War Memorial)

VENGEANCE

Builder	Laid down	Launched	Commissioned
Swan Hunter	16 Nov 42	23 Feb 44	1953

Displacement: 13,300 tons / 13,513 tonnes (standard); 18,150 tons / 18,440 tonnes (deep load).
Length: 630ft / 192.02m (pp); 650ft / 198.12m (wl); 695ft / 211.84m (oa); 680ft / 207.26m (fd).
Beam: 80ft / 24.38m (hull); 80ft / 24.38m (fd).
Draught: 18ft 6in / 5.64m (mean); 23ft 6in / 7.16m (deep load).
Machinery: Parsons geared turbines; 4 Admiralty 3-drum boilers; 2 shafts.

Performance: 40,000shp; 25kts.
Bunkerage: 3,196 tons / 3,247 tonnes.
Range: 12,000nm at 14kts.
Aircraft: 37.
Guns: 24 × 2pdr; 17 × 40mm.
Complement: 1,300.
Design The British *Colossus*-class carrier of the same name (qv), on loan to the Royal Australian Navy from early 1953 to August 1955. The ship refitted prior to transfer, receiving the Type 277Q/293Q radar outfit.
Modifications Believed none in RAN service.
Service Notes Used initially as a training carrier and from late 1953 as a front-line fleet carrier; returned

Above: A view of *Sydney* as an operational carrier. The major visible difference from the preceding photograph is the presence of a YE homing beacon, mounted on its mast abreast the funnel. (US Navy, by courtesy of A. D. Baker III)

Below: *Vengeance* in Royal Australian Navy service. This ex-*Colossus*-class vessel was closely similar in external appearance to *Sydney* (ex-*Majestic* class), differing chiefly in bridge detail, radar fit and fixed battery (note, for example, the quadruple 2pdrs and single Bofors along the deck edge). (Australian War Memorial)

prior to the transfer of *Melbourne* and subsequently sold to Brazil as *Minas Gerais* (qv).

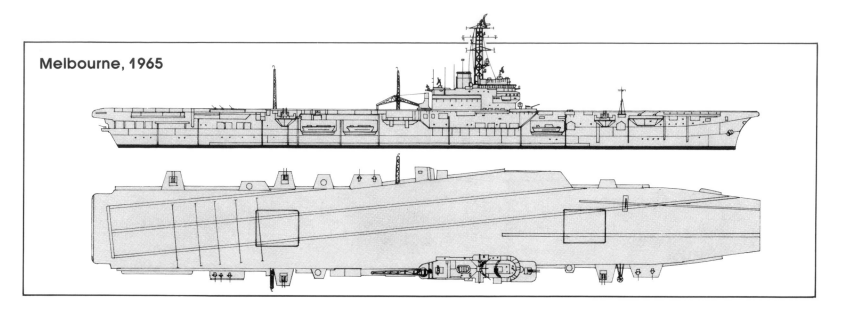

Melbourne, 1965

MELBOURNE

Builder	Laid down	Launched	Commissioned
Vickers-Armstrong (Barrow)	15 Apr 43	28 Feb 45	28 Oct 55

Displacement: 16,000 tons / 16,256 tonnes
(standard); 20,320 tons / 20,645 tonnes (deep load).
Length: 630ft / 192.02m (pp); 650ft / 198.12m (wl);
701ft 6in / 213.82m (oa); 690ft / 210.31m (fd).
Beam: 80ft / 24.38m (hull); 105ft / 32m (fd).
Draught: 25ft / 7.62m (deep load).
Machinery: Parsons geared turbines; 4 Admiralty
3-drum boilers; 2 shafts.
Performance: 40,000shp; 24.5kts.
Bunkerage: 3,000 tons / 3,048 tonnes.
Aircraft: 27.
Guns: 25 × 40mm.
Complement: 1,210.

Design The former name-ship of the British
Majestic-class light fleet carriers (qv), purchased by
Australia in 1949 and arriving in Australian waters
in May 1956. *Melbourne* was completed to a
modified *Majestic* design, featuring a 5½° angled
landing deck, new arrester gear, a mirror landing
system and a steam catapult. Her original air group
consisted of Sea Venom strike planes and ASW
Gannets, and radar Types 277Q/293Q was fitted.

Modifications The ASW role was emphasised in
1963 with the embarkation of Wessex helicopters;
the fixed battery at this time was listed as 25 × 40mm,
and Dutch main radar was fitted. An extended refit in
1967−69 equipped her for A-4 and S-2 operation,
and the radar fit now showed Dutch-built LW-01 air
search, ZW series surface search and CCA (Carrier-
Controlled Approach) sets. The flight deck was
strengthened and the catapult renewed in 1971, and
by 1976 S-2s, A-4s and ASW Sea King helicopters,
with Wessexes in the SAR role, were being operated.
By the late 1970s armament was quoted as four twin

and four single 40mm, complement as 1,335 (including air group personnel) and speed as 'more than
20kts'.

Service Notes Flagship of the Royal Australian
Navy from her commissioning. Scheduled for replacement in the early 1980s, an Italian *Garibaldi*-type
carrier first being envisaged and then the British
Invincible; however, when the latter was withdrawn
from sale in mid 1982, at which time *Melbourne* was
laid up in operational reserve, the problem of air-

capability within the RAN came under discussion
once more. The British carrier *Hermes* was offered,
but the choice would seem to lie among a Spanish
PA11-type ship, the Italian design and a converted
merchant-type V/STOL carrier, all of which were
under serious study in mid 1983.

Below: *Melbourne* shortly after receiving her new LW series
main search radar, 1965. Three ANU aerials for Type 277Q
radar are visible on the island, presumably to give
simultaneous height-finding and surface search capabilities.
Forward of and just below the ZW antenna is the 'cheese' of
the Type 293Q target-indicator. (Navy Public Relations,
Canberra, by courtesy of A. D. Baker III)

Above: By the 1970s *Melbourne* was showing a new radar/ radio fit and a new catapult; she could also operate A-4 Skyhawks, albeit in limited numbers. Note that the main search radar (LW series) has moved down to a position atop the bridge, displaced by a TACAN homing beacon. (Australian War Memorial)

Brazil

Brazil continues to operate her single carrier, another of the ubiquitous ex-British light fleets, in the ASW role.

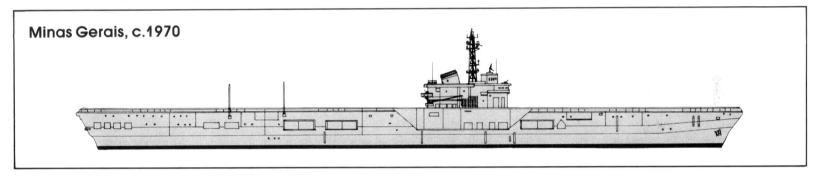

Minas Gerais, c.1970

MINAS GERAIS

Builder	Laid down	Launched	Commissioned
Swan Hunter	16 Nov 42	23 Feb 44	6 Dec 60

Displacement: 15,890 tons / 16,144 tonnes (standard); 19,900 tons / 20,218 tonnes (deep load).
Length: 630ft / 192.02m (pp); 650ft / 198.12m (wl); 695ft / 211.84m (oa); 680ft / 207.26m (fd).
Beam: 80ft / 24.38m (hull); 105ft / 32m (fd).
Draught: 21ft 4in / 6.5m (mean); 24ft / 7.32m (deep load).
Machinery: Parsons geared turbines; 4 Admiralty 3-drum boilers; 2 shafts.
Performance: 40,000shp; 24kts.
Bunkerage: 3,000 tons / 3,048 tonnes.
Range: 12,000nm at 14kts.
Aircraft: 35.
Guns: 10 × 40mm.
Complement: 1,300.

Design The ex-British *Colossus*-class carrier *Vengeance* (qv), sold to Brazil in late 1956. The ship

Left: *Minas Gerais* in the early 1960s, much changed from her configuration while serving in the RN and RAN as *Vengeance*. The island is dominated by a new lattice mast; forward of this is the large SPS-8B antenna. Note the quad 40mm mounting on the island, forward. S2F Trackers are ranged on the flight deck aft. (By courtesy of A. D. Baker III)

was extensively modernised at Verolme Dock, Rotterdam, from mid 1957 until December 1960, receiving new lifts, a strengthened flight deck with a steam catapult, new arrester gear, a deck landing mirror system, an 8½° angled landing deck and a revised AA battery of one twin and two quadruple 40mm. The island was modified and a new, raked funnel installed, while a tall lattice mast replaced the original tripod. US-built radar (SPS-12 air search, SPS-4 surface search, SPS-8B height-finder) was fitted.

Above: *Minas Gerais* in the 1970s, showing an added bridle catcher over the bows, but otherwise little changed from her appearance as first commissioned in the Brazilian Navy. (Brazilian Navy)

Modifications Extensively overhauled from 1976 to 1980. Current air complement is quoted as 20.
Service Notes Operates principally as an ASW carrier with S-2 fixed-wing aircraft and S-61 helicopters. Replacement helicopter carriers were projected in 1980, one study envisaging nuclear-powered vessels.

Canada

Canada has commissioned three carriers postwar, all ex-British light fleets. The last, the modernised *Bonaventure*, was retained for ASW until her early disposal in mid 1970.

WARRIOR

Builder	Laid down	Launched	Commissioned
Harland & Wolff	12 Dec 42	20 May 44	14 Mar 46

Displacement: 13,350 tons / 13,564 tonnes (standard); 18,300 tons / 18,593 tonnes (deep load).
Length: 630ft / 192.02m (pp); 650ft / 198.12m (wl); 695ft / 211.84m (oa); 680ft / 207.26m (fd).
Beam: 80ft / 24.38m (hull); 80ft / 24.38m (fd).
Draught: 18ft 6in / 5.64m (mean); 23ft 6in / 7.16m (deep load).
Machinery: Parsons geared turbines; 4 Admiralty 3-drum boilers; 2 shafts.
Performance: 40,000shp; 25kts.
Bunkerage: 3,196 tons / 3,247 tonnes.
Range: 12,000nm at 14kts.
Aircraft: 48.
Guns: 24 × 2pdr; 17 × 40mm.
Complement: 1,300.
Design The British-built *Colossus*-class carrier of the same name (qv), on loan to Canada from 1946 to 1948.
Modifications Believed none.
Service Notes Served until being returned to Britain in late 1948, when *Magnificent* was commissioned into the RCN.

Below: *Warrior* in April 1946, shortly after transfer to the Royal Canadian Navy. (Ministry of Defence (Navy), by courtesy of A. D. Baker III)

MAGNIFICENT

Builder	Laid down	Launched	Commissioned
Harland & Wolff	29 July 43	16 Nov 44	21 Mar 48

Displacement: 14,512 tons / 14,744 tonnes (standard); 19,550 tons / 19,863 tonnes (deep load).
Length: 630ft / 192.02m (pp); 650ft / 198.12m (wl); 698ft/212.75m (oa); 685ft / 208.79m (fd).
Beam: 80ft / 24.38m (hull); 75ft / 22.86m (fd).
Draught: 19ft 9in / 6.02m (mean); 24ft 6in / 7.47m (deep load).

Machinery: Parsons geared turbines; 4 Admiralty 3-drum boilers; 2 shafts.
Performance: 40,000shp; 25kts.
Bunkerage: 3,480 tons / 3,536 tonnes.
Range: 9,320nm at 12kts.
Aircraft: 37.
Guns: 30 × 40mm.
Complement: 1,200.
Design Completed to what was essentially the original *Majestic* design (qv) and lent to the Royal Canadian Navy in 1948. Generally similar to the

Above: *Magnificent* in March 1950, with four Fireflies ranged forward. Two of the aircraft are NF Mk 1s, distinguishable from the Mk 4/5s further aft by their three-bladed propellers, chin intakes, different fin shape and, more significantly, AI radar pods below the forward fuselage. (US Navy, by courtesy of A. D. Baker III)

RAN's *Sydney* (qv).
Modifications Believed none.
Service Notes Served until being returned to Britain in 1957; immediately placed in reserve, and sold and scrapped from July 1965.

BONAVENTURE

Builder	Laid down	Launched	Commissioned
Harland & Wolff	27 Nov 43	27 Feb 45	17 Jan 57

Displacement: 16,000 tons / 16,256 tonnes (standard); 20,000 tons / 20,320 tonnes (deep load).
Length: 630ft / 192.02m (pp); 650ft / 198.12m (wl); 704ft 10in / 214.83m (oa); 685ft / 208.79m (fd).
Beam: 80ft / 24.38m (hull); 105ft / 32m (fd).
Draught: 25ft / 7.62m (deep load).
Machinery: Parsons geared turbines; 4 Admiralty 3-drum boilers; 2 shafts.
Performance: 40,000shp; 24.5kts.
Bunkerage: 3,000 tons / 3,048 tonnes.
Aircraft: 34.
Guns: 8 × 3in.
Complement: 1,200.

Design The former *Majestic*-class light fleet carrier *Powerful* (qv), purchased by Canada in 1952, *Bonaventure* was redesigned prior to completion to accommodate an 8° angled deck, a steam catapult and a stabilised mirror landing sight. She was unique among refurbished *Majestic*s in mounting twin 3in / 50 anti-aircraft guns on four sponsons projecting a considerable distance from the hull sides (giving a maximum beam of 128ft). Her island was redesigned by having the structure extended around the funnel along the starboard side, and a tall lattice mast was erected in place of the original design's tripod. US SPS-10 surface search, SPS-12 air search and SPS-8 height-finder radar was fitted and modern arrester gear installed. The ship initially equipped with Banshee interceptors and CS2F Tracker ASW aircraft.

Modifications The carrier took on a pure ASW role from about 1961, when the fighter aircraft were landed and S-61 helicopters embarked instead. A refit in the late 1960s (Davies Shipbuilding) saw *Bonaventure* equipped with the Fresnel landing aid and improved anti-fallout facilities, and the fixed battery was reduced to 4 × 3in, the forward mountings and sponsons being removed to enhance seakeeping.

Above: *Bonaventure* after her late 1960s refit, with Trackers and Sea Kings embarked and forward sponsons removed. (Royal Canadian Navy)

Service Notes Decommissioned in July 1970 shortly after her mid-life refit and subsequently sold and broken up.

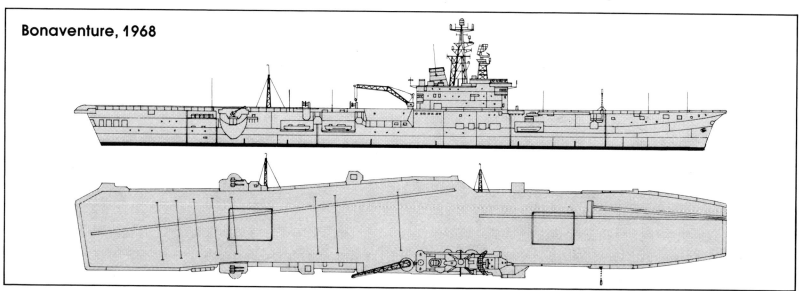

Bonaventure, 1968

France

French carrier development, pioneered by means of converted steamers during the First World War, has had a somewhat fitful history, punctuated as it has been by a large number of promising designs which for one reason or another have remained unfulfilled. The first French fleet carrier (and one of only three ever completed in France), *Béarn*, was built from a cancelled battleship hull with considerable British assistance. Early defeat in the Second World War put paid to successors, and economic difficulties and policy reassessments have resulted in only two postwar ships; these are still in service and considered to be effective assets (although limited, by US standards). However, France is still seemingly determined to maintain an attack carrier component for her navy, with the recent announcement of two nuclear-powered successors to the *Clémenceau*s.

One problem afflicting the French Navy has traditionally been the shortage of suitable indigenous naval aircraft designs, a problem not helped by the small size of the carrier component and the consequently small production runs (hence high unit cost) of dedicated carrier machines. Even today, the strike / fighter roles are combined in a single airframe the essential design of which is 30 years old; and there is no AEW element. However, the ships themselves are seen as cost-effective units (an opinion doubtless first emphasised by the performance of French-operated carrier aircraft around Indo-China during the early 1950s) and as essential to the Gaullist doctrine of complete French military independence; the strong links that France maintains with her former colonies certainly seem to validate the retention of carriers.

FOUDRE

Builder	Laid down	Launched	Commissioned
Ch de la Gironde	9 June 92	20 Oct 95	1913

Displacement: 5,971 tons / 6,067 tonnes (standard); 6,089 tons / 6,186 tonnes (deep load).
Length: 389ft 5in / 118.7m (oa).
Beam: 51ft 2in / 15.6m (hull).
Draught: 17ft 9in / 5.4m (mean); 23ft 8in / 7.2m (deep load).
Machinery: Triple-expansion reciprocating engines; 24 Lagrafel d'Allest boilers; 2 shafts.
Performance: 11,500 ihp; 19kts.
Bunkerage: 787 tons / 800 tonnes.
Range: 7,500nm at 10kts.
Aircraft: 8.
Guns: 8 × 3.9in; 4 × 65mm; 4 × 47mm.
Complement: 430.

Design Completed as a coal-burning depot ship for torpedo-boats in 1896, *Foudre*, formerly named *La Seine*, was France's earliest vessel to be provided with a realistic air capability. A succession of modifications saw her employed first as a repair ship (1907), then as a minelayer (1910), as a seaplane depot ship (1912) and finally as a *croiseur porte-avions* (1913).

As built she incorporated many cruiser characteristics, with a sloped armoured deck (maximum

Above: *Foudre* during the First World War, with makeshift hangar abaft amidships. (By courtesy of Jacques Navarret)

thickness 4.6in) and an armoured conning tower. The main armament was carried in casemate-type sponsons along the hull, with single mountings on the forepeak and right aft over the stern. After conversion she could operate a theoretical maximum of eight seaplanes, but the complement was normally four and frequently only two. On trials she made 19.57kts at 11,930ihp.

Plans to convert the protected cruiser *Forbin* (1,935 tons, 4 × 5.5in, 20kts) along similar lines were abandoned prior to the First World War and the ship served as a collier instead.

Modifications The shielded 3.9in guns were reportedly replaced by Army-pattern 3.5in weapons at the end of the First World War.

Service Notes *Foudre* was employed as a multi-purpose vessel during the First World War. She was deployed to the Mediterranean early in 1916, ferrying seaplanes to the Allied base at Port Said, and she also served as a submarine tender. She was stricken in 1921.

CAMPINAS

Laid down	Launched	Commissioned
1894	1896	1915

Displacement: 3,319 tons / 3,372 tonnes (standard).
Length: 357ft 7in / 109m (oa).
Beam: 42ft 2in / 12.85m (hull).
Draught: 23ft 3in / 7.08m (mean).
Machinery: Triple-expansion reciprocating engines; 2 boilers; 1 shaft.
Performance: 1,500ihp; 11.5kts.
Bunkerage: 984 tons / 1,000 tonnes.
Aircraft: 8.
Design A former passenger ship, completed in 1897, *Campinas* was converted in 1915 to a seaplane carrier for service in the Mediterranean. Two hangars were erected on the upper deck together with handling gear for hoisting the seaplanes, six to eight of which could be accommodated according to type. She was coal-burning.
Modifications Not known.
Service Notes Served with the Suez Canal Seaplane Flotilla from early 1916.

NORD CLASS

Ship	Laid down	Launched	Commissioned
Nord	1897	1898	1916
Pas-de-Calais	1897	1898	1916

Length: 337ft 10in / 102.97m (oa).
Beam: 34ft 11in / 10.65m (hull).
Draught: 10ft 10in / 3.3m (mean).
Machinery: Reciprocating engines; 2 paddles.
Performance: 7,800ihp; 20kts.
Aircraft: 3.
Design A pair of 1,541grt cross-Channel packets, acquired by the French Navy on the outbreak of the First World War and converted during 1915 to operate seaplanes. Both were coal-burning and both had originally been completed in 1899. Prior to conversion, *Nord* served as a cross-Channel hospital ship under the auspices of the Red Cross.
Modifications Not known.
Service Notes *Nord*: Based at Dunkirk during 1916–17. Returned to mercantile service in 1919.
Pas-de-Calais: Based at Cherbourg, operating as a patrol seaplane carrier during the First World War. Returned to mercantile service 1919.

ROUEN

Laid down	Launched	Commissioned
1911	1912	1917

Length: 301ft 10in / 92m (oa).
Beam: 34ft 8in / 10.57m (hull).
Draught: 9ft 8in / 2.95m (mean).
Machinery: Turbines; 3 shafts.
Performance: 8,000shp; 24kts.
Aircraft: 4.
Guns: 2 × 47mm.
Design A coal-burning, 1,656grt cross-Channel packet completed in 1912, *Rouen* was requisitioned by the French Navy in 1914 for service as an auxiliary cruiser to operate in the English Channel. Following mine damage in December 1916 she was repaired and given facilities for handling seaplanes.
Modifications Not known.
Service Notes *Rouen* was employed as a convoy escort in the Mediterranean during the last months of the First World War and was returned to her original owners in 1919. She was taken over again in the Second World War as an ammunition ship and in 1940 assisted in the evacuation of British forces from Dunkirk. Captured by the Germans in the summer of 1940, she was converted for minelaying (renamed *Wullenwever*). She was scrapped in 1946.

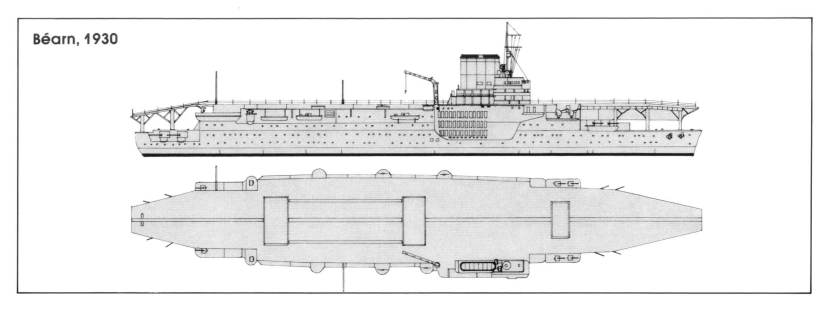

Béarn, 1930

BÉARN

Builder	Laid down	Launched	Commissioned
F Ch de la Med	10 Jan 14	Apr 20	May 27

Displacement: 22,100 tons / 22,454 tonnes
(standard); 28,400 tons / 28,854 tonnes (deep load).
Length: 559ft 9in / 170.6m (pp); 574ft 2in / 175m
(wl); 599ft 1in / 182.6m (oa); 580ft / 176.8m (fd).
Beam: 88ft 11in / 27.1m (hull); 70ft / 21.34m (fd).
Draught: 27ft 6in / 8.38m (mean); 30ft 6in / 9.3m
(deep load).
Machinery: Parsons turbines / triple-expansion
reciprocating engines; 12 du Temple small-tube

boilers; 4 shafts.
Performance: 40,000shp; 21.5kts.
Bunkerage: 2,165 tons / 2,200 tonnes.
Range: 7,000nm at 10kts.
Aircraft: 40.
Guns: 8 × 6.1in; 6 × 75mm; 8 × 37mm.
Torpedo tubes: 4 × 21.7in.
Complement: 865.
Design Early French experiments in the operation of
landplanes on board warships centred around the
trials ship *Bapaume*, a 700-ton sloop which in 1920
was fitted with a flying-off platform for Nieuport 17
fighters. Two years later authorization was given for

Above: As was the British *Eagle*, *Béarn* was a converted First
World War dreadnought hull; indeed, the French carrier,
though significantly different in general appearance, owed
much to the British design. As originally completed, she
showed a flat flight deck over the bows, as seen here, July
1928. (By courtesy of Ray Burt)

the French Navy's first full-decked aircraft carrier.

Like most early full-deck carriers, *Béarn* was an
adaptation of a capital ship design. Four *Normandie*-
class battleships (25,200 tons, 12 × 13.4in guns in
quadruple turrets, 21.5kts) were ordered under the
1913 Programme and a fifth, *Béarn*, under the 1914
Programme (ordered November 1913), but at the

outbreak of the First World War all construction work was halted as materials and labour were diverted to more immediate projects. The ships were still laid up (though in an advanced state of cannibalisation) by August 1918; there were various suggestions concerning their possible completion to modified designs, but they would have been uneconomic and outdated vessels, and their fate was finally settled by the Washington Treaty. However *Béarn*, still on the stocks, was authorised in 1922 for conversion to a carrier, and with considerable British assistance (notably plans of *Eagle*) her reconstruction began in August 1923.

The hull structure was in general retained although the bows and stern were reshaped and the armour scheme was revised: the original 11.8in-6.3in battleship belt being reduced to 3.2in, the 2.8in-1in lower deck protecting machinery and magazines being unaffected, but the 2in upper deck being abandoned and the armour redistributed to main (1in) and flight deck (1in) levels. The machinery system was also unchanged, although the actual equipment in *Béarn* came from her uncompleted sister ship *Normandie*. Of novel arrangement, the machinery consisted of geared turbines driving the inner shafts and reciprocating engines linked to the outer shafts, officially to provide alternative powerplants for high-speed sailing and cruising respectively, but probably also because French-built turbines were somewhat unreliable in service. The boilers were renewed, small-tube units replacing the designed 21 Niclausse-type coal-burners.

Workshops and stowage spaces for dismantled aircraft were built up on to the hull above which was situated a 405ft-long hangar served by three electrically-powered lifts, the wells amidships and aft measuring 27ft × 40ft and that forward 30ft × 50ft. The unusual widths were accounted for by an interesting system of hinged flaps which opened to reveal the lifts proper below, presumably to enable flight-deck operations to be conducted with the lifts lowered. This two-tiered arrangement resulted in a flight deck 51ft above the waterline in the standard condition.

The island was mounted to starboard beyond the limits of the flight deck and supported by a huge faired sponson which enclosed the boiler uptakes and featured prominent cooling vents, the gases being filtered with cold air in an effort to prevent smoke interfering with landing aircraft. A 12-ton 'gooseneck' crane was positioned abaft the island, serving the lift amidships. The flight deck had an extreme length of 600ft and was carried clear of the forecastle via supports, and an advanced Schneider-

designed transverse arrester system was installed. Aviation fuel stowage was 26,000 gallons, and the carrier was reportedly fitted with a 65ft turntable-mounted catapult.

The fixed battery consisted of single-mounted low-angle guns in casemates at forecastle deck level and on the quarters, with shielded 3in AA in pairs forward and one each side aft, below flight-deck level, and 37mm singles behind them.

Modifications *Béarn* was completed with a flat flight deck forward, but shortly afterwards this was rebuilt to give a marked downward slope. A 1935 refit saw additional vents incorporated into the island fairing and the forward flight deck overhang partially enclosed. During the Second World War the carrier had her AA battery removed at Martinique in May 1942 and from late 1943 was completely refitted as an aircraft transport at New Orleans, her French 6.1in guns being landed and four single 5in / 38, 24 × 40mm and 26 single 20mm being fitted. The flight deck was shortened forward and aft, giving an effective length of 510ft.

Service Notes Following pre-war service as a platform for the somewhat poorly equipped *Aéronavale*, *Béarn* was used as a transatlantic aircraft ferry and training carrier until being held in Martinique on US orders in June 1940 to prevent her return to France and possible take-over by the Germans. She remained in the West Indies until her US refit of 1943-44, whence she resumed her role as a transport, a task she continued after the war in the French attempt to recover their possessions in Indo-China. She was hulked in 1948, serving first as a training ship and then as a submarine depot ship; she was stricken in November 1966 and was sold for breaking up the following year.

Top left: By the early 1930s *Béarn* had a redesigned forward flight deck, the downward slope being incorporated apparently to improve air flow. The casemated battery of 6.1in guns is clearly visible. (By courtesy of Ian Sturton)

Below left: During the mid 1930s *Béarn* was further modified, with an increased number of vents amidships and the partial enclosure of the area below the forward flight deck. Note the prominent 'gooseneck' crane abaft the island. (By courtesy of Bernard Millot)

Above: *Béarn* was not employed as a front-line attack carrier during the Second World War, her slow speed and limited facilities reducing her value to the Allied fleet; however, she performed valuable service in a number of auxiliary roles. This February 1945 view show some of the changes incorporated during her US refit, notably her revised armament and shortened flight deck. (US National Archives)

COMMANDANT TESTE

Builder	Laid down	Launched	Commissioned
F Ch de la Gironde	May 27	12 Apr 29	1932

Displacement: 10,000 tons / 10,160 tonnes (standard); 11,500 tons / 11,684 tonnes (deep load).
Length: 512ft 9in / 156.3m (pp); 547ft 11in / 167m (oa).
Beam: 88ft 7in / 27m (hull).
Draught: 22ft 9in / 6.93m (mean).
Machinery: Schneider-Zoelly geared turbines; 4 Yarrow-Loire small-tube boilers; 2 shafts.
Performance: 21,000shp; 20.5kts.
Bunkerage: 290 tons / 295 tonnes.
Range: 6,000nm at 10kts.
Aircraft: 26.
Guns: 12 × 3.9in; 8 × 37mm; 12 × 13.2mm.
Complement: 642.

Design An important thread in French shipboard aviation during the inter-war years was the development of catapult flights on board capital ships and cruisers, and as early as 1926 a seaplane tender was authorised that could act as a repair and replenishment vessel in this respect, but also provide a limited airborne offensive capability.

The hull, armoured with a 2in belt and 1½in over the machinery spaces, showed a high freeboard, enclosing a 275ft-long hangar broken amidships by the boiler uptakes but extending the full beam of the ship and, with a height of 23ft, of sufficient size to accommodate not only floatplanes but also small flying boats. The aircraft were hoisted by four heavy derricks, in pairs port and starboard, each serving an adjacent catapult, and a lighter derrick on the cutdown quarterdeck enabled machines to be embarked over the stern. Half the boilers were oil-fired (bunkerage indicated in the table) and half coal, capacity for the latter being 720 tons. The aircraft complement in 1939 consisted of Latécoère 298 floatplanes and Loire-Nieuport 130 flying boats.

Modifications Pre-war modifications not known. Plans to convert *Commandant Teste* to a flush-decked aircraft carrier post-war were not proceeded with.

Service Notes *Commandant Teste* was stationed in the Mediterranean during the early months of the Second World War, launching one unsuccessful strike against Italian cruisers in June 1940. Following the fall of France she was scuttled at Toulon to forestall any take-over by German forces. Raised and basically refitted post-war, she served as a store ship until being disposed of for scrapping in May 1950.

JOFFRE CLASS

Displacement: 18,000 tons / 18,288 tonnes (standard); 20,000 tons / 20,320 tonnes (deep load).
Length: 748ft / 228m (wl); 774ft 3in / 236m (oa); 656ft 2in / 200m (fd).
Beam: 82ft / 25m (hull); 91ft 10in / 28m (fd).
Draught: 21ft 8in / 6.6m (mean).
Machinery: Parsons geared turbines; 8 Indret boilers; 4 shafts.
Performance: 120,000shp; 32kts.
Aircraft: 40.
Guns: 8 × 5.1in; 8 × 37mm; 28 × 13.2mm.
Complement: 1,250.

Design Even though the French Navy has only ever operated three indigenously-designed genuine aircraft carriers there have been a large number of stillborn projects. Among the earliest of these were studies in the early 1930s for a pair of 15,000-ton vessels with cruiser-type hulls and machinery, operating about 20-30 aircraft, and a 1936 scheme for the conversion of the cruisers *Duquesne* and *Tourville* to fast semi-carriers retaining a pair of 8in guns and deploying about a dozen aircraft. The first officially sanctioned carriers after *Béarn*, however, were a pair of most unusual ships, *Joffre* and *Painlevé*, which were laid down on 26 November 1938 and 1939 respectively, by Ateliers et Chantiers de St-Nazaire-Penhoët.

A two-storeyed hangar arrangement was selected, the upper measuring 640ft × 68ft and the lower 260ft × 50ft with heights of 16ft 6in and 14ft 6in respectively. The hangars were integrated into the hull structure and topped with a through flight deck, but the upper hangar and deck were offset to port to balance a superstructure which, although concen-trated on the starboard side, was a large, imposing feature entirely separate from the deck itself (and thus not an 'island' in the normal sense of the term) and carrying a single funnel and the new-pattern 5in / 45 dual-purpose guns, the latter in twin turrets. There were two lifts, forward and aft, and cross-deck arrester gear was to be fitted amidships.

The original air group was predicated on a com-plement made up of 25 of a new twin-engined torpedo-bomber-reconnaissance type, plus 15 fighters, but before the aircraft could be selected the Germans invaded France and all work ceased, by which time a third ship had reportedly been authorised. Both vessels were scrapped on the slips.

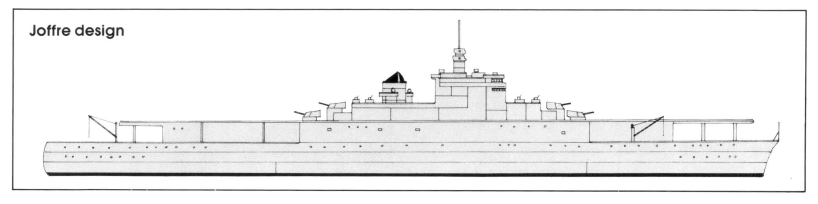

Joffre design

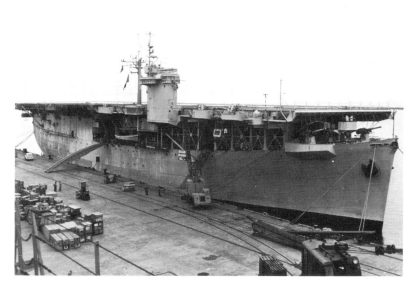

DIXMUDE

Builder	Launched	Commissioned
Sun	18 Dec 40	9 Apr 45

Displacement: 11,800 tons / 11,989 tonnes (standard); 15,126 tons / 15,368 tonnes (deep load).
Length: 465ft / 141.73m (wl); 492ft / 149.96m (oa); 440ft / 134.11m (fd).
Beam: 69ft 6in / 21.18m (hull); 78ft / 23.77m (fd).
Draught: 25ft 2in / 7.67m (deep load).
Machinery: 6-cylinder Doxford diesel engines; 1 shaft.
Performance: 8,500bhp; 16.5kts.
Bunkerage: 3,200 tons / 3,251 tonnes.

Aircraft: 20.
Guns: 3 × 4in; 10 × 20mm.
Complement: 850.
Design The former US-built British escort carrier *Biter* (qv).
Modifications On transfer to France *Dixmude* was showing US-supplied SA search radar, and the number of 20mm weapons had been reduced to thirteen. The ship appears to have been disarmed by the early 1950s, and by 1960 displacement was listed as 8,500 tons standard and speed as 16kts.
Service Notes Used principally as an aircraft transport (*transport d'aviation*) in French service.

Above left: One of the first batch of US-built escort carriers to serve with the Royal Navy (BAVGs), *Biter* was transferred to France after the war ended in Europe and renamed *Dixmude*. This 1950 view shows well two of the carrier's 4in guns, on the forecastle, with, above, a 20mm mounting; more Oerlikons are visible along the edge of the flight deck. (US Navy, by courtesy of A. D. Baker III)

Above right: *Dixmude* at New Orleans in June 1953 with Hell-divers aboard, her SA radar clearly visible at the masthead. The ship is apparently unarmed. (By courtesy of Bernard Millot)

Hulked as an accommodation ship in 1960, she was returned to US authority in mid 1966 and sub-sequently scrapped.

ARROMANCHES

Builder	Laid down	Launched	Commissioned
Vickers-Armstrong (Newcastle)	1 June 42	30 Sept 43	Aug 46

Displacement: 13,300 tons / 13,513 tonnes (standard); 18,150 tons / 18,440 tonnes (deep load).
Length: 630ft / 192.02m (pp); 650ft / 198.12m (wl); 695ft / 211.84m (oa); 680ft / 207.26m (fd).
Beam: 80ft / 24.38m (hull); 80ft / 24.38m (fd).
Draught: 18ft 6in / 5.64m (mean); 23ft 6in / 7.16m (deep load).
Machinery: Parsons geared turbines; 4 Admiralty 3-drum boilers; 2 shafts.
Performance: 40,000shp; 25kts.
Bunkerage: 3,196 tons / 3,247 tonnes.
Range: 12,000nm at 14kts.
Aircraft: 35.
Guns: 24 × 2pdr; 17 × 40mm.
Complement: 1,100.

Design The former name-ship of the British *Colossus* class of light fleet carriers (qv), loaned in August 1946 and purchased by France in 1951.
Modifications By 1953 aircraft complement consisted of 24 US-built F6F and SB2C types. *Arromanches* was reconstructed in 1957–58, receiving an angled deck (4°) and a mirror landing aid; extreme width increased from 112ft 6in to 118ft. Armament was now 43 × 40mm, but these were removed in the early 1960s, and by 1963 displacement was listed as 14,000 tons standard and 19,600 tons deep load. She was refitted again in 1968 to enable her to operate as an ASW carrier (24 helicopters), by which time French-designed DRBV-22 air warning radar had been installed.
Service Notes *Arromanches* deployed to South-East Asia from 1949, supporting French operations in Indo-China. In November 1956 she was part of the French component of the Suez task force, her aircraft attacking installations around Port Said. She was employed mainly as a training carrier from 1960, was decommissioned in 1974 and was broken up at Toulon from early 1978.

Top: One of the first British war-built light fleet carriers to be transferred to a friendly navy was *Colossus*, which served the *Marine Nationale* for almost three decades as *Arromanches*. She shows the typical late 1940s light fleet carrier battery of quadruple 2pdrs and single Bofors. (By courtesy of A. D. Baker III)

Centre: *Arromanches* at Saigon, 6 September 1952, with Hellcats and Helldivers aboard. (By courtesy of A. D. Baker III)

Left: *Arromanches* refitted as an ASW carrier, with four Breguet Alizé ASW aircraft visible. The new generation of attack aircraft (jets) available to the French Navy in the 1960s proved too heavy and powerful to be operated from the carrier without a major reconstruction, although it might be noted that one of her former sister ships, much modified, is apparently able to launch and recover successfully the French Super Étendard strike aircraft. (By courtesy of Bernard Millot)

PA28 PROJECT

Displacement: 15,700 tons / 15,951 tonnes (standard); 20,000 tons / 20,320 tonnes (deep load).
Length: 705ft 5in / 215m (wl); 754ft 7in / 230m (oa); 721ft 9in / 220m (fd).
Beam: 83ft 4in / 25.4m (hull); 98ft 5in / 30m (fd).
Draught: 21ft 4in / 6.5m (mean).
Machinery: Parsons geared turbines; 4 Indret boilers; 2 shafts.

Performance: 105,000shp; 32kts.
Aircraft: 45.
Guns: 16 × 3.9in; 16 × 57mm.
Complement: 1,800.

Design Many pre-war French carriers had proven abortive and the trend was at first continued in the post-war years. The Navy envisaged a sizeable carrier fleet in a revitalised service, and indeed quite early on the advantages of such a force were being demonstrated off Indo-China. A light fleet carrier with the specifications outlined in the table was authorised in 1947, but the conflict in the Far East, which first encouraged the programme, was ultimately a major factor in its cancellation, on grounds of cost. The name *Clémenceau* was tentatively assigned to the new carrier, which would have had a 540ft × 78ft hangar and two flight-deck catapults.

LAFAYETTE CLASS

Ship	Builder	Laid down	Launched	Commissioned
Bois Belleau	New York SB	11 Aug 41	6 Dec 42	5 Sept 53
Lafayette	New York SB	11 Apr 42	22 May 43	6 June 51

Displacement: 10,662 tons / 10,833 tonnes (standard); 14,750 tons / 14,986 tonnes (deep load).
Length: 600ft / 182.88m (wl); 622ft 6in / 189.74m (oa); 544ft / 165.81m (fd).
Beam: 71ft 6in / 21.79m (hull); 73ft / 22.25m (fd).
Draught: 21ft / 6.4m (mean); 24ft 3in / 7.39m (deep load).
Machinery: General Electric turbines; 4 Babcock & Wilcox boilers; 4 shafts.
Performance: 100,000shp; 31kts.
Bunkerage: 2,633 tons / 2,765 tonnes.
Range: 13,000nm at 15kts.
Aircraft: 30.
Guns: 28 × 40mm; 4 × 20mm.
Complement: 1,300.

Design Ex-US *Independence*-class light carriers (qv); *Lafayette* was the former *Langley* (CVL-27) and *Bois Belleau* the former *Belleau Wood* (CVL-24).

Modifications By 1952 armament was listed as 26 × 40mm and 20 × 20mm in *Lafayette*. In 1954 the radar fit consisted of SK-2 air warning and SP fighter control in *Lafayette* and SK-2 and SPS-4 surface warning in *Bois Belleau*; both ships had a lattice-type radar mast fitted between each pair of funnels the following year, carrying DRBV-22 air warning in *Bois Belleau* and its US parent SPS-6 in *Lafayette*. By 1960 displacement had risen to 11,000 tons standard and 15,800 tons deep load (draught 25ft deep load) and the 20mm guns had been landed.

Service Notes *Lafayette*: Participated as a strike carrier during the Suez crisis in 1956. Returned to the USA in March 1963 and broken up from 1964. *Bois Belleau*: Returned to the USA in September 1960, sold the same year and scrapped from 1962.

Above: During the early 1950s the French carrier fleet was given a considerable boost with the arrival of a pair of ex-wartime US light fleet carriers. This is *Lafayette*, at Toulon in September 1951, showing her original SK-2 air search radar on its stub mast amidships. The ubiquitous YE beacon tops the mainmast. (US Navy, by courtesy of Norman Friedman)

Left: *Bois Belleau* in the mid 1950s, showing the new radar mast forward of the third funnel which characterised both ex-CVLS from then on. (By courtesy of Bernard Millot)

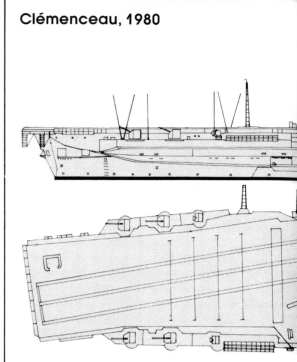

Clémenceau, 1980

Above: *Clémenceau* following her launch, December 1957. (By courtesy of A. D. Baker III)

Far right: The new French carriers were able to incorporate all the revolutionary technology that permeated carrier design during the early 1950s. This 1964 photograph clearly shows the angled deck and the pair of steam catapults installed aboard the *Clémenceau*s; note too the heavy fixed battery and the positions of the two lifts. (ECP Armées, by courtesy of A. D. Baker III)

Below: A September 1978 view of *Foch* at Toulon. The major radar antennae visible are the huge mattress of the DRBV-20C air search system; DRBI-10C height-finders at each end of the island; and DRBV-23B air search above the forward height-finder. (*Marine Nationale*, by courtesy of A. D. Baker III)

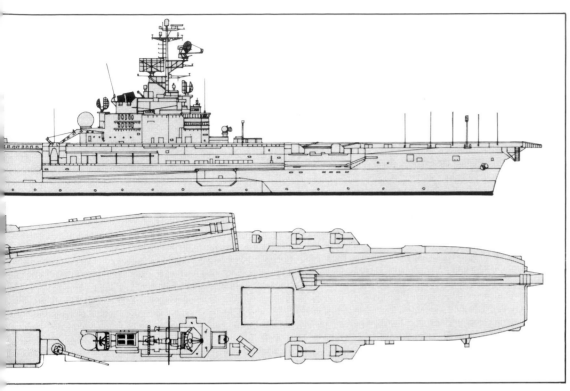

CLÉMENCEAU CLASS

Ship	Builder	Laid down	Launched	Commissioned
Clémenceau	Brest	1 Nov 55	21 Dec 57	22 Nov 61
Foch	Ch de l'Atlantique/ Brest	1 Feb 57	23 July 60	15 July 63

Displacement: 22,000 tons / 22,352 tonnes (standard); 31,000 tons / 31,496 tonnes (deep load).
Length: 780ft 10in / 238m (pp); 869ft 5in / 265m (oa); 843ft 10in / 257m (fd).
Beam: 98ft 5in / 30m (hull); 150ft / 45.72m (fd).
Draught: 24ft 7in / 7.5m (mean); 28ft 3in / 8.6m (deep load).
Machinery: Parsons geared turbines; 6 boilers; 2 shafts.
Performance: 126,000shp; 32kts.
Bunkerage: 3,720 tons / 3,780 tonnes.
Range: 7,500nm at 18kts.
Aircraft: 40.
Guns: 8 × 3.9in.
Complement: 2,200.

Design The two current French attack carriers, *Clémenceau* and *Foch*, stem from early post-war studies intended to provide the spearhead of a fleet of six units, considered the optimum number having regard to both home and colonial requirements. Even with the cancellation of PA28 in 1950 this target continued to be quoted; it was never realised, but the prospect of a new carrier was revived in the early 1950s as the post-war economy strengthened, and two units were approved in 1954 and 1955.

The design was an updated PA28, but with the advent of jet technology it also had to be considerably enlarged in order to embark an effective air group: the increased fuel requirements of jet aircraft needed greater bunkerage (317,000 gallons, one third of which was petrol for piston-engined machines) and greater flight-deck length. Hull length and displacement rose accordingly, needing more powerful machinery. The design was still tight, however, and in an effort to reduce topweight the armament, first modified from 24 × 57mm to 12 × 3.9in, was cut to that shown in the table; stability was a problem, and the second carrier, *Foch*, had to be bulged before completion (*Clémenceau* was retro-fitted) to improve things, raising beam to 104ft 1in.

The 1950s new carrier technology could be incorporated into the design, and both ships completed with an 8° angled deck and steam catapults; two of the latter were installed, one forward, to port, and one on the angled deck. The flight deck, with an extreme width of 168ft and reportedly lightly armoured, has two lifts (each 52ft 6in × 36ft), one serving the forward catapult and the other on the deck edge abaft the island; they rise from a single 590ft 6in × 78ft 9in hangar which has a height of 23ft.

The *Clémenceau* design seems to reflect British and US carrier technology of the early 1950s and no doubt was fairly heavily influenced by *Arromanches*, with an island superstructure close in general configuration to that developed for US SCB-27 reconstructions. Unusually, however, the French ships continue to carry a battery of heavy anti-aircraft weapons. The radar fit includes DRBV-20 long-range air search, DRBV-23 air search, a pair of DRBI-10 height-finders and DRBV-50 surface search; a CCA radar is carried on a dome abaft the island, and SQS-503 sonar is installed.

Modifications Both ships have been modernised to equip them for nuclear-capable Super Étendard fighter-bombers and have received a new tactical data system, SENIT-2, replacing the earlier SENIT-1. *Clémenceau*'s refit lasted throughout 1978, while work on *Foch* was carried out from July 1980 to August 1981. Externally, neither ship differs fundamentally from the original configuration, but displacement has risen, 1982 figures being quoted as 27,307 tons normal and 32,780 tons deep load.

Service Notes *Clémenceau*: Scheduled to remain in service until about 1990.

Foch: Scheduled to remain in service until about 1990.

Right: Unusually for current fleet carriers, the *Clémenceau*s retain a powerful medium-calibre gun battery, single-mounted, as seen in this photograph of the name-ship. Present policy calls for these two ships to be replaced in the 1990s with a pair of nuclear-powered carriers operating CTOL aircraft, a new generation of which is being developed by Dassault-Breguet under the designation ACM. (Avions Marcel Dassault-Breguet Aviation)

PA58 PROJECT

Displacement: 35,000 tons / 35,560 tonnes (standard); 45,500 tons / 46,228 tonnes (deep load).
Length: 859ft 7in / 262m (wl); 938ft 4in / 286m (oa); 918ft 8in / 280m (fd).
Beam: 111ft 7in / 34m (hull); 190ft 3in / 58m (fd).
Performance: 200,000shp; 33kts.
Guns: 8 × 3.9in.
Missiles: 4 Masurca.

Design With the promise of new carrier-borne heavy attack aircraft (with a nuclear capability) in the early 1960s, designs were prepared for a carrier that could deploy them: a considerably enlarged *Clémenceau*, it featured an 8° angled deck, two steam catapults and two twin Masurca launchers augmenting the heavy anti-aircraft battery. The project was cancelled on economic grounds before being authorised.

JEANNE D'ARC

Builder	Laid down	Launched	Commissioned
Brest	7 July 60	30 Sept 61	30 Jan 64

Displacement: 10,000 tons / 10,160 tonnes (standard); 13,000 tons / 13,208 tonnes (deep load).
Length: 590ft 6in / 179.98m (oa); 230ft / 70.1m (fd).
Beam: 78ft 9in / 24m (hull); 85ft / 25.91m (fd).
Draught: 20ft 4in / 6.2m (mean).
Machinery: Rateau-Bretagne geared turbines; 4 multi-tubular boilers; 2 shafts.

Performance: 40,000shp; 26.5kts.
Bunkerage: 1,360 tons / 1,382 tonnes.
Range: 6,000nm at 15kts.
Aircraft: 8.
Guns: 4 × 3.9in.
Complement: 1,050.

Design Authorised in 1957 as *La Résolue*, a training ship to replace the pre-war *Jeanne d'Arc*, this vessel was the subject of a major redesign in the late 1950s as the cancellation of PA58 led to a reassessment of French naval requirements. It appears that the commando carrier concept was being actively pursued at this time, and such a capability could be assigned to *Arromanches*, *Foch* and *Clémenceau*, the new strike carrier taking over the key fleet role. With the latter no longer available, however, the design of *La Résolue* was reworked to enable her to function as an ASW/assault ship: at once a cruiser, helicopter and commando carrier and troop transport, retaining her training role (for 192 cadets) during peacetime.

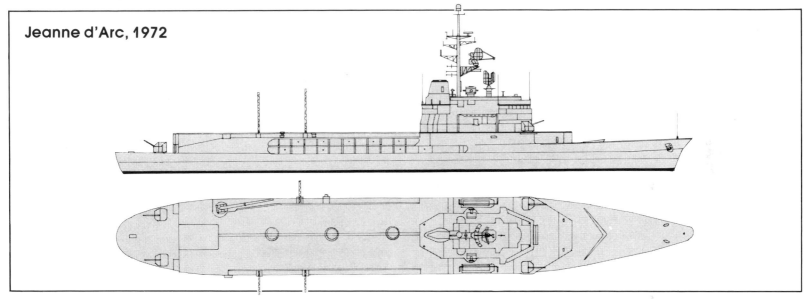

Jeanne d'Arc, 1972

Below: The multi-purpose *Jeanne d'Arc*, seen here at San Francisco in 1971. (US Navy)

The superstructure is concentrated forward, the after half of the ship being given over to a helicopter deck at the after end of which is a single lift (capacity 12 tons) serving a narrow hangar below. The specified armament originally included 6 × 3.9in guns in superfiring pairs abreast the bridge with two mountings on the quarterdeck, but the forward upper turrets were deleted prior to completion, as was a quadruple ASW mortar and its successor, a twin Masurca launcher forward.

The radar fit consists of DRBV-22 air and DRBV-50 surface search, DRBI-10 height-finder and DRBC-32A fire control systems, and SQS-503 sonar is carried. Operating in the assault role, 700 troops and their equipment can be accommodated, and eight heavy helicopters are embarked (normal peacetime complement is four). The ship was renamed *Jeanne d'Arc* on entry into service.

Modifications *Jeanne d'Arc* completed on 1 July 1963 but after trials her funnel was increased considerably in height. In 1975 six Exocet launchers were fitted before the bridge, giving an anti-ship capability for the first time. She was in refit from April 1982.

Service Notes Based at Brest.

Above left: *Jeanne d'Arc*, showing the extent of her flight deck and the position of the lift aft. (By courtesy of Bernard Millot)

Below left: Exocet was fitted to *Jeanne d'Arc* after she had been in service for some twelve years, further extending the ship's already impressive capabilities. The launchers are visible here, forward of the 3.9in mountings. (ECP Armées)

PA75 PROJECT

Displacement: 18,400 tons / 18,694 tonnes (deep load).
Length: 682ft 5in / 208m (oa); 662ft 9in / 202m (fd).
Beam: 86ft 7in / 26.4m (hull); 150ft 11in / 46m (fd).
Machinery: Geared turbines; 1 CAS230 reactor; 2 shafts.
Performance: 64,110shp; 30kts.
Aircraft: 25.
Guns: 8 × 40mm.
Missiles: 8 Crotale.
Complement: 840.

Design In 1975, with the impending retirement of *Arromanches*, the French Navy prepared plans for a new carrier which would enable it to carry out airborne ocean escort (ASW) and amphibious assault operations; a nuclear powerplant was designated, the expense being considered acceptable in view of the long range it would bestow upon the ship and the increased available internal space it would create in relation to the hull size, permitting the carrier to operate as a replenishment vessel for accompanying ships. Initial plans called for a class of four, later reduced to two on grounds of cost; some eight years after the requirement was first announced, the first ship has yet to be laid down.

Although the role of the vessel has been the subject of some redefinition since it was first conceived, the essential elements of the design have been retained: a full-length flight deck and a 275ft × 69ft hangar, 21ft 4in high, the two connected by a pair of deck-edge lifts on the starboard side abaft an island for command and control. Twenty-five Lynx helicopters would be accommodated, with various combinations of Pumas and Super Frélons as alternative, reduced complements. Since 1981 a fixed-wing V/STOL capability has been designated (resulting in a reclassification from PH to PA), although which aircraft are to make up this complement has not been explained.

The assault role is catered for by provision for embarking 1,500 troops and their equipment, and the armament shows four twin 40mm / 70 Breda and two 4-tube Crotale point-defence launchers aft. Diesel machinery would provide emergency power in the event of problems with the single reactor.

PA75 is still a 'live' project, successively redesignated through to PA83 as the years have passed, and it has been complemented by studies for a pair of nuclear-powered fleet carriers (PA88). These are considerably larger than PA75 at 35,000 tons and with a specified, and presumably conventional, fixed-wing capability. An air group of 30-40 ACX aircraft is envisaged, and the ships, first mooted in 1979, were officially announced in September 1980. The names *Provence* and *Bretagne* were, apparently, originally assigned (though the name *Charles de Gaulle* is now reported to have been selected for the first unit) and the carriers are seen as replacements for the *Clémenceaus*; work on the first is scheduled to begin at Brest in 1986, for service in the early 1990s.

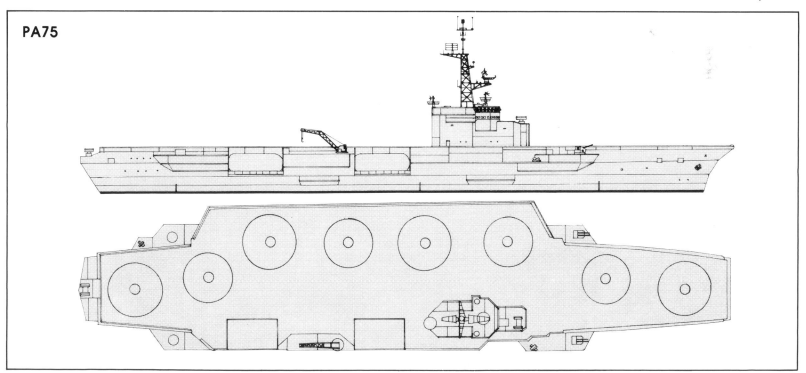

PA75

Germany

Following early flirtations with seaplane carriers during the First World War, Germany was denied any opportunity of developing a carrier force prior to the mid 1930s owing to the restrictive terms of the Versailles Treaty. The celebrated 'Z-Plan' envisaged a fleet of four carriers in service by the late 1940s, but a lack of enthusiasm shown by the Luftwaffe (who would operate the aircraft) and, as time passed, the decision to divert production energies and resources to more immediate needs meant that none was commissioned.

GRAF ZEPPELIN

Builder	Laid down	Launched
Deutschewerke	28 Dec 36	8 Dec 38

Displacement: 28,090 tons / 28,539 tonnes (standard).
Length: 820ft 3in / 250m (wl); 861ft 3in / 262.5m (oa); 787ft 5in / 240m (fd).
Beam: 103ft 4in / 31.5m (hull); 88ft 6in / 27m (fd).
Draught: 23ft 7in / 7.2m (mean); 27ft 11in / 8.5m (deep load).
Machinery: Brown-Boveri geared turbines; 16 La Mont boilers; 4 shafts.
Performance: 200,000shp; 34kts.
Bunkerage: 6,750 tons / 6,858 tonnes.
Range: 8,000nm at 19kts.
Aircraft: 42.
Guns: 16 × 5.9in; 12 × 4.1in; 22 × 37mm; 28 × 20mm.
Complement: 1,760.
Design An important feature of the German rearmament policy of the 1930s was the desire to include in the *Kriegsmarine* some form of air-capable

vessel. In 1933 a tentative design was drawn up by Wilhelm Hadeler for a full-deck carrier which could accommodate about 30 aircraft. The major problem facing the design team was a complete absence of experience in planning such a project; the German Navy of the First World War had operated seaplane carriers such as *Glyndwr*, but these were hardly comparable to the requirement under study. Not surprisingly, therefore, much reliance was placed on the assumed characteristics of carriers from other navies, in particular the Royal Navy and specifically *Courageous*, even to the extent of incorporating a double hangar and forward flying-off deck arrangement.

The air group also posed difficulties: pilots had no experience of shipboard operating procedure and, of course, there were no specialised carrier aircraft. However, it was expected that land-based aircraft could be suitably modified, given the required flight-deck catapults and arresting gear, and in the late 1930s, subsequent to the laying down of the first ship, *Graf Zeppelin*, a *Trägergruppe* of Messer-

schmitt Bf 109B fighters and Junkers Ju 87A dive-bombers had been formed for training and evaluation purposes, the ungainly Fieseler Fi 167 being the torpedo-bomber-designate that would complete the air group.

Meanwhile the Anglo-German Treaty of 1935 had settled the future size of the German Navy: excluding submarines, each type of ship could be built in numbers up to 35 per cent of the total displacement of its equivalent in the Royal Navy. For aircraft carriers this meant that 42,750 tons was theoretically available, whereas it was actually somewhat less, since the 135,000 tons permitted to Britain under the Washington Treaty had not quite been consumed. It was decided to refine Hadeler's sketches into a 'live' project, and two carriers, at 19,250 tons each, were authorised.

The design showed many 'European' features, with a high freeboard to permit good seakeeping in Atlantic conditions and a very strong defensive battery to cope with the hostile land-based aircraft that would inevitably pose a serious threat. In

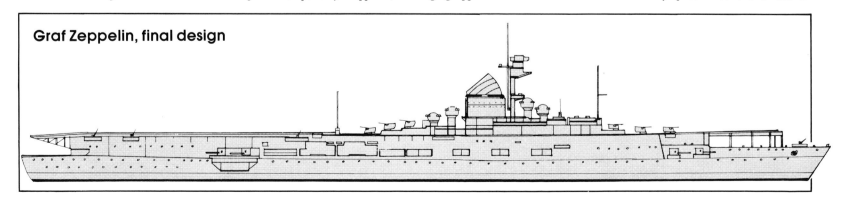

Graf Zeppelin, final design

addition, exceptionally powerful machinery was specified, which would endow the vessel with a speed in excess of that of any capital ship or carrier likely to be encountered. The flight deck, with three centreline lifts and a pair of catapults forward, extended virtually the complete length of the hull, and a low island superstructure on the starboard side carried a heavy director mast and a single massive funnel, with the heavy AA armament disposed about it forward and aft.

Progress with the design was accompanied by modifications: the carrier had already been armoured to give protection against cruiser fire (4in belt, 2½in–1½in armour deck, ¾in flight deck) but to meet a perceived destroyer threat a suite of twin 5.9in low-angle weapons was introduced forward and aft, mounted in casemates, with those at the bows being given an end-on capability reminiscent of First World War dreadnought secondary batteries. The original straight stem was modified into a 'clipper'-type bow, retractable manoeuvring propellers were fitted forward, and the funnel was heightened by means of a raked cap. Displacement escalated, from the original 19,250 tons of 1935, through 24,500 in 1936 and 27,000 in 1937, to the 1939 figure given in the table. Petrol capacity was to be about 70,000 gallons.

The air group, too, had changed. By the outbreak of war, with the carrier nearing completion, the Fi 167 requirement was abandoned and specially navalised Bf 109T and Ju 87C aircraft had been developed: the former an -E variant with a stressed airframe and with catapult points, an arrester hook, an extended wingspan for better approach characteristics and provision for manual wing-folding, and the latter a modified -B with wing-folding and arrester and catapult gear, but also a jettisonable undercarriage and flotation equipment. The 1930 complement of 30 fighters and twelve dive-bombers was reversed in 1939, by which time there was reportedly a proposal to develop a torpedo-carrying Ju 87 for use on board the carriers.

Work on both carriers was suspended in mid 1940 because of the demands of the submarine programme; the second ship, apparently to have been named *Peter Strasser*, was still on the slip at the Germaniawerft yard at Kiel and was immediately scrapped, but *Graf Zeppelin* was resumed in May 1942. Bulges were fitted but little else was done, and by early 1943 she was languishing again. She was scuttled at Stettin by the Germans a few months before the end of the war and although taken over and raised by the Russians, she was lost under tow to Leningrad in August or September 1947. (See page 190.)

Above: Bedevilled first by inter-service rivalry and later by shortages of materials and other wartime problems, the German carrier *Graf Zeppelin* was never completed. She is seen here on her slip, 8 December 1938, ready for launch. (US Naval Historical Center)

Below: By February 1942, three years after her launch, *Graf Zeppelin* was little advanced externally. Prominent in this Allied air reconnaissance view are the two catapults at the bows (right) and the openings for the three lifts. (US Naval Historical Center)

SEYDLITZ

Builder	Laid down	Launched
Deschimag	29 Dec 36	19 Jan 39

Displacement: 18,000 tons / 18,288 tonnes (standard).
Length: 654ft 6in / 199.5m (wl); 711ft 11in / 217m (oa).
Beam: 70ft 6in / 21.5m (hull).
Draught: 22ft / 6.71m (mean); 25ft 11in / 7.9m (deep load).

Machinery: Deschimag geared turbines; 12 Wagner boilers; 3 shafts.
Performance: 130,000shp; 32kts.
Bunkerage: 4,250 tons / 4,318 tonnes.
Range: 5,500nm at 18kts.
Aircraft: 18.
Guns: 10×4.1in; 8×37mm; 24×20mm.
Design Concurrent with the decision to resume work on *Graf Zeppelin* in 1942, the incomplete *Hipper*-class heavy cruiser *Seydlitz* was stripped of her super-structure with a view to commissioning her as a flush-decked carrier, but the order was rescinded in early 1943, the hull being taken to Königsberg and subsequently scuttled. It is probable that the original armour scheme (3½in maximum belt, 1½in maximum armoured deck) would have been modified had the carrier completed and that the air group would have consisted of Bf 109Ts and Ju 87Cs. Conversion of the liners *Potsdam, Europa* and *Gneisenau* was proposed but not proceeded with.

Great Britain

Although the Royal Navy fleet carrier is now a matter of history, British carrier development and technology have for seven decades provided the foundations upon which the navies of the world have built up their own sea-based aviation forces. With a few notable exceptions (for example, nuclear propulsion), the important design problems posed by the practical operation of aircraft from aboard ship have been solved by the application of British-originated concepts. The Royal Navy was the first to demonstrate the feasibility of sea-going aircraft carriers; introduced the full-length flush deck; pioneered the idea of the now-familiar 'island' superstructure; introduced aircraft lifts to bring machines from stowage areas to take-off platforms; led the way in abandoning fixed surface batteries in favour of an all-AA armament; introduced the armoured carrier; first successfully tackled the difficult problems of operating high-performance jet aircraft by means of such innovations as the steam catapult and the angled landing deck; and, even today, is leading the way in the operation of fixed-wing V / STOL aircraft from light carriers.

The early pre-eminence of British carrier development was a product of the dominant position still enjoyed by the British Fleet in the first two decades of the twentieth century. First introduced as an aid to fleet actions, during which aircraft might both reconnoitre for enemy ships and assist gunnery by observing fall of shot, aircraft-carrying ships quickly proved their capabilities in independent operations as strike platforms, carrying an airborne offensive against important land targets, and as platforms for airborne interceptors, prompted by the menace of German airships operating in the reconnaissance and strategic bombing roles. By the end of the First World War, the Royal Navy was about to introduce into service aircraft carriers whose appearance and functions would be quite recognisable today.

Development slowed considerably between the wars. Although three excellent ships, *Courageous*, *Glorious* and *Ark Royal*, were commissioned during this period, the 'levelling' effect of the 1922 Washington Treaty, and a combination of political retrenchment and problems caused by the amalgamation of both land- and sea-based military aviation under one authority, saw the Royal Navy's superiority slip at the expense of the United States and Japan. As the threat of the Second World War loomed, a large building programme was initiated, by no means all of which was realised. The armoured fleet carrier (*Illustrious* class) proved an ideal vessel for the European theatre, though aircraft capacity, limited in favour of hangar protection, would be a handicap as the need for a strong fleet fighter complement became apparent.

The small, unarmoured escort carrier was a particularly valuable component in the Atlantic war, providing an effective defence against both land-based enemy bombers and against U-boats. The most durable carrier designs of the Second World War, however, have proved to be the light fleet carriers based on the *Colossus* class: workhorses of the Royal Navy during the late 1940s and early 1950s, some are still, 40 years later, in service with foreign navies.

Despite the British technical achievements of the postwar years, not one new fleet carrier has been laid down during this period. Existing ships were modified before completion and underwent refits to bring them up to modern requirements, but with the retirement of *Ark Royal* in 1978 the size and complexity of conventional military aircraft had finally overtaken the resources available for supporting them at sea. Four years later, with massive irony, the gap in naval capabilities thus created was brought home with the outbreak of war in the South Atlantic. The small *Invincible* and the elderly *Hermes*, operating V / STOL aircraft, were the significant factor in the outcome of that campaign, demonstrating both what could be achieved with minimal carrier forces and also what might have been accomplished with fleet vessels.

HERMES

Builder	Laid down	Launched	Commissioned
Fairfield	30 Apr 97	7 Apr 98	7 May 13

Displacement: 5,650 tons / 5,740 tonnes (standard).
Length: 350ft / 106.68m (pp); 373ft / 113.69m (oa).
Beam: 54ft / 16.46m (hull).
Draught: 20ft / 6.1m (mean).
Machinery: Triple-expansion reciprocating engines; 18 Babcock small-tube boilers; 2 shafts.
Performance: 10,000ihp; 20kts.
Bunkerage: 1,100 tons / 1,118 tonnes.
Aircraft: 3.
Guns: 11 × 6in; 9 × 12pdr; 6 × 3pdr.
Torpedo tubes: 2 × 18in.
Complement: 450.

Design Early experiments in launching aircraft from ramps fitted over the forecastle decks of pre-dreadnought battleships in 1912 convinced the British Admiralty that the next logical step, the operation of aircraft in Fleet manoeuvres, should be taken as soon as practicably possible; the naval exercises in the summer of 1913 provided the ideal opportunity. The *Highflyer*-class (second-class) protected cruiser *Hermes* was selected for the experiment and in the spring of that year was temporarily rigged with canvas shelters on the forecastle and quarterdecks, the former position at least also being fitted with a railed

Left: The first ship to function primarily as a vessel deploying aircraft was Hermes, *converted from a protected cruiser in the spring of 1913. Her wartime career was short, however, and she was sunk by a German submarine in October 1914. She is seen here shortly after being torpedoed, in one of the few known photographs showing the ship in her carrier configuration. The canvas aeroplane shelter on the forecastle*

launching platform, parallel to the waterline. Whether further modifications were made to the ship is unclear, although derricks for handling the aircraft that the ship was about to embark were certainly provided.

The aircraft complement in July 1913 consisted of a Short Folder hydro-aeroplane, carried aft, and a Caudron GIII amphibian, operating forward, but provision had originally been made for three aircraft, a second seaplane (type uncertain) being envisaged aft. It is not clear whether the full suite was ever carried.

Hermes was coal-burning, and was armoured with a 3in protective deck and 3in gunshields. Although of extempore design as far as her employment as an aircraft carrier was concerned, and although owing to inclement weather she was unable to operate as

planned in the Fleet Manoeuvres, her aircraft arrangements were evidently considered acceptable since she set the pattern for the bulk of the First World War conversions which were to be undertaken during the next four years.

Modifications It is not known whether *Hermes* was modified during her brief career as a carrier.

Service Notes Precise details of *Hermes*'s activities following the July 1913 experiments are unavailable, but it is understood that she undertook a number of launching and recovery trials during the next few months, on the basis of which future conversion programmes were presumably established. She reverted to cruiser configuration in December 1913 but was employed again as a carrier on the outbreak of war and was sunk in October 1914 by *U-27*.

Hermes, 1914

can be made out; that at the stern has apparently collapsed, and the remains of what is presumably a Short Folder can be seen. Note the 6in guns trained outboard along the port side. (Fleet Air Arm Museum)

Below: Empress *after her temporary canvas shelters, hastily rigged for the carriage of aircraft at the outbreak of the 1914-18 War, had been replaced by a more substantial structure in early 1915. (By courtesy of Ray Burt)*

EMPRESS

Builder	Launched	Commissioned
Denny	13 Apr 07	Oct 14

Length: c.320ft / c.97.54m (pp).
Beam: 41ft / 12.5m (hull).
Machinery: Turbine.
Performance: 21kts.
Aircraft: 3.
Guns: Nil.
Complement: c.250.

Design The Royal Navy's first purpose-built aircraft carrier, *Ark Royal*, would be a valued addition to the Fleet but she had one major shortcoming: her low speed would prevent her operating as a unit of the battle fleet. The advantages bestowed upon a battle line by some form of aerial spotting and reconnaissance were well established, however, and to enable this task to be fulfilled the Admiralty, after the outbreak of war, requisitioned or purchased a number of faster vessels for speedy conversion to makeshift

carriers. First among these were a batch of cross-Channel packets, owned by the South Eastern and Chatham Railway Company. *Empress*, 1,695grt and marginally the largest of the three initial conversions, was given a canvas 'hangar' aft and embarked three aircraft, served by the mainmast derrick.

Modifications In early 1915 *Empress* was taken in hand for a more substantial conversion, involving the erection of a new, rigid hangar, the aftermost corners of which consisted of a pair of handling cranes; to provide the necessary room, the after superstructure was cut down and the mainmast removed. Four 12pdrs were fitted, a pair at the stern and a pair abreast the bridge, and two 3pdr anti-aircraft guns were installed at the forward end of the hangar roof. Four to six aircraft could now be carried. A flying-off deck was also fitted, date uncertain.

Service Notes Based at Harwich during 1914–15, *Empress* took part, in company with *Engadine* and *Riviera*, in a raid on Cuxhaven on 25 December 1914. Short Folders, Type 74s and Type 135s were taken on board for the purpose, but the aircraft failed in their attempt to locate their target, the German airship sheds. After her second conversion, *Empress* was based at Queenstown for much of the war, deploying to the Mediterranean in 1918. She was returned to her original owners in 1919.

ENGADINE CLASS

Ship	Builder	Launched	Commissioned
Riviera	Denny	1 Apr 11	1914
Engadine	Denny	23 Sept 11	1914

Length: 316ft / 96.32m (pp).
Beam: 41ft / 12.5m (hull).
Machinery: Turbines; 3 shafts.
Performance: 21kts.
Aircraft: 3
Guns: Nil.
Complement: c.250.

Design Two 1,676grt packets, requisitioned, like *Empress*, on 11 August 1914 and converted along similar lines. *Riviera* at least had a canvas shelter rigged on the forecastle as well as aft.

Modifications Refitted in early 1915 with a more permanent hangar aft and armed, as *Empress*.

Service Notes *Riviera* took part in the abortive Cuxhaven raid in December 1914. She was based at Harwich during the early months of her career, and from 1915 at Dover. From 1918 she operated in the Mediterranean. She was returned to her owners in 1919, and by the Second World War had been renamed *Laird's Isle*.

Engadine: Following Cuxhaven and her second conversion, *Engadine* was engaged in North Sea sweeps, generally anti-Zeppelin and ASW, for the first part of the war. She achieved fame in May 1916 at Jutland when a Short Type 184 operating from her

Top: A Sopwith Schneider nestles in *Empress*'s hangar, circa 1915. Note the pair of 12pdr guns fitted at the stern and the two cranes for hoisting the seaplane(s). (Fleet Air Arm Museum)

Above: *Engadine* deploying a Short seaplane, reputedly the machine which spotted at Jutland, May 1916. The 3pdr AA guns are visible on the hangar roof, just abaft the funnels. (Fleet Air Arm Museum)

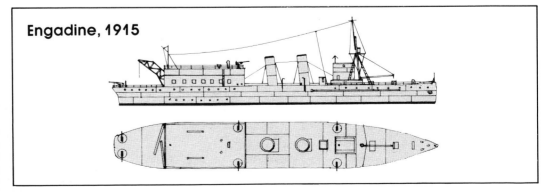

Engadine, 1915

managed to spot the High Seas Fleet, or rather part of its cruiser scouting screen; the aircraft returned to the ship, which, unfortunately, was unable to pass this information to the Fleet commander. Further North Sea patrols occupied *Engadine* until 1918, when she was moved to the Mediterranean. She was returned to her owners in December 1919.

ARK ROYAL

Builder	Laid down	Launched	Commissioned
Blyth	7 Nov 13	5 Sept 14	10 Dec 14

Displacement: 7,450 tons / 7,569 tonnes (standard).
Length: 352ft 6in / 107.44m (pp); 366ft / 111.56m (oa); 125ft / 38.1m (fd).
Beam: 50ft 10in / 15.49m (hull); 40ft / 12.19m (fd).
Draught: 18ft / 5.49m (mean).
Machinery: Vertical triple-expansion engines; 2 cylindrical boilers; 1 shaft.
Performance: 3,000ihp; 11kts.
Bunkerage: 500 tons / 508 tonnes.
Aircraft: 7.
Guns: 4 × 12pdr.
Complement: 180.

Design The evident success of *Hermes*'s experiments in late 1913 is shown in the decision to provide the Royal Navy, under the 1914/15 Estimates, with a vessel built specifically for the purposes of operating aircraft at sea, the agreement to proceed with such a ship being encouraged particularly by Churchill, then First Sea Lord. In May 1914 a collier/grain carrier, then in frame, was purchased by the Admiralty and put through a complete redesign: the original plans showed a typical layout, with machinery, funnel and main superstructure amidships and a hull with marked sheer forward and aft, but although the principal form of the hull was retained the carrier as completed bore little resemblance to them. The engines, bridge and uptake were relocated right aft, and in the forward part of the hull a large hold, 150ft long, 40ft wide and 15ft high, was provided, capable of accommodating seven seaplanes, together with workshops, bunkers for aviation fuel and ammunition and ordnance magazines; above, the flat forecastle deck was left clear for operating the aircraft, which would be hoisted out from the hold through a large hatchway by one of two steam cranes located at the deck-edge nearby. The original machinery was apparently retained, the boilers for which were coal-fired; however, there was provision for rigging a mizzen sail.

No take-off ramp was fitted, landplanes or trolley-assisted seaplanes being launched directly from the flying deck when required, although the majority of operations were conducted using seaplanes which had been hoisted out on to the water.

Modifications Various types of catapults were installed on the flying deck during the early 1930s,

Top: The first aircraft carrier capable of handling a large number of aircraft and of providing them with really comprehensive maintenance facilities was *Ark Royal*. She is seen here in 1915. (Ministry of Defence (Navy))

Above: Renamed *Pegasus*, *Ark Royal* served as a fighter catapult ship during the Second World War. Note the catapult, towards the bows, and the 12pdr guns at bows and stern. (By courtesy of A. D. Baker III)

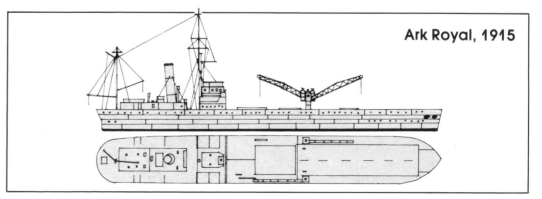

Ark Royal, 1915

Ark Royal being employed as a trials ship for equipment that would be fitted to major Fleet units. In 1940–41 (now named *Pegasus*), she was fitted with a permanent catapult for her role as a fighter-catapult ship, a stop-gap convoy escort pending the arrival of flight-deck escort carriers. Three aircraft, generally Hurricanes or Fulmars, were embarked for the purpose. She retained her 12pdr guns, but during the war received in addition 2×20mm.

Service Notes *Ark Royal* served principally in the Eastern Mediterranean for the duration of the First World War, flying spotter and reconnaissance sorties during the Dardanelles campaign and acting as a depot ship. After the war she acted as an aircraft transport during the Somaliland and Chanak crises before becoming a depot ship at Sheerness in 1923. Used experimentally in the early 1930s for both catapult trials and seaplane landing mat (Hein mat)

evaluation, she was renamed *Pegasus* in December 1934. Her 1941 employment as an active convoy escort was shortlived, and from July that year she served in a number of auxiliary roles, mainly as a transport and training vessel, before becoming an accommodation/depot ship in 1944. She reverted to mercantile status in October 1946 (*Anita I*) but was sold in June 1949 and broken up from October 1950.

BEN-MY-CHREE

Builder	Launched	Commissioned
Vickers	23 Mar 08	2 Jan 15

Displacement: 3,888 tons / 3,950 tonnes (standard).
Length: 375ft / 114.3m (pp).
Beam: 46ft / 14.02m (hull).
Machinery: Turbine.
Performance: 14,000shp; 24.5kts.
Aircraft: 4.
Guns: 2×12pdr; 2×3pdr.
Complement: c.250.

Design Encouraged by the potential shown by aircraft carriers in the early months of the First World War, the Admiralty decided that further acquisitions were called for, and three rather larger packets were commissioned into the Navy. *Ben-My-Chree*, an Isle of Man steam packet, was requisitioned in 1914, and was fitted not only with a rigid hangar aft, but also a flying-off ramp forward, enabling her to operate landplanes or amphibians as well as seaplanes. Two 12pdr guns were installed at the stern and a pair of 3pdr AA on the hangar roof. A single centreline derrick served the hangar, whilst smaller derricks were fitted forward. The aircraft complement varied, but usually included at least one Short Type 184.

Modifications It appears that *Ben-My-Chree* was not modified to any great degree during her period of service.

Service Notes *Ben-My-Chree*'s most notable feat took place in June 1915, during the Dardanelles campaign, when one of her Short Type 184s made the first successful aerial torpedo attack, striking and sinking a Turkish vessel; some weeks later, a tug was sunk by a torpedo launched from a taxying 184. She was sunk by Turkish batteries at Castellanzo in 1917 and in 1920 was raised and scrapped.

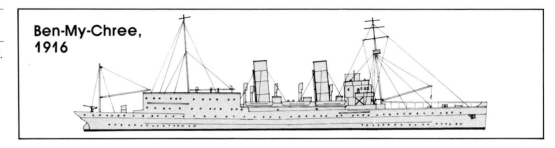

Ben-My-Chree, 1916

Below: Distinguishable from her converted predecessors by the single derrick on the quarterdeck, *Ben-My-Chree* was also somewhat larger than the ex-cross-Channel ships. Two Short 184s are seen folded in the hangar. (Fleet Air Arm Museum)

VINDEX

Builder	Launched	Commissioned
Armstrong Whitworth	7 Mar 05	26 Mar 15

Displacement: 2,950 tons / 2,997 tonnes (standard).
Length: 350ft / 106.68m (pp); 361ft / 110.03m (oa).
Beam: 42ft / 12.8m (hull).
Machinery: Turbine.

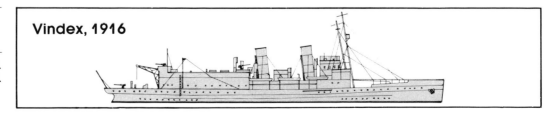

Vindex, 1916

Performance: 11,000shp; 23kts.
Aircraft: 7.
Guns: 4×12pdr; 2×3pdr.

Design A second vessel belonging to the Isle of Man Steam Packet Company was requisitioned by the Admiralty on 26 March 1915. Originally named *Viking*, she was somewhat smaller than *Ben-My-Chree*; as a merchantman she measured 1,951grt. She was converted in similar fashion, and was purchased outright for the Navy in October 1915.

Modifications *Vindex*'s forecastle flying-off deck was apparently fitted subsequent to her entry into service, but it is not known precisely when.

Service Notes *Vindex* operated out of Harwich and was part of the Nore station for most of the First World War, but served in the Mediterranean during 1918–20. She was sold back to her former owners in February 1920.

Above: Like *Ben-My-Chree*, *Vindex* featured a launching ramp over her forecastle, to enable wheeled aircraft as well as pure seaplanes to be flown off; opportunities for using the ramp proved few, however, mainly because of problems with spray and pitching. (Fleet Air Arm Museum)

CAMPANIA

Builder	Launched	Commissioned
Fairfield	8 Sept 92	17 Apr 15

Displacement: 18,000 tons / 18,288 tonnes (standard).
Length: 601ft / 183.18m (pp); 622ft / 189.59m (oa); 125ft / 38.1m (fd).
Beam: 65ft / 19.81m (hull); 35ft / 10.67m (fd).
Draught: 22ft / 6.71m (mean); 26ft / 7.92m (deep load).
Machinery: Vertical triple-expansion reciprocating engines; 13 boilers; 2 shafts.
Performance: 30,000ihp; 23kts.
Aircraft: 6.
Guns: 6×4.7in.
Complement: 550.

Design By far the largest of the merchantmen converted during the First World War for aircraft carrier service, *Campania* was the record-breaking Cunard liner of the late nineteenth century; she was scheduled for scrapping by the time war broke out, but the Admiralty purchased her in November 1914 with a view to adapting her for Fleet work, although reportedly she was first envisaged as an armed merchant cruiser.

Campania had the advantage of very high speed and, in her holds, of the capacity for stowing aircraft below. As originally converted, she was fitted with a ramp over the forecastle deck, aircraft being hoisted from the hold below the after end, just before the bridge; the ramp was parallel to the waterline and was served by a pair of derricks abreast the raised bridge. The single-mounted 4.7in guns were disposed on each side of the forecastle deck, amidships, and right aft.

Modifications *Campania*'s first conversion was not wholly satisfactory, mainly because, despite her size, she could operate no more aircraft than the modified

Below: *Campania* at Laird's yard in Birkenhead showing the modifications made during her second conversion: the forefunnel has been split to permit the original bow ramp to be extended, and a simple navigating position has been erected over the after end of the ramp. The ship's name can just be discerned below the fourth and fifth upper deck scuttles; further aft, one of the single 4.7in guns is visible. (Fleet Air Arm Museum)

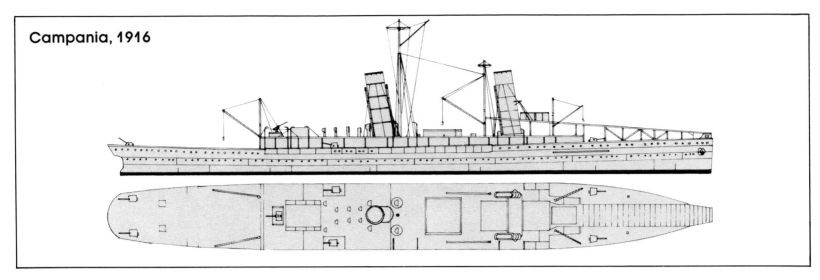

Campania, 1916

packets. She was therefore refitted in 1915–16 (at Cammell Laird's yard at Birkenhead) and given an extended, downward-sloping launching platform, room for which was made by dividing the forefunnel into two separate units, the ramp passing between them, to be serviced via a much larger hatch amidships. The bridge was raised, taking the form of a gantry before the split funnels, some 15ft above the launching ramp, which now measured 165ft in length. The pole mast aft was removed, the superstructure cut down, and a derrick added to the quarterdeck to handle both aircraft and airships. One 3in AA was installed on the superstructure aft, and *Campania* could now accommodate ten or eleven machines. This conversion was completed in April 1916.

The carrier was one of the few in history to have had an aircraft specifically designed for her use and the only one to have had one named after her. Designed during 1916 and first flown in February 1917, the Fairey Campania was a patrol seaplane and operated from the forecastle ramp using the well-tried trolley system. It is probable that *Campania*'s launching platform was extended principally to enable this aircraft to be flown from her.

Service Notes *Campania* would have been present at Jutland had it not been for a breakdown in Fleet communications which caused her to sail later than required. Most of her war service saw her operating in sweeps with the Grand Fleet in the North Sea. During a gale in November 1918 she was in collision with the large light cruiser *Glorious* and the battleship *Royal Oak* in the Firth of Forth, and was lost.

MANXMAN

Builder	Launched	Commissioned
Vickers	15 June 04	17 Apr 16

Length: 334ft / 101.8m (pp); 341ft / 103.94m (oa).
Beam: 43ft / 13.11m (hull).
Machinery: Turbine.
Performance: 21kts.
Aircraft: 8.
Guns: 2 × 12pdr; 2 × 3pdr.
Complement: c.250.

Design The last of the trio of Isle of Man steam packets taken over for use by the Royal Navy, *Manxman* (2,048grt) was generally similar to, though rather smaller than, *Vindex*. She was converted and armed at Chatham Dockyard following the established pattern, and had a ramp forward.

Modifications Not known.

Service Notes Serving at Rosyth during 1916 and 1917 and in the Mediterranean in 1918, *Manxman* was paid off in December 1919 and returned to packet duty, subsequently being renamed *Caduceus*.

Two other seaplane carriers to operate in the eastern Mediterranean were ex-German merchant vessels seized at Port Said and commissioned during the summer of 1915: *Raven II* (ex-*Rabenfels*, 4,678grt) and *Anne* (ex-*Änne Rickmers*, 4,083grt).

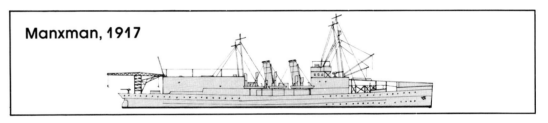

Manxman, 1917

Each was fitted with a single 12pdr and could handle two aircraft. *Raven II* was used as a troopship and collier (renamed *Ravenrock* in 1917) and *Anne* as a collier post-war.

Below: *Manxman* in 1916 or 1917. Forecastle ramps were in the main a response to the Zeppelin threat: nimble, wheeled single-seat fighters were more effective than seaplanes in combating German reconnaissance and bombing airships because they could climb faster. (Fleet Air Arm Museum)

FURIOUS

Builder	Laid down	Launched	Commissioned
Armstrong Whitworth	8 June 15	15 Aug 16	26 June 17

Displacement: 19,100 tons / 19,406 tonnes (standard); 22,400 tons / 22,758 tonnes (deep load).
Length: 735ft / 224.03m (pp); 786ft 3in / 239.65m (oa); 228ft / 69.49m (fd).
Beam: 88ft / 26.82m (hull); 55ft / 16.76m (fd).
Draught: 21ft 6in / 6.55m (mean); 25ft / 7.62m (deep load).
Machinery: Brown-Curtis geared turbines; 18 Yarrow small-tube boilers; 4 shafts.
Performance: 90,000shp; 31.5kts.
Bunkerage: 3,400 tons / 3,454 tonnes.
Range: 6,000nm at 20kts.
Aircraft: 8.
Guns: 1 × 18in; 11 × 5.5in; 4 × 3in; 4 × 3pdr.
Complement: 880.

Design The origins of the Royal Navy's best-known and most innovative carrier to take part in the First World War stretch back well into the pre-war years when Fisher was nurturing a scheme for a mass amphibious assault on Germany's Baltic coast in the event of open hostilities. With his return to power as First Sea Lord in October 1914 and warfare well in progress the plan was taken a step nearer reality: to support the landings, a squadron of fast, shallow-draught, heavily armed cruisers would be required. These vessels emerged as *Courageous*, *Glorious* and *Furious*, the first pair sister-ships but *Furious* differing principally in her main armament. Fisher's liking for, and belief in, massive artillery resulted in the installation of two single 18in / 40 gun turrets, one forward and one aft in place of the 15in twins of the earlier ships.

The project continued after Fisher's resignation from office in May 1915, but in early 1917, as

Furious was nearing completion, Admiral Beatty set up a Committee to explore the problems encountered with the seaplane carriers then in service and to make recommendations as to how the Navy might be more advantageously equipped with such ships. The perceived shortcomings of the converted packets – slow speed, too few aircraft and too little individual capacity – might be solved by the conversion of *Furious*, whose value if completed to her original design would, it was considered, be dubious at best. The Committee reported on 5 February 1917 and the order to modify the ship was made within six weeks.

The alterations were not extensive – at least not compared to the changes that would take place in later years. The forward 18in mounting and turret were removed (it is doubtful whether the gun itself was ever actually fitted), replaced by an enclosed hangar with accommodation for eight seaplanes (type not specified); a planked flying-off deck, canted downwards in the manner of *Campania* (whose configuration had the major influence on *Furious*'s modification), was erected on top, a hatch at its after end providing access below and served by a pair of 40ft wooden derricks, one each side. Workshops, petrol stowage facilities (1,200 gallons) and an ordnance magazine (converted 18in shellroom) were arranged.

Otherwise, the ship was little altered from her final light cruiser design. Her original machinery was retained, and her hull and armour protection (3in belt, 3in deck, 7in after turret) were unmodified. Her aircraft complement as completed differed from that envisaged in March 1917, four of the seaplanes being replaced by Sopwith Pups.

Above: As initially completed for service, *Furious* showed a long, downward-sloping flying-off deck forward; aft, the single massive 18in gun betrayed her 'large light cruiser' origins. The enclosed hangar is before the bridge, replacing the second single 18in mounting which featured in the original design. (Fleet Air Arm Museum)

The data given in the table refers to *Furious* as completed as a seaplane carrier in mid 1917. Her complement was made up of a ship's company of 796 plus 84 RNAS personnel.

Modifications Following deck landing trials in the summer of 1917 in which Squadron Commander Dunning lost his life attempting to place his Pup on the flying-off deck following two previously successful efforts, a September conference recommended that a landing-on deck be built over the after superstructure to enable *Furious* to retrieve aircraft from directly astern; a second hangar could be installed beneath, and aircraft complement would thereby be doubled.

In late November 1917 the carrier returned to her builder for the work to be undertaken. A 70ft × 38ft hangar was built on the quarterdeck, surmounted by a 300ft × 50ft (minimum width) landing deck which extended forward over a substructure built up over the shelter deck and connected with the flying-off area at the bows via 11ft wide ramps on each side of the funnel and bridgework. Most significantly, two electric lifts, one serving each hangar, were fitted, that aft offset to starboard. Primitive arresting gear in the form of athwartships wires weighted with sandbags at each end was embarked, and longitudinal wires ran the length of the landing-on deck forward of the lift to keep aircraft touching down on a straight course. A gantry-like structure from which was suspended a series of ropes served as a crash barrier at the forward end. As a result of the modifications, which took some four months to complete, the secondary 5.5in battery was relocated, one mounting being sacrificed.

Pups, Camels and 1½-Strutters made up the aircraft complement; seaplanes were not specified.

The reconstruction effected during 1917–18 was not an unqualified success, mainly because of the difficulties aircraft still encountered in attempting to land on, caused by eddies and currents generated by the ship's superstructure. After considerable uncertainty as to *Furious*'s future, and following experience with the flush-decked carrier *Argus*, it was decided to reconfigure her once more, this time dramatically, as outlined in a memo dated 23 March 1921 by the DNC, Sir Eustace H. Tennyson d'Eyncourt:

'The scheme provides for clearing the vessel down to the floor of the present hangar and building a double-decked hangar, with the funnels led fore and aft at the sides of these hangars, eventually discharging at the stern, somewhat as in "ARGUS".

'The upper hangar can take 33 Sopwith Torpedo Carriers folded, and the lower hangar 28, total 61, or alternatives . . .

'Two lifts are provided to serve these hangars, and in addition machines can be taken out very quickly through the forward end of the upper hangar, so that machines may get away from three positions at the same time. . . .'

It should be noted that even though the carrier was to feature a flush deck, the latter was still seen as two distinct entities, a forward flying-off deck and an after landing-on deck. The 'alternatives' would comprise varying combinations of folded or spread Sopwith fighters and Parnall Panther spotter-reconnaissance aircraft, but in the event none of the types envisaged would embark after *Furious* commissioned in her new guise.

The reconstruction was carried out at Rosyth and subsequently Devonport Dockyards, work at the former being limited to preliminaries to enable the carrier to be towed south. The main flight deck now extended for 576ft and had a usable width of 90ft. The upper hangar, 530ft × 50ft, led forward to the secondary flying-off platform which was some 200ft in length, about 50ft of this being hangar floor. The lower hangar measured 550ft × 50ft. New lifts, each capable of handling 8,000lb, were installed forward and aft, auxiliary smoke ducts being situated abreast the latter on top of the flight deck, complementing the main uptakes at the sides below. The ship was conned via a navigating position on the starboard side of the forward edge of the upper flight deck (a flying control position being provided opposite, to port), although an auxiliary retractable charthouse was located on the flight-deck centreline. Longitudinal wires were fitted along 350ft of the flight deck, and the latter was rounded off at its forward edge 'as a result of experiments at the NPL [National Physical Laboratory] which tend to show that steadier aerodynamic conditions prevail with such a form for small angles of yaw of the wind'.

The modifications raised displacement, the designed figure at legend condition, with all ammunition and 750 tons of fuel, being 22,130 tons. Draught was now 22ft 9in forward and 25ft 3in aft (legend condition, at the perpendiculars) and extreme width 107ft. Armament consisted of 10 × 5.5in in single mountings, 6 × 4in AA, four forward and two aft, and four single 2pdrs. Complement rose marginally, and 36 aircraft could be carried.

Furious was further modified during the 1930s. First, in 1931–32, her quarterdeck was raised to upper deck level and her anti-aircraft battery was revised: the four 4in weapons at the edges of the lower flying-off deck had been removed soon after she recommissioned in 1925, but two were returned in this refit, with an 8-barrelled 2pdr mounting forward of each one, while the two 4in on the quarterdeck centreline were reduced to one at the new level. Cross-deck arrester gear was fitted by the mid 1930s. In 1938–39, she was completely rearmed: the 5.5in battery was removed and six twin 4in Mk XVI were installed, two each side abaft amidships, one on the quarterdeck and one on the now disused forward flying-off platform. The single 4in were also taken out, and a third multiple 2pdr was added abaft a new low island which was fitted at the starboard flight-deck edge. Two 4in directors were added, one on the island and one abaft the forward twin 4in mounting, and a light pole mast, topped by a homing beacon, was rigged. Topweight had by this time increased considerably, and by the outbreak of war *Furious* displaced 22,450 tons standard and 28,500 tons deep load; draught was 24ft at standard displacement and 27ft 9in deep. She could make 29.5kts.

During the course of the Second World War, the defensive battery was further strengthened by the addition of a fourth 2pdr mounting, forward of the

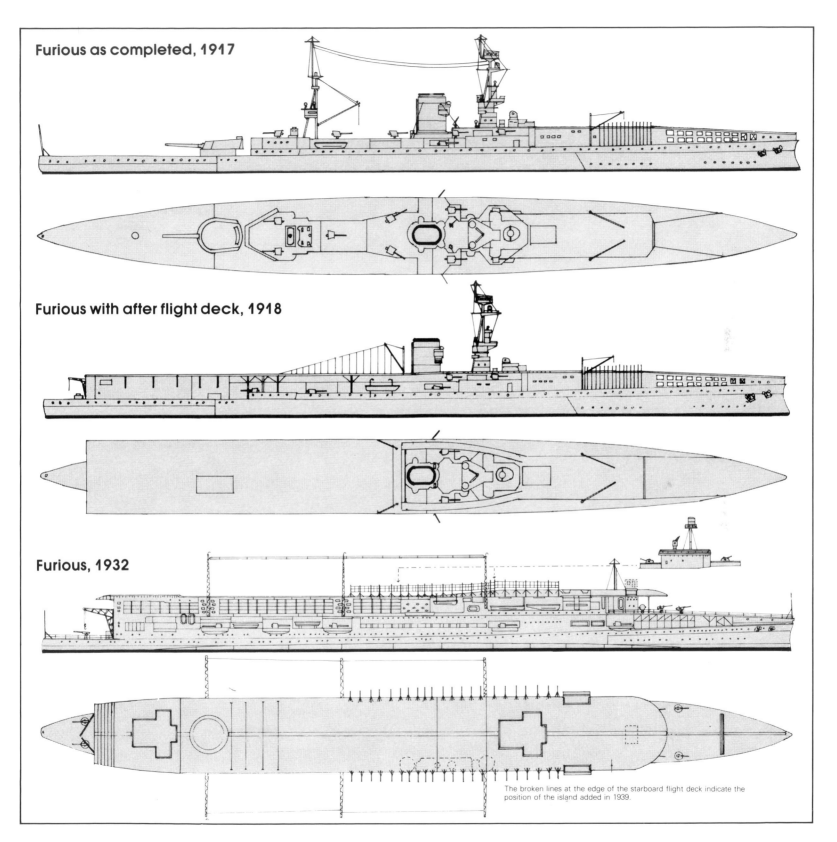

Furious as completed, 1917

Furious with after flight deck, 1918

Furious, 1932

The broken lines at the edge of the starboard flight deck indicate the
position of the island added in 1939.

island, and progressive installations of 20mms, the final number being 22. Type 285 gunnery radar was fitted, and the bulges were deepened to improve buoyancy; normal aircraft complement was now thirty.

Service Notes *Furious* recommissioned after her first reconfiguration on 15 March 1918 and although employed experimentally for much of the remainder of the war she led the celebrated Tondern raid in July 1918, sending off seven Sopwith Camels, each loaded with a pair of 50lb bombs, to strike the Zeppelin sheds there. The attacking aircraft destroyed two airships.

Her Second World War service saw her initially with the Home Fleet, engaged primarily in convoy protection and ASW duties and providing support for the Allied expeditions to Norway. Following a spell in the Mediterranean in mid 1941, she refitted in the USA that October. *Furious* took part in Operation 'Torch' (the Allied landings in North Africa) in November 1942, returning to the Home Fleet in February the following year. Strikes against German shipping, including attacks on the German battleship *Tirpitz* (lying in Altenfjord, Norway) in company with the Fleet carriers *Formidable* and *Indefatigable* and the escort carriers *Nabob* and *Trumpeter*, were to be her last major combat mission: she was reduced to reserve in September 1944, and following intermittent use as a target trials ship was sold for scrapping in 1948.

NAIRANA

Builder	Launched	Commissioned
Denny	1917	25 Aug 17

Displacement: 3,070 tons / 3,119 tonnes (standard).
Length: 315ft / 96.01m (pp); 352ft / 107.29m (oa).
Beam: 45ft 6in / 13.87m (hull).
Draught: 14ft / 4.27m (mean).
Machinery: Turbines.
Performance: 6,700shp; 19kts.
Aircraft: 7.
Guns: 2×3in; 2×12pdr.
Complement: c.250.
Design This vessel was laid down as a mail steamer, but was purchased by the Admiralty before completion. Measuring 3,547grt, she was fitted with the usual hangar aft and flight deck forward, the latter topping a second, smaller hangar, being fitted with a

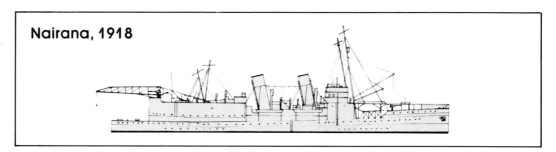

Nairana, 1918

primitive lift (the first in a Royal Navy carrier), and extending to the bridge through a dual foremast. Two handling cranes were installed aft, and 12pdr AA guns were mounted.

Modifications The original aircraft complement is not known, but by the end of the First World War *Nairana* was carrying two Sopwith Camels and five Fairey Campanias.

Service Notes Having served with the Grand Fleet in 1917–18, *Nairana* sailed with the British Expeditionary Force to North Russia in 1919. She was sold in 1921.

PEGASUS

Builder	Launched	Commissioned
John Brown	9 June 17	1917

Displacement: 3,300 tons / 3,353 tonnes (standard).
Length: 330ft / 100.58m (pp); 332ft / 101.19m (oa).
Beam: 43ft / 13.11m (hull).
Draught: 15ft / 4.57m (mean); 15ft 8in / 4.77m (deep load).
Machinery: Geared turbines; cylindrical boilers; 2 shafts.
Performance: 9,500shp; 20kts.
Bunkerage: 360 tons / 366 tonnes.
Aircraft: 9.
Guns: 2×3in; 2×12pdr.
Complement: 258.
Design The Great Eastern Railway Company's 2,450grt mail steamer *Stockholm* was purchased by the Admiralty in February 1917 and converted along similar lines to *Nairana*, with a flying-off platform, lift and hangar forward and a larger hangar, some 85ft in

Right: *Nairana* and *Pegasus* represented the ultimate development of the converted seaplane carrier in the Royal Navy and, together with *Vindex, Furious, Argus* and *Vindictive*, formed the 'Flying Squadron' of the immediate postwar years. This is *Pegasus*, little changed in general configuration from the prototypical carriers of 1914. (Fleet Air Arm Museum)

length, aft. Two heavy cranes were installed, one on each side of the after hangar entrance, and, as in *Nairana*, the foremast was split to allow the flying deck to be extended aft as far as possible. On trials *Pegasus* made 20.8kts. Her initial aircraft complement consisted of Campanias.

Modifications Not known.

Service Notes Served with the Grand Fleet during the latter months of the First World War and was retained by the Navy as an aircraft transport throughout the 1920s. Sold in August 1931 and subsequently scrapped.

Pegasus, 1917

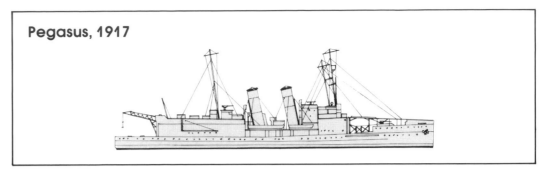

Argus, 1943

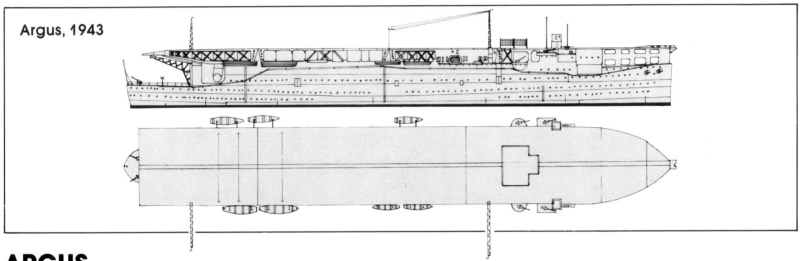

ARGUS

Builder	Laid down	Launched	Commissioned
Beardmore	1914	2 Dec 17	Sept 18

Displacement: 14,550 tons / 14,783 tonnes (standard); 17,000 tons / 17,272 tonnes (deep load).
Length: 535ft 6in / 163.22m (pp); 565ft / 172.21m (oa); 550ft / 167.64m (fd).
Beam: 68ft 6in / 20.88m (hull); 69ft / 21.03m (fd).
Draught: 21ft / 6.4m (mean); 24ft 9in / 7.54m (deep load).

Machinery: Parsons turbines; 12 cylindrical boilers; 4 shafts.
Performance: 21,500shp; 20.25kts.
Bunkerage: 2,000 tons / 2,032 tonnes.
Aircraft: 20.
Guns: 6 × 4in.
Complement: 373.

Design The origins of the Royal Navy's first flush-decked carrier are somewhat obscure. In early 1914 the merchant ship *Conte Rosso*, destined for Italian service under the Lloyd Sabaudo Line flag, was laid down at Dalmuir, but construction was suspended at the outbreak of the First World War. Beardmore had proposed an aircraft-carrying ship to the Admiralty

Below: As originally conceived, *Argus* would have been completed with a superstructure amidships and a flying-off deck forward, after the manner of early seaplane carriers, but she commissioned as a fully flush-decked ship — the world's first such carrier. Note the retractable charthouse forward, as in *Furious* after her 1920s rebuild. (Fleet Air Arm Museum)

some time beforehand, and had even drawn up detailed plans for such a vessel; on the Admiralty's purchase of the *Conte Rosso* in August 1916 these plans were translated into the vessel's design.

What is known, nevertheless, is that the ship, renamed *Argus*, turned out rather differently from the carrier that was once envisaged. At an early stage she was considered purely a seaplane carrier, but some time in 1917 it was decided to provide for land-planes, flight-deck arrangements comprising an inclined flying-off deck over the forecastle and a landing-on deck aft, the two separated by bridgework and funnel. A further development suggested a split superstructure, with the decks connected along the ship's centreline, and a crash barrier preventing landing aircraft from running over on to the forward flying-off deck. Before she was launched, and therefore for reasons unconnected with *Furious*'s experience with an after landing-on deck, and which remain somewhat difficult to unravel, it was agreed that she be completed instead with an unobstructed, full-length flight deck.

A 350ft × 68ft (48ft clear) × 20ft hangar was built up on the hull, and above this the flight deck, sloping downwards at its forward end and rounded down aft, was erected on a light, lattice-type structure. Longitudinal wires were fitted to assist landing aircraft. Navigating positions were provided below flight-deck level to port and starboard, and a retractable chart-house was installed along the flight-deck centreline. Two electrically-operated lifts, the forward unit measuring 30ft × 36ft, were installed, and two electric cranes were fitted aft on the quarterdeck, originally to handle seaplanes which could be hoisted out of the water and manoeuvred into the hangar via the open after end. Immediately forward of each crane were situated the smoke duct outlets, the ducts being led

Below: *Argus* during the Second World War, her bows semi-enclosed, her forward flight deck raised and 20mm Oerlikons fitted. (Ministry of Defence (Navy))

down on each side of the hangar from the boiler rooms.

Argus was completed as a strike carrier, with a compliment of Sopwith Cuckoo torpedo bombers and Camel fighters. Her sixth battery consisted of 4 × 4in AA, two forward behind the forecastle break and two right aft at the stern, and 2 × 4in LA in shielded mountings just abaft the conning positions.

Modifications Soon after the First World War *Argus* was fitted with a dummy (canvas) island for NPL wind-over-deck experiments in connection with the completion of *Eagle*. In 1925–26 the ship was given bulges, raising beam to 75ft 9in. In the mid 1930s she was reboiled with water-tube units taken from redundant destroyers, and her battery of 4in guns was removed. The forward 100ft of the flight deck was rebuilt, losing its downward slope and being given considerable stiffening below to enable two catapults, primarily for launching DH Queen Bee radio-controlled target aircraft, to be accommodated. Little further modification was carried out, although about 10 × 20mm were added during the Second World War to give the carrier some measure of self-defence while operating as a combat unit.

Service Notes As the only through-deck carrier in the Royal Navy until the commissioning of *Hermes* in mid 1923, *Argus* performed invaluably as a trials ship during the immediate post-war years, proving the validity of her configuration. She served with the Fleet until the mid 1930s, by which time she had been demoted from front-line status, her slow speed proving too much of a handicap. She was a training carrier by 1940, although her war service included convoy escort and aircraft ferrying; she replaced *Ark Royal* in Force H late in 1941 following that carrier's loss. She participated in Operation 'Torch', but by 1943 had reverted to her role as a training carrier. She was designated an accommodation ship in December 1944, was sold two years later, and was broken up from 1947.

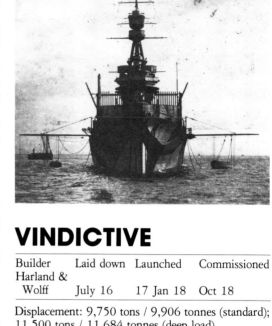

VINDICTIVE

Builder	Laid down	Launched	Commissioned
Harland & Wolff	July 16	17 Jan 18	Oct 18

Displacement: 9,750 tons / 9,906 tonnes (standard); 11,500 tons / 11,684 tonnes (deep load).
Length: 565ft / 172.21m (pp); 605ft / 184.4m (oa); 100ft / 30.48m (fwd fd), 215ft / 65.53m (aft fd).
Beam: 65ft / 19.81m (hull); 55ft / 16.76m (fwd fd), 65ft / 19.81m (aft fd).
Draught: 17ft 6in / 5.33m (mean); 20ft / 6.1m (deep load).
Machinery: Parsons geared turbines; 12 Yarrow small-tube boilers; 4 shafts.
Performance: 60,000shp; 29.5kts.
Bunkerage: 1,480 tons / 1,504 tonnes.
Aircraft: 6.
Guns: 4 × 7.5in; 4 × 3in; 4 × 12pdr.
Torpedo tubes: 6 × 21in.
Complement: 700.

Design The promise held out by the conversion of *Furious* to incorporate a landing deck aft prompted the desire to acquire further vessels of similar configuration. The cruiser *Cavendish*, ordered in April 1916, was under construction, and it was decided to complete her as a carrier that could operate with *Furious* and a fast cruiser scouting screen.

The *Hawkins* class to which she belonged saw four vessels completed to the original cruiser layout. Their armament consisted of 7 × 7.5in, 6 × 3in, 4 × 3in AA and 2 × 21in torpedo tubes. Four coal- and eight oil-fired boilers were fitted. Armour amounted to 3in maximum on the hull sides tapering to a minimum 1½in forward and aft, 1in lower and upper decks, plus anti-torpedo bulges. 1,480 tons of oil fuel and 860 tons of coal could be bunkered.

As completed, *Vindictive* (as *Cavendish* was renamed in June 1918) showed a virtually unchanged

Above left: *Vindictive* with booms rigged and wind-breaks raised, 1918–19. (Fleet Air Arm Museum)

Above: Envisaged as very much the companion to the fast carrier *Furious*, *Vindictive* was also a converted cruiser, though of smaller dimensions. The similarities between the two ships can be seen in this photograph of *Vindictive* as completed: hangars forward and aft; flying-decks forward and aft (the forward unit considerably shorter than that in *Furious*); and a 'goal-post' type crash barrier abaft the funnels. (Fleet Air Arm Museum)

hull, but two hangars were built on the upper deck: one forward, with a hatch in the roof for bringing aircraft up via a pair of derricks on each side; and a larger one aft, served by a lift. A flying-off deck was fitted forward and a landing-on deck aft, the two connected by a narrow platform along the port side. A *Furious*-type crash barrier was installed at the forward end of the landing deck.

The armament was revised, three 7.5in mountings being suppressed in order to accommodate the hangars and four additional torpedo tubes being added to the upper deck amidships, supplementing the original two submerged beam tubes (a modification also carried out on the four vessels completed as cruisers). The 3in guns were low-angle weapons and were located one on each side of the bridge and two on the quarterdeck. A platform was added between the funnels, mounting 4×12pdr (3in calibre) AA guns.

Six aircraft were at first stipulated, but it was generally found that two fighters and six spotter-reconnaissance aircraft could be accommodated.

Modifications Some unofficial sources state that *Vindictive* received four machine-guns (type not specified) for anti-aircraft use in 1919. With the decision in favour of flush-decked carriers arising, in the first instance, from the problematic deck-landing

trials experienced with separated flight decks, the ship became something of a liability: very little actual flying had been conducted from her, and it was decided to reconvert her to cruiser configuration, retaining, however, the forward hangar. The work was carried out between 1923 and 1925 and included also the installation of a catapult on the hangar roof, together with a lattice-type handling crane, so that *Vindictive* retained a limited air capability, albeit experimental.

Service Notes *Vindictive*'s service career was less than fortunate. She ran aground in the Baltic in the summer of 1919, requiring extensive repairs at Portsmouth Dockyard at a cost of £200,000. She rejoined the Fleet in 1921. She became a training ship in 1937 and was a repair ship during the Second World War. She was sold in February 1946 and subsequently broken up.

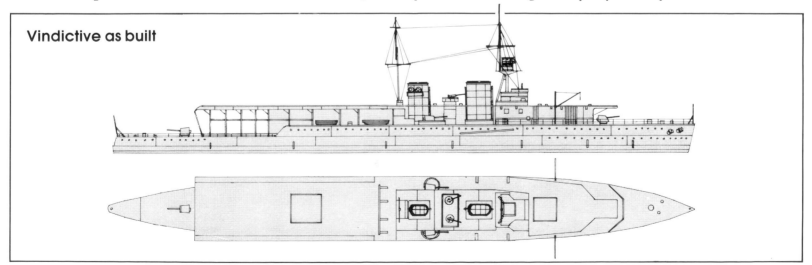

Vindictive as built

HERMES

Builder	Laid down	Launched	Commissioned
Armstrong Whitworth	15 Jan 18	11 Sept 19	July 23

Displacement: 10,850 tons / 11,024 tonnes (standard); 13,000 tons / 13,208 tonnes (deep load).
Length: 548ft / 167.03m (pp); 600ft / 182.88m (oa); 580ft / 176.78m (fd).
Beam: 70ft 3in / 21.41m (hull); 65ft / 19.81m (fd).
Draught: 18ft 9in / 5.71m (mean); 21ft 6in / 6.55m (deep load).
Machinery: Parsons geared turbines; 6 Yarrow small-tube boilers; 2 shafts.
Performance: 40,000shp; 25kts.
Aircraft: 20.
Guns: 6 × 5.5in; 3 × 4in.
Complement: 664.

Design The ordering of *Hermes* in July 1917 was a decision of considerable significance since for the first time the Navy would receive a carrier designed from scratch – and she would remain the only such ship in service for fifteen years. Whatever changes might be incorporated as construction proceeded, the purpose of the new carrier was clear: she was to act in concert with cruisers, fulfilling the function of a cruiser, the only difference being that her reconnaissance task could be carried out at increased range by means of her 25 aircraft. Accordingly, she was built along the lines of a light cruiser, in terms of her size, strength (scantlings), armour protection, machinery and speed.

The hull was also of cruiser form, with the main deck as the strength deck, above which was built a hangar approximately 400ft in length, surmounted by a full flight deck. The flight deck itself showed a considerable rise aft, a feature adopted following NPL research, and the single lift was located in the centre of this; longitudinal wires stretched along the landing area. The hull was plated right up to flight-deck level, and given an exaggerated flare forward to permit the maximum flight-deck width possible at the bows. Vertical protection consisted of a 3in belt diminishing to 1½in-2in at the ends, and horizontal protection consisted of 1in decks (main deck forward, over the magazines, and upper deck amidships, over the machinery spaces). The hull was bulged.

The armament consisted of six low-angle 5.5in in single mountings (similar to those installed aboard *Furious*), disposed in openings cut in the hull plating amidships, and three single 4in AA in unshielded mountings, two before and one, beneath a large crane, abaft the island.

The latter was adopted without precedent, and whether it was a feature of the original design is uncertain; however, it was a massive structure for a ship of this size, at least in the light of future trends, and, topped with a sturdy tripod mast and an impressive foretop, it caused some problems. Further difficulties arose from the fact that *Hermes* trimmed by the bow. A July 1928 note from the ship's CO while at Wei-Hai-Wei to the C-in-C China Station elucidated:

'Oil Fuel tanks 166–186 Starboard are now permanently in use to correct trim, thus increasing the fuel capacity by 64 tons to 1956 tons.
'Port bulges 166–204 are permanently flooded to correct for Superstructure.
'Watertight compartments 248–258 are permanently flooded to correct for trim.
'Oil Fuel tanks 48–94 are always emptied first to assist trim of ship.'

In fact, the balance was so delicate that allowances had to be made according to whether 'Trinidad' (specific gravity 0.96) or 'Persian' (0.89) oil was being burned.

Modifications Interwar modifications were fairly limited, involving the installation of a second, forward, lift, transverse arrester gear and a catapult.

By later standards, *Hermes* was an extremely small carrier with an extremely small aircraft capacity, and her limitations were severe by the 1930s. Aircraft capacity in October 1930 consisted of eight 'assembled' Fairey IIIFs, four 'assembled' Ripons and seven unrigged Flycatchers; because of the restricted hangar width, 'no more space could be made available by unrigging further aircraft. Ripons packed in cases could only be taken on Flying D^k but it is unpracticable [*sic*] owing to strain on Flying D^k . . .' By the mid 1930s, capacity was down to fifteen and by the Second World War to twelve.

Particular anxieties were expressed about her lifts. They were of reasonable capacity at five tons and moved at 35ft per minute, but their dimensions were unsuited to aircraft then coming into service. An Admiralty inquiry elicited the information that the forward lift was 36ft 1¾in long and the after lift 36ft 6½in, and in 1938 a flat mould of a Swordfish aircraft was produced and revealed a 1in clearance at each end for the forward unit.

Following a Devonport refit in 1934, *Hermes*'s armament consisted of 6 × 5.5in, 3 × 4in and 2 × 0.5in (4-barrelled), but photographs indicate that a fourth 4in was added some distance abaft that already installed behind the island for a period. In 1937 it was proposed to rearm her by removing the 5.5in and 4in single mountings and fitting 4 × 4in

Below: Flycatcher floatplanes aboard *Hermes* in the Far East, where the carrier spent much of her peacetime service. The ship's massive island superstructure is seen to good effect, and her single 4in guns are visible before and abaft it; below and further aft are three of the 5.5in low-angle mountings. (Fleet Air Arm Museum)

Mk XVI twins and two 8-barrelled 2pdr 'M' mountings, but this scheme was cancelled and the carrier received only one 4-barrelled 2pdr and about half a dozen 20mms during the Second World War.
Service Notes *Hermes* served mainly on the China Station throughout her career, but the outbreak of war saw her dispatched to the Atlantic, hunting raiders. In mid 1940 she collided with the AMC *Corfu*, seriously damaging herself forward. Following repairs in South Africa she carried out strikes off East Africa against German positions and shipping and also in the Middle East. She was caught and sunk by Japanese aircraft from the carriers *Soryu*, *Hiryu* and *Akagi* off Ceylon on 9 April 1942.

Above: Hermes, a tiny carrier by modern standards, but a pace-setter in her day: she was the first purpose-designed carrier to be built, although not the first to enter service. Note the extreme flare forward, adopted to maximise the width of the flight deck at the bows and to help minimise interference from spray. (Fleet Air Arm Museum)

Hermes, 1933

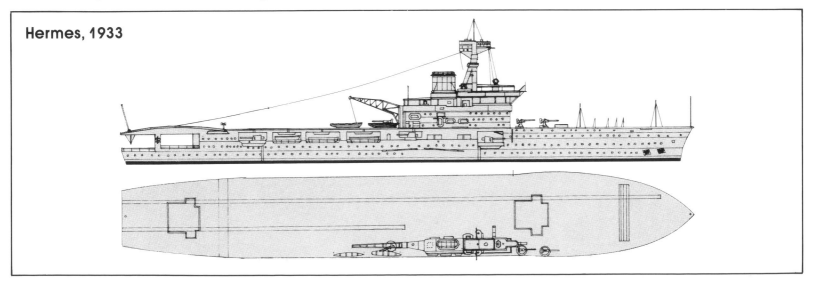

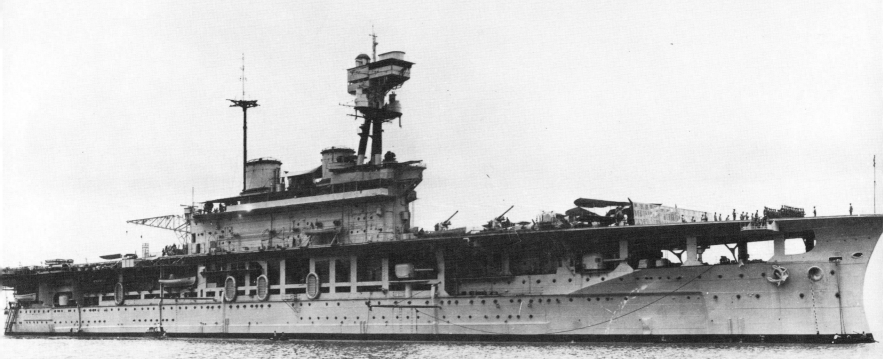

EAGLE

Builder	Laid down	Launched	Commissioned
Armstrong Whitworth	20 Feb 13	8 June 18	26 Feb 24

Displacement: 21,850 tons / 22,200 tonnes
(standard); 26,800 tons / 27,229 tonnes (deep load).
Length: 627ft 1in / 191.13m (pp); 667ft 6in /
203.45m (oa); 652ft / 198.73m (fd).
Beam: 105ft 2in / 32.06m (hull); 95ft / 28.96m (fd).
Draught: 21ft 9in / 6.63m (mean); 26ft 6in / 8.08m
(deep load).
Machinery: Brown-Curtis / Parsons turbines;
32 Yarrow boilers; 4 shafts.
Performance: 50,000shp; 24kts.
Bunkerage: 3,750 tons / 3,810 tonnes.
Range: 4,000nm at 18kts.
Aircraft: 24.
Guns: 9 × 6in; 5 × 4in; 4 × 3pdr.
Complement: 834.

Left: Like the French *Béarn*, *Eagle* was a converted First World War battleship hull and consequently retained battleship features of the period: massive weight and slow speed. *Hermes*, at half her displacement, could accommodate almost as many aircraft. *Eagle* is seen here in the 1930s, her multiple pompom fitted to her island and her HACS director in place on the foretop. Note the smoke streamer at the stem. (Fleet Air Arm Museum)

Below left: *Eagle* prior to the outbreak of the Second World War. The lines of a typical dreadnought hull are plain to see, in particular the cut-away forecastle which enabled the battleship's secondary batteries to achieve some measure of ahead fire. Swordfish are ranged on deck, protected by the raised windscreen. Even *Eagle* was originally designated a 'seaplane carrier', a reminder being the heavy lattice crane abaft the island, the primary task of which was to hoist aboard or deploy floatplanes. (Fleet Air Arm Museum)

Design 'It has been decided subject to satisfactory arrangements being made that the Chilean Battleship ALMIRANTE COCHRANE now building at Elswick shall be converted into a seaplane carrier for service in H.M. Navy . . .'

By January 1918 the Board of Admiralty was fully convinced of the value of seaplane carriers and little effort was spared in scouring the country for suitable hulls for conversion. The incomplete Chilean battleship *Almirante Cochrane*, on which work had stopped at the outbreak of war and whose sister-ship, *Almirante Latorre*, had been completed for Royal Navy service as *Canada* (28,600 tons, 10 × 14in, 22kts), was still on the ways pending a decision as to her future. Her designed strength and protection, it was felt, would make her suitable for use as a strike carrier; her heavy scantlings, in fact, proved to be an unnecessary burden, but it must be remembered that the concept around which she was completed was as yet untried.

When it became apparent that the war against Germany would end before she could be brought into service, her completion was pursued in a very leisurely (indeed uncertain) fashion – there was considerable doubt as to whether she would actually commission as a carrier until the official sanction came on 24 September 1920, and it was widely felt that she should be reconverted to her original state and sold to Chile as first arranged.

During the first half of 1918, however, conversion plans had been moving with almost indecent haste. The original flight-deck arrangements had much in common with those mooted at one stage for *Argus* (and presumably influenced by *Campania*): the

minutes of an Admiralty meeting on 4 February 1918 record that the bridge structure would be '. . . divided into two islands standing about 110-ft long and about 68-ft apart. These islands accommodate the funnel uptakes, W/T offices, Coding and decoding rooms and sea cabins.

'The two islands are cross connected at the top with heavy bracing which is plated over to form a Navigating Platform and cover in and protect the assembly space beneath. On this platform the Charthouse, Wheel House, and usual Bridge Equipment are arranged as well as sea cabins. There will be a clear height of 20-ft between the framing of the platform and the flying deck. . . .

'Two tripod masts are provided – one on each island. These are staggered and confused with funnels for anti-submarine effect.'

The following month, a single island, bridge and mast had been settled on.

A 20ft 6in high hangar some 400ft long was provided, with a lift well at each end (47ft × 46ft forward, 33ft × 46ft aft); on top, a 100-ton flight deck of maximum 1in plate, squared off at its forward end, was fitted. Armour distribution remained much as in the battleship design: the belt was thinner, at 4½in, but bulkheads were 4in, main deck 1½in and hangar (upper) deck 1½in. The ship was designed to burn both oil and coal, 1,750 tons of the latter being accommodated in addition to the oil capacity given in the table.

The carrier was fitted out for flying trials before being completed, and was moved to Portsmouth in the spring of 1920, where a section of the flight deck was fitted with 190ft long fore-and-aft guidance wires.

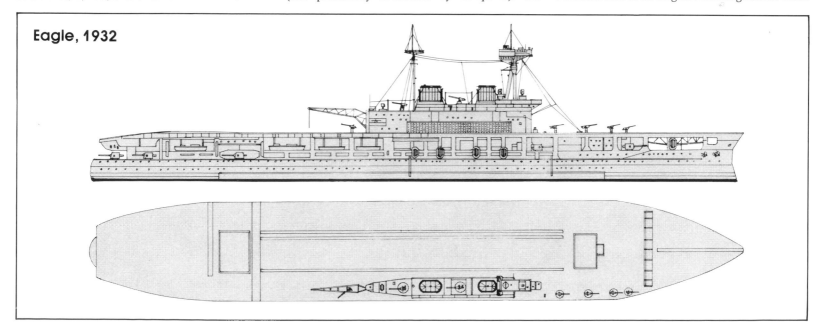

Eagle, 1932

After the order to complete the following September, *Eagle* was taken in hand at Portsmouth. The hull was bulged as an anti-torpedo measure (as in contemporary capital ships) and was expected to withstand a 750lb detonation of TNT as a result. The armament was installed and the island completed (the ship had received only one funnel prior to her passage south), and the flight deck was lengthened forward and the space below enclosed. Torpedo tubes, stipulated in early designs, were not fitted, neither was a sixth 4in AA. New longitudinal wires (328ft) were installed and, after considerable delays caused by electrical problems (in particular concerning the lifts), the ship was completed.

Modifications The longitudinal wires were removed from *Eagle* in 1926 and the ship operated without any deck landing aids until the installation of a cross-deck arrester system in 1936. Armament changes comprised the addition of two single 2pdr guns in 1926; the substitution of an 8-barrelled 2pdr for the 4in gun on the island top, between the uptakes, in 1931–32; a further multiple 2pdr before the island in 1936; and about a dozen 20mms during the Second World War. She was reboilered in 1931–32 and just prior to the outbreak of war had a high-angle director system fitted on the foremast. Complement rose with these additions, and still more during the war with the installation of Types 290 warning and 285 gunnery radar.

Service Notes *Eagle* served mostly in the Mediterranean for the early part of her career, but from 1934 operated principally on the China Station. She carried out anti-raider sweeps and troop convoy escort in the Indian Ocean following the outbreak of war, and in March 1940 suffered an internal explosion in one of her bomb rooms and was at Singapore for some weeks for repair. Moving to the Mediterranean, she carried out strikes against enemy-held positions in North Africa from May 1940, but for much of 1941 was assigned to the Atlantic, mainly covering convoys. During Operation 'Pedestal', the supply of aircraft reinforcements to Malta, she was hit by four torpedoes fired from the submarine *U-73* on 11 August 1942, and sank within five minutes.

Left: At full speed during flying operations, *Eagle* is shown here with her new four-barrelled 2pdr pompom forward of the bridge. The practice of painting part of the mast black — to mask staining from the funnel — was typical of the period. (Fleet Air Arm Museum)

Right: *Courageous* and *Glorious* were semi-sisters to *Furious*, but upon conversion were considerably different in appearance, mainly because of their island superstructures. The windscreen visible here is erected on the forward (auxiliary) flying-off deck, from which fleet fighters could operate while the upper flight deck was in use. Note, too, the prominent anti-torpedo bulge at the waterline in this photograph of *Courageous*, circa 1930. (Fleet Air Arm Museum)

COURAGEOUS CLASS

Ship	Builder	Laid down	Launched	Commissioned
Courageous	Armstrong Whitworth	28 Mar 15	5 Feb 16	5 May 28
Glorious	Harland & Wolff	1 May 15	20 Apr 16	10 Mar 30

Displacement: 22,000 tons / 22,352 tonnes (standard); 26,100 tons / 26,518 tonnes (deep load).
Length: 735ft / 224.03m (pp); 786ft 6in / 239.73m (oa); 530ft / 161.54m (fd).
Beam: 90ft 6in / 27.58m (hull); 84ft 6in / 25.76m (fd).

Draught: 24ft / 7.32m (mean); 27ft 3in / 8.31m (deep load).
Machinery: Parsons geared turbines; 18 Yarrow small-tube boilers; 4 shafts.
Performance: 90,000shp; 30.5kts.
Bunkerage: 3,800 tons / 3,861 tonnes.

Range: 5,860nm at 16kts.
Aircraft: 48.
Guns: 16 × 4.7in.
Complement: 1,200.

Design Conceived, with *Furious*, as an outgrowth of Fisher's Baltic scheme (see p. 85), *Courageous* and *Glorious* were completed early in 1917 as 18,600-ton 'large light cruisers' mounting 4 × 15in in twin turrets, 18 × 4in in triples and 2 × 3in AA. Armour protection was similar to that of *Furious*,

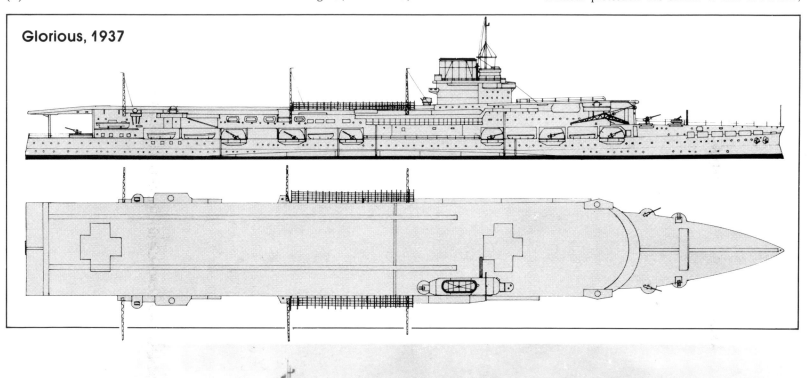

Glorious, 1937

with 3in sides and decks and 7in turrets. Whatever doubts were cast about their value as fighting units – and they were hotly ridiculed in this respect – they possessed the virtues of large hull size and high speed, which made them viable candidates for conversion to carriers. There was some discussion following the Washington Treaty of 1922 as to whether the pair should be scrapped, but with *Furious* the only 30kt carrier in prospect, the advantages of three such vessels forming a roughly homogeneous 'fast flying squadron' proved irresistible, and work started in 1923.

The superstructure was razed, 'all bulkheads; shelter deck; conning tower; director towers; masts; main derrick; bridges; funnel and uptakes and boiler room vents down to main deck; all guns and boats'

and 'various fittings on forecastle deck' being removed. Two superimposed, 550ft long hangars, the upper one opening on to a short auxiliary flying-off deck, were built on to the hull, two 46ft × 48ft lifts bringing up aircraft to the main flight deck. The vertical and horizontal protection was retained, but the defensive battery was revised. Consideration was given early on to the possibility of mounting single 8in guns, the heaviest carrier weapon permissible under Washington, but this was changed, first to 10 × 5.5in, 6 × 4in HA and four Mk 'M' pompoms, and finally to an all-AA battery as indicated in the table. The hull bulges, deepened to improve buoyancy, were designed to defeat 440lb of TNT. Petrol stowage totalled 34,500 gallons.

An island and uptake were located on the starboard

deck-edge, and the flight deck itself incorporated a ramp forward to assist take-offs. This was the subject of some discussion, as an Admiralty letter of April 1924 noted:
'. . . from a flying point of view a 4' 6" ramp was not required and there would be no objection to this height being modified. The one requirement is that the arresting gear [longitudinal] should not be more than 15" from the deck. In view of this, the run-up of the flight deck is being arranged to start at 105 station which becomes the forward end of the fixed ramp.'
Courageous was converted from June 1924 at Devonport and *Glorious* from 1925, first at Rosyth and then at Devonport. The two carriers were easily the most satisfactory such vessels in Royal Navy service up to the late 1930s. They had a good speed,

Left: *Glorious* displays her flight-deck features: the gently undulating profile and cruciform lifts. Both ships showed a pair of catapults by the late 1930s; they are evident in this photograph. (By courtesy of Ian Sturton)

Top right: *Glorious* in February 1937, 2pdrs fitted to her former flying-off deck. The navigating platform extending across the flight deck folded back along the funnel when not in use. (By courtesy of Ray Burt)

Centre right: Originally, *Glorious* (shown) could be distinguished from her sister ship by her slightly longer flight deck aft. The sponsons at lower hangar deck level indicate the locations of the 4.7in AA guns; a pair were also fitted on the forward flying-off deck, with two more, as can be seen, at the stern. Inevitably most of these guns had poor sky arcs. (Fleet Air Arm Museum)

Below right: Later, *Glorious*'s flight deck was extended to overhang the stern, and her quarterdeck was raised, making the distinction much more pronounced. This photograph is dated 1935. (Ministry of Defence (Navy))

and a realistic fixed battery, given the changing requirements for carrier employment. Their aircraft capacity, while hardly large by US standards, provided for a balanced air group, officially (at first) sixteen Flycatchers, sixteen IIIF spotter-reconnaissance aircraft and sixteen Ripon torpedo planes.

Modifications Four single 'M' 2pdr pompoms were fitted to each carrier in the early 1930s, at which time cross-deck arrester gear was also installed. In 1934 the question of air turbulence around the stern was the subject of a study; accordingly, *Glorious* was refitted in 1935 with a lengthened and more pronounced round-down (flight deck now 570ft overall), a modification that was considered also for *Courageous* in 1937 but not carried out. At the same time *Glorious* had her quarterdeck raised and each ship received a pair of hydraulic catapults forward; three 8-barrelled 2pdr pompoms were fitted (one abaft the island and two on the slip deck, which latter was made redundant), and *Courageous* was fitted with a tripod mast, replacing the original pole, and a charthouse on the island. By 1939 *Glorious* displaced 22,500 tons legend and 26,500 tons deep load.

Service Notes *Courageous*: As a light cruiser, *Courageous* served with the Grand Fleet's 1st Cruiser Squadron from 1917 until 1918, and during the interwar years, following conversion, she operated mainly with the Home Fleet. She was sunk soon after the outbreak of the Second World War by two torpedoes from *U-20* in the South-West Approaches, 17 September 1939.

Glorious: First World War service generally followed that of *Courageous*, but subsequent to conversion *Glorious* spent much of her time in the Mediterranean. She conducted a series of successful strikes with Skuas and Gladiators off Norway during early 1940, but on 18 June that year, with a deck-load of Hurricanes and Gladiators evacuated during the Allied withdrawal from that theatre, she was caught by the German battlecruisers *Scharnhorst* and *Gneisenau* and sunk by gunfire.

ALBATROSS

Builder	Laid down	Launched	Commissioned
Cockatoo	5 May 26	23 Feb 28	Sept 38

Displacement: 4,800 tons / 4,877 tonnes (standard); 6,000 tons / 6,096 tonnes (deep load).
Length: 422ft / 128.63m (pp); 443ft 9in / 135.26m (oa).
Beam: 60ft 10in / 18.54m (hull).
Draught: 13ft 9in / 4.19m (mean); 16ft 3in / 4.95m (deep load).
Machinery: Parsons geared turbines; 4 Yarrow small-tube boilers; 2 shafts.
Performance: 12,000shp; 20kts.
Bunkerage: 1,000 tons / 1,016 tonnes.
Aircraft: 9.
Guns: 4 × 4.7in; 4 × 2pdr.
Complement: 450.
Design The ex-Royal Australian Navy seaplane carrier of the same name (qv).
Modifications In late 1940 the catapult was replaced by a more up-to-date explosive type and a tripod mast carrying air warning radar replaced the original pole.

Below: *Albatross* in Royal Navy service, her catapult removed. (Fleet Air Arm Museum)

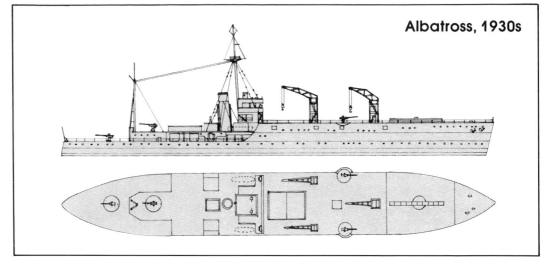

Albatross, 1930s

By 1943 the ship had been converted to a maintenance vessel for escorts and minesweepers: all her aircraft equipment and light AA were removed and two quadruple 2pdr and 6 × 20mm were added.
Service Notes During the early part of the Second World War *Albatross* was employed off West Africa and later in the Indian Ocean, operating Walrus amphibians in the trade protection role. She also provided Fleet spotting facilities during the occupation of Madagascar in October 1942. She was hit by a torpedo in August 1944 and although not seriously damaged was not repaired. By 1946 she had been converted to a merchantman (*Hellenic Prince*) and was broken up at Hong Kong from mid 1964.

ARK ROYAL

Builder	Laid down	Launched	Commissioned
Cammell Laird	16 Sept 35	13 Apr 37	16 Nov 38

Displacement: 22,000 tons / 22,352 tonnes (standard); 27,700 tons / 28,143 tonnes (deep load).
Length: 685ft / 208.79m (pp); 721ft 6in / 219.91m (wl); 800ft / 243.84m (oa); 780ft / 237.74m (fd).
Beam: 94ft 9in / 28.88m (hull); 96ft / 29.26m (fd).
Draught: 22ft 9in / 6.93m (mean); 27ft 9in / 8.46m (deep load).

Machinery: Parsons geared turbines; 6 Admiralty 3-drum boilers; 3 shafts.
Performance: 102,000shp; 31kts.
Bunkerage: 4,600 tons / 4,673 tonnes.
Range: 7,600nm at 20kts.
Aircraft: 60.
Guns: 16 × 4.5in; 48 × 2pdr; 32 × 0.5in.
Complement: 1,600.
Design *Ark Royal* was the first large British carrier to be designed from scratch, and although she was predicated on experience gained from existing

Above: *Ark Royal* awaits launch, April 1937, heralding a new era in Royal Navy carrier construction. The two protuberances over the bows will support the ship's catapults (strictly 'accelerators'), while discernible amidships, along the waterline demarcation, is the 4in armour belt. (By courtesy of John Roberts)

(converted) vessels and thus was able to incorporate all the technical operating facilities that had proven their worth during the late 1920s and early 1930s, her constructors were exploring new territory and her appearance was singularly distinctive. She was

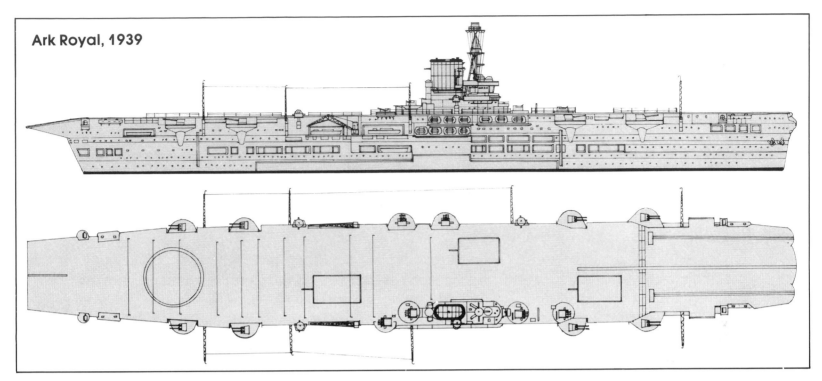

Ark Royal, 1939

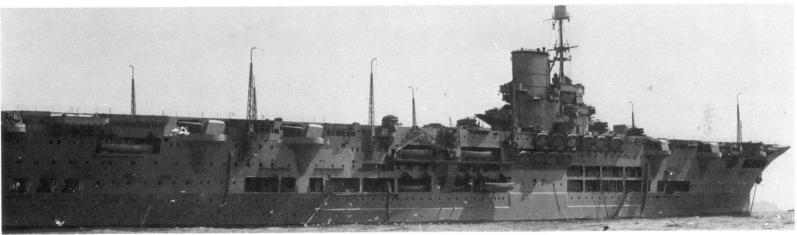

designed in 1934 to a hoped-for Treaty limit of 22,000 tons (in fact the subsequent Second London Treaty would allow 23,000 tons), and was formally ordered in 1935.

The hull was the maximum length permitted by drydocking and was plated up to the level of the flight deck, openings being let in for boat stowage, etc. The machinery arrangements, in a choice which was to prove unfortunate, consisted of three turbine spaces and three boiler rooms situated abreast one another, the uptakes being carried low down and vented through a single large funnel on the starboard side. The hull was given a 4½in armour belt amidships, with a 3½in armour deck covering boiler rooms and

Above: Responding to the ever-growing threat from the air, *Ark Royal*'s designers incorporated an impressive AA battery in the ship. The twin 4.5in were sited along the flight-deck edge, giving good sky arcs, and eight-barrelled 2pdr pompoms were clustered around the island; two further pompom mountings were fitted amidships on the port side. Note the carrier's high freeboard, demanded by the double hangar arrangement, but also by the requirement for good seakeeping. (By courtesy of Ray Burt)

magazines. Anti-torpedo protection was afforded by a new system of double-layering the hull skinning.

For the first time in a British carrier the designers were able to make the flight deck the principal strength deck of the vessel, which contributed significantly to the overall rigidity of the hull. In order

to preserve this strength longitudinally, the three lift wells had to be offset from the centreline, and all had to be extremely narrow. Two (45ft × 22ft) were positioned to starboard, one at each end of the hangar area, and the third (45ft × 25ft) was positioned to port amidships. As in *Courageous*, two hangar levels were arranged (although the upper one was totally enclosed), 568ft long above and 452ft below, each being 60ft wide and 16ft high.

The flight deck itself was given a huge overhang at the stern (the latter enclosed) to give extra length, and two hydraulic catapults were installed forward, each capable of assisting a 12,000lb aircraft. Cross-deck arrester gear was fitted, and the compact island, aero-

dynamically designed, supported a tripod mast topped by a radio homing beacon.

The armament incorporated the new twin 4.5in mounting, located high up just below flight-deck level and therefore commanding good sky arcs and obviating problems of working the weapons in heavy

ILLUSTRIOUS CLASS

Ship	Builder	Laid down	Launched	Commissioned
Illustrious	Vickers-Armstrong (Barrow)	27 Apr 37	5 Apr 39	25 May 40
Formidable	Harland & Wolff	17 June 37	17 Aug 39	24 Nov 40
Victorious	Vickers-Armstrong (Newcastle)	4 May 37	14 Sept 39	15 May 41
Indomitable	Vickers-Armstrong (Barrow)	10 Nov 37	26 Mar 40	10 Oct 41

Displacement: 23,000 tons / 23,368 tonnes (standard); 28,210 tons / 28,661 tonnes (deep load).
Length: 673ft / 205.13m (pp); 743ft 9in / 226.69m (oa); 650ft / 198.12m (fd).
Beam: 95ft 9in / 29.18m (hull); 80ft / 24.38m (fd).
Draught: 24ft / 7.32m (mean); 28ft / 8.53m (deep load).
Machinery: Parsons geared turbines; 6 Admiralty 3-drum boilers; 3 shafts.
Performance: 111,000shp; 30.5kts.
Bunkerage: 4,850 tons / 4,928 tonnes.
Range: 11,000nm at 14kts.
Aircraft: 36.
Guns: 16 × 4.5in; 48 × 2pdr.
Complement: 1,200.
Design The 1936 Programme provided for the construction of two carriers for the Royal Navy. The 23,000-ton limit set by the Second London Treaty was in force, and it seemed at first that the basic *Ark Royal* design could be taken, the extra 1,000 tons available being used to incorporate improvements. The spectre of a European war loomed large, however, and with it the realisation that the Royal Navy would be forced to operate under constant threat of land-based air attack, particularly in the Mediterranean – where Italy's intentions had been unpredictable since the early 1930s – and in the North Sea.

A novel approach, guided by the strong representations of Rear-Admiral Henderson, the Third Sea Lord, was adopted to meet the threat: the

seas. The six 2pdr mountings were situated two amidships at the port-side deck edge and four on the flight deck before and abaft the superstructure. The eight multiple machine-guns were positioned at the corners of the flight deck, on small sponsons.

The carrier was designed to operate in the strike role; complement as of 1937 was stated to be 48 Swordfish and 24 of the new multi-role (fighter/dive-bomber) Skuas, although initially Ospreys were embarked in place of the latter. Aviation fuel capacity was 100,000 gallons.

Modifications Little in the way of modification was carried out in *Ark Royal* before her loss, although her funnel was raised 8ft before commissioning to overcome downdraught problems posed to landing aircraft. Two multiple 2pdr pompoms were added to the fixed battery in May 1941.

carriers should be given an unprecedented measure of passive defence, in the form of extensive armouring, plus a heavy anti-aircraft battery, much as in *Ark Royal*. The primary task was to preserve the carrier's main armament – her strike aircraft – and so the stowage area was designed as an armoured 'box' intended to be proof against 500lb bombs and 6in shells. As in *Ark Royal*, belt, bulkhead and armour deck protection for machinery and magazines was also to be incorporated.

The problem was one of accomplishing all this within the Treaty displacement limits; clearly, something had to be sacrificed, and the victim was the two-storeyed hangar arrangement of the earlier design. This would save not only weight in itself, but also top-weight, ensuring the stability of the hull, whose dimensions were more or less fixed for the same reasons as were *Ark Royal*'s.

As finalised, the hangar was provided with 4½in armoured sides, a 3in roof (forming part of the flight deck) and 4½in bulkheads forward and aft, a 3in armoured deck acting as the hangar floor and extending to the 4½in main belt which was itself closed by armoured bulkheads. Additional armour was included to protect the steering compartments (3in), the flight deck before and abaft the hangar limits (1½in) and the hangar deck ends (1in). The dimensions of the hangar were 458ft × 62ft, with a height of 16ft, providing accommodation for thirty torpedo-bombers and six fighter/dive-bombers, a total capacity half that of *Ark Royal*'s originally specified

complement. The weak spots in an otherwise totally protected enclosure were the 45ft × 22ft lifts, which could not be armoured because of the weight penalty that would be exacted, but movable armoured screens were provided at each end of the hangar, by the lift wells. The armoured hangar concept proved its worth in the Far East where kamikazes caused damage above but not within it, thus not interfering significantly with aircraft operation; this contrasted sharply with US experience.

A three-shaft machinery arrangement was installed, as in *Ark Royal*, and to counter the weight of the island structure the hull was widened to port. The fixed battery consisted of eight powered 4.5in turrets, their crowns level with the flight deck and hence providing, theoretically, some measure of cross-deck fire. They were controlled by Mk IV directors. One hydraulic catapult (14,000lb capability) was fitted on the flight deck, forward and to port, and six wires aft formed the arresting system. Petrol stowage totalled 50,540 gallons.

Illustrious and *Victorious* were the two carriers provided under the 1936 Programme, the second pair under the 1937 Programme. *Indomitable*'s design, however, was modified before she completed. Second thoughts were expressed about the size of the air group, and it was decided to revert to a two-level hangar arrangement, the lower one extending beneath the after half of the upper, 168ft long. The 16ft height was retained below, but the upper hangar was reduced to 14ft. The price for this increase in capacity was a reduction in the thickness of the hangar sides to 1½in, but even so *Indomitable*'s displacement rose to 24,680 tons standard and 29,730 deep load. However, 48 aircraft could be accommodated. She received 8 × 20mm before completion, and complement stood at 1,592.

Modifications Wartime modifications were many and varied. The major structural change was a rebuilding of the flight deck forward and aft, giving an increased usable length of 740ft (745ft in *Indomitable*). The defensive battery was progressively augmented, first by the addition of 20mms and subsequently by installing 40mms in quadruple, twin and single mountings. By 1945, for example, *Illustrious* was showing more than fifty of the former and three Bofors, and *Victorious*, 45 × 20mm and 21 × 40mm. The adoption of an aircraft deck park

system (outriggers were fitted from the flight deck to support aircraft tailwheels) enabled the air group to be increased to 54 machines.

Radar was progressively updated, starting with Type 79 warning and moving through Types 281 (air warning) and 285 (4.5in gunnery) to Types 277 (height-finder) and 960 (air warning). *Indomitable* had a US SM-1 (CXBL) fighter control set fitted

1945–48, but the equipment proved too heavy (the antenna assembly weighed 2 tons) and it was not selected for the rest of the class. Arrester wires were strengthened and increased in number to cope with new, more demanding aircraft, for which reason some, including *Illustrious*, had their lifts stressed and enlarged. By 1945, complement had risen to about 2,000, and a typical air group was 36 Corsairs and sixteen Avengers.

Victorious was the subject of a major reconstruction post-war. She was taken in hand at Portsmouth Dockyard in October 1950 for a modernisation which would prove to be an extremely protracted affair as attempts were made to keep pace with swiftly changing technologies. By the time she recommissioned in January 1958 she had been completely gutted and rebuilt from the hangar deck up. Hangar height had been increased to 17ft 6in (length 360ft × 65ft 6in, single level), the flight deck had been lengthened to 775ft and provided with an angled (8¾°) landing area, the lifts had been renewed (58ft × 40ft forward, 54ft × 34ft aft, 40,000lb capacity), new arresting gear fitted, and two BS4 steam catapults added forward. The carrier was reboilered (Foster Wheeler), rearmed (12 × 3in / 50, 6 × 40mm) and had radar Types 984 (3-D, fighter control), 293Q (height-finding) and 974 (surface warning), plus CCA, installed. Displacement was now 30,530 tons standard and 35,500 tons deep load; dimensions 781ft (overall), 103ft 4in beam (157ft overall flight-deck width) and 31ft draught; output 110,000shp (giving 31kts) and complement 2,200; 35 aircraft were accommodated.

Service Notes *Illustrious* joined the Fleet in August 1940, carrying out anti-shipping strikes (two Italian destroyers sunk) and convoy cover in the Mediterranean, and raids on North African enemy positions. Her most famous exploit took place on 10–11 November when in a night attack on Taranto her aircraft sank the Italian battleship *Conte di Cavour* and damaged *Littorio* and *Caio Duilio*. In June 1941 she was hit by eight 500kg and 100kg bombs from German land-based aircraft and was put out of action; one bomb actually penetrated the armoured hangar, but exploded before passing through the hangar deck into the ship's vitals. Following temporary repairs at Alexandria she moved to the USA for rebuilding and did not rejoin combat until May 1942, taking part in the Madagascar landings. The year 1943 was spent mainly in home waters and the Mediterranean, but by early 1944 *Illustrious* had joined the Eastern Fleet, carrying out

Left: The four units of the *Illustrious* class were a development of the *Ark Royal* design, although they sacrificed aircraft capacity (one-storey hangar only) in the interests of armouring the hangar. The design has been heavily criticised on these grounds, but it must be remembered that the ships were seen as operating within close range of large numbers of land-based strike aircraft. The name-ship is shown, early in her career. (Fleet Air Arm Museum)

strikes against Japanese-held positions in the East Indies. She joined the newly-formed British Pacific Fleet early in 1945, being hit by kamikazes during April and May which caused some damage, but not enough to put her out of action. After the war she operated as a trials carrier, but was placed in reserve at the end of 1954 and was sold for breaking up on 3 November 1956.

Victorious: Within a few days of commissioning, *Victorious* was involved in the *Bismarck* chase, one of her TSRs scoring a hit and slowing the German battleship. Following escort and ferrying operations, she was engaged in strikes against Norway and cover for Russia convoys which included an abortive attack on *Tirpitz*. Further Malta convoys came in mid 1942, and the carrier was refitted at Norfolk Navy

Yard during the winter of 1942–43, subsequently operating 'on loan' to the US fleet in the Pacific before being relieved by *Essex*. A further attack was carried out on *Tirpitz* in the spring of 1944 while returned to the Home Fleet after a refit, but by July 1944 she was in the Far East, forming part of the British Pacific Fleet in 1945. She was hit by two kamikazes in May 1945, which necessitated repairs

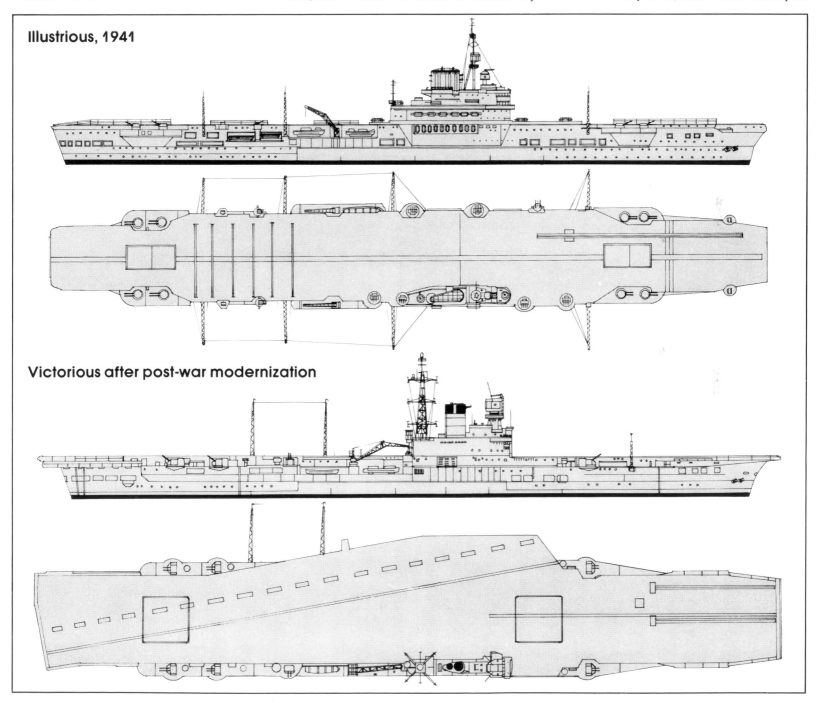

Illustrious, 1941

Victorious after post-war modernization

in Australia. Following reconstruction, *Victorious* was refitted in 1960 and again in 1967, but before work was completed during the second a minor fire broke out and it was decided that the ship should not recommission. She was sold in July 1969 and broken up.

Formidable: On commissioning, *Formidable* replaced *Illustrious* in the Mediterranean in early 1941, one of her aircraft scoring a hit on the Italian battleship *Vittorio Veneto*, 28 March. She contributed to the destruction of three Italian cruisers the following day (Matapan) by stopping *Pola* with an airborne torpedo and enabling British battleships to close. She was hit and seriously damaged by two 1,000kg bombs on 26 May 1941 and was out of action for six months. She continued in service in the Mediterranean until the autumn of 1944, whence she joined other carriers of her class in the Far East, being hit but not disabled by a kamikaze in May 1945. Placed in reserve in 1947, she was sold in 1953, being scrapped from November 1956.

Indomitable was also a victim of bomb attack in the Mediterranean when during Operation 'Pedestal' she was struck by two 500kg projectiles and was obliged to return to Britain for repairs. She helped cover operations off Sicily in the spring of 1943, but was torpedoed on 16 July; repaired and refitted in the USA, she joined the British forces in the Far East in July 1944, suffering kamikaze hits on 4 May the following year. Post-war she continued in service with the Mediterranean and Home Fleets, but was sold for scrapping in May 1953.

Top: *Victorious* in 1942, with Albacores on deck. (Fleet Air Arm Museum)

Above: *Indomitable* in 1941. Note the extra half-hangar, allowing her an air group of 48. (Fleet Air Arm Museum)

Above: The limited aircraft facilities of the *Illustrious* class was the major reason why the carriers were not retained in commission for long after the Second World War; the short-coming in capacity was appreciated very early on, however, and various expedients were pursued in order to get more aircraft aboard. Outriggers, to take tailwheels off the flight deck, were successfully employed, and two of the Sea Hurricanes visible in this photograph of *Indomitable* are parked in this way. (Fleet Air Arm Museum)

Above: *Indomitable* postwar. Two Sea Hornet twin-engined fighters are on deck, and the 'dishes' of her Type 277Q radar can be seen at each end of the island. Note also the rebuilt forward flight deck. (Fleet Air Arm Museum)

Below: Of the war-built fleet carriers, only *Victorious* was recommissioned into the Royal Navy, reconfigured to operate jet aircraft. Her silhouette was changed dramatically by the installation of the massive Type 984 radar system above the bridge; not evident here are the wealth of modifications aimed at improving her aircraft-handling capabilities — angled landing deck, stronger arrester gear, steam catapults and, significantly, increased hangar height. (Fleet Air Arm Museum)

AUDACITY

Builder	Launched	Commissioned
Bremer Vulkan	29 Mar 39	June 41

Displacement: 10,231 tons / 10,395 tonnes (deep load).
Length: 434ft 9in / 132.51m (pp); 435ft 6in / 132.74m (wl); 467ft 3in / 142.42m (oa); 450ft / 137.16m (fd).
Beam: 56ft / 17.07m (hull); 60ft / 18.29m (fd).
Draught: 21ft 7in / 6.58m (deep load).
Machinery: 7-cylinder MAN diesel engines; 1 shaft.
Performance: 5,200bhp; 15kts.
Bunkerage: 694 tons / 705 tonnes.
Range: 12,000nm.
Aircraft: 6.
Guns: 1 × 4in; 4 × 2pdr; 4 × 20mm.

Design One of the most serious problems facing Great Britain from mid 1940 was that, with the availability to the Germans of air bases along the European coastline, merchant shipping had come within striking distance of enemy aircraft, in particular the long-range Focke-Wulf Fw 200 bomber. The initial reaction was to equip a number of merchantmen each with a catapult forward on which an adapted Hurricane fighter would perch, ready to be launched on an interception mission should an enemy aircraft be detected; the fighter would endeavour to make for the nearest landfall once the threat had been removed. A more satisfactory counter, however, would be the fitting of full-length flight decks to merchant hulls: the ships could act as convoy escorts, providing not

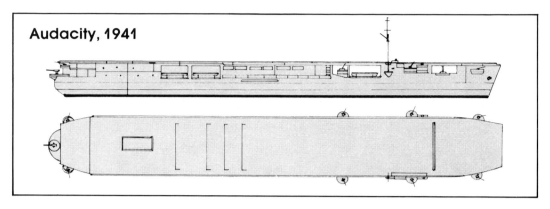

Audacity, 1941

one-shot interception attempts but some semblance of fighter cover; if TBRs could also be accommodated, some effort could be made to deal with U-boats as well.

The Norddeutscher Line's 5,500grt passenger-cargo ship *Hannover* had been captured in the West Indies in March 1940 and brought back to Britain; in January 1941 she was converted to a flush-decked carrier by the Blyth Shipbuilding Company. Her superstructure, funnel and masts were stripped off, her uptake diverted to discharge horizontally, and two arrester wires aft, a safety wire amidships and a crash barrier forward were installed on the flight deck; there was no hangar and consequently no lift, and the detachment of aircraft (initially Martlets) was thus permanently topside, parked forward at the bows during landing and right aft for take-offs. Navigation

and air control were achieved via a rudimentary platform to starboard.

The 4in / 45 DP gun was mounted at the stern, the single 2pdrs forward and aft at the flight-deck edge, and the 20mm singles forward of amidships; there were also six Hotchkiss light guns and, anticipating the ASW role, four depth-charge projectors aft. An acoustic hammer was fitted over the bows. Average action displacement was 9,811 tons and 10,000 gallons of petrol could be stowed. Conversion was completed in June 1941.

Modifications Two additional arrester wires were installed during service, probably in November 1941. It is not known whether radar was fitted.

Service Notes Employed in convoy protection duty to and from Gibraltar, and sunk by torpedoes from *U-751* off Portugal, 20 December 1941.

ARCHER

Builder	Launched	Commissioned
Sun	14 Dec 39	17 Nov 41

Displacement: 10,220 tons / 10,384 tonnes (standard); 12,860 tons / 13,066 tonnes (deep load).
Length: 465ft / 141.73m (pp); 492ft / 149.96m (oa); 410ft / 124.97m (fd).
Beam: 69ft 6in / 21.18m (hull); 70ft / 21.34m (fd).
Draught: 22ft / 6.71m (deep load).
Machinery: 7-cylinder Sulzer diesel engine; 1 shaft.
Performance: 8,500bhp; 16.5kts.
Bunkerage: 1,400 tons / 1,422 tonnes.
Aircraft: 16.
Guns: 3 × 4in; 15 × 20mm.
Complement: 555.

Design The problem of commissioning additional flight decks into the Royal Navy to meet the Atlantic threat was to be solved principally by the supply of US-built converted merchant designs.* The first of these, *Archer* (BAVG-1†), was one of the six originally ordered by the US Navy, but she was transferred under Lend-Lease.

Converted from a C3 hull at Newport News,

Archer (ex-*Mormacland*) was fitted with a wooden planked flight deck on the starboard side of which was positioned a small platform for navigation and air control. Arrester gear was fitted aft and, unlike *Audacity*, a hydraulic catapult was installed on the port side, forward. A more fundamental difference from the British-converted ship was the provision of a quarter-length hangar (height 18ft 9in), access to the flight deck being via a 38ft × 34ft lift (capacity 12,000lb).

The machinery was complex, consisting of four engines linked to a single shaft, and the carrier was to gain a notorious reputation in this respect, leading to her premature retirement from front-line service on account of too-frequent mechanical failure. There were also problems initially with her petrol stowage arrangements, the Royal Navy insisting that permanent ballast be carried to maintain stability instead of the US practice of replacing used fuel with seawater, and objecting to what they interpreted as casual safety precautions; as a result, the ship carried less than half her total capacity of some 85,000 gallons.

The 4in armament was disposed one mounting at the stern and one each side on the forecastle; two twin 20mm were fitted below each after corner of the flight deck, with seven singles along the port and starboard sides.

Modifications In late 1942 the US 4in / 50 guns were exchanged for British-designed Mk Vs of the same calibre, and the flight deck was lengthened to 440ft; two twin Bofors were installed in March 1943, and air and surface warning radars were fitted at this time.

Service Notes *Archer*'s service career was a catalogue of mishaps punctuated by one claim to fame. Her first catapult shot ended in disaster when in late 1941 a Martlet dropped into the sea, and the following month she was involved in a collision with a Peruvian merchantman out of Norfolk, Virginia. Runs to Sierra Leone and South Africa were followed by participation in Operation 'Torch' in November 1942, and in May 1943, on ASW duty in the Atlantic, one of her TBRs scored the first-ever U-boat kill with rocket fire. Continual engine trouble caused her to be laid up as a stores ship in August 1943, and

Top: The prototype British escort carrier, *Audacity*, showing her single 4in gun at the stern and the acoustic hammer over the bows. (US Navy)

Centre: *Archer* could be distinguished from later US-built Royal Navy escort carriers by the absence of an island. She is seen here in about early 1943. The enclosed area aft is the aircraft hangar. (Ministry of Defence (Navy), by courtesy of Ray Burt)

Right: A mutilated photograph of *Archer* which does, however, show her navigating and air control facilities. Note the standard carrier Type 271 surface warning radar in its characteristic 'lantern'. (Fleet Air Arm Museum)

she formally decommissioned in March 1945. She was returned to the USA in January 1946 and reconverted to merchant configuration, becoming *Empire Lagan* (1946), *Anne Salem* (1949), *Tasmania* (1955) and *Union Reliance* (1961); she was scrapped from March 1962.

*See US section for further details.
†For convenience all US designations in the British section are shown in the form in force when the ships were ordered; all US-built escort carriers were designated ACV on 20 August 1942, and CVE on 15 July 1943.

AVENGER CLASS

Ship	Builder	Launched	Commissioned
Avenger	Sun	27 Nov 40	2 Mar 42
Biter	Sun	18 Dec 40	1 May 42
Dasher	Sun	12 Apr 41	1 July 42

Displacement: 10,366 tons / 10,532 tonnes (standard); 15,120 tons / 15,362 tonnes (deep load).
Length: 465ft / 141.73m (pp); 465ft / 141.73m (wl); 492ft / 149.96m (oa); 410ft / 124.97m (fd).
Beam: 69ft 6in / 21.18m (hull); 78ft / 23.77m (fd).
Draught: 21ft / 6.4m (mean); 25ft 2in / 7.67m (deep load).
Machinery: 6-cylinder Doxford diesel engine; 1 shaft.
Performance: 8,500bhp; 16.5kts.
Bunkerage: 3,000 tons / 3,048 tonnes.
Aircraft: 15.
Guns: 3×4in; 19×20mm.
Complement: 555.

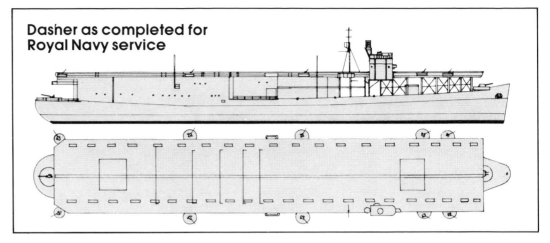

Dasher as completed for Royal Navy service

Design These three ships were part of the initial batch of six escort carriers built in the USA and were supplied under Lend-Lease; they were generally similar to the US-retained *Charger* (qv), but ballasted as in *Archer* with a consequent reduction in petrol bunkerage to 36,000 gallons, modifications which delayed their entry into service. Type 79 series air warning and Type 271 series surface warning radars were fitted. The flight decks were extended to 440ft on arrival in Great Britain.

Modifications *Biter* and *Dasher* had their US-pattern 4in guns exchanged for 4in Mk Vs in the autumn of 1942. An HF/DF mast was added forward of the island.

Service Notes *Avenger*: The former *Rio Hudson*, designated BAVG-2 and converted by Bethlehem (Staten Island), *Avenger* carried out Sea Hurricane deck-landing trials in the summer of 1942, subsequently covering convoys in the North Atlantic. She participated in Operation 'Torch', the Allied landings in North Africa, in November 1942, but was sunk the following month (15th) by *U-155* off Gibraltar when a torpedo hit started a fire and set off explosions.

Biter: Converted by Atlantic Basin Iron Works, *Biter* was used almost exclusively in convoy escort duties during her Royal Navy service, apart from a deployment to North Africa for 'Torch', November 1942. One incident in November 1943 saw her rudder damaged when a torpedo from one of her own Swordfish struck the carrier after the aircraft had ditched nearby. Her original merchant name was *Rio Parana*, and she was designated BAVG-3 in US terminology. She was returned to US custody on 9 April 1945 and immediately transferred to France as *Dixmude* (qv).

Dasher: Ex-*Rio de Janeiro*, US designation BAVG-5, and converted by Tietjen & Lang, *Dasher* took part in 'Torch' and served in the Atlantic for a brief period in early 1943 before being sunk by a petrol explosion during aircraft refuelling in the Firth of Clyde, 27 March 1943.

Below left: Like *Archer*, the *Avenger*s were generally similar to the US *Charger*, itself an improved version of *Long Island*. This is *Dasher* in 1942, showing her single lift. The port-side catapult can just be made out forward on the camouflaged flight deck. Note the single US-pattern 4in gun at the stern. (US National Archives)

Below: A Swordfish ASW aircraft departs *Biter*, circa 1943. The 4in guns below the flight-deck overhang are British Mk Vs, and one of the carrier's 20mm Oerlikons can be seen in a deck-edge tub. (Fleet Air Arm Museum)

Bottom right: Another view of *Biter*, showing the stern sponson carrying the after 4in gun. The boot-topping appears to have been applied crudely. (Fleet Air Arm Museum)

ACTIVITY

Builder	Laid down	Launched	Commissioned
Caledon	1 Feb 40	30 May 42	29 Sept 42

Displacement: 11,800 tons / 11,989 tonnes
(standard); 14,300 tons / 14,529 tonnes (deep load).
Length: 475ft / 144.78m (pp); 512ft 9in / 156.29m
(oa); 490ft / 149.35m (fd).
Beam: 66ft 6in / 20.27m (hull); 66ft / 20.12m (fd).
Draught: 26ft 1in / 7.95m (deep load).
Machinery: 6-cylinder Burmeister & Wain diesel
engines; 2 shafts.
Performance: 12,000bhp; 18kts.
Bunkerage: 2,000 tons / 2,032 tonnes.
Aircraft: 10.
Guns: 2 × 4in; 24 × 20mm.
Complement: 700.

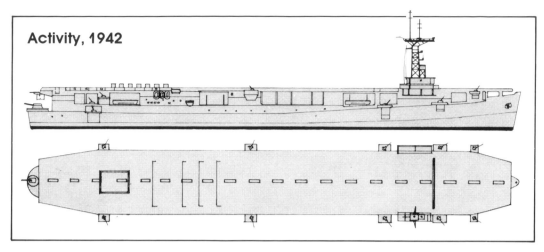

Activity, 1942

Design Originally the fast refrigerated ship
Telemachus, *Activity* was converted by her builders,
before completion as a merchantman, to one of the
few British-built escort carriers. She was initially
designated 'Auxiliary Aircraft Carrier Type "C"'.

The hangar, although 21ft high, was well under
100ft long, which compared unfavourably with US-
built BAVGs and permitted only a relatively small
number of aircraft to be accommodated. The steel

flight deck had four arrester wires and a barrier and
safety wire forward as in *Audacity*; the lift, aft,
measured 42ft × 20ft and could handle a 10,000lb
load. No catapult was fitted.

The armament consisted of a twin 4in / 45 at the
stern and ten twin 20mm (four sponsoned out just
below flight-deck level and six at upper-deck level) and

four single 20mm on sponsons. The official aircraft
complement was either six TBRs and four fighters or
four TBRs and six fighters, for which 20,000 gallons
of petrol was stowed, together with a specified list of
10 × 18in torpedoes, 36 × 500lb SAP and 96 × 250lb
SAP bombs and 144 Mk XI depth-charges.

Modifications Not known.

Service Notes Used for deck-landing training during
1943, *Activity* spent her combat career on Atlantic
and Russia convoy duty, frequently operating as an
oiler. She carried replacement aircraft to the Far East
in 1945. After the war she was reconverted for
mercantile service and renamed *Breconshire*.

Left: *Biter* in May 1943. As in US Navy escort carriers of the
time, the island is fitted to the side of, rather than on, the
flight deck. Note the 'huff-duff' aerial post forward. (Ministry
of Defence (Navy), by courtesy of Ray Burt)

Below: *Activity* in 1944, showing almost her entire air group
topside; note the Swordfish TBR on its way down to or up
from the hangar, riding the carrier's lift. (Fleet Air Arm
Museum)

ATTACKER CLASS

Ship	Builder	Laid down	Launched	Commissioned
Attacker	Western Pipe	17 Apr 41	17 Sept 41	10 Oct 42
Chaser	Ingalls	28 June 41	15 Jan 42	9 Apr 43
Stalker	Western Pipe	6 Oct 41	5 Mar 42	30 Dec 42
Tracker	Seattle-Tacoma	3 Nov 41	7 Mar 42	31 Jan 43
Battler	Ingalls	15 Apr 41	4 Apr 42	15 Nov 42
Fencer	Western Pipe	5 Sept 41	4 Apr 42	20 Feb 43
Striker	Western Pipe	15 Dec 41	7 May 42	29 Apr 43
Hunter	Ingalls	15 May 41	22 May 42	11 Jan 43
Searcher	Seattle-Tacoma	20 Feb 42	20 June 42	8 Apr 43
Ravager	Seattle-Tacoma	11 Apr 42	16 July 42	26 Apr 43
Pursuer	Ingalls	31 July 41	18 July 42	14 June 43

Displacement: 10,200 tons / 10,363 tonnes (standard); 14,400 tons / 14,630 tonnes (deep load).
Length: 465ft / 141.73m (pp); 496ft / 151.18m (oa); 440ft / 134.11m (fd).
Beam: 69ft 6in / 21.18m (hull); 82ft / 24.99m (fd).
Draught: 23ft 3in / 7.09m (mean); 26ft / 7.92m (deep load).
Machinery: General Electric geared turbine; 2 Foster Wheeler boilers; 1 shaft.
Performances: 8,500shp; 18.5kts.
Bunkerage: 3,100 tons / 3,150 tonnes.
Aircraft: 20.
Guns: 2 × 4in; 14 × 20mm.
Complement: 646.

Design US *Bogue*-class carriers (qv) transferred to the Royal Navy under Lend-Lease and modified by having petrol stowage reduced to about 50,000 gallons (ballasted in compensation with about 1,000 tons) and US 4in / 50 guns instead of the original US 5in / 38s. Later ships completed with four twin 40mm (eight in *Searcher*) and extra 20mms. *Battler*, *Chaser*, *Hunter* and *Pursuer* had Westinghouse turbines instead of General Electric. Radar generally consisted of Types 79 / 279 air warning and 271 / 272 (lantern-enclosed) surface warning systems. *Battler*, *Chaser*, *Fencer*, *Striker*, *Pursuer* and *Tracker* at least had HF / DF installed. One catapult was fitted.

Modifications Soon after commissioning *Battler* exchanged her US-pattern 4in guns for British Mk Vs. Many of the other ships had their original single 20mms replaced by twins, and *Fencer*, *Pursuer* and *Striker* at least had additional single 40mms in place by the end of the war.

Service Notes *Attacker*: Originally named *Steel Artisan*, but renamed *Barnes* (AVG-7) for US Navy service and on transfer to the Royal Navy named *Attacker*. She spent much of her service career in the Mediterranean, taking part in the Allied invasion of Italy in the autumn of 1943 and the landings in southern France in the summer of 1944. She deployed to the Eastern Mediterranean in September of that year prior to joining the British Pacific Fleet. *Attacker* was returned to the USA on 5 January 1946 and was reconverted for merchant service, being progressively renamed *Castel Forte* (1948), *Fairsky* (1970s) and *Philippine Tourist* (1977). She was broken up in 1980.

Chaser was laid down as the merchantman *Mormacgulf* (*Breton*, AVG-10, before transfer to Britain) and was the first British escort carrier to embark an Avenger squadron, May 1943. She was employed mainly in convoy escort, including duties to northern Russia in February and March 1944, but was later transferred to the Pacific as a transport / fighter carrier. Returned to the USA on 12 May 1946, she became the merchantman *Aagtekerk* in

Below: *Attacker*, shortly after commissioning. The eleven carriers of her class were RN versions of the US *Bogue*s; the enlarged hangars of these vessels are delineated by the two lifts. (US Navy, by courtesy of A. D. Baker III)

Top right: *Chaser*, 20 June 1943, showing single 20mms on her forecastle and twin 40mms in the forward deck-edge sponsons. Avenger strike aircraft are ranged aft. (US National Archives)

Below right: *Stalker* raises steam, March 1943. (Ministry of Defence (Navy), by courtesy of Ray Burt)

△1

△2

△3 ▽4

△5

△6

△7

△8 ▽9

1948, renamed *E Yung* in 1967. She was damaged beyond repair on 20 December 1972, at Kaoksiung, Taiwan, and scrapped.

Stalker: The former *Hamlin* (AVG-15), *Stalker* took part as a fighter support carrier in the Allied landings in Italy in September 1943. She was in the Mediterranean for much of 1944, before transferring to the Pacific. Following her return to the USA on 29 December 1945 she was reconfigured as a merchant ship and operated under the names *Riouw* (in 1948)

and, finally, *Lobito* before being scrapped in 1975.

Tracker: Completed by Willamette Iron and Steel and designated BAVG-6 by the US Navy, *Tracker* was used for Atlantic and Russia convoy escort throughout her career. Transferred back to the USA on 29 November 1945, she was modified for merchant service and was named *Corrientes* in the late 1940s. She was broken up in Portugal from August 1964.

Battler: Designated AVG-6 in US classification and

named originally *Altamaha* (ex-*Mormactern*), *Battler* covered Gibraltar convoys for much of the summer of 1943 and assisted in Operation 'Avalanche', the Allied invasion of Italy. She transferred to the Indian Ocean in October 1943 and subsequently joined the British forces in the Pacific. Relinquished in February 1946, she was quickly sold and scrapped.

Fencer: Named *Croatan* (AVG-14) before joining the Royal Navy, *Fencer* enjoyed a varied service career, taking part in Operation 'Alacrity' (the setting up of an Allied base in the Azores) in October 1943 and in the attacks on the German battleship *Tirpitz* in April 1944 ('Tungsten') as well as routine convoy escort in the Atlantic and on the Russian and West African runs. She was transferred to the British Pacific Fleet in 1945, and was returned to the USA at the end of 1946. She was subsequently converted for merchant service and was not broken up until 1975, having served successively as *Sydney* (1948), *Roma* (1968), *Galaxy Queen*, *Lady Dina* and *Caribia*.

Striker: Formerly the US *Prince William* (AVG-19), *Striker* was another escort carrier retained principally for ASW duty in the North Atlantic, before moving to the Pacific in November 1944 for service as a transport and fighter support carrier. She was restored to US Navy command on 12 February 1946 and was sold for breaking up four months later.

Hunter was employed as a fighter support carrier

1: A view of *Stalker* off San Francisco, 15 January 1943. At the masthead are the horizontal dipoles of Type 79 long-range warning radar; below, over the bridge, is the Type 271 series lantern. (US Department of Defense, by courtesy of A. D. Baker III)

2: Unlike the *Avenger*s, the *Attacker*-class escort carriers had two medium-calibre guns installed on the quarters, with anti-aircraft armament in a pair of stern tubs, as can be seen in this view of *Tracker* in August 1943. (US National Archives)

3: *Battler* just after commissioning. (Ministry of Defence (Navy), by courtesy of Ray Burt)

4: *Searcher* in late 1943 showing the pair of 40mm sponsons forward more typical of the *Ameer*-class carriers (qv). (Fleet Air Arm Museum)

5: A May 1943 photograph of *Battler*. Note the US-developed YE radio homing beacon, not fitted at the masthead as in US escort carriers since the main radar already occupies that

position. (Ministry of Defence (Navy), by courtesy of Ray Burt)

6: Another view of *Battler*, taken at the same time as the previous photograph. Note that the flight deck has been lengthened compared to 1942. (Ministry of Defence (Navy), by courtesy of Ray Burt)

7: *Striker*, with 40mm Bofors fitted at the stern and in the forward deck-edge gun tubs. The HF/DF mast is prominent before the bridge. (By courtesy of Ray Burt)

8: *Hunter* in January 1943. (Ministry of Defence (Navy), by courtesy of Ray Burt)

9: *Fencer*, 26 March 1943. (US National Archives)

Below: As were US Navy escort carriers, Royal Navy *Attacker*s and *Ameer*s were also used as aircraft transports. Fulfilling the role in this photograph is *Ravager*, 11 November 1944, with a deck load of Fleet Air Arm Avengers and Corsairs. (US National Archives)

during the Allied landings in Italy in autumn 1943 and also during the landings in southern France ('Dragoon') in August the following year. Her service also included convoy protection duties in 1943. She deployed to the Pacific during the last months of the war and was present at the surrender of Penang in September 1945. She was laid down as the merchantman *Mormacpenn*, was renamed *Block Island* (AVG-8) on transfer to US Navy control and was originally to have been named *Trailer* in Royal Navy service. She was handed back to US Navy authority on 29 December 1945 and was modified for merchant service as *Almdijk*, a name which she apparently retained until being sold in October 1965 and scrapped in Spain.

Searcher (US designation AVG-22) was completed by Commercial Iron Works and was employed mainly in home waters during the Second World War. She did, however, participate in the attack on *Tirpitz* in April 1944 and in the invasion of southern France later that year; during the Normandy invasion in June 1944 she functioned as an ASW patrol vessel. Handed back to the USA in November 1945, she became the merchantman *Captain Theo* in 1947, and during the 1970s operated as *Oriental Banker*. She was scrapped in 1976.

Ravager: AVG-24 was completed as an escort carrier by Willamette Iron and Steel and during her service with the Royal Navy was used mainly for training. Returned to US authority in February 1946, she became the merchantman *Robin Trent* (1948) and subsequently *Trent*.

Pursuer: Originally *Mormacland*, then *St George* (AVG-17), *Pursuer* was a regular partner of *Searcher* during the Second World War and operated in many missions in which that carrier was employed. Unlike *Searcher*, she did not survive for long after being handed back to US authority in February 1946, being sold that May and scrapped.

Top right: *Pursuer* in July 1943, acting as transport for her maiden crossing to the UK. Note that the fins of the P-47s on deck have been removed in order to accommodate more aircraft. The meaning of the rectangle in the US wing insignia position on each aircraft is unclear. (US National Archives)

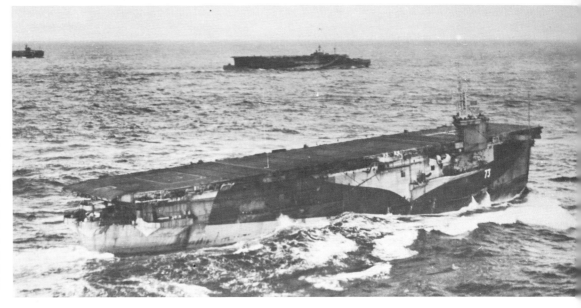

Centre right: A March 1944 photograph of *Pursuer*, in company with *Furious* and an unidentifiable escort carrier (but one of *Searcher*, *Fencer* or *Emperor*), on Operation 'Tungsten', the strike against the German battleship *Tirpitz*. (Ministry of Defence (Navy), by courtesy of Ray Burt)

Right: *Unicorn* was initially envisaged as a support and repair ship for the *Illustrious*-class carriers; she indeed functioned as such, but also saw service as an escort, transport and attack carrier. She is shown here at Trincomalee in April 1944, with Barracuda strike aircraft and Corsair fighters on board. In the background are the battlecruiser *Renown*, the carrier *Illustrious* and a *Fiji*-class cruiser.

Far right: *Unicorn* served in the Korean War as a resupply and maintenance vessel. Her high freeboard reflected her double-storeyed hangar and recalled *Ark Royal's* appearance. Note that the ship retains her Second World War armament. (US Navy, by courtesy of A. D. Baker III)

UNICORN

Builder	Laid down	Launched	Commissioned
Harland & Wolff	29 June 39	20 Nov 41	12 Mar 43

Displacement: 16,530 tons / 16,794 tonnes (standard); 20,300 tons / 20,625 tonnes (deep load).
Length: 564ft / 171.91m (pp); 575ft / 175.26m (wl); 646ft / 196.9m (oa); 610ft / 185.93m (fd).
Beam: 90ft / 27.43m (hull); 80ft / 24.38m (fd).
Draught: 20ft 6in / 6.25m (mean); 24ft / 7.32m (deep load).
Machinery: Parsons geared turbines; 4 Admiralty 3-drum boilers; 2 shafts.
Performance: 40,000shp; 24kts.

Bunkerage: 3,000 tons / 3,048 tonnes.
Range: 11,000nm at 13.5kts.
Aircraft: 36.
Guns: 8 × 4in; 16 × 2pdr; 13 × 20mm.
Complement: 1,094.

Design Begun under the 1938 Programme as a depot/maintenance support ship, *Unicorn* was modified during construction and emerged, somewhat delayed, as a vessel equipped to function as an aircraft carrier if necessary. Her general appearance owed something to the *Ark Royal* design, mainly as a result of the decision to incorporate a double-storeyed hangar; with her shortened hull, this gave the ship a decidedly cumbrous appearance.

The hangar lengths were restricted to about 300ft to provide additional space for internal workshop facilities; each was given a height of 16ft 6in to enable floatplanes to be accommodated, these being brought aboard by means of a pair of cranes serving the after lift or via the open stern. The lifts themselves, reflecting hangar length, were each placed towards amidships, and were offset to starboard; the after unit measured 46ft × 24ft and that forward 46ft × 33ft, and each could handle 20,000lb loads. A catapult was fitted forward.

Unicorn's primary role showed in the decision to fit low-power machinery, with two boiler rooms and two engine rooms enabling greater workshop space to

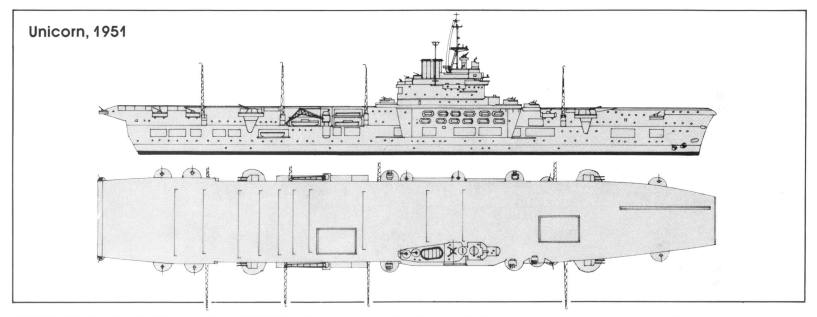

Unicorn, 1951

be put into the design. Armament was also reduced, one twin 4in mounting being installed at each corner of the flight deck and supplemented by four quadruple pompoms (2pdr), before and abaft the island and on the port side amidships. Armour protection was relatively comprehensive: there was no armoured 'box' as such, but the flight deck comprised 2in NC and the magazines were closed by 2in thicknesses forward and 2½–3in aft and topped by a 2in armour deck. A 1½in bulkhead protected the machinery spaces against torpedo hits. Air warning radar (probably Type 281B) was carried.

Modifications There is evidence that *Unicorn* received an additional multiple 2pdr mounting during the war, and it is believed that a number of 40mm single Bofors and additional 20mm were embarked prior to the ship's deployment to the Far East.

Service Notes Operating Seafires, *Unicorn*'s first combat mission took place in mid 1943 when the carrier supported the Allied landings at Salerno. Following escort duties in the Atlantic, she deployed to the Pacific where she participated in the invasion of Okinawa. In reserve from 1946 until 1949, she was recommissioned as a transport carrier, ferrying aircraft and *matériel* to the Far East, where she remained during the Korean conflict, acting as a resupply, repair and occasional troop ship out of Singapore and Hong Kong. She returned to reserve in 1953, and was sold and broken up in 1959–60.

Above right: Another photograph of *Unicorn* taken during the Korean War. She is shown here in Japanese waters, circa 1951, with Fireflies, a Sea Fury and a DUKW on the flight deck. Note the open stern. (Fleet Air Arm Museum)

Right: *Pretoria Castle* in August 1943. Note the paravane slung between the forward sponsons. (Ministry of Defence, by courtesy of Ray Burt)

EMPIRE MacALPINE CLASS

Ship	Builder	Launched	Commissioned
Empire MacAlpine	Burntisland	23 Dec 42	14 Apr 43
Empire MacKendrick	Burntisland	29 Sept 43	Dec 43

Length: 412ft 6in / 125.73m (pp); 459ft / 139.9m (oa); 400ft / 121.92m (fd).
Beam: 56ft 9in / 17.3m (hull); 60ft / 18.29m (fd).
Draught: 24ft / 7.32m (mean).
Machinery: 4-cylinder Doxford diesel engine; 1 shaft.
Performance: 3,500bhp; 12.5kts.
Aircraft: 4.
Guns: 1 × 4in; 2 × 40mm; 4 × 20mm.
Complement: 107.

Design In order to boost convoy protection pending the completion of US-built escort carriers, a number of bulk grain carriers were authorised by the Admiralty for conversion. Their suitability for the role stemmed from the fact that they had little superstructure and their cargo was loaded and discharged via hoses. The addition of a flight deck would have a minimal effect on their carrying capacity; the insistence on the provision of a hangar and other facilities, however, meant that some cargo space had to be given up, and deadweight tonnage was reduced from about 9,500 to 6,500. The conversion scheme was initiated in mid 1942 and originally covered two 7,950grt ships.

There was a full-length steel flight deck with a 42ft × 22ft lift aft capable of raising 10,000lb, and the usual arrester gear and safety barrier were installed. The armament consisted of a single 4in Mk IV gun on the quarterdeck and single Bofors and Oerlikons just below flight-deck level. An acoustic hammer was fitted over the bows. Hangar height was 24ft, accommodating four folded Swordfish TBRs which were the only aircraft that could realistically be operated from the carriers, given the latter's low speed and short deck. Petrol bunkerage was 5,000 gallons. A small island fitted with Type 271M surface warning radar carried a tall pole mast topped with a Type 79 series air warning antenna. When loaded the ships made quite stable flying-off platforms, but topweight was a severe problem in other conditions.

Modifications Not known.

Service Notes *Empire MacAlpine*: Convoy duty from May 1943. Collided with *Empire Ibex* in June 1943, but managed to return to the UK with a badly leaking hull. Reconverted after the war and renamed successively *Derrynane*, *Huntsbrook* (1950s), *Djatingaleh*, *San Ernesto*, *Suva Breeze* and *Pacific Endeavour*.

Empire MacKendrick: Atlantic convoy duty. Returned to mercantile service post-war and named *Granpond* (1948), *Condor* (1951), *Saltersgate* (late 1950s) and *Vassil Levsky* (1950; trapped in the Bitter Lakes during the Arab-Israeli 'Six-Day War', 1967).

PRETORIA CASTLE

Builder	Launched	Commissioned
Harland & Wolff	12 Oct 38	9 Apr 43

Displacement: 19,650 tons / 19,964 tonnes (standard); 23,450 tons / 23,825 tonnes (deep load).
Length: 560ft / 170.69m (pp); 594ft 7in / 181.23m (oa); 550ft / 167.64m (fd).
Beam: 76ft 6in / 23.32m (hull); 75ft / 22.86m (fd).
Draught: 28ft / 8.53m (deep load).
Machinery: 8-cylinder Burmeister & Wain diesel engines; 2 shafts.
Performance: 21,869bhp; 18kts.
Bunkerage: 2,430 tons / 2,469 tonnes.
Aircraft: 21.
Guns: 4×4in; 16×2pdr; 20×20mm.

Design By far the largest escort carrier in Royal Navy service during the Second World War, *Pretoria Castle* was the ex-Union Castle passenger liner (17,392grt) which had been converted to an AMC at the outbreak of war. She was acquired by the Admiralty in mid 1942 and subsequently converted to a carrier at Swan Hunter's yard, her superstructure and funnel being razed and a full-length flight deck added. A large, 17ft 6in high hangar was installed on the upper deck, served by the standard 45ft × 34ft lift at the forward end, and there was a single catapult on the centreline. Extreme beam was 98ft 6in, and there was a low island forward for navigational purposes and air control, with the usual air and surface warning radar.

Armament consisted of two twin 4in / 45 Mk XVI on the stern, and ten twin 20mm and four quadruple 2pdrs were officially listed as escort carrier armament, with the direction that the 2pdrs be exchanged for eight single Oerlikons when used in the training role; she completed with the latter suite of close-range weapons. As an operational escort carrier she would have carried fifteen TBRs and six fighters, with 75,000 gallons of aviation fuel and 54 × 500lb and 144 × 250lb SAP bombs, 21 × 18in torpedoes and 216 Mk XI depth-charges. Draught at light condition was 23ft. Type 279 series and 281 series radar systems were carried.

Modifications Not known.

Service Notes Used exclusively as a trials and training carrier. Reconverted for mercantile use by 1947 (renamed *Warwick Castle*) and scrapped in 1962–63.

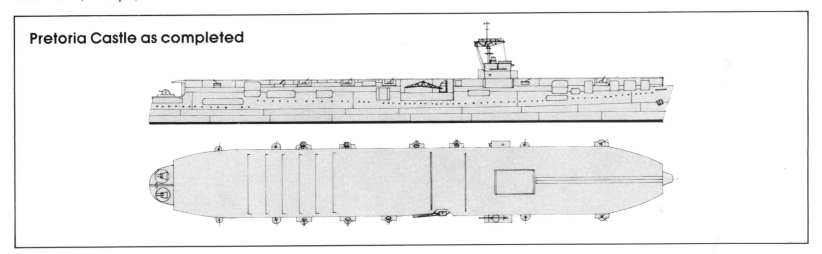

Pretoria Castle as completed

RAPANA CLASS

Ship	Builder	Launched	Commissioned
Ancylus	Swan Hunter	9 Oct 34	Oct 43
Acavus	Workman Clark	24 Nov 34	Oct 43
Amastra	Lithgow	18 Dec 34	1943
Alexia	Bremer Vulkan	20 Dec 34	Dec 43
Rapana	Witton-Fijenoord	Apr 35	July 43
Miralda	Nederlandse Dok	July 36	Jan 44
Adula	Blythswood	28 Jan 37	Feb 44

Displacement: 16,000 tons / 16,256 tonnes (deep load).
Length: 463ft / 141.12m (pp); 481ft / 146.61m (oa); 460ft / 140.21m (fd).
Beam: 59ft 3in / 18.06m (hull); 60ft / 18.29m (fd).
Draught: 27ft 6in / 8.38m (mean).
Machinery: 8-cylinder Sulzer diesel engine; 1 shaft.
Performance: 4,000bhp; 11.5kts.
Aircraft: 4.
Guns: 1×4in; 2×40mm; 6×20mm.
Complement: 118.

Design At about the same time that grain carriers were being considered for conversion to merchant aircraft carriers, John Lamb of the Anglo-Saxon Petroleum Company was quite independently preparing plans for the conversion of tankers along similar lines. The Admiralty, fearing particularly that such vessels would constitute a grave fire risk, at first turned down the scheme, but in September 1942 decided to proceed with the project.

The company's 12,000dwt tankers provided the most suitable hulls, and by reducing the bridge and after superstructure, removing the funnel and venting off the gases to discharge at the sides a full-length flight deck could be built on a supporting structure of some 800 tons of steel girders. There was no hangar (hence no lift), but arrester gear and a safety barrier were installed, together with a system of screens and palisades to afford some protection to the 3–5 Swordfish lashed on deck. The modifications reduced oil capacity by about 1,000 tons only, and speed by about ½kt; after conversion, 'black oil' was carried exclusively, in order to minimise the risk of fire, and the ships frequently acted as oilers for convoy escort vessels, carrying out underway replenishment. Petrol stowage for the aircraft was approximately 5,000 gallons.

A small island for navigation and air control was fitted well forward, and radar generally comprised a Type 271M surface set and, probably, a Type 79 / 279 air warning set, plus HF / DF. The 4in / 40 was at the stern and the single 40mm and 20mm on sponsors faired into the hull plating just below flight-deck level.

Acavus, *Adula*, *Amastra* and *Ancylus* differed slightly in being 465ft pp and with 3,500bhp.

Modifications Not known.

Service Notes *Ancylus*: Operated as Atlantic escort carrier and occasional transport. Reconfigured to merchant tanker post-war and served as *Imbricaria* from 1952; scrapped in Italy during 1955.

Acavus: Converted to carrier configuration at Falmouth and served in the North Atlantic. Rebuilt post-war as a standard tanker and by 1952 was renamed *Iacara*. Sold and broken up in 1963.

Amastra: Converted at Smith's Dock. *Amastra* conducted trials with Martlet aircraft, but the type was not adopted for operation aboard MAC ships. Atlantic escort duties from 1944. Reconverted post-war and served from the early 1950s as *Idas*. Scrapped 1955.

Alexia: North Atlantic escort duty. Reconverted to standard configuration post-war and renamed *Ianthina* in 1951. Sold in the early 1950s and broken up from August 1954.

Rapana: Rebuilt at Smith's Dock, and the first ex-tanker Merchant Aircraft Carrier to see service. Convoy protection duty from September 1943. Flight deck and aircraft facilities removed post-war and served as *Rotula* from 1950. Broken up at Hong Kong in 1958.

Miralda: Atlantic escort duty from spring 1944. Reconverted post-war; known as *Marisa* in 1950. Broken up at Hong Kong from late 1960.

Adula: Escort duty from spring 1944. Sold and broken up 1953 following post-war reconversion.

Top right: Their original role relatively little impaired by conversion to escort carriers, the *Rapana*s were another of the emergency wartime projects to get flight decks to sea. The tanker hull is clearly evident in this photograph of *Amastra*, shortly after completion. (Shell)

Centre right: *Amastra* with wind-breaks raised and betraying the position of her funnel. Like *Audacity*, the tanker MAC-ships had no hangar, with all the problems of a limited air group — and maintaining it — that that entailed. (Shell)

Right: The ex-grain carrier *Empire MacAndrew*, July 1943. Note the very spartan AA battery: a single 4in at the stern, two 20mm abaft amidships (on each side) and the single 40mm sponson (each side) forward. (Ministry of Defence (Navy), by courtesy of Ray Burt)

EMPIRE MacANDREW CLASS

Ship	Builder	Launched	Commissioned
Empire MacAndrew	Denny	3 May 43	July 43
Empire MacDermott	Denny	24 Jan 44	Mar 44

Length: 425ft / 129.54m (pp); 448ft 6in / 136.7m (oa); 400ft / 121.92m (fd).
Beam: 56ft / 17.07m (hull); 60ft / 18.29m (fd).
Draught: 24ft 6in / 7.47m (mean).
Machinery: 6-cylinder Burmeister & Wain diesel engine; 1 shaft.
Performance: 3,300bhp; 12.5kts.
Aircraft: 4.
Guns: 1 × 4in; 2 × 40mm; 4 × 20mm.
Complement: 107.
Design Ex-grain carriers, 7,950grt, generally similar to *Empire MacAlpine*.

Modifications Not known.

Service Notes *Empire MacAndrew*: Atlantic convoy escort duty. Reconverted post-war and in service as *Derryheen* (1940s), *Cape Grafton* (1950s), *Patricia* (from 1964). Sold for scrapping October 1970.

Empire MacDermott: Atlantic escort duty. Reconverted from late 1945 and renamed *La Cumbre* in 1948, *Parnon* in the 1960s and *Starlight* from 1969.

AMEER CLASS

Ship	Builder	Laid down	Launched	Commissioned
Atheling	Seattle-Tacoma	9 June 42	7 Sept 42	1 Aug 43
Emperor	Seattle-Tacoma	23 June 42	7 Oct 42	6 Aug 43
Ameer	Seattle-Tacoma	18 July 42	18 Oct 42	20 July 43
Begum	Seattle-Tacoma	3 Aug 42	11 Nov 42	3 Aug 43
Slinger	Seattle-Tacoma	25 May 42	15 Dec 42	11 Aug 43
Trumpeter	Seattle-Tacoma	25 Aug 42	15 Dec 42	4 Aug 43
Khedive	Seattle-Tacoma	22 Sept 42	27 Dec 42	23 Aug 43
Empress	Seattle-Tacoma	9 Sept 42	30 Dec 42	13 Aug 43
Speaker	Seattle-Tacoma	9 Oct 42	20 Feb 43	20 Nov 43
Nabob	Seattle-Tacoma	20 Oct 42	9 Mar 43	7 Sept 43
Premier	Seattle-Tacoma	31 Oct 42	22 Mar 43	3 Nov 43
Shah	Seattle-Tacoma	13 Nov 42	21 Apr 43	27 Sept 43
Patroller	Seattle-Tacoma	27 Nov 42	6 May 43	25 Oct 43
Rajah	Seattle-Tacoma	17 Dec 42	18 May 43	17 Jan 44
Ranee	Seattle-Tacoma	5 Jan 43	2 June 43	8 Nov 43
Trouncer	Seattle-Tacoma	1 Feb 43	16 June 43	31 Jan 44
Thane	Seattle-Tacoma	23 Feb 43	15 July 43	19 Nov 43
Queen	Seattle-Tacoma	12 Mar 43	31 July 43	7 Dec 43
Ruler	Seattle-Tacoma	25 Mar 43	21 Aug 43	22 Dec 43
Arbiter	Seattle-Tacoma	26 Apr 43	9 Sept 43	31 Dec 43
Smiter	Seattle-Tacoma	10 May 43	27 Sept 43	20 Jan 44
Puncher	Seattle-Tacoma	21 May 43	8 Nov 43	5 Feb 44
Reaper	Seattle-Tacoma	5 June 43	22 Nov 43	21 Feb 44

Displacement: 11,400 tons / 11,582 tonnes (standard); 15,400 tons / 15,646 tonnes (deep load).
Length: 465ft / 141.73m (pp); 494ft 9in / 150.8m (oa); 438ft / 133.5m (fd).
Beam: 69ft 6in / 21.18m (hull); 88ft / 26.82m (fd).
Draught: 23ft / 7.01m (mean); 25ft 6in / 7.77m (deep load).
Machinery: General Electric geared turbine; 2 Foster Wheeler boilers; 1 shaft.
Performance: 8,500shp; 18kts.
Bunkerage: 3,100 tons / 3,150 tonnes.
Aircraft: 20.

Guns: 2 × 5in; 16 × 40mm; 20 × 20mm.
Complement: 646.

Design Very similar to the *Attacker* class and hence to the US *Bogue*s (qv), but laid down as carriers rather than being converted. The original US-pattern 5in / 38 surface-action guns were retained, however, and not all had their flight decks lengthened, although aviation fuel capacity was reduced as was customary, a typical gallonage being 35,000. A more powerful catapult capable of launching Avenger TBRs was fitted on the port side of the flight deck forward, and the anti-aircraft battery was strengthened by the addition of eight twin 40mm; 20mm armament varied, some ships completing with as few as ten singles and others with up to 28 barrels in single and twin mountings.

Rajah, *Slinger* and *Speaker* were completed by Willamette Iron & Steel at Portland and *Trouncer* and *Trumpeter* by Commercial Iron Works, also at Portland. Some of the class had Allis-Chalmers machinery.

As with the *Attacker*s, the ships were fitted before completion (many in Canada) according to the different primary duties envisaged for them – *Atheling*, *Begum*, *Nabob*, *Premier*, *Puncher*, *Queen*, *Shah*, *Smiter* and *Trumpeter* as ASW escort vessels, *Ameer*, *Emperor*, *Empress*, *Khedive*, *Ruler* and *Speaker* as strike/CAP carriers and the rest as aircraft transports though retaining a strike capability which could be invoked if required. It appears that most if not all were equipped with US SK and SG radar.

Modifications Carriers assigned to the Pacific in 1944–45 generally received additional single 40mm (displacing 20mms): for example, by the end of the war *Arbiter* was showing four such weapons. Some reportedly had their 5in guns replaced by 5in / 38 DPs prior to delivery to the Royal Navy.

Service Notes *Atheling*: Named *Glacier* (AVG-33) before being handed over to the Royal Navy, *Atheling* was employed in the Indian Ocean from 1944, serving out the war in the Far East. Returned to US control on 13 December 1946, she was converted for mercantile service and renamed *Roma* by 1950; she was scrapped in Italy in 1967–68.

Below: *Trouncer* ferries Fleet Air Arm Corsairs, which are painted in a mix of the old Dark Sea Grey/Dark Slate Grey/Sky scheme and the new Sea Blue Gloss, 10 October 1944. Note the single Oerlikons facing the camera at hangar-deck level, beneath the island. (US National Archives)

Emperor (ex-*Phybus*, AVG-34) was retained in European waters for the first part of her career, providing fighter cover in the strikes against *Tirpitz* in early April 1944, being employed in ASW patrols during the D-Day operations, and participating in the invasion of southern France two months later in August 1944; following strikes in the Eastern Mediterranean, she deployed to the Far East, where she assisted in the occupation of Rangoon (Operation 'Dracula'). *Emperor* was transferred back to US authority in February 1946 and by May that year had been sold for breaking up.

Ameer: The former US *Baffins* (AVG-35), *Ameer* was deployed to the Far East during the last year of the war, taking part in strikes along the Arakan coast, in ASW sweeps and in CAP missions during minesweeping and assault operations. On her return to the USA (January 1946) she was converted to merchant configuration, being renamed *Robin Kirk* in 1948. She was broken up in about 1969.

Begum: Ex-*Bolinas* (AVG-36). Served with the British Eastern and Pacific Fleets from March 1944. Restored to US control on 4 January 1946 and modified for merchant service as *Raki* (late 1940s), being renamed *I Yung* in 1966. She was scrapped in 1974.

Slinger: Laid down as the US escort carrier *Chatham* (AVG-32), *Slinger* was employed mainly as an aircraft transport and CAP (fighter) escort in the Pacific during her Second World War career, having been disabled by a mine in February 1944 which put her out of action for most of that year. After the war she was handed back to the US Navy (February 1946), converted to merchant configuration and served as the *Robin Mowbray*.

Trumpeter: Formerly *Bastian* (AVG-37) and reportedly to have been named *Lucifer* in Royal Navy service before her name was changed to *Trumpeter*, this carrier was on convoy escort duty in the European theatre as late as March 1945, and struck

enemy shipping off Norway as late as May that year, before being sent to join the British Pacific Fleet for the remainder of the war. Following transfer back to the USA, she was refitted as the merchantman *Alblasserdijk* (1948) and was still in service as *Irene Valmas* in the mid 1960s.

Khedive: Laid down as *Cordova* (AVG-39), *Khedive* was crewed by the Royal Canadian Navy for much of the war. She participated in the landings in southern France in August 1944 (Operation 'Dragoon') and then moved to the eastern Mediterranean where in company with *Attacker*, *Pursuer* and *Emperor* she carried out strikes and provided fighter cover in operations against enemy-held targets. She moved on to the Pacific, where she took part in the liberation of Rangoon. She was returned to the USA on 26 January 1946, and after reconfiguration for merchant service she was renamed *Rempang* in 1948 and later *Daphne*.

Empress: Laid down as the US *Carnegie* and designated AVG-38. Served with the British Eastern and Pacific Fleets, including participation in the occupation of Rangoon; not converted post-war and sold for breaking up during 1946 after reverting to US Navy control.

Speaker: One of several British escort carriers modified in Canada to British requirements by Burrards (Vancouver) before being commissioned into Royal Navy service, *Speaker* was frequently in use as an aircraft ferry and CAP carrier with the British Pacific Fleet during the latter stages of the war. Her original designation was AVG-40 (US name *Delgada*), and on her return to the USA in the summer of 1946 was converted for merchant service, being renamed *Lancero* and subsequently *Lucky Three* and *President Osmena*. She was broken up in Taiwan in 1972.

Nabob: The RCN-crewed *Nabob* was laid down as the US escort carrier *Edisto* (AVG-41), but her

combat career was cut short in August 1944 when she was torpedoed by *U-354* off the North Cape. She was considered a write-off and took no further part in the war, but on her return to the USA before the end of the war in Europe she survived to be converted for merchant service. She kept her RN name until the late 1960s when she was renamed *Glory*. She was broken up in 1977.

Premier: Ex-*Estero*, AVG-42. Retained in European waters until the cessation of hostilities, mainly for escort duty. Restored to US control on 12 April 1946, she was converted to a merchantman, renamed *Rhodesia Star* and then *Hongkong Knight* in the late 1960s; she was scrapped in Taiwan in 1974.

Shah: First designated AVG-43 (USS *Jamaica*), *Shah* operated with the British Eastern Fleet from March 1944 (occupation of Rangoon, May 1945) and was handed back to the US Navy in December 1945. After conversion she served as *Salta* until being sold for scrapping in 1967.

Patroller: In service with the British Pacific Fleet, 1945. Originally named *Keeweenaw* and designated AVG-44 under the US system, she became the mercantile *Almkerk* post-war, being renamed *Pacific Reliance* in 1969; she was scrapped in 1974.

Rajah: AVG-45 was first named *McClure* in US charge, but was renamed *Prince* prior to launch; her name was changed again in January 1944 on entry

1: *Trumpeter*, 6 October 1943. In contrast to earlier US-built Royal Navy escort carriers, the *Ameer*s were almost all fitted with US radar systems: the big SK mattress is clearly visible here. (US National Archives)

2: *Premier* in February 1944. (US National Archives)

3: *Ameer* shows the considerable overhang of the flight deck and island of the ships of her class. The starboard forecastle 20mm is clearly visible, together with its 'stop' rail, fitted to prevent any chance of the weapons being fired towards the carrier's flight deck. (By courtesy of Ted Barlow)

4: *Puncher*, 1944. In this class, the sheer of the hangar deck, made evident by the line of the sponsons, caused some problems when manoeuvring aircraft below. (By courtesy of Ray Burt)

5: An August 1944 photograph of *Empress*, a fake hull painted on the side as a camouflage measure. The carrier appears to be trimming by the stern, suggesting that she is not fully fuelled. (Ministry of Defence (Navy), by courtesy of Ray Burt)

6: *Arbiter* in Far Eastern waters, February 1945. (By courtesy of Ray Burt)

7: *Ranee*, together with other carriers, was employed as a troopship postwar, returning servicemen from the Far East to their home bases. Note the covered gun mountings and the life rafts on deck in this November 1945 photograph. (Ministry of Defence, by courtesy of Ray Burt)

8: *Puncher* in June 1944, with a Blackburn Shark on the flight deck. Sharks were in use as trainers until the last year of the war, and it was in support of these that *Puncher* was presumably operating here. (US Department of Defense, by courtesy of A. D. Baker III)

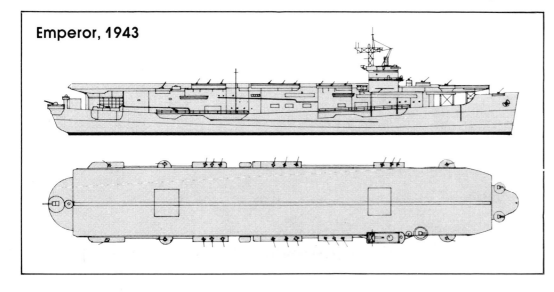

Emperor, 1943

4△

5△

1△

6△

2△ 3▽

7△ 8▽

into RN service. She joined the British Eastern Fleet in March 1944 and remained in the Far East for the duration of the war. On her return to the USA at the end of 1946 she was modified for merchant service, being renamed successively *Drente* (1948), *Lambros* (1967) and *Ulysses* (1969).

Ranee: An assault carrier fitted out in Canada prior to commissioning; with the British Pacific Fleet from 1945. Returned 21 November 1946, converted, renamed *Friesland* and broken up as *Pacific Breeze* in 1974. US designation AVG-46 (*Niantic*).

Trouncer: Formerly *Perdito* (AVG-47). Operated with the British forces in the Indian and Pacific Oceans, 1944–45. Returned to US control in March 1946 and modified for use as a merchant ship, being renamed *Greystoke Castle* (1949), *Gallic* (1954) and *Benrinnes* (1959) before being scrapped in 1973.

Thane: An assault carrier completed in Canada, *Thane* was torpedoed by *U-482* in the Firth of Clyde on 15 January 1945 and was written off; although technically returned to US authority during 1945, she was not repaired and was scrapped in Britain during 1946. Her original designation was AVG-48 (*Sunset*).

Queen: Designated AVG-49 and named *St Andrew* by the US Navy, *Queen* was an assault carrier fitted out in Canada; she took part in the last FAA European operations of the war, a strike against German shipping off Norway in May 1945, and continued to act as a convoy escort to Russia for some weeks afterwards, as a precaution. Returned to US control in October 1946, she became the merchantman *Roebiah* and subsequently *President Marcos* (mid 1960s) and *Lucky One*, under which name she was scrapped in Taiwan in 1972.

Ruler: Ex-*St Joseph* (AVG-50), *Ruler* was another of her class to be fitted out in Canada and subsequently converted for the assault role, and she served with the British Pacific Fleet towards the end of the war, often as a transport and fighter support carrier. She was not adapted for use as a merchantman after the war and was sold for breaking up in 1946.

Arbiter: Designated AVG-51 and originally to have been named *St Simon* for US service, *Arbiter* was used to evaluate the US Helldiver strike aircraft for

Royal Navy use in July 1944, but the aircraft was rejected. The carrier was subsequently deployed to the Far East, where she was engaged mainly in ferrying and CAP duties. After the war she became the merchantman *Coracero*, renamed *President Macapagal* in the mid 1960s and *Lucky Two* in the late 1960s. She was broken up in 1972.

Smiter: US designation AVG-52 (*Vermillion*). Converted to an assault carrier before delivery to the Royal Navy. Served as an Atlantic escort carrier (ASW) from 1944. Returned to US control in April 1946, converted, and renamed *Artillero* and *President Garcia* (1965); ran aground off Guernsey in July 1967 and was a constructive total loss.

EMPIRE MacRAE CLASS

Ship	Builder	Launched	Commissioned
Empire MacRae	Lithgow	21 June 43	Sept 43
Empire MacCallum	Lithgow	12 Oct 43	Dec 43

Length: 425ft / 129.54m (pp); 446ft 6in / 136.09m (oa); 400ft / 121.92m (fd).
Beam: 57ft 9in / 17.6m (hull); 60ft / 18.29m (fd).
Draught: 24ft 6in / 7.47m (mean).
Machinery: 6-cylinder Burmeister & Wain diesel engine; 1 shaft.
Performance: 3,300bhp; 12.5kts.
Aircraft: 4.
Guns: 1 × 4in; 2 × 40mm; 4 × 20mm.

EMPIRE MACKAY

Builder	Launched	Commissioned
Harland & Wolff	17 June 43	Oct 43

Length: 460ft / 140.21m (pp); 479ft 6in / 146.15m (oa); 450ft / 137.16m (fd).
Beam: 61ft / 18.59m (hull); 60ft / 18.29m (fd).
Draught: 27ft 3in / 8.31m (mean).
Machinery: 6-cylinder Burmeister & Wain diesel engine; 1 shaft.
Performance: 3,300bhp; 11kts.
Aircraft: 4.

EMPIRE MacCOLL

Builder	Launched	Commissioned
Cammell Laird	24 July 43	Nov 43

Length: 463ft / 141.12m (pp); 481ft 6in / 146.76m (oa); 450ft / 137.16m (fd).
Beam: 61ft 9in / 18.82m (hull); 60ft / 18.29m (fd).
Draught: 27ft 9in / 8.46m (mean).
Machinery: 6-cylinder Burmeister & Wain diesel engine; 1 shaft.
Performance: 3,300bhp; 11kts.

Puncher: Completed by Burrards of Vancouver and modified in Britain for the assault role, *Puncher* was used primarily as an Atlantic ASW carrier from mid 1944, and was also employed in training. Her US designation was AVG-53 – *Willapa* – and on return to US control early in 1946 she was converted for mercantile service as *Muncaster Castle*, subsequently being renamed *Bardic* (1954) and *Ben Nevis* (1959).

Reaper: Ex-*Winjah* (AVG-54), fitted out in Canada prior to delivery to the Royal Navy, and served as a fighter support carrier and aircraft transport in the Pacific during 1945. Returned in May 1946, converted for mercantile service and renamed *South Africa Star*; sold for breaking up in March 1962.

Complement: 107.
Design Ex-grain carriers, 8,250grt, generally similar to *Empire MacAlpine*.
Modifications Not known.
Service Notes *Empire MacRae*: Converted by builders. Atlantic convoy escort duty from autumn 1943. Reconfigured post-war and renamed *Alpha Zambesi* (1948), *Tobon* (mid 1950s) and *Despina* (1967).
Empire MacCallum: Converted by builders and served in North Atlantic. Reconverted post-war, being renamed successively *Doris Clunies* (1947), *Sunrover* (1951), *Eudoxia* (1959) and *Phorkyss* before being scrapped in Japan from November 1960.

Guns: 1 × 4in; 8 × 20mm.
Complement: 122.
Design Ex-oil tanker, 8,908grt, slightly slower than but otherwise generally similar to the *Rapana*-class carriers. BP-owned.
Modifications Not known.
Service Notes North Atlantic escort duty. *Mackay* was the carrier from which the last operational Swordfish flight was made, and after reconversion she was appropriately named *British Swordfish*. She survived until being scrapped at Rotterdam in 1960.

Aircraft: 4.
Guns: 1 × 4in; 8 × 20mm.
Complement: 122.
Design Ex-oil tanker, 9,133grt. Generally similar to *Empire Mackay*. BP-owned.
Modifications Not known.
Service Notes Converted while under construction. Atlantic convoy escort duty. Reconfigured post-war and served under the name *British Pilot* until being scrapped from August 1962.

NAIRANA CLASS

Ship	Builder	Laid down	Launched	Commissioned
Vindex	Swan Hunter	1 July 42	4 May 43	3 Dec 43
Nairana	John Brown	1942	20 May 43	12 Dec 43

Displacement: 13,825 tons / 14,046 tonnes (standard); 16,980 tons / 17,252 tonnes (deep load).
Length: 498ft 3in / 151.87m (pp); 528ft 6in / 161.09m (oa); 495ft / 150.88m (fd).
Beam: 68ft / 20.73m (hull); 65ft / 19.81m (fd).
Draught: 23ft 6in / 7.16m (mean); 25ft 8in / 7.82m (deep load).
Machinery: 5-cylinder Doxford diesel engines; 2 shafts.
Performance: 10,700bhp; 16kts.
Bunkerage: 1,655 tons / 1,681 tonnes.
Aircraft: 21.
Guns: 2 × 4in; 16 × 2pdr; 16 × 20mm.
Complement: 700.

Design These two escort carriers were, like *Activity*, converted from fast refrigerated cargo ships and although not very much larger than that vessel were considerably improved designs. No catapult was fitted, but the 45ft × 34ft lift led down to a hangar which, despite being reduced in height to 17ft 6in, was significantly more capacious. The ship was designed to carry fifteen TBRs and six fighters, but in practice this complement was reduced.

The usual British-built escort carrier features – all-riveted hull, steel flight deck, plated hangar sides – were retained and there was a small island well forward supporting a tall lattice mast. Armament consisted of one twin 4in DP, four quadruple 2pdrs and eight twin 20mm. Designed petrol bunkerage was 52,000 gallons and specified ordnance (escort role) was 68 × 500lb SAP, 180 × 250lb SAP and 58 × 500lb MC bombs, 21 × 18in torpedoes and 270 Mk XII depth-charges.

Vindex differed marginally from *Nairana* (data given), displacing 13,445 tons standard and 16,830 tons deep load, for a deep load draught of 25ft 2in. *Nairana*'s radar suite included Type 281B, Type 277 and Type 293, the Type 277 low-angle search system being fitted on a stub mast abaft the island. However, it is not clear whether these sets were installed when the ship first commissioned.

Modifications Not known.

Service Notes *Nairana* operated as a 'hunter-killer' unit in the North Atlantic from early 1944 (often in company with *Activity*) and was employed on convoy protection duties, particularly on the Russian run. She was transferred to the Royal Netherlands Navy in 1946 and renamed *Karel Doorman* (qv).

Vindex served as an ASW and convoy escort carrier in the North Atlantic. In 1944–45 she operated an interesting variety of aircraft, including a pair of Fireflies (the first to be embarked on an escort carrier) and also Fulmars, the latter as night-fighters on the Russian run. She was converted for mercantile service post-war, under the name *Port Vindex*, and was broken up in 1971.

Below: *Vindex*, with Swordfish and a Martlet (virtually obscured) ranged aft, shows her rudimentary island. Topping the mast is a YE homing beacon; below is what appears to be the antenna assembly for Type 281 air warning radar. (Fleet Air Arm Museum)

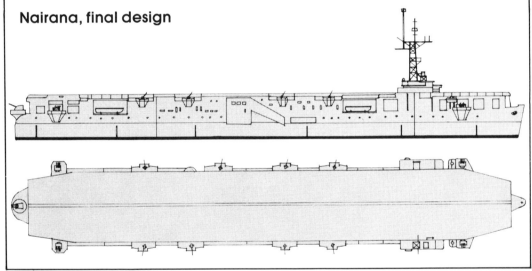

Nairana, final design

Above: *Nairana* in January 1944. (Ministry of Defence (Navy), by courtesy of Ray Burt)

EMPIRE MacMAHON

Builder	Launched	Commissioned
Swan Hunter	2 July 43	Dec 43

Length: 460ft / 140.21m (pp); 483ft / 147.22m (oa); 450ft / 137.16m (fd).
Beam: 59ft / 17.98m (hull); 60ft / 18.29m (fd).
Draught: 27ft 6in / 8.38m (mean).
Machinery: 8-cylinder Werkspoor diesel engine; 1 shaft.
Performance: 3,300bhp; 11kts.
Aircraft: 4.
Guns: 1 × 4in; 8 × 20mm.
Complement: 122.
Design Ex-tanker, 8,856grt, generally similar to *Mackay*.
Modifications Not known.
Service Notes Converted by builders. Atlantic escort duty. Reconverted post-war and renamed *Navinia*; scrapped in 1960.

EMPIRE MacCABE

Builder	Launched	Commissioned
Swan Hunter	18 May 43	Dec 43

Length: 463ft / 141.12m (pp); 485ft 9in / 148.06m (oa); 450ft / 137.16m (fd).
Beam: 61ft 9in / 18.82m (hull); 60ft / 18.29m (fd).
Draught: 27ft 6in / 8.38m (mean).
Machinery: 4-cylinder Doxford diesel engine; 1 shaft.
Performance: 3,300bhp; 11kts.
Aircraft: 4.
Guns: 1 × 4in; 8 × 20mm.
Complement: 122.
Design BP-owned, 9,249grt ex-tanker, generally similar to *Mackay*.
Modifications Not known.
Service Notes Atlantic convoy protection duties from spring 1944. Renamed *British Escort* following reconversion (1946) and *Easthill Escort* from 1959. Broken up in 1962.

CAMPANIA

Builder	Laid down	Launched	Commissioned
Harland & Wolff	12 Aug 41	17 June 43	7 Mar 44

Displacement: 12,450 tons / 12,649 tonnes (standard); 15,970 tons / 16,226 tonnes (deep load).
Length: 510ft / 155.45m (pp); 540ft / 164.59m (oa); 510ft / 155.45m (fd).
Beam: 70ft / 21.34m (hull); 70ft / 21.34m (fd).
Draught: 19ft / 5.79m (mean); 22ft 10in / 6.96m (deep load).
Machinery: 6-cylinder Burmeister & Wain diesel engines; 2 shafts.
Performance: 10,700bhp; 16kts.
Bunkerage: 2,230 tons / 2,266 tonnes.
Aircraft: 18.
Guns: 2 × 4in; 16 × 2pdr; 16 × 20mm.
Complement: 700.
Design Generally very similar to the *Nairana*s, though with a slightly longer, beamier hull and a reduced draught. Fitted with Type 277 radar. Notable for being the first British escort carrier with AIO (Action Information Organisation).
Modifications An additional quadruple 2pdr was added by mid-1944.
Service Notes Engaged principally in escort duties with Russia convoys and ASW operations in the Arctic. She deployed to the Baltic after the German surrender. Post-war she was used in promoting the Festival of Britain, 1949–51, and following participation in the British Pacific nuclear tests in 1952 was placed in reserve. She was scrapped from November 1955.

Left: Campania closely resembled the *Nairana*s and, like them, was a most successful escort carrier conversion. Note in this 1944 view the large sponson aft supporting one of the 2pdr mountings, and the smoke drift across the flight deck, a problem which no escort carrier design completely overcame. (Ministry of Defence (Navy), by courtesy of Antony Preston)

Below: Campania, in June 1944. (By courtesy of Ray Burt)

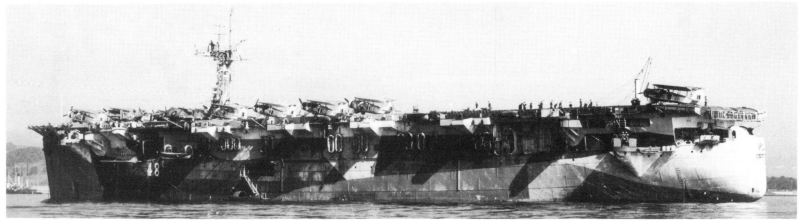

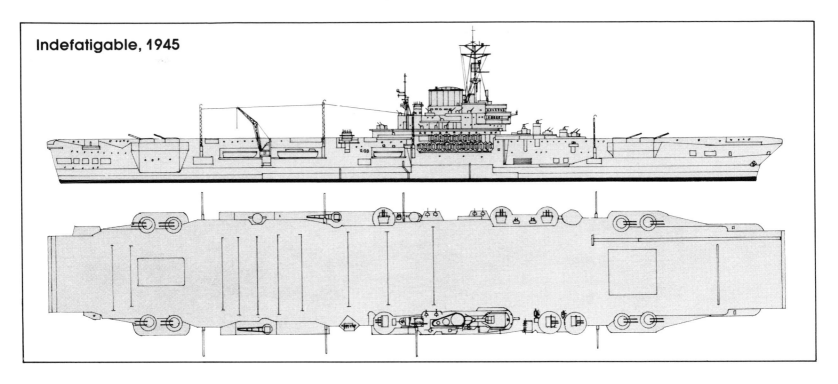

Indefatigable, 1945

IMPLACABLE CLASS

Ship	Builder	Laid down	Launched	Commissioned
Indefatigable	John Brown	3 Nov 39	8 Dec 42	3 May 44
Implacable	Fairfield	21 Feb 39	10 Dec 42	28 Aug 44

Displacement: 23,450 tons / 23,825 tonnes (standard); 32,110 tons / 32,624 tonnes (deep load).
Length: 673ft / 205.13m (pp); 766ft 6in / 233.63m (oa); 750ft / 228.6m (fd).
Beam: 95ft 9in / 29.18m (hull); 80ft / 24.38m (fd).
Draught: 26ft / 7.92m (mean); 28ft 11in / 8.81m (deep load).

Machinery: Parsons geared turbines; 8 Admiralty 3-drum boilers; 4 shafts.
Performance: 148,000shp; 32kts.
Bunkerage: 4,690 tons / 4,765 tonnes.
Range: 11,000nm at 14kts.
Aircraft: 54.
Guns: 16 × 4.5in; 48 × 2pdr; 37 × 20mm.

Complement: 1,400.
Design Two more aircraft carriers were provided for under the 1938 Programme, essentially repeat *Illustrious*-class ships, but with the modifications worked into *Indomitable* taken a stage further. The effects of the London Naval Treaty were by now, however, causing very serious design problems, and it was clear

Below: *Implacable* at Sydney, late 1945. Eight- and four-barrelled 2pdr pompoms can be made out amidships, while on the island, abaft the funnel, are a pair of single Bofors. (By courtesy of Ray Burt)

that the limitations laid down would have to be breached. Moreover:

'. . . the Staff Requirements called for only 1½" NC plating for the hangar sides, stating that this was "estimated to be capable of withstanding 500lbs SAP low level and dive-bombing".

'It is considered that developments in low level bombing have rendered that estimation incorrect.

'. . . the hangar side armour in Implacable should be increased to 2" and it is understood that there is still time to arrange this . . .

'To enable this to be done, two alternative courses offer themselves: (A) to increase the ship's displacement above the Treaty limitation (B) to reduce the height of the lower hangar to the same as that of the upper hangar, viz. 14'-0" under the beams and 16'-6" from deck to deck head.

'The implications of course (B) are that the Implacable would not be able to house floatplanes in her hangars . . . This is considered technically acceptable.'

Thus at the price of hangar height, which would have an adverse impact by the end of the Second World War, the lower hangar could be extended to 208ft and hangar side armour be increased by ½in over Indomitable. As in the latter, the lower hangar would of course be served only by the after lift.

Apart from this, the '1938 Aircraft Carrier' differed from Indomitable and her sister-ships in having a four-shaft machinery arrangement, with four engine rooms and four boiler rooms (as against three and three), on the 'unit' system. Power correspondingly rose by about one-third. Mainly to accommodate this, the hull was slightly longer; the bow form also differed from Indomitable as built. The fixed battery was enhanced by two quadruple 2pdr pompoms, and Mk V directors were fitted for the 4.5in guns. Petrol stowage was increased to 94,650 gallons. A stronger catapult was installed, capable of launching a 20,000lb aircraft, and a crash barrier was fitted at mid-length, as in the earlier ships. Radar comprised the Types 281/277/293 system.

Modifications Wartime modifications were limited because of the carriers' short combat careers; however, additional AA weapons were fitted – both were carrying more than 60 single and twin 20mm by the end of 1944, and some of these were displaced by 40mm Bofors (four in Implacable, ten in Indefatigable) by the time the carriers deployed to the Pacific. By means of a deck park, 81 aircraft could be carried by the end of the war, and complement had risen to 2,467. Post-war reconstruction was contemplated, but the 14ft high hangars proved too much of a handicap.

Service Notes *Implacable*: Having served in the British Pacific Fleet at the end of the war, *Implacable* was refitted in 1948–49, but employed mainly in training duties from 1952. She was placed in reserve in mid 1954, sold, and broken up from November 1955.

Indefatigable: Before departing to join the British fleet in the Pacific, *Indefatigable* took part in an attack against *Tirpitz* (with *Furious* and *Formidable*) in August 1944. In the Pacific, she suffered one kamikaze hit which caused superficial damage. In reserve from 1946 to 1949, she was used for training from 1950 to 1954, but was sold and broken up in 1956–57.

COLOSSUS CLASS

Ship	Builder	Laid down	Launched	Commissioned
Colossus	Vickers-Armstrong (Newcastle)	1 June 42	30 Sept 43	16 Dec 44
Glory	Harland & Wolff	27 Aug 42	27 Nov 43	2 Apr 45
Venerable	Cammell Laird	3 Dec 42	30 Dec 43	17 Jan 45
Vengeance	Swan Hunter	16 Nov 42	23 Feb 44	15 Jan 45
Perseus	Vickers-Armstrong (Newcastle)	1 June 42	26 Mar 44	19 Oct 45
Pioneer	Vickers-Armstrong (Barrow)	2 Dec 42	20 May 44	8 Feb 45
Warrior	Harland & Wolff	12 Dec 42	20 May 44	Nov 48
Theseus	Fairfield	6 Jan 43	6 July 44	9 Feb 46
Ocean	Stephen	8 Nov 42	8 July 44	8 Aug 45
Triumph	Hawthorn Leslie	27 Jan 43	2 Oct 44	9 May 46

Displacement: 13,190 tons / 13,401 tonnes (standard); 18,040 tons / 18,329 tonnes (deep load).
Length: 630ft / 192.02m (pp); 650ft / 198.12m (wl); 695ft / 211.84m (oa); 680ft / 207.26m (fd).
Beam: 80ft / 24.38m (hull); 80ft / 24.38m (fd).
Draught: 18ft 6in / 5.64m (mean); 23ft 6in / 7.16m (deep load).
Machinery: Parsons geared turbines; 4 Admiralty 3-drum boilers; 2 shafts.
Performance: 40,000shp; 25kts.
Bunkerage: 3,196 tons / 3,247 tonnes.

Range: 12,000nm at 14kts.
Aircraft: 48.
Guns: 24 × 2pdr; 32 × 20mm.
Complement: 1,300.

Design By late 1941 all major British naval yards were fully occupied in warship construction, yet with

Below: *Glory* as completed, spring 1945; she was one of four light fleet carriers completed in time to deploy to the Far East before the end of the war. These ships are sometimes inaccurately described as converted merchant ship designs. (Ministry of Defence (Navy), by courtesy of Ray Burt)

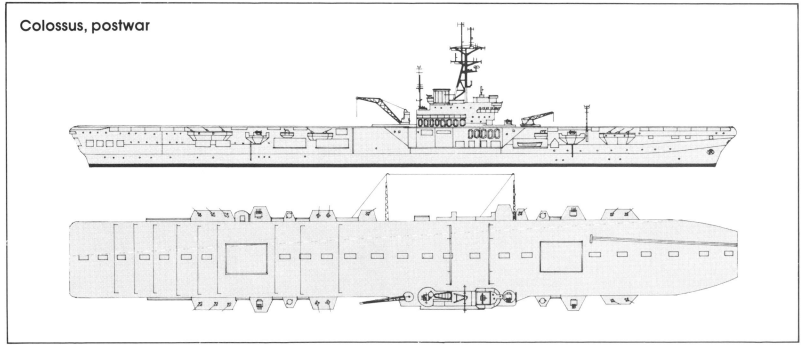

Colossus, postwar

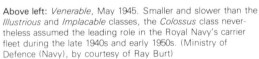

Above left: *Venerable*, May 1945. Smaller and slower than the *Illustrious* and *Implacable* classes, the *Colossus* class nevertheless assumed the leading role in the Royal Navy's carrier fleet during the late 1940s and early 1950s. (Ministry of Defence (Navy), by courtesy of Ray Burt)

Top right: The newly completed *Triumph*, May 1946, shows her AA battery: multiple pompoms before the island, on the aftermost bow sponson, abaft the funnel and at the deck edge abaft amidships; and single 40mm Bofors on three deck-edge sponsons, one forward and two abaft amidships. Note the YE homing antenna attached to a stub mast by the funnel, a somewhat lower position than was normal. (Ministry of Defence (Navy), by courtesy of Ray Burt)

Above right: Four vessels of the *Colossus* class saw front-line service as combat carriers during the Korean War in the early 1950s; this is one of them, *Ocean*. Typically, she has Sea Furies and Fireflies embarked. The track of the bow catapult can be traced: note that it is angled from the centreline, in order to clear both the lift and the port-side deck-edge. (Fleet Air Arm Museum)

signs that the war was about to expand into a worldwide conflict there was plainly an urgent need for more carriers in commission, especially as new fleet units, then in design, could not expect to complete until 1945 at the earliest. One solution was the escort carrier, but its low speed and limited capacity was hardly suited to a role which had been proved necessary following experience in the Mediterranean and made desperate by the loss of two capital ships in the Far East – providing fighter cover for fleet operations. Various options were considered, including the conversion of existing but obsolete fast warships (the ex-carrier, now reconverted cruiser *Vindictive* was reportedly a prime candidate) and the conversion of passenger liners, but in the end it was decided to design a new class of vessel, with a merchantman's scantlings to enable the ships to be constructed by merchant divisions of leading yards. The result was a low-cost unit which could be built within two years in some numbers, but the question of an air group remained; however, when the viability of operating contemporary landplanes from carrier decks was shown, first with the Hurricane and then in late 1941 with 'hooked' Spitfires, it was decided to equip the carriers with such aircraft, a choice aided by the lessening of the daylight German airborne threat over the British Isles and the consequent freeing of RAF home defence machines. This would call for a considerably enlarged flight deck, however, and so in 1942 the design was reviewed, delaying keel-laying by some months.

As finalised, the *Colossus* design in some ways resembled a scaled-down *Illustrious*, but with a single 445ft × 52ft hangar, 17ft 6in high, no armour at all, and an armament restricted to light AA weapons. The machinery selected was a modified cruiser set with boilers and engine spaces set *en échelon* to reduce the effects of a serious hit, and with no longitudinal subdivision, the loss of *Ark Royal* having shown that such an arrangement, limiting flooding to one side as it could, might have disastrous consequences. The boiler uptakes were led between main and hangar decks and vented through a single funnel on the starboard side. Two lifts were provided, each 45ft × 34ft and capable of raising 15,000lb, and there was a single hydraulic catapult forward.

The 1942 armament scheme of the 'Intermediate Aircraft Carrier' (thereafter generally referred to as a 'light fleet carrier') showed six quadruple 2pdr pompoms, eleven quadruple 20mms and eight twin 20mms, with the provision of twins instead of quads pending availability. As completed, however, ships differed, early units showing the outfit indicated in the table; later carriers would have seventeen single and twin 40mm Bofors instead. Radar generally comprised the Type 79 series/281 system, although *Ocean* had the US SM-1 fighter control set.

Perseus and *Pioneer* completed as maintenance carriers, unable to operate in a combat role: aircraft would be taken aboard by sheerlegs. The pair were fitted with two quadruple 2pdr mountings and 12×20mm only, all on the flight deck instead of outboard in galleries. Displacement fell, to 12,000/16,500 tons.

Air groups in the light fleet carriers differed, reflecting different roles: *Glory*, for example, was equipped initially as a night-fighter carrier, with 32 Hellcats and Fireflies; *Vengeance* commissioned with Barracuda strike aircraft and Fireflies; and *Colossus* equipped with Corsairs and Fireflies.

Modifications In the post-war years, the *Colossus* class proved in many ways the most effective carriers in Royal Navy service, and they were employed both as trials and as combat vessels, their economical running costs being especially attractive. Radar installations were improved through to the 1950s, the standard suite for active carriers being the Types 277 / 293 tracking / target indicator system. *Warrior* received the upgraded 277Q / 293Q during a 1952−53 refit, which also saw a reconfigured bridge and a new lattice-type foremast; a further refit in 1955−56 equipped her with a partially angled deck and heavier arrester gear, with armament now reduced to 8×40mm. The 20mm and 2pdr batteries disappeared from early vessels, *Perseus* and *Pioneer* being disarmed completely.

Three ships were the subject of major changes of configuration in Royal Navy service. In late 1948 *Warrior* was fitted with a mattress-like inflated rubber landing deck aft in order to test the concept of retrieving undercarriage-less (and of course propeller-less) jet aircraft which, freed of such weight penalties, could thus carry more fuel and thereby increase their range; a converted Vampire was used, but the system proved unworkable even though the landings themselves were successful. *Perseus* was refitted in 1950 to test the newly-invented steam catapult. The forward half of the flight deck was built up with a centreline platform within which the BXS-1 installation was incorporated, and a deckhouse was added aft. Following trials in 1950−51 the system was taken to the USA, leading to its adoption in US Navy carriers. In the late 1950s and early 1960s, *Triumph* was converted to a heavy repair ship with additional flight-deck superstructure. Details following conversion

Right: *Glory* in the early 1950s, showing how the islands of the light fleet carriers were sponsored away from the flight deck in order to provide maximum flight-deck width amidships. (Fleet Air Arm Museum)

Far right, top: *Pioneer* was also completed as a support ship, this February 1945 view showing the additional accommodation installed on the flight deck and the uncluttered lines of the upper hull. The ship is wearing the Admiralty Standard camouflage scheme, with its distinctive hull panel. (US Navy, by courtesy of A. D. Baker III)

Far right, below: *Warrior* shows her new angled deck, 1956. The structural alterations involved in achieving this were minimal, as can be seen by comparing this photograph with that of *Venerable*. (Fleet Air Arm Museum)

were: displacement 13,500 tons standard, 17,500 tons deep load; 699ft overall length, 112ft 6in maximum flight-deck width and 23ft 8in draught; 4×40mm; speed 24.25kts; bunkerage 3,000 tons and range 10,000nm at 14kts; and complement 500 plus 285 maintenance crew. Catapult, wires and other air-operation fittings were removed, although three helicopters were carried.

Service Notes *Colossus*: Deployed to the British Pacific Fleet in mid 1945 just too late to see combat, *Colossus* returned to Britain twelve months later and was immediately transferred on loan to France as *Arromanches* (qv), being purchased outright in 1951.

Glory: Arriving in the Far East too late to take part in active combat, *Glory* moved to New Guinea to accept the surrender of Japanese forces there in late September 1945. She was active during the Korean conflict from April 1951 to the spring of 1953, and against Malayan Communists in late 1952. She was stricken in the late 1950s, sold, and broken up from autumn 1961.

Venerable: Having served in the Far East as part of the 11th Carrier Squadron with *Colossus*, *Glory* and *Vengeance* and been employed in 'mopping up' duties after the Japanese surrender, *Venerable* was sold in 1948 to the Dutch and renamed *Karel Doorman* (qv).

Vengeance: Following a brief spell in the Mediterranean in early 1945, *Vengeance* moved to the Far East and served with the British Pacific Fleet, based at Hong Kong. She was employed in cold-weather trials in the Arctic in 1948–49, was refitted in the early 1950s and transferred to the Royal Australian Navy (qv). Returning in 1955, she was placed in reserve until being sold to Brazil as *Minas Gerais* (qv).

Perseus: Originally named *Edgar*, but rechristened in 1944, *Perseus* was used for steam catapult trials from the summer of 1950. She was sold in the late 1950s and scrapped from May 1958.

Pioneer: First designated *Ethalion*, then *Mars*, but renamed *Pioneer* in 1944. Continued as a maintenance support ship until sold for scrapping in 1954.

Warrior: Ex-*Brave*. In Royal Canadian Navy service following completion and not commissioned into the Royal Navy until late 1948 when used for 'flexideck' trials, *Warrior* was first employed as an operational front-line carrier during the Korean conflict, although she was mainly used as a transport. She participated in the British nuclear tests at Christmas Island in 1957, and the following year was sold to Argentina as *Independencia* (qv).

Theseus: Following brief spells in the Far East and in home waters, *Theseus* was used in mid 1950 for jet night landing trials. She served one tour in Korea, 1950–51. Used mainly for training from 1954, she was employed as a makeshift assault carrier during the 1956 Suez crisis, landing men via helicopter at Port Said. In reserve from 1957, she was sold in 1960 and scrapped from May 1962.

Ocean provided the flight deck for the world's first carrier landing by a jet aircraft, the third prototype DH Vampire, 3 December 1945. A spell in the Mediterranean as a supply ship during the Palestine crisis was followed by deployment to the Far East. She served in the Korean War from the spring of 1952 until late in 1953, returning to the Mediterranean in 1955 and operating as an *ad hoc* commando carrier during the Suez landings in November 1956. *Ocean* was placed in reserve in 1957, sold with *Theseus* in 1960, and broken up in 1962.

Triumph: The last of the *Colossus*-class carriers to complete, *Triumph* was used as a trials carrier for twin-engined aircraft, and in 1949 was deployed to Malaya to assist in combating Communist insurgency. She was the first British carrier to arrive off Korea (June 1950), subsequently being engaged as a training ship until being placed in reserve in the mid 1950s. During this latter period she tested an extempore angled deck layout by having a line canted at 10° from the fore-and-aft axis painted on her flight deck. Following conversion to a repair ship, she moved to the Far East again, acting as a support ship during the Indonesian confrontation (1966), based at Singapore. She took part in the Beira Patrol in the late 1960s, and following a refit in 1972 continued in service until being placed in reserve in 1975. She was sold and broken up in 1981–82.

MAJESTIC CLASS

Ship	Builder	Laid down	Launched
Terrible	Devonport	19 Apr 43	30 Sept 44
Magnificent	Harland & Wolff	29 July 43	16 Nov 44
Powerful	Harland & Wolff	27 Nov 43	27 Feb 45
Majestic	Vickers-Armstrong (Barrow)	15 Apr 43	28 Feb 45
Leviathan	Swan Hunter	18 Oct 43	7 June 45
Hercules	Vickers-Armstrong (Newcastle)	12 Oct 43	22 Sept 45

Displacement: 14,000 tons / 14,224 tonnes (standard); 17,800 tons / 18,085 tonnes (deep load).
Length: 630ft / 192.02m (pp); 650ft / 198.12m (wl); 695ft / 211.84m (oa); 680ft / 207.26m (fd).
Beam: 80ft / 24.38m (hull); 75ft / 22.86m (fd).
Draught: 23ft 6in / 17.16m (deep load).
Machinery: Parsons geared turbines; 4 Admiralty 3-drum boilers; 2 shafts.
Performance: 40,000shp; 25kts.
Bunkerage: 3,000 tons / 3,048 tonnes.
Aircraft: 37.
Guns: 24 × 2pdr; 19 × 40mm.
Complement: 1,100.
Design The *Colossus* class were ordered as a batch of sixteen vessels, but the last six were modified to a revised design which took account of the need to operate heavier aircraft with higher landing speeds. As a result, the flight decks were stressed and, as weight compensation, fuel bunkerage was reduced; even so, displacement rose compared to the earlier carriers. Improved subdivision was worked into the hull, and the fixed defensive battery was designed to incorporate 40mm Bofors in single and twin mountings (see table); ultimately, these replaced the 2pdrs too, and a typical installation on the ships' completion was six twin and eighteen single 40mm.

With the end of the war, building was halted until a decision as to the carriers' future could be made; in the event, none saw service with the Royal Navy, but five of the six were completed later and sold to foreign navies.
Modifications See under navies to which ships were transferred.
Service Notes *Terrible*: Purchased by Australia in 1948 and transferred the following year. Renamed *Sydney* (qv).
Magnificent: Completed in 1946–47 for the Royal Canadian Navy, lent to that service and subsequently sold (qv).
Powerful: Sold to Canada in 1952 and completed to a modified design; transferred in January 1957, renamed *Bonaventure* (qv).
Majestic: Completed to a modified design for the Royal Australian Navy in 1955. Renamed *Melbourne* (qv).
Leviathan: Not completed. Hull scrapped from May 1968.
Hercules: Sold to India, completed to a modified design by Harland & Wolff and transferred as *Vikrant* (qv) in 1961.

EAGLE CLASS

Ship	Builder	Laid down	Launched	Commissioned
Eagle	Harland & Wolff	24 Oct 42	19 Mar 46	1 Oct 51
Ark Royal	Cammell Laird	3 May 43	3 Mar 50	25 Feb 55

Displacement: 36,800 tons / 37,389 tonnes (standard); 45,720 tons / 46,452 tonnes (deep load).
Length: 720ft / 219.46m (pp); 750ft / 228.6m (wl); 803ft 9in / 244.98m (oa); 775ft / 236.22m (fd).
Beam: 112ft 9in / 34.37m (hull); 105ft / 32m (fd).
Draught: 33ft 3in / 10.13m (mean); 36ft / 10.97m (deep load).
Machinery: Parsons geared turbines; 8 Admiralty 3-drum boilers; 4 shafts.
Performance: 152,000shp; 31.5kts.
Bunkerage: 6,500 tons / 6,604 tonnes.
Range: 5,000nm at 24kts.
Aircraft: 80.
Guns: 16 × 4.5in; 32 × 40mm.
Complement: 2,250.
Design With the completion of the 1936 and 1937 aircraft carriers (*Illustrious* class) and the construction of the 1938 ships in progress, tentative designs were put in hand early in 1942 for successors. The first sketch designs showed a logical extension of the *Implacable* concept, essentially a repeat of the class, but with the provision of two complete hangars; displacement, on a slightly larger hull to accommodate the increased weights, was expected to work out at about 24,000 tons. A revision saw the flight deck stressed and catapults and arrester gear improved to handle the 30,000lb aircraft expected in service; however, hangar height was only 14ft 6in. Hull length increased to 790ft, displacement advanced to 31,500 tons, and armament would consist of 16 × 4.5in in twin mountings and 64 × 2pdr in 8-barrelled mountings. The 1in steel flight deck would have 4in (160lb) armour to defeat 1,000lb bombs, the armoured hangar 'box' would have 1½in (60lb) sides and ends, and an armoured hangar deck (2½in, 100lb) would be closed by 4½in-1½in (180-60lb) bulkheads; steering gear was protected by 4in (100lb) NC and there was a 4in (160lb) belt and a 1½in (60lb) underwater bulkhead for anti-torpedo protection. In all, armour would account for about 20 per cent of the total weight of the ship, compared to some 15 per cent in *Implacable*. A total of 78 aircraft could be carried, some permanently on deck. Oil fuel bunkerage was 5,500 tons.

The realisation that the hangar height, though suitable for contemporary naval fighters and such strike aircraft as the Swordfish (just; the Albacore would be a problem), would be inadequate for new types* led to a major redesign just as the ships were ordered in mid 1942: hangar height (each level) was raised to 17ft 6in, the additional topweight requiring

*The claim that hangar height was increased to allow US-built FAA aircraft to be struck below is misleading: the modification was necessary rather to accommodate the Barracuda strike bomber, of which much was anticipated in 1942.

Above: *Eagle* as first completed, with an axial flight deck. The lifts are offset from the centreline, to provide adequate room for trunking the boiler gases higher in the ship than was the case with earlier fleet carriers. (Ministry of Defence (Navy))

an increase in beam to maintain stability, thereby increasing hangar capacity by enabling aircraft to be stowed four abreast instead of three, and allowing additional fuel (6,960 tons total) to be carried. The air group now stood at 100, and petrol capacity was 103,300 gallons.

Machinery was arranged on the 'unit' system, and the plant was similar to that employed in the *Implacable*s, though with slightly increased power to keep the drop in sea speed to a minimum. The flight deck featured two lifts, each 54ft × 44ft and offset to port but central with regard to the hangar, itself offset to permit the boiler room trunking to be carried over at a higher relative level in the ship, in the light of experience with *Ark Royal*. Overall flight-deck dimensions were 795ft × 115ft, and two hydraulic catapults (strictly 'accelerators', as in previous carriers) were fitted forward and eight wires aft. Displacement on this revised design had risen to 33,000 tons standard and 42,390 tons deep load, with a 25ft 6in mean draught and a range, thanks to the increased bunkerage, of 6,000nm at 24kts. A war complement of 2,688 was provided for.

The armament also showed some changes. The eight twin 4.5in were retained, but the 2pdrs were first augmented by 60 × 20mm, then removed altogether, the new suite comprising 1 × 40mm 'Buster', 7 × 40mm Mk VI, 24 × 20mm twins and 12 × 20mm singles; and the final battery consisted of eight 6-barrelled 40mm (before and abaft the island, along the port side, and on the starboard side aft), two twin 40mm (at the stern) and twelve single 40mm (on the port side forward, and on the island), plus eighteen single 20mm. Twelve Mk V directors would give excellent control facilities.

Three ships were under construction by the time the Second World War was brought to a close (a fourth, reportedly to be named *Africa*, had been abandoned earlier and the name transferred to a *Malta*-class vessel). One ship, to be named *Eagle* (laid down April 1944 at the Vickers-Armstrong yard on the Tyne) was not particularly advanced and was cancelled in January 1946, her name being taken over by *Audacious*, building at Belfast; work on the remaining pair was halted for three years during a reassessment of post-war carrier requirements.

It was eventually decided to proceed with the completion of *Eagle* (ex-*Audacious*) and the launching of *Ark Royal*, and the former was commissioned much to the final 1945 condition, except for a reduced armament (see table), US Mk 37 directors and more advanced radar (Types 960 surveillance, 982 fighter control, 983 height-finder). The first air group consisted of Firebrand strike fighters and the new jet Attackers.

Left: Ark Royal was completed (1955) with an angled deck and a deck-edge lift, the latter a result of US influence on the design. When this photograph was taken, almost twelve years had elapsed since her keel was laid. (Ministry of Defence (Navy))

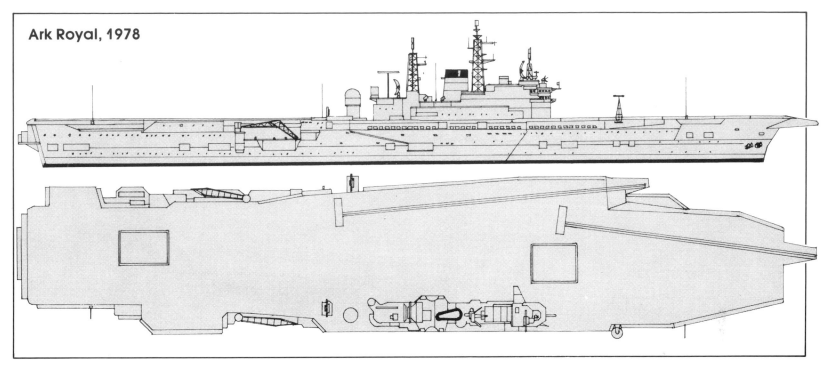

Ark Royal, 1978

Ark Royal completed to a different configuration, with a pair of the new steam catapults, a partially angled deck (5½°), a mirror landing device and a port-side deck-edge lift; also unlike *Eagle*, she showed no multiple 40mm abaft the island. The flight-deck dimensions were 800ft × 112ft and her air group consisted of Sea Hawks, Gannet ASW and Skyraider AEW aircraft, plus helicopters.

Modifications *Eagle* received a partially angled deck (5½°) in a 1954–55 refit. In 1956 *Ark Royal* had her forward 4.5in turrets on the port side removed since they were proving a handicap to air operations; in 1959 the deck-edge lift was taken out for the same reason, at which time the remaining forward 4.5in were also suppressed. *Eagle* again refitted from 1959 to 1964, when an 8½° angled deck was added, all the

Left: Another 1955 view of *Ark Royal*, her steam catapults prominent. Radars visible here are the two Type 982 'troughs', air warning; Type 293Q on the yardarm above, target indicator; and one of the Type 983s somewhat obscured by the funnel abaft it, height-finder. The wartime YE homing beacon is still in use, at the masthead. (Ministry of Defence (Navy))

Inset: *Eagle* in 1956, showing her re-aligned landing deck. Wyvern attack aircraft and Skyraider AEW aircraft can be seen aft; Sea Hawk and Sea Venom fighters line the port side of the flight deck; and Gannets (ASW) are along the island. Note that the crowns of the 4.5in mountings form, in effect, part of the flight deck. (Fleet Air Arm Museum)

Right: By 1964 *Eagle* had received a more thorough refit, with a rebuilt flight deck (at some expense in the heavy AA battery) and an upgraded radar suite, the latter including the massive 3-D Type 984 and the double 'mattress' (AKE-2) of Type 965. (Ministry of Defence (Navy))

forward 4.5in and all 40mm were removed and a lattice mast substituted for the tripod. New flight-deck armour was fitted, and the deck was extended outboard of the island to permit fore-and-aft movement along the starboard deck edge. Two steam catapults replaced the BH5s, and the radar suite was upgraded with Types 984 and 965 search and Type 963 CCA. Six Seacat missile launchers were fitted, and 42 aircraft, plus helicopters, were embarked. Displacement was now 44,100 tons standard and 54,100 tons deep load, extreme dimensions being 803ft 9in × 166ft 9in and mean draught 36ft.

Ark Royal meanwhile (1962) had been fitted for Buccaneer operation and by 1964 had had her 40mm and her remaining 4.5in mountings removed, Type 965 radar fitted, and sponsons added for Seacat missiles, although the latter were not installed. Displacement was now 43,340 tons standard and 53,340 tons deep load, length overall 808ft 8in, flight-deck width 160ft 6in overall and draught 36ft mean.

In 1966−67 *Eagle* had a waist catapult added and was fitted for Buccaneer operation, and by 1970 had embarked ASW helicopters. *Ark Royal* underwent a further refit from March 1967 until February 1970 to equip her for F-4s: she received an 8.5° angled deck, new catapults (including a third, waist, unit) and arrester gear, bridle catchers (increasing overall length to 845ft), a reconfigured island, and radar Types 965 air warning (AKE-2 array), 982 / 983

Below: *Ark Royal* in company with *Eagle*, c. 1970. Although nominally sister ships, the two carriers were always readily distinguishable: at this time, and even at this distance, the catapult bridles and the differing radar systems (including a prominent CCA abaft the island) of *Ark Royal* are plain to the eye. (Ministry of Defence (Navy), by courtesy of Ian Sturton)

fighter-direction / height-finder, and CCA. A flight of ASW Sea Kings was embarked, and fixed-wing capacity dropped to thirty. Displacement (as of 1978) was 43,060 tons standard and 50,786 tons deep load. **Service Notes** *Eagle* carried out flying trials in the early months of 1952. In late 1956 she participated in the Suez campaign, but was reduced to one catapult when mechanical faults developed. She embarked the first Royal Navy carrier-borne tanker flight (Scimitars) in the mid 1960s, and by the spring of 1966 was on patrol off East Africa enforcing the Rhodesian blockade. She covered the British withdrawal from Aden in November 1967, and following a deployment to the Far East was engaged in trials with F-4 Phantoms in March 1969. She was decommissioned in January 1972, stricken, and broken up from October 1978.

Ark Royal: Although some reports indicate that the name *Irresistible* was originally allocated to *Ark Royal*, there appears to be no official evidence for this. The ship was involved in post-refit trials during the Suez operations. She carried out P1127 V/STOL aircraft trials in February 1963. Originally scheduled to be scrapped in the mid 1970s, she was granted a reprieve and kept in service by obtaining spares from the redundant *Eagle*. Her condition was quite desperate by the time she paid off in February 1979; she was scrapped from 1980.

Below: *Ark Royal* launches a Buccaneer from her waist catapult. Large by the wartime standards to which she was originally designed, by the early 1970s *Ark Royal* was in reality the minimum platform that could support the new generation of supersonic fighters, represented here by Phantoms; even the latter were by this time being phased out by the US Navy in favour of still heavier types. Note that the ship retains some elements of her original radar suite. (Fleet Air Arm Museum)

MALTA CLASS

Displacement: 46,900 tons / 47,650 tonnes (standard); 56,800 tons / 57,709 tonnes (deep load).
Length: 820ft / 249.94m (pp); 916ft 6in / 279.35m (oa); 900ft / 274.32m (fd).
Beam: 115ft 9in / 35.28m (hull); 136ft / 41.46m (fd).
Draught: 29ft 6in / 8.99m (mean); 34ft 6in / 10.52m (deep load).
Machinery: Parsons geared turbines; 8 Admiralty 3-drum boilers; 4 shafts.
Performance: 200,000shp; 33kts.
Bunkerage: 6,000 tons / 6,096 tonnes.
Aircraft: 80.
Guns: 16×4.5in; 55×40mm.
Complement: 3,520.

Design The design for follow-ups to the *Eagle*s, ordered in the summer of 1943, marked a departure from earlier practice in British carriers. Although first studies had seen the ships as essentially enlarged 1942 carriers, with double-storeyed armoured hangars, the design as finalised showed a single hangar 460ft long, the additional beam giving an overall hangar area not too different from that of the *Eagle*s, but with 17ft 6in deck to deck-head specified from the start. As well as two centreline lifts, each 54ft×46ft in dimensions, there were, for the first time in a British carrier, two deck-edge units (56ft×35ft), which rather ruled out the armoured 'box' principle of the *Implacable*s; in fact, the plans went a stage farther and incorporated an open-sided hangar, permitting aircraft struck below to warm up before being taken topside for take-off. It is possible that this arrangement was influenced by US practice, but close comparisons are not entirely appropriate since the hull, it appears, would be plated up to flight-deck level for much of its length and the bows would be totally enclosed.

Armour protection was not abandoned altogether: there was the usual box (4in) over the steering compartment, protective citadels forward and aft over the magazines and a protective deck over the machinery spaces enclosed by a 4½in belt extended to cover the petrol bunkers and closed by armoured bulkheads; three armoured longitudinal bulkheads provided anti-torpedo defence. There were four machinery spaces and four boiler rooms.

Longitudinal strength was effected by the hangar deck rather than by the flight deck on account of the 'open hangar' arrangement, and the flight deck itself was of 1in (40lb) steel and showed two 160ft hydraulic catapults converging at the bows. The island was of novel design, providing a large extension aft carrying a mast for Type 960 radar.

The heavy dual-purpose battery of 4.5in guns was retained (improved Mk V weapons instead of Mk IV), supplemented by eight 6-barrelled Bofors disposed on and before the island, a pair at the stern and one on each quarter at hangar-deck level, and a pair at the same height on the port side; several single 40mms were also to have been fitted.

Two of the four, *Gibraltar* (Vickers-Armstrong, Tyne) and *Africa* (Fairfield) were cancelled immediately after the war, while the remaining pair, *Malta* (John Brown) and *New Zealand* (Harland & Wolff) lasted only until January 1946; none was laid down.

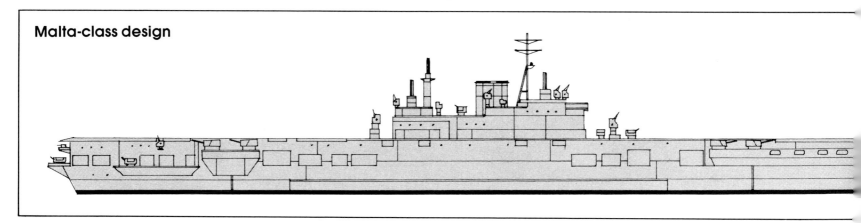

Malta-class design

CENTAUR CLASS

Ship	Builder	Laid down	Launched	Commissioned
Centaur	Harland & Wolff	30 May 44	22 Apr 47	1 Sept 53
Albion	Swan Hunter	23 Mar 44	6 May 47	26 May 54
Bulwark	Harland & Wolff	10 May 45	22 June 48	4 Nov 54
Hermes	Vickers-Armstrong (Barrow)	21 June 44	16 Feb 53	18 Nov 59

Displacement: 18,300 tons / 18,593 tonnes (standard); 24,500 tons / 24,892 tonnes (deep load).
Length: 650ft / 198.12m (pp); 686ft / 209.1m (wl); 737ft / 224.64m (oa); 710ft / 216.41m (fd).
Beam: 90ft / 27.43m (hull); 100ft / 30.48m (fd).
Draught: 22ft / 6.71m (mean); 27ft / 8.23m (deep load).
Machinery: Parsons geared turbines; 4 Admiralty 3-drum boilers; 2 shafts.
Performance: 80,000shp; 29.5kts.
Bunkerage: 4,000 tons / 4,064 tonnes.
Range: 6,000nm at 20kts.
Aircraft: 42.
Guns: 32×40mm.
Complement: 1,390.

Design In 1943, design began on a class of eight carriers based on and which would resemble *Colossus*-class ships, but with significantly improved capabilities. Most importantly, they were to receive machinery twice as powerful, giving them the requisite speed to act in concert with the *Illustrious*-class fleet carriers; in addition, they would be better protected, with 2in (80lb) magazine and 1in (40lb) machinery crowns, and 1in (40lb) sides to the magazines and machinery spaces plus an internal (40lb) belt and improved compartmentation. The flight deck was stressed for 30,000lb aircraft, as were the two 54ft×44ft lifts and the single hydraulic catapult forward. The one-storey, 17ft 6in high hangar would enable the latest types of aircraft to be accommodated, and four twin 4.5in mountings would give an enhanced fixed battery with a return to an anti-surface capability. To accommodate the added weights, the hull dimensions were increased.

With the end of the Second World War construction slowed, and at one stage it was mooted that the

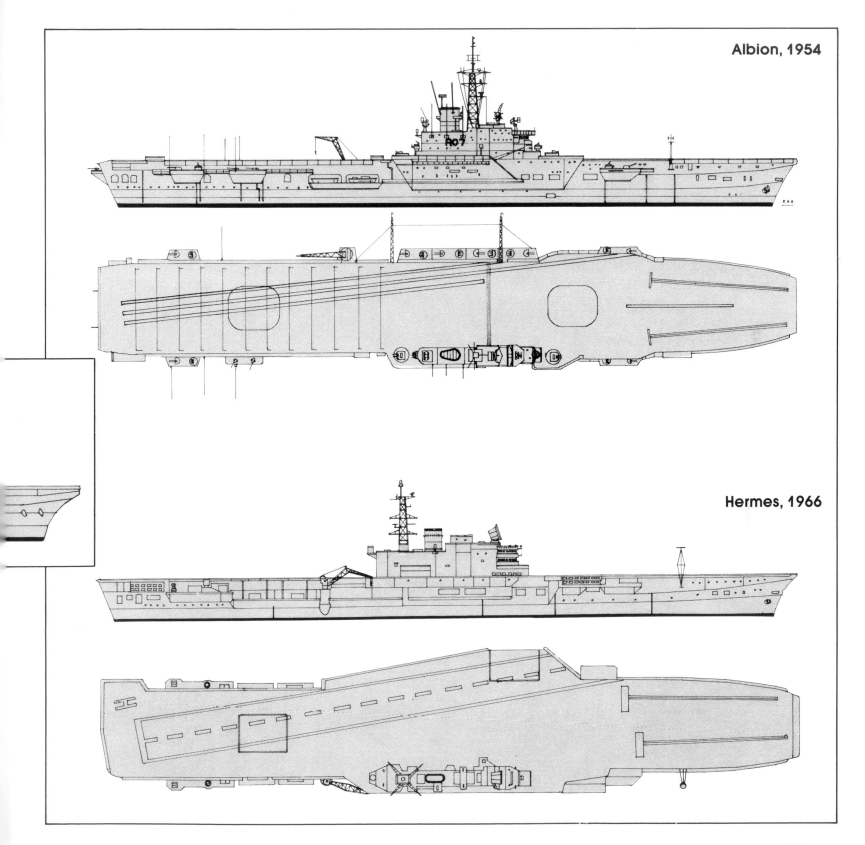

Albion, 1954

Hermes, 1966

four ships already laid down (four were cancelled because of the end of hostilities) be dismantled on the slips; when it was realised, however, that, with the *Illustrious* carriers seriously handicapped by their limited hangar depth and thus requiring extensive reconstruction to operate the new generation of naval aircraft (jets) then in prospect (plans were drawn up in 1947–48), the early 1950s would see only the two remaining *Eagle*s as viable fleet carriers, it was decided to complete them to a slightly revised design. In the event, only one, *Centaur*, was to be thus commissioned, the other three incorporating a series of further modifications which reflected the introduction into service of high-speed jet aircraft and the new carrier technologies that would accompany them.

The new plans (1951) showed the carriers with a standard displacement of 20,260 tons (26,118 tons deep load), an extreme width across the flight deck of 120ft 6in and a draught of 21ft 8½in mean at standard displacement and 26ft 6in at deep. The two-shaft machinery arrangement would produce 76,000shp and 29kts at standard displacement, oil fuel was 4,145 tons (including diesel fuel), and armament two 6-barrelled Bofors (before and abaft the island), eight twin 40mm (six on the port-side deck edge, two to starboard) and four single 40mm (two to starboard and two at the stern). The air group would consist of sixteen Sea Hawks (fighter-bomber), sixteen Fireflies (fighter-reconnaissance) and four Avengers (AEW), air ordnance comprising 'bombs, rockets, "Red Angels" and torpedoes'. *Centaur* emerged in this configuration if not with this air group, having additionally a 5½° line painted along her landing area in an early form of angled deck.

Bulwark and *Albion* were able to take better account of developing technology, being completed with an 'interim', 5¾° angled landing area which involved the physical extension of the flight deck on the port side, increasing maximum width to 123ft, but losing three twin 40mm as a result of the overhang. Two hydraulic catapults were fitted. Radar suites for all three carriers completed in 1953–54 comprised Types 982 and 960 (air surveillance), 983 (height-finder) and 277Q (fighter direction).

Hermes was completed some years later to a much-modified design which included an enlarged island, a 6½° angled deck, steam catapults and a mirror

Below: *Hermes* entered service as the most capable of the *Centaur*-class carriers; some of the significant improvements are visible in this photograph of the ship as first commissioned. Note particularly the heavy Type 984 radar, the TACAN dome atop the lattice mast, and the landing sight amidships. (Vickers Ltd)

Right: Sea Hawks, Sea Venoms, Gannets and Skyraiders ranged aboard *Albion*, October 1957. (By courtesy of John Halstead)

Far right: Three of the four *Centaur*-class carriers eventually saw service as Commando carriers; *Bulwark* was the first, recommissioning in 1960. The Suez experience of 1956 had prompted such conversions. (Ministry of Defence (Navy))

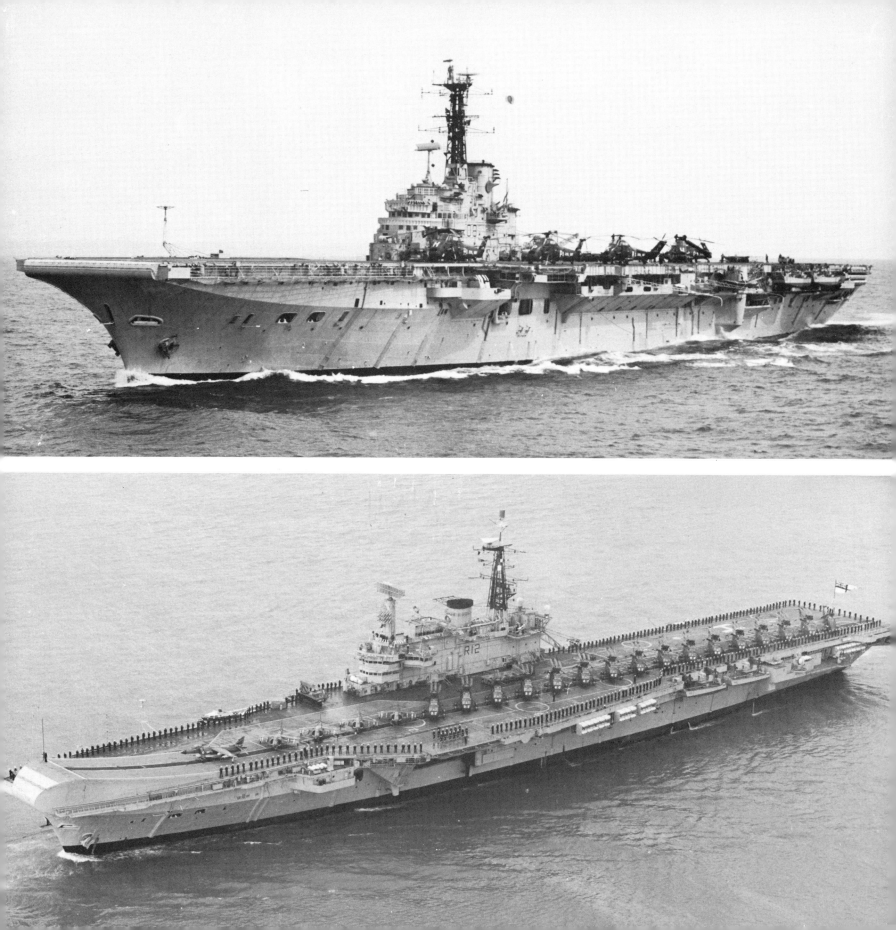

landing sight. She was given anti-fallout protection and automatic boiler feed. The forward lift was moved out to the port-side deck edge, after the fashion of US carriers, and atop her island was the massive 3-dimensional Type 984 radar, which combined surveillance, tracking, height-finding and fighter direction (also fitted to *Victorious* and *Eagle*); Types 293Q target-indicator and 963 CCA were also installed. Displacement as completed was 23,000 tons standard and 27,800 tons deep load; length overall was 744ft 3in, maximum flight-deck width 144ft 6in and mean draught 28ft; armament consisted of 10×40mm; and complement was 1,834. Twenty aircraft could be accommodated (Scimitars and Sea Vixens), plus AEW Gannets and ASR helicopters.

The four ships not proceeded with (cancelled October 1945 prior to laying down) were *Arrogant*

(to be built by Swan Hunter), *Hermes* (Cammell Laird; the ship of the same name completed in 1959 was originally named *Elephant*), *Monmouth* (Fairfield) and *Polyphemus* (Devonport Dockyard).

Modifications *Centaur* was refitted in the late 1950s to incorporate a pair of steam catapults. By 1960 she displaced 22,000 tons standard and 27,000 tons deep; measured 737ft 9in overall and had a maximum beam of 123ft and a mean draught of 27ft; carried 20×40mm; and could embark 21 aircraft. In the 1950s *Bulwark* was fitted with a deck landing mirror for trials purposes. Following the success of *Ocean* and *Theseus* at Suez late in 1956, both she and *Albion* were converted to commando carriers in the late 1950s and early 1960s. *Bulwark*'s refit took from January 1959 to January 1960 and involved the removal of the catapults, arrester gear and most of the 40mm (reduced to eight barrels). Sixteen Whirlwind helicopters and a Commando of 750 men could be accommodated, four landing craft being carried in davits. Ship's complement was reduced to 1,037. The work was carried out at Devonport, and on completion displacement stood at 22,300 / 27,300 tons. She retained an ASW capability, which could be called upon if required. *Albion* was similarly reconfigured (February 1961–August 1962) but was equipped to carry Wessex helicopters. *Bulwark* was further modified in 1963 to accommodate Wessexes and Sioux, with 900 troops. Deep load displacement rose to 17,700 tons.

Since first commissioning, *Hermes* has seen a succession of refits reflecting changes in naval strategy and economic 'squeezes'. She was first refitted in 1964–66 to operate Sea Vixen and Buccaneer aircraft, having her flight deck widened (now 160ft maximum) to starboard of the island in an 'Alaskan highway'. In 1971 she was taken in hand for conversion to an amphibious assault ship (to replace *Albion*), catapults and arrester gear being landed and provision for the transport of 750 troops and their equipment being made. The flight deck was strengthened at the same time, anticipating the embarkation of Harrier V/STOL aircraft. She completed in August 1973. Delays in the *Invincible* programme prompted her modification in 1976–77 to enable her to operate as an ASW unit with a squadron of Wessex and one of Sea King helicopters, although the assault role was preserved. A 'ski-jump' was added at the forward end of the flight deck, faired into the bows, to permit fully loaded Sea Harriers to be flown off, thereby endowing the carrier with a limited strike and air defence capability. Two quadruple Seacat launchers were fitted aft, and displacement rose to 23,900 / 28,700 tons.

Service Notes *Centaur*: Deployed mainly in the Mediterranean and Far East during her service career, including operations off Aden. She became a depot ship in 1966, first at Devonport and then at Portsmouth. She was stricken in 1971 and scrapped from 1972.

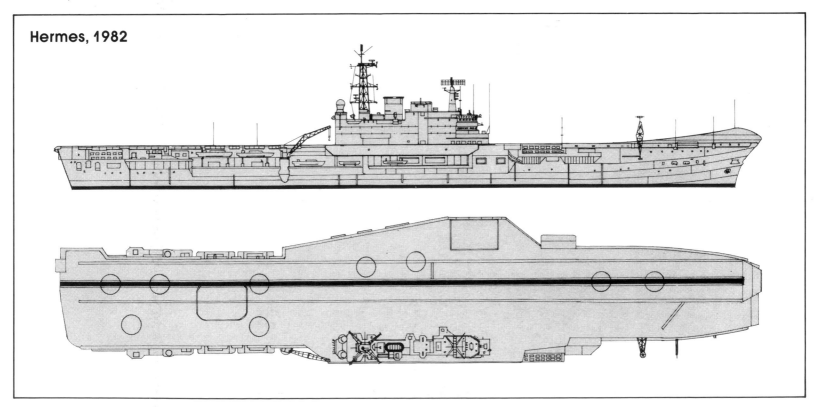

Hermes, 1982

Above: Commando carriers required not only an airborne assault capability: seaborne beachhead operations were also encompassed, for which landing craft were carried aft, in davits, as seen in this photograph of *Albion*. (Fleet Air Arm Museum)

Albion operated as a fighter carrier (Sea Hawks, Sea Venoms) during the Suez operations in November 1956, and during the 1960s was employed mainly in the Far East, being present during the Indonesian confrontation in 1966. She operated as a Commando carrier from mid 1962, and was stricken in 1972 and broken up.

Bulwark: After a brief spell as a special trials carrier, *Bulwark* was sent to the eastern Mediterranean during the Suez crisis, operating Sea Hawks and Avengers. She was a training ship in 1957, but recommissioned as a combat carrier in the late 1950s. Following conversion to a Commando carrier, she operated in the Far East and Mediterranean and was on duty during the Indonesian confrontation. Designated a reserve anti-submarine carrier in April 1976, *Bulwark* was refitted the following year as a full ASW carrier, recommissioning in 1979. With the entry into service of *Invincible* in 1980 she was reduced to reserve once more (formally decommissioned in March 1981), in which state she currently (1983) remains.

Hermes: Deployed 'east of Suez' from 1960, with subsequent service in the Far East and Mediterranean. After conversion to an interim ASW carrier, she was assigned to the Atlantic. Sea Harrier trials were conducted in late 1978. She operated as flagship of the Falklands Task Force in action after the Argentine invasion of the islands in the spring of 1982. After her last operational deployment, in November 1983 she went to Devonport for a minor refit before entering the reserve in spring 1984.

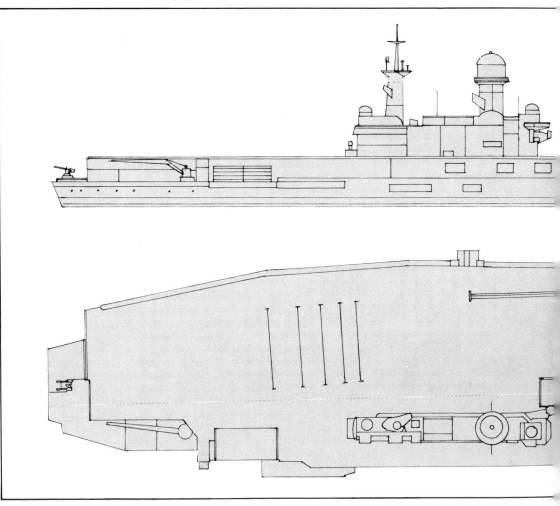

CVA-01

Displacement: 50,000 tons / 50,800 tonnes
(standard); 54,500 tons / 55,372 tonnes (deep load).
Length: 890ft / 271.27m (pp); 890ft / 271.27m (wl);
963ft / 293.52m (oa); 884ft / 269.44m (fd).
Beam: 122ft / 37.19m (hull); 191ft / 58.22m (fd).
Draught: 32ft / 9.75m (deep load).
Machinery: Turbines; 6 boilers; 3 shafts.
Performance: 135,000shp.
Aircraft: 45.
Missiles: 2 Sea Dart.
Complement: 3,230.

Design By the late 1950s the Royal Navy's carrier fleet numbered five vessels, *Ark Royal*, *Eagle*, *Victorious*, *Hermes* and *Centaur* (*Albion* and *Bulwark* were earmarked for conversion to amphibious assault ships), and in 1959 proposals were formulated for a new generation of vessels which would replace what were in reality Second World War designs. In its final form the design was radical.

The fully angled flight deck concept was abandoned in favour of a 'three lane' arrangement which would provide a landing area (3½° off the fore-and-aft axis) on the port side, occupying about half the flight-deck width, and a two-way marshalling / taxying area to starboard, split physically amidships by the 200ft × 18ft island which would have access tunnels athwartships to permit movement of deck vehicles and flight-deck personnel (see the introductory chapters for a more detailed discussion). Two 250ft catapults were to be fitted, at the waist and right forward, to starboard, with a centreline lift amidships and a deck-edge lift aft on the starboard side. At the stern, a 'fantail' opened from the 650ft × 80ft hangar to permit aircraft engines to be run without interfering with flight-deck operations; the fixed battery, one twin Sea Dart system, was also located here, the principal area defence being entrusted to the ship's aircraft in the outer layer and specially built Type 82 surface escorts in an inner ring (one of the latter, *Bristol*, was completed), much as in US task force organisation. Radar would include the Anglo-Dutch Type 988 search / target tracking system and Type 909 for missile control, while the air group would be made up of eighteen F-4s, eighteen Buccaneers, four Gannet AEW and five Sea King ASW helicopters, with, presumably, an additional SAR flight.

CVA-01 was cancelled with the publication of the 1966 British Defence White Paper; the much-quoted name *Furious* appears to have been purely a speculative designation.

Below: An artist's impression of CVA-01, showing the angled landing area to port and the two-lane 'taxyway' either side of the island. (Ministry of Defence (Navy))

Bottom: CVA-01 was to have featured an innovative 'warm-up' facility right aft, jet exhausts venting through the opening at the end of the hangar. The carrier's fixed battery, a twin Sea Dart launcher, can be made out at the stern. (Ministry of Defence (Navy))

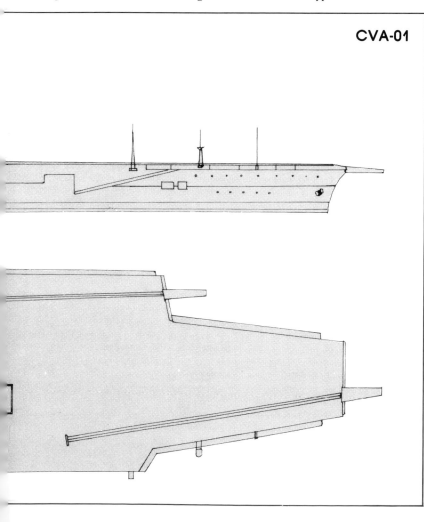

CVA-01

INVINCIBLE CLASS

Ship	Builder	Laid down	Launched	Commissioned
Invincible	Vickers (Barrow)	20 July 73	3 May 77	11 July 80
Illustrious	Swan Hunter	7 June 76	1 Dec 78	18 June 82
Ark Royal	Swan Hunter	14 Dec 78	2 June 81	

Displacement: 16,000 tons / 16,256 tonnes (standard); 19,500 tons / 19,812 tonnes (deep load).
Length: 632ft / 192.63m (pp); 677ft / 206.35m (oa); 550ft / 167.64m (fd).
Beam: 90ft / 27.43m (hull); 115ft / 35.05m (fd).
Draught: 24ft / 7.32m (mean).
Machinery: 4 Olympus gas turbines; 2 shafts.
Performance: 112,000shp; 28kts.
Range: 5,000nm at 18kts.
Aircraft: 14.
Missiles: 2 Sea Dart.
Complement: 900.

Design The *Invincible*s reflect in dramatic terms the shift in British naval policy over the last two decades, with the abandonment of a worldwide strike capability and a concentration on Atlantic ASW within the NATO framework. Their design period was protracted as political uncertainties surrounded the project and subsequently new demands were made of it.

The origins lie in a 1966 decision to replace the two *Tiger*-class vessels that were being converted to command cruisers with a new design to act as ASW escorts for the new fleet carrier CVA-01. With the cancellation of the latter, the design emerged in 1970 as a 'through-deck cruiser', primarily a helicopter carrier, but with provision for operating V / STOL Harrier aircraft should such a requirement be directed. The first ship was ordered in April 1973, and the original scheme foresaw all being built at

Barrow; however, in mid 1975 it was decided that the second and third units should be built on the Tyne.

The choice of gas turbine propulsion imposed limits on both hangar and flight-deck dimensions, since considerable internal volume and large uptakes are required; command facilities also reduce the amount of space available for air operations, and these factors go some way to explain the apparently small aircraft complement in terms of the displacement. The flight deck itself is a 42ft-wide runway angled ½° to port, leaving little room for a deck park. There are two lifts, but no catapults or arrester gear.

Early sketch designs reportedly included the installation of a quadruple Exocet SSM launcher in the bows, and a Sea Wolf SAM system was apparently also a feature at one stage. Among the design changes that have certainly been made are the requirement that the ships be capable of functioning as amphibious assault carriers, and if needed they can accommodate 1,000 troops together with their equipment. Externally, *Invincible* was fitted with a 6½° 'ski-jump' (installed from September 1977) to enable Harriers to leave the ship with enhanced payloads; *Illustrious* also has a 6½° ramp. The latter commissioned with a pair of US CIWS (Phalanx) 20mm systems, in the bows and on the starboard flight-deck edge, right aft, while *Ark Royal* has received a 15° 'ski-jump' via an extended forward flight deck. Radar consists of Type 1022 long-range

air warning, Type 992 target indication and Type 909 for Sea Dart control; *Illustrious* has, in addition, integral Phalanx radar with her CIWS.

Modifications It was decided that, in the light of combat experience in the South Atlantic, *Invincible* would be retro-fitted with Phalanx, and the question of incorporating the Sea Wolf point-defence system has also been raised again.

Service Notes *Invincible*: Deployed to the South Atlantic in April 1982, operating as an ASW / air defence / strike carrier against Argentine forces (nine Sea Kings, eight Sea Harriers / Harrier GR3s) off the Falkland Islands.

Illustrious: Deployed to the South Atlantic, July 1982.

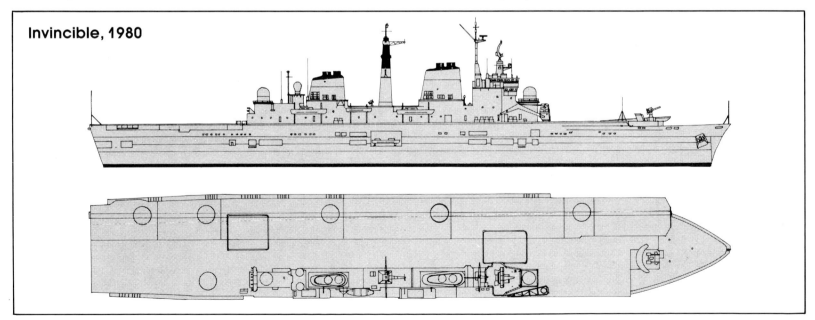

Invincible, 1980

India

The sole Indian Navy carrier, *Vikrant*, remains in service and is currently being modified for V / STOL aircraft operation.

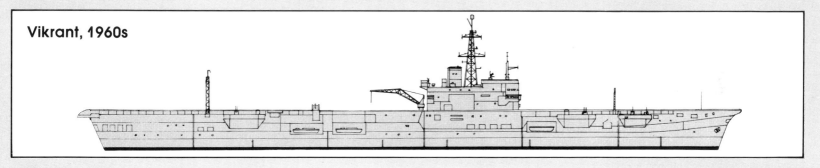

Vikrant, 1960s

VIKRANT

Ship	Builder	Laid down	Launched	Commissioned
Vikrant	Vickers-Armstrong (Newcastle)	14 Oct 43	22 Sept 45	4 Mar 61

Displacement: 16,000 tons / 16,256 tonnes (standard); 19,550 tons / 19,863 tonnes (deep load).
Length: 630ft / 192.02m (pp); 650ft / 198.12m (wl); 700ft / 213.36m (oa); 680ft / 207.26m (fd).
Beam: 80ft / 24.38m (hull); 105ft / 32m (fd).
Draught: 24ft / 7.32m (deep load).
Machinery: Parsons geared turbines; 4 Admiralty 3-drum boilers; 2 shafts.
Performance: 42,000shp; 24.5kts.
Bunkerage: 3,000 tons / 3,048 tonnes.
Aircraft: 21.

Guns: 15 × 40mm.
Complement: 1,343.
Design Originally one of the six British *Majestic*-class carriers, *Hercules* (qv) was laid up for ten years before being purchased by the Indian Government in January 1957. She was taken in hand by Harland & Wolff immediately after completion of the Canadian *Bonaventure* and reconstructed along broadly similar lines, with a reconfigured island and lattice mast, an angled landing deck, a steam catapult and advanced landing aids, though lacking the Canadian carrier's

deepened hull sponsons. In addition, she was fully air-conditioned and received the Type 277Q / 293Q radar fit. She commissioned as *Vikrant*, with Sea Hawk strike aircraft and French-built Alizé ASW aircraft. The anti-aircraft battery consisted of four twin and seven single 40mm.
Modifications Refitted 1979–82 to operate Sea Harriers. 'Ski-jump' modification began in 1983.
Service Notes *Vikrant* saw combat in the December 1971 war with Pakistan, her Sea Hawks striking coastal installations and shipping in the Chittagong area and her Alizés carrying out mining and bombing missions. The carrier is expected to remain in service until the early 1990s.

Below: Vikrant as completed, spring 1961. She was the last *Majestic*-class vessel to be completed and is one of three ex-British light fleet carriers still (1984) in front-line service. (By courtesy of Ian Sturton)

Italy

Plans to commission Italian carriers during the Second World War were thwarted by Italy's continuing military setbacks and eventual defeat, but the revitalised postwar navy has been a consistent champion of shipboard aviation. The proven value of multi-role helicopter carriers has finally resulted in a full-deck vessel, *Giuseppe Garibaldi*, which is currently nearing completion.

GIUSEPPE MIRAGLIA

Launched	Commissioned
20 Dec 23	1927

Displacement: 4,880 tons / 4,958 tonnes (standard).
Length: 377ft 4in / 115m (pp).
Beam: 49ft 3in / 15m (hull).
Draught: 17ft 1in / 5.2m (mean).
Machinery: Parsons geared turbines; 8 Yarrow boilers.
Performance: 12,000shp; 21kts.
Bunkerage: 430 tons / 437 tonnes.
Aircraft: 20.
Guns: 4 × 4in.
Complement: 180.

Design Italy's first effective seaplane carrier was the ex-merchantman *Citta de Messina*, converted at La Spezia Navy Yard in the mid 1920s and renamed *Giuseppe Miraglia*. Hangars were installed before and abaft the midships superstructure across the former well decks, the hull plating being carried right up to the roofs and pierced at each end by doors to port and starboard to enable the aircraft to be hoisted from the water, via hinged gantries. A catapult was installed over the forecastle and a second one over the poop, the seaplanes being readied for launch by means of derricks which lifted them from the hangars. The four single 4in guns were disposed abreast each catapult. Aircraft complement varied, but a typical figure, indicated in the table, numbered four large and sixteen medium-sized machines, repair facilities for which were also provided by the ship.

Modifications By the mid 1930s 11 × 14pdr AA were listed in addition to the 4in battery.

Service Notes Employed generally as an experimental catapult ship for much of her career, *Giuseppe Miraglia* was designated a transport by 1940 and acted as a seaplane tender to Italian capital ships and cruisers, and as a training ship. Following the Italian surrender in September 1943 she was a submarine depot ship for a period. Her ultimate fate is uncertain.

Below left: Giuseppe Miraglia raises steam. This photograph clearly shows the ship's forward catapult, the forward hangar doors and the gantries above for hoisting aircraft to and from the water. Abreast the after end of the catapult, on a small platform sponsored out over the hull, is one of the carrier's 4in guns. (By courtesy of A. D. Baker III)

Below: Miraglia's high freeboard amidships disguised her original lines: the hull plating was extended upwards during conversion, to enclose the seaplane hangars. (By courtesy of Ian Sturton)

AQUILA

Builder	Launched
Ansaldo	1926

Displacement: 23,350 tons / 23,724 tonnes (standard); 27,800 tons / 28,245 tonnes (deep load).
Length: 680ft 1in / 207.3m (pp); 759ft 2in / 231.6m (oa); 700ft / 213.35m (fd).
Beam: 96ft 6in / 29.41m (hull); 83ft / 25.3m (fd).
Draught: 24ft / 7.31m (mean).
Machinery: Belluzzo geared turbines; 8 Thornycroft boilers; 4 shafts.
Performance: 140,000shp; 30kts.
Bunkerage: 2,800 tons / 2,845 tonnes.
Range: 4,000nm at 18kts.
Aircraft: 36.
Guns: 8 × 5.3in; 12 × 65mm; 132 × 20mm.
Complement: 1,420.

Design The 32,580grt passenger liner *Roma* provided the foundation for Italy's first full-deck carrier project. She was originally (in the mid 1930s) envisaged as the basis for an austere conversion with little internal modification, the superstructure being razed, the boiler uptakes re-routed and a flight deck being added, but in the event a more far-reaching reconstruction was effected, the hull being gutted and an island and funnel superstructure mounted on the starboard deck edge. The hull was first lengthened and then bulged (to improve stability), reinforced-concrete being introduced to the bulges to afford some degrees of protection to the machinery (now two sets of cruiser plant), while a partial 3.1in armoured deck was worked in over the petrol bunkers (total capacity 72,000 gallons) and magazines.

Much assistance was obtained from the Germans, particularly in respect of flight-deck equipment such as the twin catapults and two lifts, although *Aquila* differed from *Graf Zeppelin* in having only a single hangar (525ft × 60ft). Non-folding Re 2001 fighters were to make up the air group (in anticipation of which two examples were fitted with arrester hooks and another experimentally fitted with a torpedo to test the aircraft as a strike plane, Re 2001G), which limited internal capacity in terms of numbers of aircraft although it was envisaged that the carrier

Above: A view of *Aquila* following the Italian surrender, in damaged condition in 1944. Note the particularly massive bulge, which was expected to improve both stability and underwater defence. (By courtesy of A. D. Baker III)

would commission with a folding version and hence embark a larger complement. The 5.3in / 45 guns were single-mounted, low-angle weapons to give some defence against surface units, while the 2.6in / 64 were single- and the 20mm sextuple-mounted; originally the battery was seen as having 8 × 6in / 55, 12 × 3.5in heavy AA and 104 × 37mm AA.

Aquila never entered service: conversion began in mid 1941 and the carrier was virtually complete at the time of the Italian capitulation in September 1943. She was immediately taken over by the Germans, but damage, first in an Allied air raid and subsequently by human torpedoes, led to any plans to commission her being abandoned, and she was finally scuttled. Refloated post-war, she was taken to La Spezia for refitting, but in the event she was broken up in 1951–52.

SPARVIERO

Launched 1927

Length: 664ft 2in / 202.43m (wl); 600ft / 182.88m (fd).
Beam: 82ft 10in / 25.24m (hull).
Draught: 30ft 2in / 9.2m (mean).
Machinery: Diesel engines; 4 shafts.
Performance: 28,000bhp; 18kts.
Guns: 6 × 6in; 4 × 4in.
Design In 1936 the 30,418grt passenger vessel *Augustus* was suggested as the possible basis for a future aircraft carrier, and although initially rejected

the proposal was taken up in 1942 to provide an auxiliary carrier generally similar in configuration to that first envisaged for *Aquila*. Renamed *Falco*, and then *Sparviero*, the ship would comprise the merchant hull, which internally would be essentially unaltered (though featuring deep, concrete-reinforced bulges to give some measure of protection and improved stability); a single hangar, served by two lifts well amidships and topped by a flight deck terminating some 150ft from the bow (to be replaced by a narrow flying-off deck that extended to the stem), was to be substituted for the former superstructure.

The single-mounted armament was to be disposed on each side of the forecastle, at hangar-deck level below the flight-deck overhang, and at the stern. No island was featured, the diesel engines exhausting below flight-deck level to port and starboard amidships.

Conversion began at the Ansaldo yard, Genoa, in September 1942, but proceeded at pedestrian pace, the only signs of change by the time of the Armistice, a year later, being the removal of the upperworks. The hull was requisitioned by the Germans along with *Aquila* and was subsequently scuttled to block the harbour entrance.

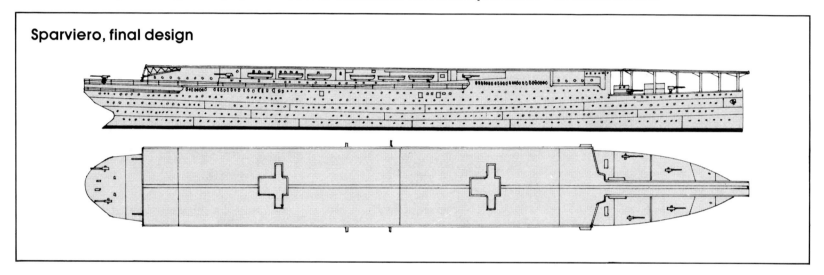

Sparviero, final design

GIUSEPPE GARIBALDI

Builder	Laid down	Launched
CRDA	June 81	11 June 83

Displacement: 10,000 tons / 10,160 tonnes (standard); 13,370 tons / 13,584 tonnes (deep load).
Length: 590ft 6in / 180m (oa); 570ft 10in / 174m (fd).
Beam: 77ft 1in / 23.5m (hull); 99ft 9in / 30.4m (fd).
Draught: 22ft / 6.7m (mean).
Machinery: 4 General Electric gas turbines; 2 shafts.
Performance: 80,000shp; 30kts.
Range: 7,000nm at 20 kts.
Aircraft: 18.
Guns: 6 × 40mm.
Torpedo tubes: 6 × 12.75in.
Missiles: 4 Teseo, 16 Albatros.
Complement: 825.
Design Authorised in late 1977 and currently (1983) under construction, the carrier *Giuseppe Garibaldi* will be the first full-deck air-capable ship to see service with the Italian Navy. The design is more properly that of a helicopter cruiser, however, since it is directly descended from the ASW / AAW (Terrier)

7,500-ton *Vittorio Veneto*, built in the late 1960s with a 130ft × 60ft landing deck aft and operating nine helicopters, and thus indirectly from the earlier and much smaller *Caio Duilio*s which themselves were an adaptation of a destroyer design and could handle four helicopters.

Despite her primary ASW function, for which eighteen Sea King helicopters will be embarked (twelve of them can be accommodated in the 360ft × 49ft hangar below the flight deck), *Giuseppe Garibaldi* shows a meaningful anti-air and anti-surface armament, with two twin Teseo launchers (Otomat SSMs) at the stern and two 8-cell Albatros launchers (Aspide SAMs) before and abaft the starboard-mounted island, supplemented by three twin 40mm / 70 disposed two forward and one aft. The ASW element is boosted by the provision of a pair of triple torpedo tubes and a DE-1160 sonar system. Two lifts, offset to starboard but sited well amidships, handle helicopter stowage. The radar fit is not yet finalised, but will presumably include RAN-3L and RAN-10 (search), RTN-10X / Orion (20mm) and RTN(NA)-30 (Albatros), plus Otomat systems.

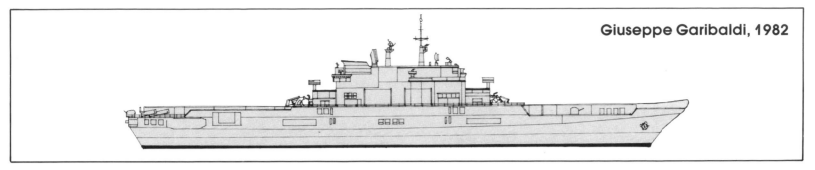

Giuseppe Garibaldi, 1982

Below: The new Italian carrier *Giuseppe Garibaldi*, shortly after launch. (By courtesy of British Aerospace)

Bottom of page: An official model of *Giuseppe Garibaldi*, currently (1984) fitting out. (Italian Navy)

Japan

Relations between the Imperial Japanese Navy and the Royal Navy were close during the late nineteenth and early twentieth centuries – indeed, the two services were drawn together by their countries' defence treaty – and it is thus not surprising that Japanese warship development showed a marked British influence. This carried over to shipboard aviation, particularly with regard to operating procedure and the types of aircraft embarked.

Japanese seaplane carrier operations began in earnest as early as 1914, with an attack on the German enclave at Tsingtao. The first through-deck carrier, *Hosho*, commissioned in 1922. In common with the two other major navies, hulls laid up as a result of the Washington agreement were utilised for pioneer large fleet carriers (*Akagi*, *Kaga*), and throughout the 1930s much effort went into devising the best means of utilising the remaining carrier tonnage allocated under Washington. Unique to the Japanese Navy, however, was the construction of the so-called 'shadow' carrier fleet. As an insurance against the smaller Japanese carrier force (in

relation to those of the Royal and US Navies) dictated by naval agreements and the consequent disadvantages should hostilities break out, a large number of ships were designed for ready conversion to carriers should the latter be required – as in fact turned out to be the case.

Tactically, the Japanese placed emphasis on seaborne air strike, as did the US Navy, spotting / reconnaissance being more the province of catapult-launched floatplanes operating from other units. Dispersal rather than concentration of carriers formed the basic battle doctrine following the spectacularly successful carrier raid on Pearl Harbor in 1941. However, full-scale sea warfare from mid 1942, as US industry responded to the requirement for mass production of matériel, left the Japanese unable to compete – if not at a technological level, then certainly in terms of the amount of equipment they could organise and the numbers of trained crew to operate it. It was this disadvantage which, in the main, contributed to the extinction of the Japanese carrier force in 1945, and indeed of the Imperial Japanese Navy in its entirety.

WAKAMIYA

Builder	Laid down	Launched	Commissioned
Duncan	1900	21 Sept 01	17 Aug 14

Displacement: 7,720 tons / 7,844 tonnes (standard).
Length: 365ft / 111.25m (pp).
Beam: 48ft 2in / 14.68m (hull).
Draught: 19ft / 5.79m (mean).
Machinery: Vertical triple-expansion reciprocating engines; 3 boilers; 1 shaft.
Performance: 1,600ihp; 9.5kts.
Bunkerage: 851 tons / 865 tonnes.
Aircraft: 4.
Guns: 2×3in; 2×47mm.
Design The first vessel in the Imperial Japanese Navy to have any major air capability was the former *Lethington*, a coal-burning, British-built, 4,421grt cargo vessel captured by the Japanese in 1905 during the war with Russia and used initially as a naval

Right: The ex-merchantman *Wakamiya*, the first seaplane carrier of the Imperial Japanese Navy, showing the positions of the aircraft bays and the derricks that serviced them. The carrier's 3in guns are just discernible, forward and aft. (Japanese Official)

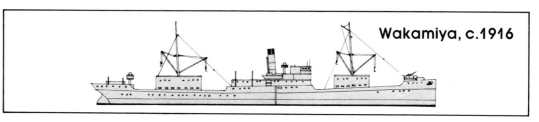

Wakamiya, c.1916

transport. Conversion details encompassed the fitting of temporary canvas shelters over her well decks in the summer of 1914 to afford protection for four seaplanes, which were hoisted aboard by derricks. It is not clear whether she was armed upon commissioning or whether guns were added later; however, they appear to have been in place by the end of the First World War, the 3in weapons being located one on the forecastle and one on the poop.

Modifications In the summer of 1920 *Wakamiya* was fitted with a planked take-off deck over the forecastle for operating Sopwith Pups.

Service Notes *Wakamiya* carried out a raid on German-held Tsingtao in the autumn of 1914, her seaplanes sinking one minelayer and causing superficial damage to shore installations. She was officially classified as an aircraft carrier (in the precise sense of the term) in April 1920 and following use as a trials vessel was stricken in April 1931 and subsequently broken up.

Below: The diminutive *Hosho* in her early configuration, with small rounded island and tripod mast; note, too, the pronounced downward slope of the forward flight deck, and the positions of the two lifts. A single aircraft, probably a Sopwith type, is parked forward. One of the 5.5in mountings is clearly visible. (By courtesy of Ray Burt)

Bottom: For flying operations, *Hosho*'s tall pole mast (fitted when the island was removed) hinged downwards, as seen in this photograph. Smoke drift was also a problem, and the funnels discharged horizontally. (By courtesy of Ray Burt)

HOSHO

Builder	Laid down	Launched	Commissioned
Asano	16 Dec 19	13 Nov 21	27 Dec 22

Displacement: 7,470 tons / 7,590 tonnes (standard); 10,000 tons / 10,160 tonnes (deep load).
Length: 510ft / 155.45m (pp); 541ft 4in / 165m (wl); 551ft 6in / 168.1m (oa); 520ft / 158.5m (fd).
Beam: 59ft 1in / 18m (hull); 70ft / 21.34m (fd).
Draught: 20ft 3in / 6.17m (mean).
Machinery: Parsons geared turbines; 12 Kampon boilers; 2 shafts.
Performance: 30,000shp; 25kts.
Bunkerage: 2,695 tons / 2,738 tonnes.
Range: 8,000nm at 15kts.
Aircraft: 26.
Guns: 4 × 5.5in; 2 × 80mm.
Complement: 550.

Design *Hosho* is frequently the subject of such phraseology as 'first carrier in the world to be designed from the keel up', 'first true aircraft carrier to enter service' and 'first carrier with an island superstructure', but these laudatory attributes require qualification. There is strong evidence to suggest that the ship was laid down as an oiler (named *Hiryu*) or at most that her design was that of an adapted oiler, while without the assistance of the British (an official technical mission, in all probability armed with details of *Hermes* and *Eagle*) it is doubtful whether she would have commissioned in the form she did, or so quickly.

As completed, however, the hull showed very little sheer, and it was topped by a half-length hangar amidships at each end of which was a lift, about 26ft × 33ft forward and 43ft × 28ft aft. The spaces abreast the hangar were open, apart from right aft where the hull plating was carried up to flight-deck level, and the main armament was single-mounted in shields at hangar-deck level, one pair forward and the other just abaft amidships.

A full-length flight deck of 74ft 6in extreme width was carried over the forecastle, inclined downwards and supported by stanchions clear of the anchor gear. A longitudinal arrester-wire system was installed before the after lift and reportedly *Hosho* carried a

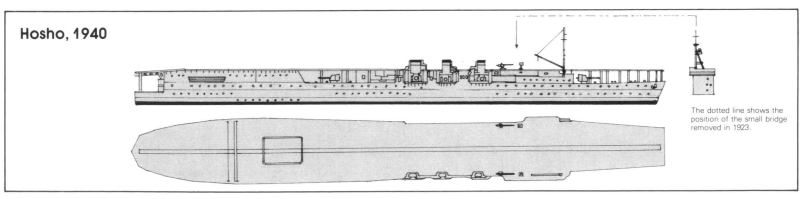

Hosho, 1940

The dotted line shows the position of the small bridge removed in 1923.

primitive deck-landing aid in the form of a row (or rows) of lights. In addition to the oil bunkerage indicated in the table, 940 tons of coal could be carried, suggesting a mixture of oil-burning and coal-burning (probably oil-sprayed) boilers as in later Japanese carriers. The boiler uptakes were trunked over to the starboard side and emerged via three funnels which could be hinged sideways during flying operations. A rather basic, rounded island was fitted on the starboard deck edge for navigation and flight control. The original air group probably consisted of British-built Gloster Mars (Sparrowhawk) types, considerable numbers of which were supplied to the Japanese. Trial displacement was 9,330 tons.*

Modifications Within a year of commissioning, *Hosho* had her island removed, apparently because of turbulence causing smoke drift — it had been positioned within a few yards of the foremost funnel; instead, an open platform was added to the starboard side at about the same station, a tall pole mast replaced the original tripod, and the forward section of the flight deck was modified to remove its downward slope. In the early 1930s the funnels were modified and could thereafter discharge only horizontally, and by the outbreak of the Second World War the two 3.1in AA had been removed and four twin 25mm added. By the end of the war the flight deck was reportedly extended aft, and had its forward section removed completely post-war. An additional four twin 25mms were fitted in 1942, when the 5.5in guns were landed, but only 6×25mm are listed for 1945. The advent of progressively larger aircraft saw a continuous decrease in capacity: by 1934 the figure was 21 and by the outbreak of the Second World War the total had dropped to only eleven.

Service Notes As the first Japanese full-decked carrier, *Hosho* was involved in a great deal of pioneering flight-deck training and experimental work during the 1920s, but by the end of 1933 had been relegated to secondary roles. With the advent of war, however, she was employed once more as a front-line unit and was part of Yamamoto's fleet at Midway though did not see action. She was struck by US aircraft during 1945 while at Kure, but survived through to the summer of 1946 as a post-war repatriation transport. She was scrapped in 1947.

*It was Japanese practice to calculate 'trial' displacements of warships, based on the standard displacement plus two-thirds of the maximum ordnance, fuel, stores and other provisions necessary for full combat readiness.

NOTORO CLASS

Ship	Builder	Laid down	Launched	Commissioned
Notoro	Kawasaki	24 Nov 19	3 May 20	1924
Tsurumi	Osaka	1921	29 Sept 21	1924

Displacement: 14,050 tons / 14,275 tonnes (standard).
Length: 456ft / 139m (pp).
Beam: 58ft / 17.68m (hull).
Draught: 26ft 6in / 8.08m (mean).
Machinery: Vertical triple-expansion reciprocating engines; 4 Miyabara boilers; 2 shafts.
Performance: 5,850ihp; 12kts.

Bunkerage: 1,000 tons / 1,016 tonnes.
Aircraft: 10.
Guns: 2×4.7in; 2×80mm.
Complement: 155.
Design Two *Shiretoko*-type fleet oilers were adapted for use as seaplane carriers-cum-transports in 1924. Conversion work was minimal, the two well decks before and abaft the bridge being covered with platforms and sturdy handling derricks added; the ships' tanker functions were unimpaired.

Modifications Not known.

Service Notes *Notoro*: Originally completed (as an oiler) on 10 August 1920. Used in combat during the Sino-Japanese War in 1937, equipped with Nakajima E8N floatplanes. Handling gear removed 1942, the ship retaining only oiling capabilities. Broken up in 1947.

Tsurumi: Completed as an oiler on 14 March 1922; reconverted for exclusively tanker duties in 1931 and torpedoed and sunk in August 1942.

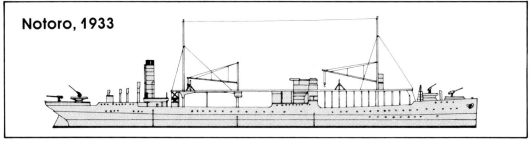

Notoro, 1933

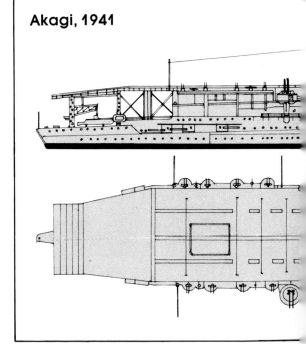

Akagi, 1941

Above: *Notoro* at Chefoo, June 1928, showing the minimal nature of her modification. (US National Archives)

AKAGI

Builder	Laid down	Launched	Commissioned
Kure	6 Dec 20	22 Apr 25	25 Mar 27

Displacement: 29,600 tons / 30,074 tonnes
(standard).
Length: 770ft / 234.7m (pp); 816ft 9in / 248.95m
(wl); 857ft / 261.21m (oa); 624ft / 190.2m (fd).
Beam: 95ft / 28.96m (hull); 100ft / 30.48m (fd).
Draught: 26ft 6in / 8.08m (mean).
Machinery: Gijutsu-Hombu turbines; 19 Kampon
boilers; 4 shafts.
Performance: 131,000shp; 32.5kts.

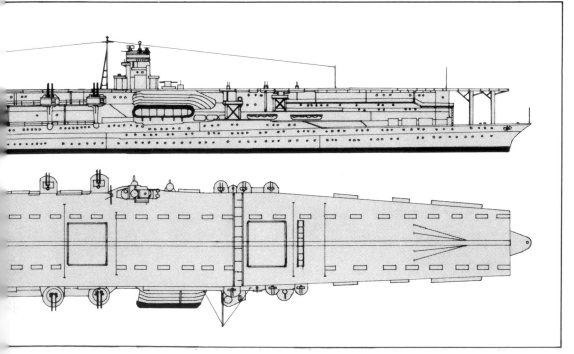

Bunkerage: 3,900 tons / 3,962 tonnes.
Range: 8,000nm at 14kts.
Aircraft: 60.
Guns: 10 × 8in; 12 × 4.7in.
Complement: 1,600.

Design As was the case in the USA, Japan's first fast fleet carriers were a direct product of the Washington Treaty of 1922. Under the terms of the agreement, Japan's total allowable capital ship tonnage was 315,000 (maximum ten vessels), but more pertinently no new construction was permitted. However, 81,000 tons were available to the Navy for

Above: A photograph of *Akagi*, taken in 1928. The three flying-off decks gave both *Akagi* and *Kaga* a distinctive silhouette; however, the middle deck, only some 50ft long, was rarely used, and by the time the carriers were in commission it was becoming patently clear that the larger and heavier aircraft then in prospect would render such auxiliary take-off platforms redundant. (By courtesy of Ray Burt)

establishing a carrier fleet, the displacement of individual units being restricted to 27,000 tons apart from two which could be built up to 33,000.

By late 1921 Japan was well advanced with her '8-8' programme, a scheme that was to equip the Navy with eight modern battleships and eight modern battlecruisers by the early 1930s, and when this was swept away by Washington there remained four partially constructed *Amagi*-class battlecruiser hulls (original specification 41,200 tons, 10 × 16in guns) on various slips; *Amagi* and *Akagi*, the more advanced pair, seemed to offer the chance of providing Japan with two carriers that would rival the US *Lexington*s, ordered for conversion in November 1922. As designs were being finalised, however, an earthquake struck the Yokosuka area and wrecked the hull of *Amagi* beyond economic salvage.

Work began on the reconfiguration of *Akagi* late in 1923. The essential structure of the hull was retained, but in order to extract the maximum air capability from the design some modifications were necessary: a double-decked hangar arrangement might be possible if hull weights could be reduced, and accordingly the original battlecruiser armour was reorganised. The waterline belt was reduced in thickness from 10in to 6in and the armoured deck from 3.8in to 3.1in, while to help compensate for the topweight of the hangars the latter was moved down, in effect, from upper to main deck, requiring a lowering of the main belt itself and a reshaping of the anti-torpedo bulge. The bow was modified to clipper form.

The conversion apparently had little other impact on the hull design, although there were some changes internally, not least the rearrangement of the boiler uptakes. There was also a reduction in coal capacity of some 15 per cent to 2,100 tons (no significant loss in combat radius resulted, because of the smaller displacement), although the original oil capacity (data in table) was retained. Boilers consisted of eight coal- and eleven sprayed coal-burners, and the battlecruiser geared turbine machinery was unaltered. The boilers were trunked over to starboard, gases discharging via a large, downward-angled funnel supplemented by a smaller, upward-pointing stack further aft.

Apparently quite independently, the Japanese had come to the conclusion that the two-storey hangar arrangement not only offered the best opportunity for providing a very large air group, but also enabled it to be deployed in combat extremely efficiently, since each hangar deck opened out on to a short (50ft upper, 175ft lower) auxiliary flying-off deck, giving the carrier a 'stepped' profile. The upper auxiliary deck was flanked by twin 8in turrets and the height of the upper hangar was restricted by a conning position below the forward edge of the main flight deck (one of the reasons the arrangement was dispensed with later). The latter was uniquely contoured, sloping forward and aft from a point about the position of the uptakes, apparently to assist take-off and landing. There were two lifts, 38ft 6in × 42ft 6in forward and 42ft × 27ft 6in aft, and between each an arresting system of longitudinal wires occupied some 300ft of deck.

Six single-mounted 8in were located in casemates right aft, and the 4.7in AA were twin-mounted and sited on sponsons amidships, just below flight-deck level. The official standard displacement figure was 26,900 tons, but it is generally accepted that, in reality, this was a considerable understatement.

Modifications Quite early after completion *Akagi* received an auxiliary navigation platform on the starboard side forward, just beneath the flight-deck edge, and in 1931 new cross-deck arrester gear was fitted.

From October 1935 she was reconstructed on a major scale to enable her to operate more aircraft more effectively. Rising dimensions and increased weights of aircraft had signalled the impracticality of the short forward flying-off platforms: the 8in turrets were removed; the lower deck was shortened and the upper one extended and both were enclosed to form additional hangarage; and the main flight deck was built out over the forecastle to give a total length of 817ft. A new lift, approximately 37ft 6in × 41ft 3in, was added amidships, and the flight deck was widened

Above: Another pre-reconstruction view of *Akagi*, with a deck load of Mitsubishi Type 87 torpedo-bombers. The carrier appears to have had a small island superstructure installed along the starboard deck edge, forward. (Japanese Official)

Below: A 1940 photograph of *Akagi*, showing the port-side island; she was one of only two carriers to have this feature. Boiler gases still discharged to starboard, however, via a massive downward-curved funnel, visible here. (By courtesy of Pierre Hervieux)

locally to port and the hull stressed below to accommodate a small island superstructure. The 4.7in armament remained unchanged except that the starboard mountings were enclosed in protective turrets to help combat the exhaust fumes which were now vented through a single, enlarged, downward-discharging funnel. The close-range anti-aircraft battery was enhanced by the installation of fourteen twin 25mm mountings, added in new platforms sponsoned out below the flight deck forward and aft. The ship was reboilered (coal fuel being dispensed with and oil bunkerage correspondingly increased, to 5,770 tons) and the flight deck was strengthened. All these modifications leading to a significant rise in displacement, to 36,500 tons standard and 42,750 tons deep load (trial displacement, originally 33,821 tons, rose to 40,650) and requiring modification to the underwater bulges which increased beam to 103ft and reduced full-power speed to 31.5kts, mean draught now registering 28ft 6in. On completion of the refit, in August 1938, the air group stood at eighteen Aichi D1A 'Susie' dive-bombers, 36 Yokosuka B4Y 'Jean' torpedo-bombers and eighteen Mitsubishi A5M 'Claude' fighters; reserve aircraft could be embarked to give a theoretical maximum capacity of 91 aircraft.

Service Notes *Akagi* took part in the Sino-Japanese War in 1937 and led the task force which attacked Pearl Harbor. Operations in the South Pacific against Rabaul and Darwin were followed by a move in April 1942 into the Indian Ocean, where the carrier's aircraft helped sink the British cruisers *Dorsetshire* and *Cornwall*, hit installations in Ceylon and helped sink the carrier *Hermes*. Two months later *Akagi* was hit by two bombs delivered by SBDs from the US carrier *Enterprise*, one of which penetrated the flight deck and exploded in the upper hangar, detonating bombs and torpedoes within, the other hitting the flight deck and causing explosions and severe damage to parked aircraft. Uncontrollable fires developed and some eighteen hours later the carrier was scuttled by torpedoes from the destroyers *Arashi*, *Hagikaze*, *Maikaze* and *Nowake*, 5 June 1942.

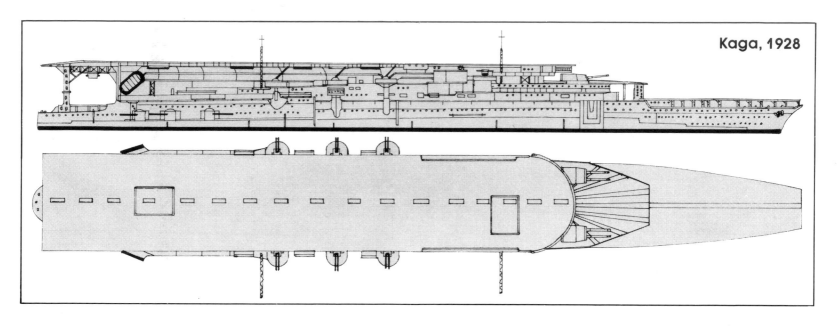

Kaga, 1928

KAGA

Builder	Laid down	Launched	Commissioned
Kawasaki/			
Yokosuka	19 July 20	17 Nov 21	31 Mar 28

Displacement: 29,600 tons / 30,074 tonnes (standard).
Length: 715ft / 217.93m (pp); 754ft 7in / 230m (wl); 782ft 6in / 238.51m (oa); 560ft / 170.69m (fd).
Beam: 97ft / 29.57m (hull); 100ft / 30.48m (fd).
Draught: 26ft / 7.92m (mean).
Machinery: Brown-Curtis turbines; 12 Kampon boilers; 4 shafts.
Performance: 91,000shp; 27.5kts.
Bunkerage: 3,600 tons / 3,658 tonnes.
Range: 8,000nm at 14kts.
Aircraft: 60.
Guns: 10 × 8in; 12 × 4.7in.
Complement: 1,340.

Design The wrecking of *Amagi* in the 1923 earthquake left the Japanese with the prospect of commissioning only one major fleet carrier in the post-Washington reorganisation, and so alternatives were sought: the most advanced hull available was that of the '8-8' battleship *Kaga*, one of two projected 40,000-ton vessels armed with 10 × 16in guns and with a speed of 26.5kts, whose enforced cancellation had resulted in *Kaga*'s hull being laid up prior to scrapping. The keels of *Atago* and *Takao*, sister ships to *Amagi*, were still on the slips, but on grounds of economy it was decided to modify *Kaga*, despite the disadvantages of a lower fleet speed brought about by a bluffer hull form and less powerful machinery.

Below: As first completed, *Kaga* resembled *Akagi* in general configuration, although a notable distinguishing point was the former's extended funnel casings, discharging towards the stern. (By courtesy of Ray Burt)

The conversion scheme, authorised at the same time that *Akagi*'s was officially ordered, followed the same principles as that of the battlecruiser, with a modified armour system (11in belt reduced to 6in as in *Akagi* and the 4in armour deck to 1½in; the latter did not need to be relocated), two auxiliary flying-off decks and an island-less flight deck with two lifts of similar dimensions to those installed in the other carrier; the armament was virtually identical, both in calibre and in disposition, while there was a similar bridge arrangement below the forward edge of the main flight deck. The original battleship machinery was retained, eight of the boilers being oil-fired and four oil-sprayed coal. *Kaga* differed in three important respects, however, reportedly in the cause of comparative evaluation: the flight deck was quite horizontal throughout its entire length, apart from a gentle round-down at the stern; a cross-deck arrester

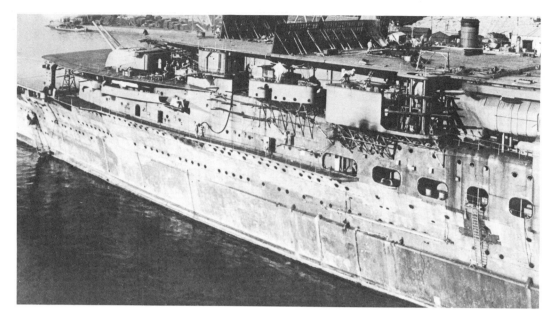

system of French origin was installed; and the boiler gases were discharged via prominent, 300ft long, external tubular ducts extending horizontally on each side just below flight-deck level. The initial air group consisted of 24 Nakajima A1N fighters and 36 Mitsubishi B1M strike aircraft.

Modifications Officially commissioned on the date indicated in the table, *Kaga*, nevertheless, was not ready for front-line service until some time later, and by early 1934 it was decided that she should be reconstructed, mainly with a view to making her

Below: *Kaga* after her mid 1930s reconstruction, with an extended flight deck, deletion of the forward auxiliary flying-off decks, lengthened hangar and island superstructure (conventionally, on the starboard side). Not evident in this photograph are other significant modifications: new lifts, a new arrester system, new machinery and a new AA battery. (US Naval Historical Center)

Above: Characteristic of both *Akagi* and *Kaga* was a heavy fixed anti-surface battery, four of the 8in guns being disposed in twin turrets forward, as seen in this photograph of *Kaga* under construction. The weapons were considered necessary in order to deal with surprise attacks from cruisers, whose armament had been maximised at 8in calibre by Washington. (Japanese Official)

more compatible with *Akagi*, whose modernisation, although begun later, was conceived at the same time. An increase in aircraft capacity to 72 (plus eighteen reserves) was effected by extending both hangars forward and enclosing them, at the expense of the auxiliary flying-off decks and the two 8in turrets, the guns from which were simply relocated aft, forward of the existing casemates. The flight deck was carried forward over the hangar extensions and also aft, additional supports being provided via a reconstructed stern, which was lengthened by some 40ft. An extra

lift was located forward of amidships, the existing units being enlarged, and new cross-deck arrester gear was installed. Eight new boilers and new, more powerful turbines were fitted, producing 127,500shp but a speed advantage of only 1kt since displacement rose dramatically to 38,200 tons standard and 43,650 tons deep load (41,869 tons trial, against the previous 33,161), and to maintain stability the bulges had to be enlarged. Oil fuel capacity was now 7,500 tons.

A new dual-purpose armament of 16×5in / 40 weapons in twin mountings was disposed a pair forward on the starboard side and a pair (enclosed) abaft the reconfigured single funnel, three on the port side amidships and one forward. In addition, 22×25mm AA in twin mountings were positioned along and just below the flight-deck edge. An island was fitted to starboard, forward of amidships and abreast the new centreline lift. The new air group consisted of 24 D1A, 36 D4Y and 12 A5M.

By the time of the attack on Pearl Harbor *Kaga* had had her arrester wires replaced again, and a further four twin 25mm added; with the appearance of the Nakajima B5N ('Kate') torpedo-bomber in 1938 the air group dropped to 66, plus reserves.

Service Notes *Kaga*'s aircraft took a leading part in the offensive against Shanghai in January 1932 ('Shanghai Incident') and were involved against the Chinese again after the carrier's reconstruction when from August 1939 they conducted raids on Hangchou, Nanking and Canton. *Kaga* was part of the First Air Fleet which struck Pearl Harbor in December 1941, and she subsequently participated in the raid on Darwin, Australia (19 February 1942), and helped provide distant cover for the Japanese landings in Rabaul (March). She was sunk at Midway on 4 June of that year when, struck by four bombs from *Enterprise*'s aircraft, she was engulfed in flames and exploded some eight hours later when the fires reached the petrol bunkers.

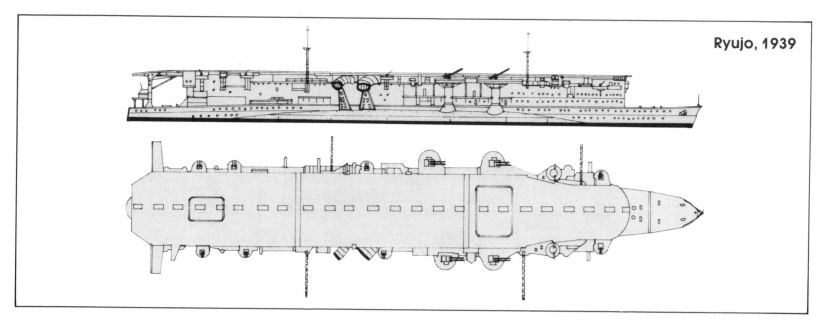

RYUJO

Builder	Laid down	Launched	Commissioned
Yokohama	26 Nov 29	2 Apr 31	9 May 33

Displacement: 8,000 tons / 8,128 tonnes (standard).
Length: 548ft 7in / 168.48m (pp); 575ft 5in / 175.39m (wl); 590ft 3in / 179.9m (oa); 513ft 6in / 156.5m (fd).
Beam: 66ft 8in / 20.32m (hull); 75ft 6in / 23m (fd).
Draught: 18ft 3in / 5.56m (mean).
Machinery: Geared turbines; 6 Kampon boilers; 2 shafts.
Performance: 65,000shp; 29kts.
Bunkerage: 2,490 tons / 2,530 tonnes.
Range: 10,000nm at 14kts.
Aircraft: 48.

Guns: 12 × 5in.
Complement: 600.

Design The construction of *Akagi* and *Kaga* used up a nominal 53,800 tons of Japan's Washington-allocated carrier tonnage; *Hosho*, under 10,000 tons, was discounted, and for her next vessel Japan chose to build, under the 1927 Programme, a further unit which would not be subject to treaty restrictions. The result was a rather unsatisfactory design in which somewhat ambitious aircraft facilities were married to a hull which, having much in common with those of contemporary cruisers (less their armour), plainly could not cope with the demands made of it.

The original plans called for a single, full-length hangar, but with the realisation that this would restrict the embarked air group to something less than thirty machines, the design was hastily re-jigged by the straightforward expedient of adding a second hangar above the first. Displacement was kept at about 8,000 tons (9,990 tons trial) by restricting protection practically to nil, but stability suffered as a result of the added topweight, relative and real, and the carrier was back in dockyard hands for modification within eighteen months of first commissioning.

Below: *Ryujo* at speed, 1934. The massive sponsons forward of amidships support the ship's 5in battery; by this time the additional mountings aft had been removed. The bridge, as can be seen, was situated immediately below the forward edge of the flight deck. (By courtesy of A. D. Baker III)

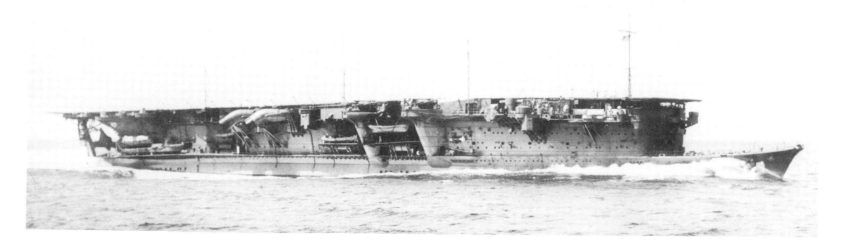

Unlike her larger predecessors, *Ryujo* did not have extended hangar decks in the form of flying-off platforms, and her single flight deck terminated some 70ft from the bows, affording the bridge below the forward edge an unrestricted field of view, but minimising an already short runway. There was a large lift forward and a smaller one aft, and arresting gear of the transverse type was installed. The boiler uptakes were routed over to the starboard side to discharge in two downward-canted funnels abaft amidships, and the six twin 5in guns, mounted on sponsons below the level of the flight deck and commanding good sky arcs, were supplemented by two dozen 13.2mm machine-guns.

Modifications *Ryujo* was refitted at Yokosuka from 1934 to 1936 in an attempt to overcome the stability problems. The hull was strengthened and ballasted, and the bulges were widened, giving a beam of 68ft 2in. In a desperate move to reduce topweight, the aftermost 5in mountings and their sponsons were landed and a pair of twin 25mm installed. The modifications increased displacement to 10,800 tons standard and 13,650 tons deep load (12,531 tons trial), but the inevitable effect was a dramatic increase in draught (to 23ft 3in mean), and the consequent reduction in freeboard meant that the carrier was quickly back for still further modifications: her forecastle was raised, and at the same time, the bridge was reshaped to more aerodynamic contours. During early 1942 the close-range battery was improved by the addition of six extra 25mm (triple) mountings, by which time the air group consisted of B5Ns and A5Ms; she had re-equipped with 27 A6Ms ('Zeke', one-third of which were employed in the fighter-bomber role) and six B5N ('Kate') torpedo-bombers by the time of her loss.

Service Notes A busy first six months of the Second World War saw *Ryujo*'s aircraft in action covering the landings on the Philippines (December 1941) and in the East Indies (January 1942), carrying out attacks on shipping (US destroyer *Pope* sunk, March) and striking at installations in the Aleutians (June). On 24 August of that year, while operating off Guadalcanal, she was hit by SBDs and TBFs from the US carrier *Saratoga*, was set afire, and sank.

Left: The light carrier *Ryujo* suffered from stability problems, stemming largely from the topweight of a double hangar upon what was in essence a slim cruiser hull. This photograph emphasises the carrier's top-heavy appearance. (Japanese Official)

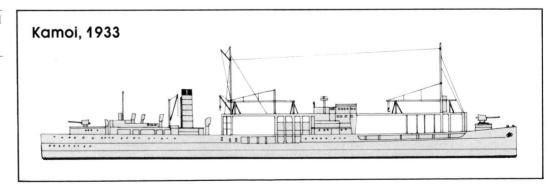

Below: The seaplane carrier *Kamoi* as originally completed, owing much to earlier Japanese designs for such ships in that her conversion entailed principally the erection of roofed platforms over the well decks and the installation of a small defensive gun battery. (By courtesy of Ray Burt)

KAMOI

Builder	Laid down	Launched	Commissioned
New York SB	14 Sept 21	8 June 22	1933

Displacement: 17,000 tons / 17,272 tonnes (standard).
Length: 488ft 6in / 148.9m (pp); 496ft / 151.18m (wl); 496ft / 151.18m (oa).
Beam: 67ft / 20.42m (hull).
Draught: 27ft 8in / 8.43m (mean).
Machinery: Curtis turbo-electric drive; 2 Yarrow boilers; 2 shafts.
Performance: 9,000shp; 15kts.
Bunkerage: 2,500 tons / 2,540 tonnes.
Aircraft: 12.
Guns: 2 × 5.5in; 2 × 80mm.

Design A coal-burning ex-oiler, 10,222grt and built in the USA, *Kamoi* was converted to a seaplane carrier at Tokyo in 1932–33. Platforms were erected across the well decks, and floatplanes were handled by derricks. The single 5.5in guns were mounted one

Kamoi, 1933

well forward on the forecastle and the other on the after superstructure; the 3in AA were also aft. Her role as an oiler was virtually unimpaired, and her bunkers could accommodate 10,000 tons of oil and 2,500 tons of coal.

Modifications *Kamoi* was modified in the mid 1930s for over-the-stern (Hein mat) recovery experiments, when a winch and a third, heavy derrick appeared right aft, the adjacent 5.5in gun apparently being landed.

Service Notes *Kamoi* was designated a flying boat tender in 1940, but surrendered all aircraft handling capabilities in 1943. She was sunk at Hong Kong during an air attack, date uncertain.

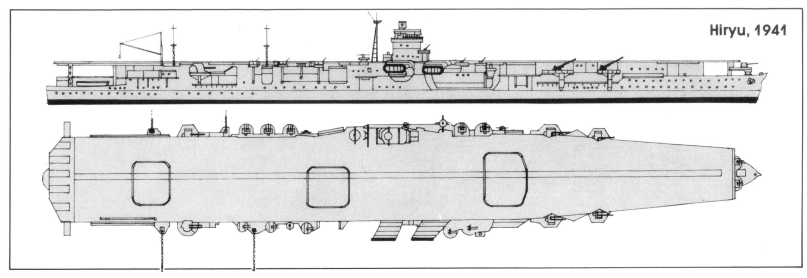

Hiryu, 1941

SORYU CLASS

Ship	Builder	Laid down	Launched	Commissioned
Soryu	Kure	20 Nov 34	21 Dec 35	29 Jan 37
Hiryu	Yokosuka	8 July 36	16 Nov 37	5 July 39

Above left: *Soryu* fitting out, late 1936. As in US carriers of the time, the hangar accommodation was built over the hull as a separate unit, the main deck rather than the flight deck providing rigidity. Note the AA platform above the forecastle. (Japanese Official)

Above right: *Hiryu* as completed, 1939. (Japanese Official)

Displacement: 15,900 tons / 16,154 tonnes
(standard); 19,800 tons / 20,117 tonnes (deep load).
Length: 677ft 6in / 206.5m (pp); 728ft 4in / 222m
(wl); 746ft 5in / 227.5m (oa); 705ft 6in / 215m (fd).
Beam: 69ft 11in / 21.3m (hull); 85ft 6in / 26m (fd).
Draught: 25ft / 7.62m (mean).
Machinery: Geared turbines; 8 Kampon boilers;
4 shafts.
Performance: 152,000shp; 34.5kts.
Bunkerage: 3,670 tons / 3,729 tonnes.
Range: 7,750nm at 18kts.
Aircraft: 71.
Guns: 12 × 5in; 28 × 25mm.
Complement: 1,100.

Design Although the carriers *Soryu* and *Hiryu* are generally grouped together they were, from the point of view of design, individually rather different. The starting-point for a particular class of carrier is frequently difficult to determine, given that warship development is generally an evolutionary, rarely revolutionary, process, but the origins of *Soryu* seem to lie with an innovative warship type which never actually materialised.

The Washington Treaty was still very much in force in 1930, and with the commissioning in the late 1920s of the first generation of fast fleet carriers, albeit all of them conversions of battleship or battlecruiser (strictly, in the case of the Royal Navy, 'large light cruiser') designs, the planning of additional units was well advanced. For the Japanese, however, there was a problem inasmuch as the first two ships, *Akagi* and *Kaga*, had, as suggested earlier, eaten up a very large slice of their allocated carrier tonnage. *Ryujo* was an interesting experiment, but by

1931 it was becoming apparent that she would have serious deficiencies. One solution was probably prompted at the 1930 London Naval Conference. The US delegation reminded all present that an aircraft carrier, in order to be thus defined, was a vessel designed expressly for the purpose of carrying aircraft; by implication, therefore, a ship that was really a gun platform but was fitted with, say, a 600ft flight deck as a sort of afterthought was not.[*]

Such a design was finalised in Japan in 1932 – a 17,500-ton vessel armed with 6 × 8in guns in three

[*] At about the same time a 'flight-deck cruiser' was a serious proposal in the United States, though with a less blatant air capability.

twin turrets in stacked, superfiring positions forward. With an island superstructure and a downward-venting funnel amidships, it was less of a gun platform than *Akagi* and *Kaga*, although it did sacrifice auxiliary flying-off decks (which were rapidly becoming an unattractive proposition anyway). The following year another design was prepared, this time with a full-length flight deck and a vast vertical uptake, but otherwise with the same general characteristics as its predecessor although, interestingly, it did incorporate a stern plated up to flight-deck level.

Apparently, at about this time Japan made up its mind to abrogate the Treaty, since the future direction of the carrier fleet was finalised by the ordering, under the 1931–32 Supplementary Programme, of a pair of carriers, based on the preliminary conceptions described above, whose combined displacements would take its total tonnage over the 81,000 limit, although the first, *Soryu*, would on its own not violate international agreement. They would set the pattern for all future Japanese vessels.

The hull was a very light structure for a ship of *Soryu*'s size, and since powerful, cruiser-type machinery was selected the carrier proved to be exceptionally fast. Protection was limited, the machinery receiving 1.8in armour along the belt and a 1in deck above, and the magazines 2.2in horizontal armour. The cruiser-calibre armament of the preliminary designs was rejected completely, an all-DP/AA battery of six twin 5in / 40 and fourteen twin 25mm mountings being fitted, three of the latter being installed over the bows, just below the flight-deck edge. All the weapons along the starboard side abaft the two downward-pointing funnels were enclosed, to protect the crews from boiler gases.

The 'double-decked' hangar arrangement was retained in *Soryu*, although this was not readily conveyed by the carrier's external appearance; designed as a carrier, as opposed to being an adaptation of some other type, she was able to integrate the lower hangar well within the hull structure instead of having it superimposed on top of the hull. The upper hangar was somewhat longer than the lower (about 520ft, compared to about 420ft), reflecting the fining of the bows, and there were three lifts: a large one forward, abreast the starboard-sited island, and two smaller units, offset to starboard, further aft. Initially, *Soryu* carried 63 operational aircraft with nine in reserve, and petrol capacity was about 150,000 gallons.

Some six months after *Soryu*'s launch the keel for *Hiryu* was laid, but during the building of the first ship some fundamental modifications had been made to the design. Apparently as a result of storm damage which afflicted the Japanese Fourth Fleet in 1935, the hull was strengthened and the forecastle heightened, and at the same time beam was increased, protection enhanced (belt to 3.5in across the machinery and 5.9in along the magazines; horizontal protection was unchanged) and the defensive battery redistributed. The data in the table refer to *Soryu*; *Hiryu* displaced 17,300 tons standard and 21,900 tons deep load, measured 688ft 9in pp, 731ft 9in wl and 745ft oa with a 73ft 3in beam (flight deck 88ft 6in) and 25ft 9in mean draught, had an oil bunkerage of 4,400 tons and could operate 64 aircraft (maximum capacity 73). More noticeably, *Hiryu* had her island to port, as did *Akagi* following modernisation. Unlike *Soryu* also, the fixed DP battery was disposed symmetrically, four pairs forward and two aft, and the bow and port-side Hotchkiss-type 25mm weapons apparently com-

Top: A January 1938 photograph of *Soryu*. Not obvious in this view is the fact that the carrier's island is situated to starboard; her semi-sister's differed in being disposed to port. (US Naval Historical Center)

Above: An important visual difference between *Hiryu* (shown) and *Soryu* was the degree of freeboard accorded to the hull, a point borne out by comparing this photograph with the previous one. (By courtesy of A. D. Baker III)

prised the new triple mountings. Funnels discharged to starboard, as in the earlier carrier.

Modifications Believed none.

Service Notes *Soryu* took part in operations against the Chinese in 1939, and following her involvement in the attack on Pearl Harbor she supported Japanese progress through the Western Pacific, striking at Wake Island and supporting landings through the East Indies. In February 1942 she assisted in the strike on Port Darwin and operated in the Indian Ocean during the following month, her aircraft taking part in the attacks on the British cruisers *Cornwall* and *Dorsetshire* and on the carrier *Hermes*. On 4 June, at Midway, she was hit by three bombs from *Yorktown*'s aircraft; two penetrated into the upper hangar, setting off fires which eventually overtook the carrier and culminated in a violent explosion as she went down.

Hiryu: Throughout her career the partner of *Soryu*, joining in the same actions, *Hiryu* was also lost at Midway, on 5 June 1942, when she was surprised by a force of US SBDs from *Enterprise* and *Hornet*. Set afire by four bombs, the enveloping flames were uncontrollable and the carrier was abandoned and deliberately torpedoed by the Japanese destroyer *Makigumo*; it is not clear whether the scuttling attempt was conclusive, since several hours elapsed before *Hiryu* sank.

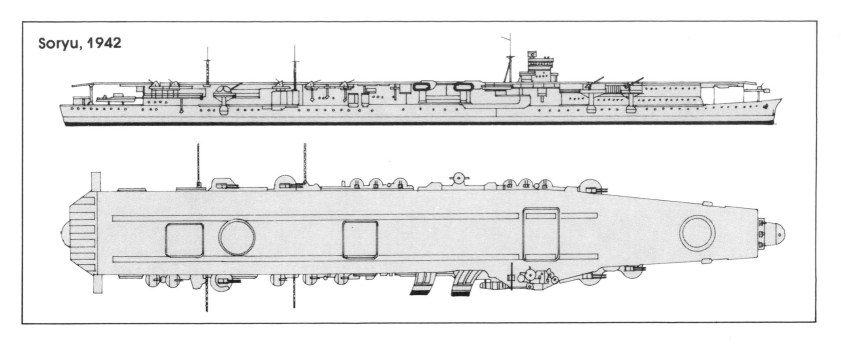

Soryu, 1942

CHITOSE CLASS

Ship	Builder	Laid down	Launched	Commissioned
Chitose	Kure	26 Nov 34	29 Nov 36	25 July 38
Chiyoda	Kure	14 Dec 36	19 Nov 37	15 Dec 38

Displacement: 11,023 tons / 11,199 tonnes (standard).
Length: 570ft 10in / 174m (pp); 603ft 4in / 183.9m (wl); 631ft 7in / 192.5m (oa).
Beam: 61ft 8in / 18.8m (hull).
Draught: 23ft 8in / 7.21m (mean).
Machinery: Geared turbines / diesel engines; 4 Kampon boilers; 2 shafts.
Performance: 44,000shp / 12,800bhp; 29kts.
Bunkerage: 3,500 tons / 3,556 tonnes.
Range: 8,000nm at 18kts.
Aircraft: 24.
Guns: 4 × 5in; 12 × 25mm.
Design From about 1934 Japanese warship construction took on a new slant. By this time Japan

had determined that conflict in the Pacific, or at least in the Western Pacific, was extremely likely in the future, and began to take some precautions. In order not to advertise her intentions too baldly, however, she instituted a policy of 'shadow' building programmes whereby a number of vessels were laid down to designs that permitted rapid adaptation for an alternative role should the need arise; in particular, Japan was looking towards a carrier fleet which could be quickly mobilised.

The first such ships were a pair of vessels which, ostensibly, were seaplane carriers/tenders, but which could with relative ease be configured into oilers, submarine depot ships or (as events would prove) fully flush-decked aircraft carriers. Ordered in the

1931–32 Supplementary Programme, they were to be the forerunners of a small group of singularly unusual ships. Mixed propulsion was selected, giving both good speed and a high cruising range, but the ships were more evidently remarkable for their profile: a neat, compact bridge superstructure well forward with a single funnel abaft it, behind which was a flat upper deck almost 400ft long, relieved amidships by a huge 125ft × 60ft platform covering a servicing area and supported on four substantial pillars. These doubled as diesel uptake casings (forward pair) and as machinery rooms for two heavy cranes (after pair). A derrick was sited adjacent to each pillar and a fifth unit was positioned right at the stern, offset to port. The upper deck itself was covered in a system of tracks and turntables for the movement of floatplanes, which could be launched via four catapults, a pair abreast the funnel and a pair abaft the platform, flanking a lift serving a below-decks hangar.

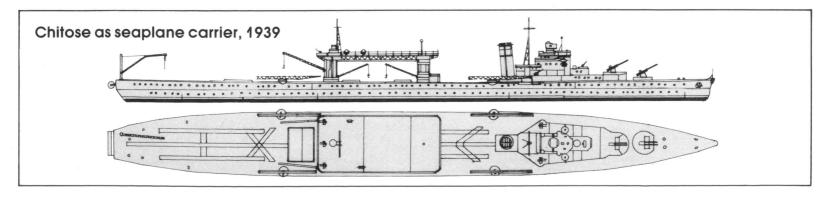

Chitose as seaplane carrier, 1939

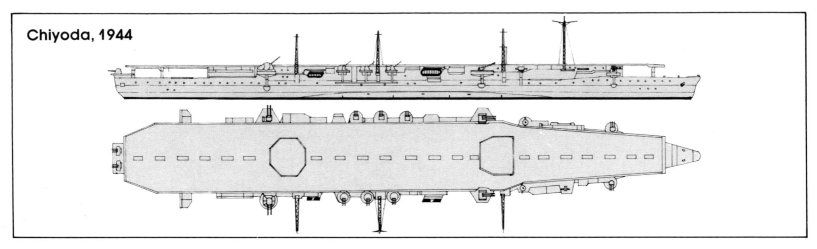

Chiyoda, 1944

Hein mat recovery gear was fitted at the ships' stern.
Modifications The data in the table refer to *Chitose*
and *Chiyoda* as first completed, but in 1941 each had
the stern modified to permit the launching of midget
submarines, twelve of which could be stowed in the
adapted hangar and discharged via a pair of doors.
Seaplane complement was reduced to twelve as a
result of this modification. Both vessels underwent a
more far-reaching conversion in 1942–44 to refit
them as conventional aircraft carriers. The hull was

modified by additional bulging to maintain stability
(beam increased to 68ft 3in), and a hangar
approximately 300ft long was built on top of the
upper deck, boiler trunking being carried over to the
starboard side to discharge via a single downward-
canted funnel. The flight deck (590ft 6in × 75ft) was
served by two lifts, and thirty aircraft could be
accommodated, while gun armament consisted of
8 × 5in / 40 DP in twin mountings and 30 × 25mm
in triple mounts, all in deck-edge sponsons, those aft

on the starboard side being enclosed as was normal
practice; two of the 25mm mountings were located at
the stern. With the removal of the midships platform
and its associated machinery, displacement did not
increase dramatically, the carriers showing 11,190
tons standard, 13,431 tons trial and 15,300 tons
deep load following reconstruction with a waterline
length of 610ft and a mean draught of 24ft 8in.
Complement reached 800 and oil fuel bunkerage
dropped to 1,000 tons.

Chitose was converted at Sasebo, recommissioning
on 1 January 1944; *Chiyoda* completed about two
months earlier, 31 October 1943, at Yokosuka Navy
Yard. By the time they were lost each had received an
additional six triple 25mm mountings.
Service Notes *Chitose* received her first taste of
action on 4 January 1942 when she sustained
superficial damage from B-17 bombs at Davao,
Philippines. She subsequently helped cover Japanese
landings in the East Indies and Gilbert Islands.
Damaged at the Battle of Eastern Solomons, August
1942, she was repaired and then taken in hand for
reconstruction. She was lost off Cape Engaño,
Northern Philippines, on 25 October 1944 when,
during an attack carried out by aircraft from *Essex* and
Lexington, a bomb struck her aft.
Chiyoda, like *Chitose*, was part of Yamamoto's
reserve at Midway, but took no effective part in the
battle. She too was lost off Cape Engaño, sunk by
cruiser fire and destroyer torpedoes in a confrontation
with units from Task Force 38, 25 October 1944.

Above: *Chitose* as first completed, her lines dominated by the
distinctive platform amidships. Three of the carrier's catapults
can be traced, seemingly covered with protective material. (By
courtesy of Ray Burt)

Left: A feature of Japanese shipbuilding during the late 1930s
was the provision in certain ships for rapid reconfiguration to
aircraft carriers should the need arise — the so-called
'shadow' programme. Both units of the *Chitose* class were
built with this in mind, and both were subsequently converted
to full-deck carriers. Here *Chitose* shows her new look, 1944.
(Japanese Official)

MIZUHO

Builder	Laid down	Launched	Commissioned
Kawasaki	1 May 37	6 May 38	25 Feb 39

Displacement: 10,929 tons / 11,104 tonnes (standard).
Length: 570ft 10in / 174m (pp); 603ft 4in / 183.9m (wl); 631ft 6in / 192.5m (oa).
Beam: 61ft 8in / 18.8m (hull).
Draught: 23ft 4in / 7.1m (mean).
Machinery: 4-cylinder diesel engines; 2 shafts.
Performance: 15,200shp; 22kts.
Bunkerage: 3,600 tons / 3,658 tonnes.
Range: 8,000nm at 16kts.
Aircraft: 24.
Guns: 6 × 5in; 12 × 25mm.

Design Virtually a repeat *Chitose* with an almost identical hull and layout, *Mizuho* was, however, rather more heavily armed and was purely diesel-powered, resulting in a considerable drop in speed. Her bridge configuration was similar to *Chitose*'s but she lacked the latter's funnel, the diesel engines exhausting via the pillars, each pair of which were joined athwartships by a narrow platform but did not support a complete roof. The 5in twin mountings were disposed one well forward on the forecastle and a pair abreast the bridge. The decrease in topweight led

to a shallower draught and a lesser displacement (11,960 tons trial) over the earlier design.

Mizuho was conceived under the 1937 Programme, and although plans existed for her full conversion to aircraft carrier configuration these were never put into effect.

Modifications In 1944 she was modified, as *Chitose*, to operate a dozen midget submarines, her stern seaplane recovery gear was landed, and two additional triple 25mms were installed.

Above: *Mizuho* at Tsingtao, 1939. (US Naval Historical Center)

Service Notes *Mizuho* helped cover the landings in the Philippines and on Ambon (with *Chitose*, December 1941–January 1942) and subsequent Japanese invasions, but was sunk by torpedoes from the US submarine *Drum*, 2 May 1942, off Cape Omai-Zake, Southern Honshu.

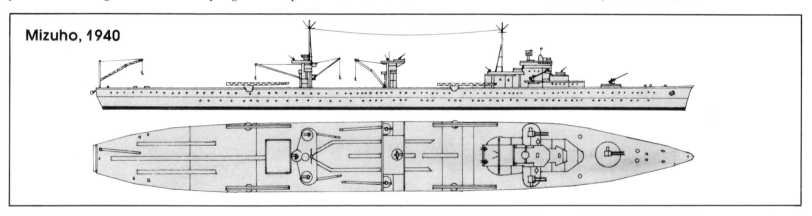

Mizuho, 1940

SHOHO CLASS

Ship	Builder	Laid down	Launched	Commissioned
Shoho	Yokosuka	3 Dec 34	1 June 35	26 Jan 42
Zuiho	Yokosuka	20 June 35	19 June 36	27 Dec 40

Displacement: 11,262 tons / 11,442 tonnes (standard); 14,200 tons / 14,427 tonnes (deep load).
Length: 606ft 11in / 185m (pp); 660ft 11in / 201.45m (wl); 674ft 3in / 205.5m (oa); 590ft 6in / 180m (fd).
Beam: 59ft 9in / 18.2m (hull); 75ft 6in / 23m (fd).
Draught: 21ft 7in / 6.58m (mean).
Machinery: Geared turbines; 4 Kampon boilers; 2 shafts.

Performance: 52,000shp; 28kts.
Bunkerage: 2,500 tons / 2,540 tonnes.
Range: 7,800nm at 18kts.
Aircraft: 30.
Guns: 8 × 5in; 8 × 25mm.
Complement: 785.

Design Further products of the Japanese 'shadow' programmes were a pair of 9,500-ton (standard displacement) submarine depot ships, *Tsurugisaki* and

Takasaki, which were designed with the capacity for future conversion to either oilers or fully fledged aircraft carriers. Only the former completed for her original role, showing a built-up superstructure and a single, raked funnel amidships. She could handle three floatplanes which were hoisted by derricks abaft the bridge and stowed in an enclosed hangar built on to the upper deck. A pair of twin 5in / 40 weapons were carried, one forward and one aft, and there were also 12 × 13.2mm machine-guns. She completed for service in January 1939, but two years later was taken in hand for conversion to a flush-decked aircraft carrier, to be renamed *Shoho*. *Takasaki* was modified

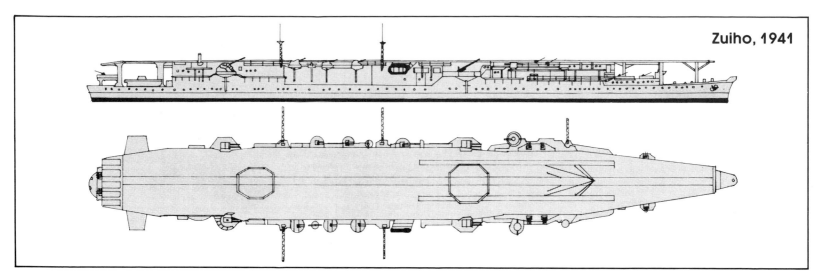

Zuiho, 1941

Above: *Shoho* in late 1941, just prior to commissioning, her flight-deck profile broken only by her radio masts and auxiliary uptake right aft. The smoke plume, incidentally, is not being generated by the carrier, but by (presumably) another ship hidden from the camera. (By courtesy of A. D. Baker III)

Left: A much-published but nevertheless interesting photograph of *Zuiho* under attack by US aircraft in the Philippine Sea, October 1944. Camouflaging carrier flight decks was ever a difficulty: if too effective it would be distinctly unhelpful to friendly aircraft. (US National Archives)

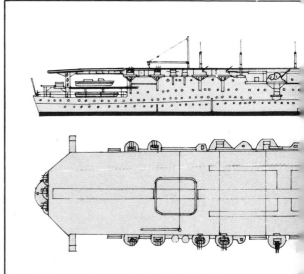

prior to completion as a depot ship, her reconstruction occupying some four years; she was renamed *Zuiho*.

In their guise as carriers both ships featured a single hangar some 350ft long, adapted from the original short seaplane hangar, and the earlier 56,000bhp diesels were replaced by destroyer-type machinery in order to retain the speed required on the increased displacement. Two lifts served the flight deck, which narrowed considerably towards the bows; there was no island, and the funnel was sited below the starboard deck-edge in the usual manner. A characteristic feature was a small, hinged stack right aft on the starboard side connected to an auxiliary boiler. The 5in guns were twin-mounted abreast the

lifts and there were two pairs of twin 25mm amidships.

Modifications In 1943 *Zuiho* received additional 25mm guns in the form of half a dozen triple mountings, enhanced in the following year by a further twenty barrels, at which time six 8-barrelled rocket-launchers were also fitted to strengthen the anti-aircraft defence. The flight deck was extended over the forecastle, giving an overall deck length of 632ft.

Service Notes *Shoho* was an early war loss, sunk by bombs and torpedoes from *Yorktown*'s aircraft at the Battle of the Coral Sea on 7 May 1942: she was quickly engulfed in flames and went down within minutes.

Zuiho helped to provide distant cover during the invasions in the East Indies in early 1942, and suffered serious bomb damage at Santa Cruz on 25 October 1942, under attack from *Enterprise*'s aircraft. Following repairs, she participated in operations off Guadalcanal (December 1942) and the Marianas (June 1943), but was sunk at Cape Engaño on 25 October 1944 during the Leyte Gulf campaign, hit by bombs and four hours later struck by torpedoes and further bombs directed by aircraft from Task Force 38.

SHOKAKU CLASS

Ship	Builder	Laid down	Launched	Commissioned
Shokaku	Yokosuka	12 Dec 37	1 June 39	8 Aug 41
Zuikaku	Kawasaki	25 May 38	27 Nov 39	25 Sept 41

Displacement: 25,675 tons / 26,086 tonnes (standard); 32,105 tons / 32,619 tonnes (deep load).
Length: 774ft 3in / 236m (pp); 820ft 3in / 250m (wl); 844ft 10in / 257.5m (oa); 787ft / 240m (fd).
Beam: 85ft 4in / 26m (hull); 95ft / 29m (fd).
Draught: 29ft / 8.85m (mean).
Machinery: Geared turbines; 8 Kampon boilers; 4 shafts.
Performance: 160,000shp; 34.25kts.
Bunkerage: 5,300 tons / 5,385 tonnes.
Range: 10,000nm at 18kts.
Aircraft: 84.
Guns: 16 × 5in; 36 × 25mm.
Complement: 1,660.

Design The two fleet carriers designed in 1936–37 were without question the most successful operated by the Imperial Japanese Navy; they had all the virtues and few of the vices of the *Soryus* and were, moreover, considerably larger, better armed and more heavily armoured, and could accommodate a larger air group. Their one principal defect was the light construction of the flight deck, aggravated by totally enclosed yet unprotected double hangars and unsatisfactory petrol bunkerage, but of course the proof of this was not available at the time of their conception.

A longer, beamier hull allowed the provision of heavy-cruiser type 6.5in belt armour along the

magazines, reinforced with a further 1.8in across the machinery spaces, with a 3.9in armour deck over the latter and 5.1in over the former. The bulged clipper bow which would also be a feature of the *Yamato*-class battleships was also incorporated, while extremely powerful machinery bestowed a high sustained sea speed. The original design reportedly envisaged islands to port on one ship and to starboard on the other, together with a funnel to port and to starboard on each, but the ships as completed were generally similar, with both superstructure and uptakes on the starboard side.

The wooden flight deck, planked except in the region of the two converging catapult tracks forward and over the boiler uptakes, was serviced by three lifts measuring 42ft 6in × 52ft 6in (forward), 42ft 6in × 39ft 4in (amidships) and 38ft 6in × 42ft 6in (aft), and there were eight transverse arrester wires aft and three further forward, with a hinged screen abaft the catapults to provide a wind break. Eight twin 5in / 40 were disposed along the deck edge in pairs forward and aft, and the 25mm triple mountings were distributed along the flight-deck edge, those abaft the funnel on the starboard side being enclosed as in most other Japanese carriers.

The original designed air group numbered 96 machines (24 B5N torpedo-bombers, 24 D1A dive-bombers, twelve A5M fighters, twelve C3N reconnaissance planes, 24 reserves), but with the cancellation of the C3N and the phasing out of the D1A and A5M the air group upon completion consisted of 27 B5N, 27 D3A ('Val') dive-bombers and eighteen A6M fighters, with twelve machines in reserve. Trial displacement for each carrier was 29,330 tons.

Modifications As was the pattern in the US and Royal Navies, wartime modifications to the surviving units of Japan's carrier fleet were concerned principally with the upgrading of the anti-aircraft battery. By the summer of 1942 both *Shokaku* and

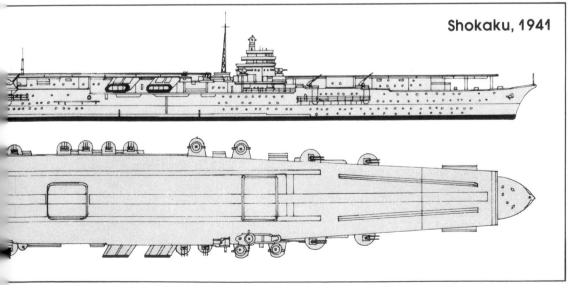

Shokaku, 1941

Zuikaku had had two additional triple 25mm mountings added at the stern and two at the bows, bolstered later that year with a third at both bow and stern and sixteen single 25mms forward. By the time of her loss Zuikaku had received even more weapons – two more triples, one before and one abaft the island, and twenty more singles, half of which were portable and, operating independently of the ship's power supply, were dispersed about the flight deck during periods when aircraft were not operating; there were also six 28-barrelled rocket-launchers forward. At some time during 1943–44 both carriers received Type 13 air warning and Type 21 air/surface warning radar systems,* and following her near-loss in May 1944 Zuikaku had her petrol bunkers reinforced with concrete in an effort to exclude air from the spaces surrounding them and hence mixing with the vapour.

*Some writers refer to the Type 13 as 'Type 3 Mk 1' and to the Type 21 as 'Type 2 Mk 2'.

Service Notes *Shokaku*: It seems likely that the timing of the Japanese attack on Pearl Harbor, 7 December 1941, was determined partly by the fact that both *Shokaku* and *Zuikaku* would by then be ready for combat, and both carriers played a leading role in that venture. *Shokaku* carried out raids on New Guinea the following month, and in May 1942 was seriously damaged in the Coral Sea when hit by three bombs; her aircraft accounted for *Lexington* during that action, but on her return to Japan for repairs she almost sank. She was hit once during the Battle of Eastern Solomons (August 1942), and very badly damaged during her next major engagement, Santa Cruz (October 1942), when she was caught by aircraft from *Hornet* and received six direct bomb hits. On 19 June 1944, in the Battle of the Philippine Sea, she was sunk by four torpedoes fired by the submarine *Cavalla*: afire and badly listing, she eventually turned turtle.

Zuikaku's career followed that of her sister-ship for

Top: The *Shokaku*s were in many respects the most successful Japanese carriers of the Second World War. This is the name-ship, shortly after commissioning. Note the enclosed gun mountings abaft the funnels, affording a measure of habitability to the crews. (By courtesy of A. D. Baker III)

Above: *Zuikaku*, 25 September 1941. (US Naval Historical Center)

the first six months of the war, her aircraft also being involved in the sinking of *Lexington*. She escaped damage in that action, and subsequently took part in the Aleutians operations. *Zuikaku* was seriously mauled during the Battle of the Philippine Sea, but her crew managed to overcome the fires which threatened to engulf the carrier. In October 1944, however, while assisting in feints to draw the US carriers supporting the Leyte Gulf landings (Cape Engaño), she was hit first by one torpedo and later by a further six torpedoes and seven bombs and was sunk (25th).

TAIYO CLASS

Ship	Builder	Laid down	Launched	Commissioned
Taiyo	Mitsubishi	6 Jan 40	19 Sept 40	15 Sept 41
Unyo	Mitsubishi	14 Dec 38	31 Oct 39	31 May 42
Chuyo	Mitsubishi	9 May 38	20 May 39	25 Nov 42

Displacement: 17,830 tons / 18,115 tonnes (standard).
Length: 551ft 2in / 168m (pp); 569ft 11in / 173.7m (wl); 591ft 4in / 180.24m (oa); 492ft / 150m (fd).
Beam: 73ft 10in / 22.5m (hull); 75ft 6in / 23m (fd).
Draught: 25ft 5in / 7.75m (mean).
Machinery: Geared turbines; 4 boilers; 2 shafts.
Performance: 25,200shp; 21kts.
Range: 6,500nm at 18kts.
Aircraft: 27.
Guns: 6×4.7in; 8×25mm.
Complement: 747.

Design From about 1940, in common with the other two major navies, the Japanese Navy had a pressing need for as large a number of flight decks as possible and, as in the USA and Great Britain, a number of merchantmen were taken over for conversion. Three 21–22kt, 17,100grt passenger liners were first modified – *Kasuga Maru* (at Sasebo Navy Yard), *Yawata Maru* and *Nitta Maru* (Kure Navy Yard), renamed *Taiyo*, *Unyo* and *Chuyo* respectively – and

were commissioned as the rough equivalent of the early Allied escort carriers, though considerably larger.

The conversions were not major undertakings, the work in essence involving the re-routing of the boiler uptakes to starboard, discharging via the familiar downward-curved funnel amidships; the addition of a single 300ft hangar on the upper deck; the fitting of a flight deck; and the addition of some elderly medium-calibre AA and a few 25mm (although *Unyo* and *Chuyo* would receive 8×5in / 40 DP in twin mountings instead of the single 4.7s). There were two lifts, but no catapult and no arrester gear, while the requirement for a bow and a stern AA capability restricted flight-deck length. Each conversion occupied about six months and was expedited by the fact that none of the vessels had actually been completed for their original role and retained the original machinery.

Modifications By late 1943 additional light anti-aircraft weapons had been installed (16×25mm in

Taiyo and *Unyo*, 14×25mm and 5×13.2mm in *Chuyo*), and Type 21 radar was evident, mounted, since there was no island, directly on the starboard deck-edge. *Unyo* had half her DP battery removed and *Taiyo* had exchanged her 4.7in guns for two twin 5in / 40s by mid 1944, and both carriers were showing 64×25mm and 10×13.2mm AA.

Service Notes *Taiyo*: Used mainly for transport and training duties throughout her wartime career, but sailed with *Yamato* in a supporting role for the Eastern Solomons engagement, August 1942. Sunk by the US submarine *Rasher*, 18 August 1944, off Luzon, Philippines.

Unyo: Employed exclusively for transport and training. Sunk by torpedoes from the submarine *Barb* near Hong Kong, 16 September 1944.

Chuyo: Used as a transport and training carrier and sunk by the submarine *Sailfish* off Yokosuka, 4 December 1943.

Below: The urgency to commission the largest possible number of flight decks during the Second World War exercised the Japanese as well as the British and US Navies, and for all three services a number of mercantile hulls served as the basis for bringing such programmes into being. Among the earliest such undertakings were the three units of the *Taiyo* class. *Taiyo* is shown here; just visible, forward, is her Type 21 radar antenna. (Japanese Official)

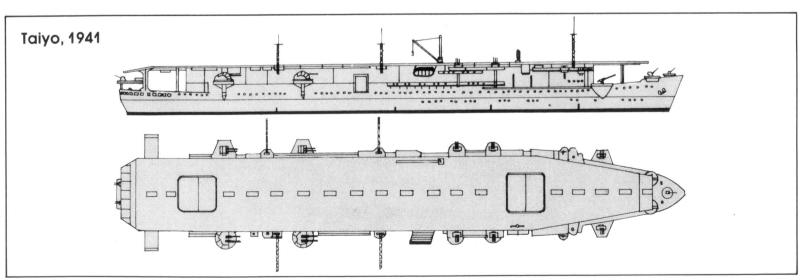

Taiyo, 1941

AKITSU MARU CLASS

Ship	Builder	Laid down	Launched	Commissioned
Akitsu Maru	Harima	17 Sept 39	24 Sept 41	30 Jan 42
Nigitsu Maru	Harima	June 41	1942	Mar 43

Displacement: 11,800 tons / 11,989 tonnes (standard).
Length: 471ft 7in / 143.75m (pp); 498ft 8in / 152m (wl); 404ft / 123m (fd).
Beam: 64ft / 19.5m (hull); 74ft / 22.5m (fd).
Draught: 25ft 9in / 7.85m (mean).
Machinery: Geared turbines; 4 boilers; 2 shafts.
Performance: 7,500shp; 20kts.
Aircraft: 20.
Guns: 12 × 3in.

Design The Navy was not the only Japanese service to operate combat ships during the Second World War. In order to support any progress through the East Indies and islands in the Western Pacific, the Army had concluded before the outbreak of war that an independently operated assault ship, under their command, might be more usefully employed if in addition to its carrying troops and equipment it were to be fitted with a flight deck so that JAAF aircraft could not only be transported with a landing force, but also flown off the vessel to assist in the rapid establishment of a land-based air defence unit.

Hence a number of merchantmen were requisitioned for conversion, the first pair being *Akitsu Maru* (9,186grt) and *Nigitsu Maru* (9,547grt), both ex-passenger vessels. Reconstruction was limited to redirecting the boiler uptakes to the starboard side to emerge as a single funnel, decking over the superstructure, installing a pair of handling derricks and adding 2 × 3in AA and 10 × 3in Army-type ex-field guns, the latter presumably for shore bombardment. A basic lift was installed aft to bring up aircraft from beneath the flight deck (there was no hangar in the usual sense of the word); an alternative cargo would be twenty standard (46ft) landing craft, in which case fewer aircraft could, of course, be carried.

Modifications Plans formulated in early 1944 to extend *Akitsu Maru*'s flying-off deck over the stern were not proceeded with.

Service Notes *Akitsu Maru*: Details of wartime operations not known. Sunk by torpedoes from the US submarine *Queenfish* off Kyushu, 15 November 1944.

Nigitsu Maru: Details of wartime operations not known. Sunk by the submarine *Hake*, 12 January 1944, about 700 miles east of Formosa.

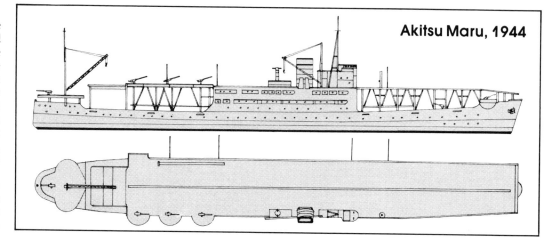

Akitsu Maru, 1944

NISSHIN

Builder	Laid down	Launched	Commissioned
Kure	Nov 38	30 Nov 39	27 Feb 42

Displacement: 11,317 tons / 11,498 tonnes (standard).
Length: 570ft 10in / 174m (pp); 616ft 10in / 188m (wl); 636ft 6in / 194m (oa).
Beam: 64ft 8in / 19.7m (hull).
Draught: 23ft / 7m (mean).
Machinery: 6-cylinder diesel engines; 2 shafts.
Performance: 47,000bhp; 28kts.
Range: 11,000nm at 18kts.
Aircraft: 25.
Guns: 6 × 5in; 18 × 25mm.

Above: The seaplane carrier *Nisshin* continued with the distinctive configuration established by earlier Japanese vessels of her genre; note, however, the three twin turrets forward. Like her predecessors, she was equipped also to operate midget submarines. (Japanese Official)

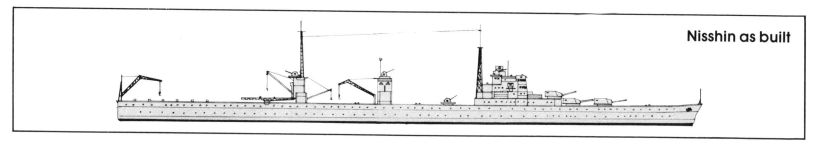

Nisshin as built

Design A further development of the *Chitose* design, the seaplane carrier *Nisshin* was ordered under the 1937 Programme. As with *Mizuho*, she lacked the original high platform aft, but she was equipped with only two catapults and her 5in armament was grouped in three centreline turrets forward. She was also larger than *Mizuho* (trial displacement 12,300 tons) and was fitted for minelaying, capacity being 700 mines, replacing all aircraft and discharging by means of doors at the stern. Considerably more powerful machinery was installed, tripling the shaft horsepower compared to *Mizuho* and raising speed by about 6kts.

Two improved *Nisshin*s (13,500 tons standard) were planned in 1942, but not proceeded with.

Modifications New ramps were fitted in the stern some time in 1942 to enable the ship to operate midget submarines.

Service Notes Part of Yamamoto's 'Special Duty' force, with *Chiyoda, Nisshin* was available for the Midway battle in June 1942, but was not actually involved. She was sunk off the west coast of Bougainville by US aircraft while bringing up troop reinforcements, 22 July 1943.

HIYO CLASS

Ship	Builder	Laid down	Launched	Commissioned
Hiyo	Kawasaki	30 Nov 39	24 June 41	31 July 42
Junyo	Mitsubishi	20 Mar 39	26 June 41	5 May 42

Displacement: 24,140 tons / 24,526 tonnes (standard); 29,000 tons / 29,464 tonnes (deep load).
Length: 675ft 10in / 206m (pp); 706ft 4in / 215.3m (wl); 719ft 6in / 219.3m (oa); 689ft / 210m (fd).
Beam: 87ft 7in / 26.7m (hull); 89ft 6in / 27.25m (fd).
Draught: 26ft 9in / 8.15m (mean).
Machinery: Geared turbines; 6 Kampon boilers; 2 shafts.
Performance: 56,250shp; 25.5kts.
Bunkerage: 3,000 tons / 3,048 tonnes.
Aircraft: 53.
Guns: 12 × 5in; 24 × 25mm.
Complement: 1,200.

Design Further products of the pre-war Japanese 'shadow' programme, these two ships were designed ostensibly as 27,500grt passenger liners for the North American route, but about a year prior to launch they were reportedly taken over by the Navy for completion as carriers. Doubts have been expressed as to whether there was any intention to complete them as merchant ships, but the names *Izumo Maru* (for *Hiyo*) and *Kashiwara Maru* (*Junyo*) had apparently been assigned and the mercantile origins of the vessels are clearly evident: a clean hull, a good sheer forward, armour protection limited to 1in over the machinery spaces, as a sort of after-thought, and subdivision within the hull which clearly would have been unacceptable in a purpose-designed warship. A further problem was topweight. The relatively light scantlings were not entirely suited to a two-hangar arrangement, but a single hangar would have accommodated a quite inadequate air group. A compromise was achieved by severely restricting hangar height, to only 10ft 6in clear in the case of the lower level, which was barely sufficient for the A6M, but virtually impossible for any of the current range of strike aircraft, even were propellers to be swung.

For the first time in a Japanese carrier the boiler uptakes were trunked together and routed through an island superstructure, gases emerging through a lofty funnel some 50ft above flight-deck level and angled outboard about 25° to keep fumes as far away from aircraft as possible and permitting open-type deck-edge battery mountings along the starboard side aft. *Junyo*'s boilers differed from those of *Hiyo* (data given), consisting of four Kampon and two Mitsubishi units; all were types used in destroyers, although the turbines themselves were part of the mercantile design.

The wood-planked flight deck reached maximum width throughout most of its length since the island was sponsored out from the hull and barely encroached on the flying platform proper, and it appears that the hull was asymmetrically bulged to compensate for the weight. The defensive battery – twin 5in / 40 and triple 25mm – was also sited on hull-mounted sponsons. There were two lifts, each about 45ft × 45ft, and the original assigned air group was made up of eighteen D3A, eighteen B5N and twelve A6M, plus two, five and three respectively as a

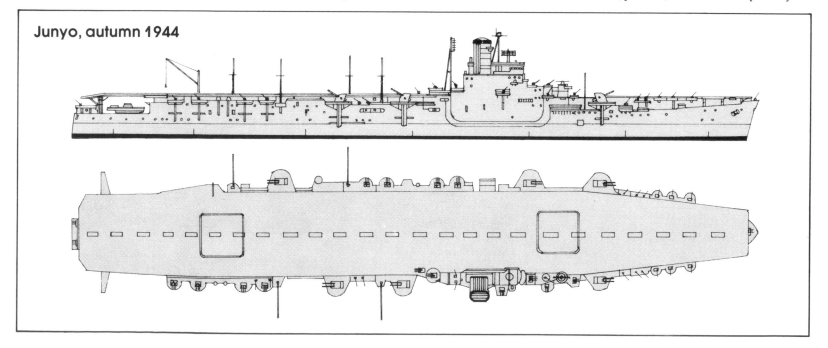

Junyo, autumn 1944

reserve, although, in the event, rather fewer of the latter were embarked.

Modifications During its second year of service each ship received an additional 16×25mm AA and by mid 1944 *Junyo* was showing 76×25mm total, many of the additional mountings being portable, single-barrelled weapons. Like *Zuikaku*, *Junyo* received concrete protection around her aviation fuel tanks before the end of her career, by which time she was fitted with Type 13 (on a tripod mast abaft the island) and Type 21 (atop the island and on the port-side flight-deck edge, aft) radar antennae. *Hiyo* was operating 27 A6M, six B6N and eighteen D3A by 1944; *Junyo* had a mix of D3A and D4Y dive-bombers at this time.

Service Notes *Hiyo*: In October 1942 *Hiyo*'s aircraft were engaged in attacking US warships in the Guadalcanal area, accounting for the destroyer *Meredith*, but the carrier suffered engine trouble soon afterwards and did not take part in the ensuing Santa Cruz action. She returned to Guadalcanal within a few weeks, however, escorting convoys and launching largely unsuccessful strikes against US shipping, including the carrier *Enterprise*. During the Battle of the Philippine Sea she was hit by torpedoes delivered by aircraft from the light carrier *Belleau Wood* and sank, 20 June 1944.

Junyo took part in the Aleutians attacks in June 1942, and prior to the Battle of Santa Cruz, during which she was engaged in strikes against the carrier *Enterprise* and the battleship *South Dakota* and cruiser *San Juan*, she assisted *Hiyo* in the despatch of the destroyer *Meredith*. She operated off Guadalcanal during the 'Tokyo Express' evacuations, January–February 1943. *Junyo* was seriously damaged during the Philippine Sea action and suffered further damage in December 1944 when she was hit by torpedoes from the submarines *Redfish* and *Sea Devil* off Nagasaki; she was never repaired and was laid up for the duration of the war, to be scrapped in 1947.

Left: The *Hiyo*s, for the first time in Japanese carrier design, incorporated their funnels within the island superstructure, although, still wary of the effects of smoke drift over the flight deck, the designers canted the uptake well over to starboard. *Junyo* is seen here at the end of the war, laid up in a damaged condition. (US Navy)

Below: Another view of *Junyo* after the close of hostilities, disarmed but otherwise relatively intact, even to the extent of her two Type 21 radar aerials. Note the flight deck wind-break, folded just ahead of the forward lift. (US Navy, by courtesy of A. D. Baker III)

RYUHO

Builder	Laid down	Launched	Commissioned
Yokosuka	12 Apr 33	16 Nov 33	28 Nov 42

Displacement: 13,360 tons / 13,574 tonnes
(standard); 16,500 tons / 16,764 tonnes (deep load).
Length: 647ft 4in / 197.3m (pp); 689ft / 210m (wl);
707ft 4in / 215.6m (oa); 607ft / 185m (fd).
Beam: 64ft 3in / 19.58m (hull); 75ft 6in / 23m (fd).
Draught: 21ft 9in / 6.63m (mean).
Machinery: Geared turbines; 4 Kampon boilers;
2 shafts.
Performance: 52,000shp; 26.5kts.
Bunkerage: 2,900 tons / 2,946 tonnes.
Range: 8,000nm at 18kts.
Aircraft: 31.
Guns: 8 × 5in; 38 × 25mm.
Complement: 989.

Design This carrier, like those of the *Shoho* class, was originally a submarine depot ship, but an earlier design, somewhat larger (10,000 tons standard) but much less powerfully engined (4 diesels, 14,000bhp, 20kts). As first completed (as *Taigei*, March 1934), she generally resembled *Tsurigisaki*, but was fitted with a pair of derricks aft. Two catapults were installed for launching her three scout floatplanes. She was hastily built and structurally defective, and in 1936–37 had to have her hull stressed and bulges added to improve stability.

She was deemed suitable for conversion to a carrier, however, and in 1942 was rebuilt at Yokosuka Navy Yard along the lines of *Shoho*, receiving destroyer-type machinery instead of her original diesels, a single hangar, a wooden flight deck terminating some 60ft from the stem and two lifts disposed one amidships and one well aft, larger than those fitted in the earlier ex-submarine tender conversions. There was no island, the ship being conned from a position below the forward flight deck in typical Japanese style. The funnel uptake was configured to starboard in the familiar way, and the twin 5in / 40 were sponson-mounted along the sides of the hull; six triple 25mm mountings were located abaft amidships below flight-deck level, the balance of the battery being made up of single mountings in bow, stern and deck-edge positions, plus a pair on the flight deck itself. Protection was limited to a ½in deck across the machinery spaces and magazines. Trial displacement was 15,060 tons.

Below: *Ryuho* at Kure, October 1945. The installation of turbine machinery caused delays and indeed gave considerable trouble to the ship in service. (US National Archives)

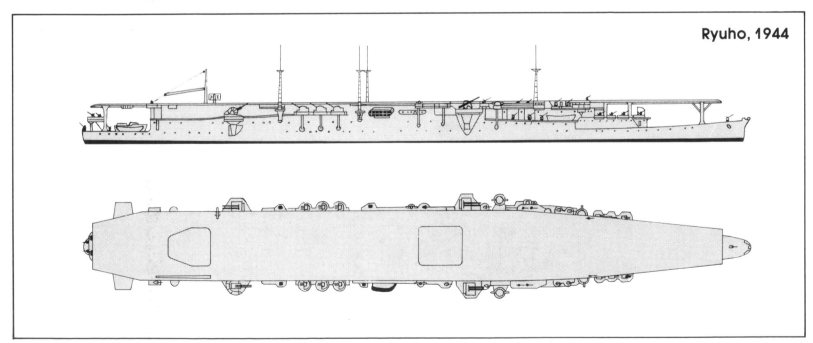

Ryuho, 1944

Modifications The light anti-aircraft battery was augmented in 1943 (to 42 × 25mm and 6 × 13.2mm) and again in 1944 (to 61 × 25mm, 21 × 13.2mm and six 28-barrelled rocket-launchers). The flight deck was extended over the forecastle in 1944, extreme dimensions now being 650ft × 75ft 6in, and a Type 21 warning radar set was added.

KAIYO

Builder	Laid down	Launched	Commissioned
Mitsubishi	22 Feb 38	9 Dec 38	23 Nov 43

Displacement: 13,600 tons / 13,818 tonnes (standard).
Length: 508ft 6in / 155m (pp); 523ft 7in / 159.6m (wl); 546ft 5in / 166.55m (oa); 492ft / 150m (fd).
Beam: 71ft 10in / 21.9m (hull); 72ft / 22m (fd).
Draught: 27ft / 8.25m (mean).
Machinery: Kampon geared turbines; 4 boilers; 2 shafts.
Performance: 52,000shp; 24kts.
Aircraft: 24.
Guns: 8 × 5in; 24 × 25mm.
Complement: 829.
Design The 12,755grt passenger liner *Argentina Maru* was first taken over by the Imperial Japanese

Navy in late 1941 for use as a troop transport, but during 1942 it became apparent that she might be more useful if converted to a carrier, albeit a rather small one which would have little practical use in a fast carrier fleet.

As with *Taiyo*, the conversion, which began late in 1942, was austere: the original diesel machinery was taken out and destroyer-type turbines substituted; the boilers were trunked over to starboard, venting in a downward-canted funnel; a hangar was built over the upper deck; a light wooden flight deck was erected on top; two lifts were installed; and a number of sponsons were built out around the hull to accommodate four twin 5in and six triple 25mm Hotchkiss, two further 25mm being located on a platform over the stern, below the flight-deck round-down. There was no island and there were no catapults, but the ship,

renamed *Kaiyo*, completed with a Type 21 radar antenna on the starboard flight-deck edge. Trial displacement was 16,483 tons.

It had been planned to convert a sister-ship, *Brazil Maru*, but she was lost in August 1942.
Modifications In mid 1944 *Kaiyo* was fitted with twenty further 25mm barrels and some 8-barrelled rocket-launchers, and she reportedly carried depth-charges for a limited ASW role.
Service Notes *Kaiyo* was generally employed as an aircraft transport up to mid 1944 and thereafter was used for air-crew training. She was disabled by aircraft from the British carriers *Formidable*, *Indefatigable* and *Victorious* off Beppu, Kyushu, on 24 July 1945 and was scrapped post-war.

SHINYO

Builder	Launched	Commissioned
Deschimag	14 Dec 34	15 Dec 43

Displacement: 17,500 tons / 17,780 tonnes (standard).
Length: 606ft 11in / 185m (pp); 621ft 3in / 189.35m (oa); 553ft / 168.5m (fd).
Beam: 84ft / 25.6m (hull); 80ft / 24.5m (fd).
Draught: 26ft 9in / 8.15m (mean).
Machinery: AEG geared turbines; 4 water-tube boilers; 2 shafts.
Performance: 26,000shp; 22kts.
Aircraft: 33.
Guns: 8 × 5in; 30 × 25mm.
Complement: 942.
Design The German (Norddeutscher Line) passenger

liner *Scharnhorst* (18,184grt), at Kobe when war broke out in Europe, was acquired by the Japanese Navy early in 1942 for possible use as a troop transport; with the disastrous losses at Midway, however, the ship was rapidly taken in for conversion to a makeshift aircraft carrier, mainly for the purposes of training fresh crews to replace lost pilots. So urgent was the need for additional flight decks at this time that battleship construction was halted (notably that of the fourth *Yamato*-class unit) and materials diverted to expedite carrier construction.

In general *Scharnhorst*'s conversion followed that of earlier, similar projects except that there was a particular problem caused by the pronounced sheer line of the hull which meant that the hangar deck had to be carried somewhat higher; this created some

instability, and as a result the hull was fitted with prominent bulges. The original German machinery was retained. The ship was conned from a bridge forward, below the flight deck, but there was a flight control position on the starboard flight-deck edge which could be retracted during flying operations. Type 21 radar was carried. The armament was the standard fit of twin 5in and triple 25mm, and there were two lifts.
Modifications The anti-aircraft battery was increased to 42 × 25mm in early 1944 and to 50 × 25mm by mid 1944.
Service Notes Used principally for training. Sunk 17 November 1944 by torpedoes from the submarine *Spadefish*, in the Yellow Sea.

KAMAKURA MARU PROJECT

Builder	Laid down	Launched
Yokohama	1928	1929

Displacement: 16,800 tons / 17,069 tonnes (standard).
Length: 560ft / 170.7m (pp); 565ft 11in / 172.5m (wl); 575ft 9in / 175.5m (oa); 500ft / 152.5m (fd).
Beam: 73ft 10in / 22.5m (hull).
Draught: 27ft 7in / 8.4m (mean).
Machinery: 8-cylinder Burmeister & Wain diesel engines; 2 shafts.
Performance: 16,000bhp; 20kts.
Bunkerage: 3,190 tons / 3,241 tonnes.
Aircraft: 38.
Guns: 8 × 5in; 24 × 25mm.
Design The former liner *Chichiba Maru* (17,526grt) was acquired by the Imperial Japanese Navy in 1941 as a hospital ship and general transport. Her

conversion to a carrier was planned during 1942, but she was sunk in April 1943 by the submarine *Gudgeon* before work could be put in hand. As completed she would have generally resembled other mercantile conversions though with her twin 5in at upper deck level forward and, according to some sources, an open-sided hangar arrangement.

Top: The ex-liner *Kaiyo*, beached at Beppu Bay postwar and apparently in the process of being broken up. Her original mercantile livery is clearly evident. (US Naval Historical Center)

Centre: *Shinyo* on trials in the Inland Sea, November 1943. (By courtesy of A. D. Baker III)

Bottom: One of the last big fleet carriers to be commissioned into the Imperial Japanese Navy was *Taiho*. This vessel was innovative in several respects: she featured an armoured flight deck, introduced the new 3.9in AA gun to the carrier fleet and, as can be seen in the photograph, was fitted with an enclosed bow. (US Navy)

TAIHO

Builder	Laid down	Launched	Commissioned
Kawasaki	10 July 41	7 Apr 43	7 Mar 44

Displacement: 29,300 tons / 29,769 tonnes (standard); 37,270 tons / 37,866 tonnes (deep load).
Length: 780ft 10in / 238m (pp); 830ft 1in / 253m (wl); 855ft / 260.6m (oa); 843ft / 257m (fd).
Beam: 90ft 11in / 27.7m (hull); 98ft 6in / 30m (fd).
Draught: 31ft 6in / 9.59m (mean).

Machinery: Geared turbines; 8 Kampon boilers; 4 shafts.
Performance: 160,000shp; 33.33kts.
Bunkerage: 5,700 tons / 5,791 tonnes.
Range: 8,000nm at 18kts.
Aircraft: 60.
Guns: 12 × 100mm; 71 × 25mm.
Complement: 1,751.
Design The largest and in many ways the most

advanced Japanese purpose-built aircraft carrier, *Taiho* was a developed *Shokaku*, but introduced a number of innovative features; it is not certain that the earliest sketch designs showed these, and the ship's somewhat extended building period may reflect design modifications worked in as construction progressed.

Taiho was Japan's first carrier to feature an armoured flight deck; consisting of 3in plate and intended to stop a 1,000lb bomb, this was also the longest to see Japanese service. Comparisons with the British *Illustrious* class are often made, but *Taiho* was in reality quite different in concept, the two-storey hangars being unprotected at the sides and hence in themselves not completing an armoured 'box' within the hull structure; clearly, the Japanese would have been unaware of the *Midway*-class design, but comparisons with this US carrier are perhaps more valid.

The armoured flight deck contributed substantially to the rigidity of the hull, but the main strength member was the lower hangar deck, 4.9in plate and extending across the machinery spaces and boiler rooms, and enclosed by a 5.9in belt; armour protection in total accounted for 8,800 tons, or 30 per cent of the entire weight of the ship – almost certainly the highest proportion in any carrier design with the exception of the converted battleship *Shinano*. The topweight of the flight deck forced a compromise of course, and this manifested itself in the elimination of one deck compared to *Shokaku*, in order to keep freeboard down.

The official capacity of 60 aircraft seems somewhat low, given the size of the hangars (each not much less than 500ft long and with a height of 16ft 6in), but may reflect the fact that the ship was designed to embark the new Aichi B7A heavy torpedo / dive-bomber, which it never had the chance to do; in service an air group comprising 75 aircraft could be accommodated.

A further innovation was the plating of the bows up to flight-deck level, a unique Japanese instance though of course standard practice in the Royal Navy's carriers. As in the *Hiyo*s, there was a substantial island superstructure, with a funnel canted to starboard, sponsoned out from the hull to permit maximum flight-deck width. Two lifts were fitted,

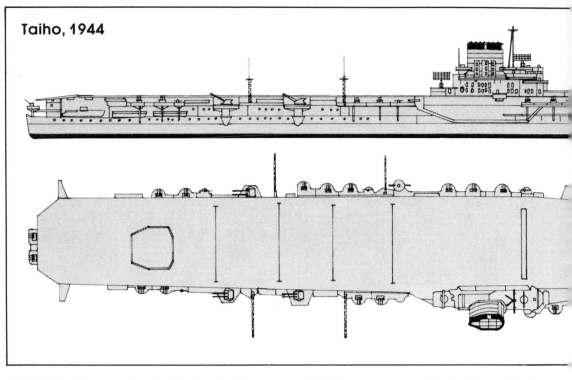

Taiho, 1944

that aft being offset to starboard and equipped with an adjacent derrick, presumably for handling floatplanes. Type 21 radar was installed, one set at each end of the island providing 360° coverage.

Taiho introduced the new 65-calibre 3.9in anti-aircraft gun into the carrier fleet, six such mountings being distributed on hull sponsons.

Two slightly larger, more heavily armed *Taiho*s (hull nos. 801 and 802) were ordered during the war, but before construction began the design was upgraded into a programme of five further modified vessels, none of which was ever laid down although one was reportedly ordered.

Modifications Believed none.

Service Notes *Taiho* was sunk within a few weeks of completing her shake-down when, at the Battle of the Philippine Sea, she was hit by torpedoes fired from the submarine *Albacore* on 19 June 1944, petrol vapour igniting some hours later and causing a massive explosion.

IBUKI

Builder	Launched	Commissioned
Kure	24 Apr 42	21 May 43

Displacement: 12,500 tons / 12,700 tonnes (standard).
Length: 616ft 2in / 187.8m (pp); 650ft 9in / 198.35m (wl); 672ft 7in / 205m (oa); 660ft / 201m (fd).
Beam: 69ft 7in / 21.2m (hull); 75ft 6in / 23m (fd).
Draught: 20ft 8in / 6.3m (mean).
Machinery: Geared turbines; 4 boilers; 2 shafts.
Performance: 72,000shp; 29kts.
Aircraft: 27.
Guns: 4 × 76mm; 48 × 25mm.
Missiles: 168 rocket launchers.
Complement: 1,015.

Design By 1943 the Japanese carrier force was reduced to two fast attack units, two large but slow fleet carriers adapted from merchant designs, and three light carriers, one of which was held for training; further fleet units were building and several conversions were in hand, but if losses were to continue at the rate sustained during the second half of 1942 it was clear that replacements would be required at a furious rate. A crash programme of carrier construction was instituted; as the Japanese position became ever more desperate, many of the projects were not realised, including a scheme for modifying a heavy cruiser.

Details of the original design are scarce, but it appears that this was to be a 12,200-ton vessel mounting 10 × 8in guns, a development of the *Mogami* type with 3.9in belt armour increasing to 4.9in along the magazines, together with 2.4in–1.4in armour decks; whether this standard of protection was to be retained in the carrier conversion is unclear, but the hull was substantially bulged, presumably to improve stability on what would be a lively cruiser platform.

An island well over to starboard was a feature of the revised design, with a downward-venting funnel aft and the usual battery of 25mm AA along the deck edge. Heavy AA fire would be provided by two twin 3in / 60 forward, and provision was apparently made for the installation of rocket-launchers. There was a single hangar, served by two lifts, and in order to accommodate additional fuel half the boilers were removed.

Ibuki's conversion was ordered in the autumn of 1943 and the incomplete hull was towed to Sasebo. Work proceeded somewhat fitfully and stopped altogether in March 1945 with no real prospect of completion. The hull was broken up in the post-war period.

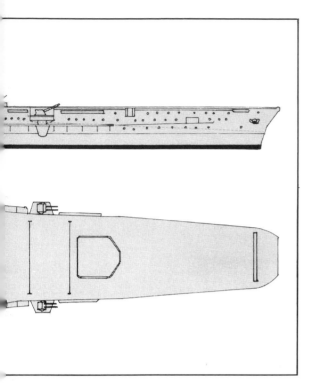

Above: A November 1945 view of *Ibuki* showing the prominent hull bulge and the numerous AA, etc., sponsons along the flight-deck edge. The three submarines alongside are small, utility Type SS transport vessels, with US personnel aboard. (US National Archives)

Ibuki, final design

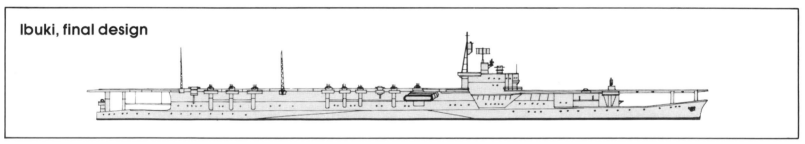

Below: *Ibuki* at Sasebo, September 1945. (US National Archives)

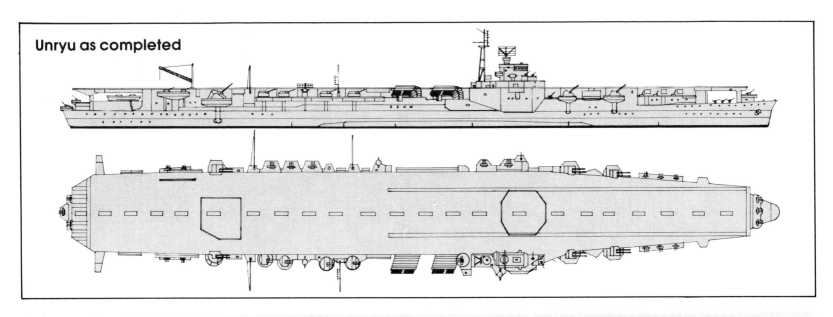

Unryu as completed

UNRYU CLASS

Ship	Builder	Laid down	Launched	Commissioned
Unryu	Yokosuka	1 Aug 42	25 Sept 43	6 Aug 44
Amagi	Mitsubishi	1 Oct 42	15 Oct 43	10 Aug 44
Katsuragi	Kure	8 Dec 42	19 Jan 44	
Kasagi	Mitsubishi	14 Apr 43	19 Oct 44	
Aso	Kure	8 June 43	1 Nov 44	
Ikoma	Kawasaki	5 July 43	17 Nov 44	

Displacement: 17,150 tons / 17,424 tonnes
(standard); 22,500 tons / 22,860 tonnes (deep load).
Length: 679ft 2in / 207m (pp); 731ft 8in / 223m
(wl); 745ft 11in / 227.35m (oa); 712ft / 217m (fd).
Beam: 72ft 2in / 22m (hull); 88ft 6in / 27m (fd).
Draught: 25ft 9in / 7.85m (mean).
Machinery: Geared turbines; 8 Kampon boilers;
4 shafts.
Performance: 152,000shp; 34kts.
Bunkerage: 3,670 tons / 3,729 tonnes.
Range: 8,000nm at 18kts.

Aircraft: 65.
Guns: 12 × 5in; 51 × 25mm.
Complement: 1,595.
Design The ultimate expression of Japanese carrier
construction during the Second World War was a
group of vessels based on one design, generally an
improved *Soryu* and bearing a close resemblance to
that ship, but with individual units differing in detail
reflecting the changing circumstances as the conflict
in the Pacific approached its conclusion. *Unryu* was
ordered under the 1941 Programme and was to be

Above: *Unryu* just prior to commissioning. Ambitious plans
envisaged more than a dozen of these fast fleet carriers, but
even if the Japanese had had the materials to complete them
and the oil to fuel them it is doubtful whether sufficient
trained pilots could have been mustered in order to turn them
into effective battle units. (By courtesy of A. D. Baker III)

followed by a sister carrier, but the latter was
cancelled in 1942 and a batch of seven authorised in
its place, to be followed by a further eight featuring a
slightly enlarged hull; in the event only five of the
first follow-up group were laid down, two of which (in
addition to the lead ship) were completed.

To ease construction, cruiser machinery was
installed, but a shortage of parts led to *Aso* and
Katsuragi receiving destroyer turbines, reducing
power output by one-third and maximum speed by
2kts. Machinery and magazines were protected by
1.8in and 5.9in (belt) and 1in and 2.2in (deck)
armour respectively, and uptake, island, flight deck

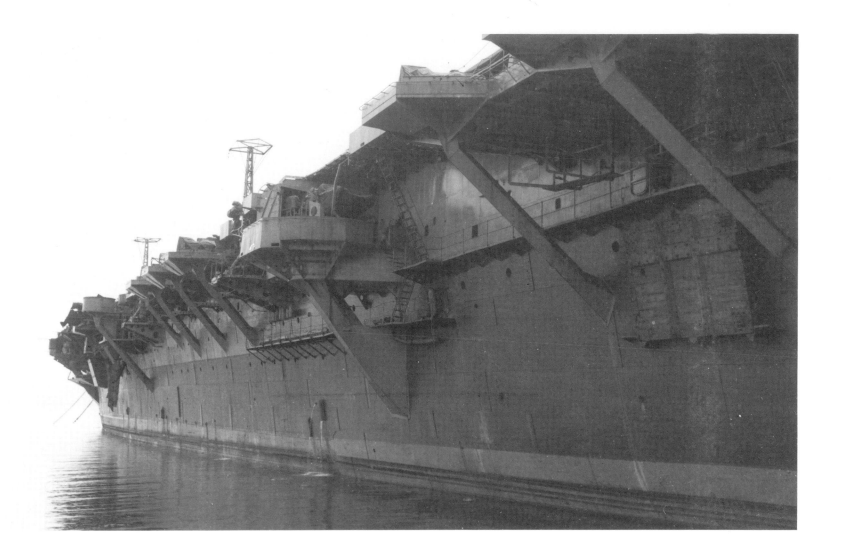

Above: *Katsuragi* survived the war to be used for repatriation duties; she is seen here in October 1945, still, rather surprisingly, armed although hardly ammunitioned. Note the comparatively lightweight sponson construction. (US National Archives)

and armament followed the well-tried pattern although, unlike *Soryu* (which had three), only two lifts were fitted.

The *Unryu*s did not have armoured flight decks, which is partially explained by the fact that they were not really envisaged as fleet carriers in the classical sense of the term: rather, they were to form the cores of anti-convoy strike groups, screened by heavy cruisers and not expected to bear the brunt of fleet actions, for which the armoured carriers in prospect would be employed. Their light construction would not in any case have permitted the effective operation of large numbers of heavy strike aircraft (B7A, B6N) required to penetrate US carrier air defences, although they were seen as suitable platforms for launching kamikaze attacks.

The data in the table refer specifically to *Unryu*; displacement variations were shown by *Amagi* (17,460 / 22,800 tons) and *Katsuragi* (17,260 /

22,530 tons), and the latter's flight deck measured 703ft 9in effective length; trial displacements ranged from 19,780 tons (*Unryu*, *Katsuragi*, *Aso*) to 20,020 tons (*Kasagi*) and 20,120 (*Amagi*, *Ikoma*); the fixed battery in *Amagi* and *Katsuragi* showed 89×25mm upon completion; and aircraft complements varied, *Ikoma* being credited with only 53 machines and *Kasagi*, *Katsuragi* and *Aso* with 64, probably reflecting variations in types to be embarked rather than any great differences in hangar dimensions. Type 21 (two antennae, one on the island and one on the starboard deck edge, aft) and Type 13 warning radars were fitted.

Aso, *Ikoma* and *Kasagi* were never completed: work was halted early in 1945 and all the hulls were scrapped after the war, *Aso* first being used by the Japanese for experiments with suicide weapons.

Modifications By the end of the war the three vessels in commission were showing 89×25mm (22

triple and 23 portable single mountings), plus six 8-barrelled rocket-launchers.

Service Notes *Unryu*: Not used in action because of shortages of aircraft and fuel, although reportedly some A6Ms and B6Ns had embarked for the ship to be involved in patrols during the autumn of 1944. Sunk by torpedoes from the submarine *Redfish* off Shanghai, 19 December 1944.

Amagi: Not deployed in combat. Sunk by bombing near Kure, 27 July 1945; hulk scrapped post-war.

Katsuragi: Not deployed. Damaged in an air raid at Kure on two occasions late in the war, but sufficiently seaworthy to be used as a repatriation vessel. Broken up post-war.

Above: *Amagi*, keeled over, three months after being disabled in a US air attack in July 1945. The structure angled to port by the mast is a Type 13 air-warning antenna. (US National Archives)

Above right: *Kasagi*, one of three *Unryu*s incomplete at the end of the war. The photograph was taken at Sasebo, 19 October 1945. (US Army, by courtesy of A. D. Baker III)

Below: *Ikoma* as she appeared at the close of hostilities, in distinctive camouflage. The apparently odd bow profile is caused by the starboard hawser swinging free. Note the uptake stowed on the flight deck. (US Navy)

Bottom: The hulk of the foundered *Aso*, complete only to hangar-deck level, but showing the flight-deck support structure at the stern. (US Navy)

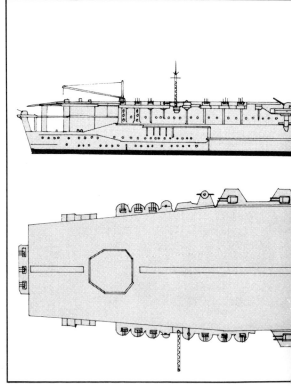

SHINANO

Builder	Laid down	Launched
Yokosuka	4 May 40	8 Oct 44

Displacement: 64,800 tons / 65,837 tonnes
(standard); 71,890 tons / 73,040 tonnes (deep load).
Length: 800ft 6in / 244m (pp); 839ft 11in / 256m
(wl); 872ft 8in / 266m (oa); 827ft / 252m (fd).
Beam: 119ft 1in / 36.3m (hull); 131ft / 40m (fd).
Draught: 33ft 10in / 10.3m (mean).
Machinery: Kampon geared turbines; 12 Kampon
boilers; 4 shafts.
Performance: 150,000shp; 27kts.
Bunkerage: 8,904 tons / 9,046 tonnes.
Range: 10,000nm at 18kts.

Aircraft: 120.
Guns: 16 × 5in; 145 × 25mm.
Missiles: 336 rocket launchers.
Complement: 2,400.

Design The early exchanges of the Pacific War very
quickly established the ascendancy of air over heavy-
gun power and one immediate result of this in Japan
was the cessation of all work on capital ships. This
decision directly affected the construction of the
Yamato-class battleships, one of which had been
completed by mid 1942 with a second almost ready
for sea and a third whose hull was virtually complete
on the slips.

The last offered the prospect of an enormous

platform for air operations and one, moreover, that
would be prodigiously armoured. It also suggested an
internal volume that could accommodate vast
quantities of fuel and ordnance, and it was this
capacity which led to the idea that the converted
vessel might be very usefully employed as a support
ship for replenishing fleet combat carriers without
their having to return home; replacement aircraft
would also be embarked, but they would not form a
combat air group for the carrier herself.

The battleship hull was essentially retained *in toto*,
with its armour and underwater protection, although
the belt was reduced from 15.7in to 8.1in except
along the magazines where it kept its original
thickness. The principal horizontal protection
consisted of a 7.5in armour deck, but sources differ as
to whether this was at main deck level, as in the
original battleship design, or raised to hangar deck (*ie*
former upper deck) level. The hangar itself was a
single-storey unit some 550ft long, built up over the
forecastle deck, open for much of its length (roller
shutters for enclosure), served by two lifts, and
surmounted by a 3.1in armoured flight deck. The
island, sponsoned out to starboard, was generally
similar to though considerably larger than that
evolved for the *Hiyo*s, with a single large uptake
angled over to starboard. Types 13 and 22 radars are
believed to have been fitted.

Shinano would have been equipped with an air
group of 40–50 planes (the initial scheme was revised
during conversion), stowed forward in the hangar, but
the bulk of the capacity would be given over to
replacement aircraft for fleet carriers and forward land
bases. However, the ship never entered service: while
moving to Kure for final fitting out she was struck by
four torpedoes from the US submarine *Archerfish* (29
November 1944). Damage control facilities in the
form of pumps and watertight doors had not been
completed, and flooding spread from the starboard
engine room and empty petrol bunkers, sinking the
vessel some seven hours after being hit.

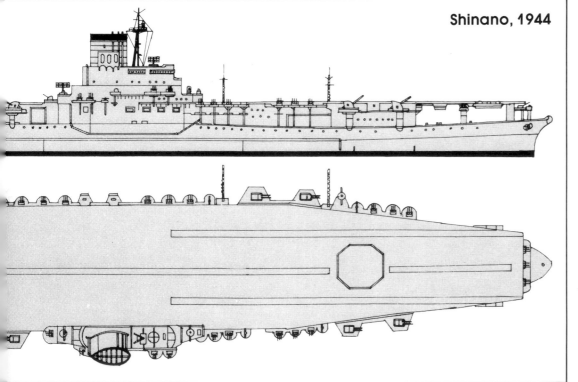

Shinano, 1944

YAMASHIRO MARU CLASS

Ship	Builder	Laid down	Launched	Commissioned
Yamashiro Maru	Mitsubishi	19 July 44	14 Nov 44	27 Jan 45
Chigusa Maru	Mitsubishi	11 Sept 44	29 Dec 44	

Length: 485ft 7in / 148m (pp); 516ft 9in / 157.5m (oa); 410ft / 125m (fd).
Beam: 66ft 11in / 20.4m (hull); 75ft 6in / 23m (fd).
Draught: 29ft 6in / 9m (mean).
Machinery: Geared turbines; 2 boilers; 1 shaft.
Performance: 4,500shp; 15kts.
Range: 9,000nm at 13kts.
Aircraft: 8.
Guns: 16 × 25mm.
Complement: 221.
Design Following the acquisition of two liners for conversion to flight-decked assault ships (*Akitsu* *Maru* class), the Imperial Japanese Army took matters a step further in 1944 and chartered a pair of 10,100grt Type 2TL tankers for conversion to escort carriers to operate JAAF aircraft (probably Ki-44s, which would have been light enough) in a limited air defence role over troop convoys. There was neither hangar nor lift, the aircraft to be spotted aft for take-off and manhandled back along the flight deck after landing. An ASW projector was fitted on the fore-castle, and there was stowage for 120 depth-charges.

Chigusa Maru was never completed as a carrier, but served post-war as a tanker (10,325grt).
Modifications Believed none.
Service Notes *Yamashiro Maru*: Not used as a carrier. Sunk by US aircraft at Yokohama, 17 February 1945, the hulk being scrapped post-war.

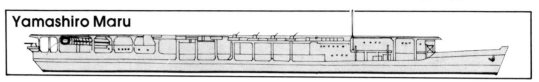
Yamashiro Maru

SHIMANE MARU CLASS

Ship	Builder	Laid down	Launched	Commissioned
Shimane Maru	Kawasaki	8 June 44	17 Dec 44	28 Feb 45
Otakisan Maru	Kawasaki	18 Sept 44	14 Jan 45	

Displacement: 11,800 tons / 11,989 tonnes (standard).
Length: 492ft 2in / 150m (pp); 502ft / 153m (wl); 526ft 7in / 160.5m (oa); 500ft / 152.5m (fd).
Beam: 65ft 7in / 20m (hull); 75ft 6in / 23m (fd).
Draught: 29ft 10in / 9.1m (mean).
Machinery: Geared turbines; 2 boilers; 1 shaft.
Performance: 8,600shp; 18.5kts.
Range: 10,000nm at 14kts.
Aircraft: 12.
Guns: 2 × 4.7in; 52 × 25mm.
Design Two Type 1TL tankers were acquired by the Japanese Navy in late 1944 for rapid conversion to auxiliary convoy escort carriers. A hangar was built up on to the well deck amidships, a single lift bringing aircraft up to the flight deck. There was no island, and the mercantile hull was unmodified save for the trunking of the boilers over to starboard, discharging aft via a downward-angled funnel. A lattice-type mast outboard of the island carried a Type 13 radar antenna, and the flight deck forward was flanked by a pair of single 4.7in guns, nine triple and 25 single 25mm of the standard Hotchkiss type being strung along the deck edge.

Otakisan Maru was never completed for service, and she drifted on to a mine at Kobe soon after the war ended (25 August 1945); the hulk was later scrapped. Two further 1TL conversions were planned but not proceeded with.
Modifications Believed none.
Service Notes *Shimane Maru*: Not deployed operationally. Sunk by US aircraft, 24 July 1945, off Takamatsu, Shikoku.

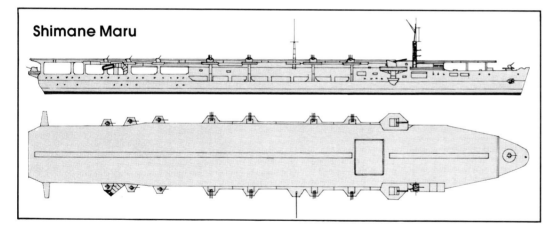
Shimane Maru

KUMANO MARU

Builder	Laid down	Launched	Commissioned
Hitachi	15 Aug 44	28 Jan 45	30 Mar 45

Displacement: 8,000 tons / 8,128 tonnes (standard).
Length: 465ft 9in / 141.96m (pp); 501ft / 152.7m (oa); 361ft / 110m (fd).
Beam: 64ft 3in / 19.58m (hull); 70ft 6in / 21.5m (fd).
Draught: 23ft / 7m (mean).
Machinery: Geared turbines; 4 boilers; 2 shafts.
Performance: 10,000shp; 19kts.
Range: 6,000nm at 17kts.
Aircraft: 37.
Guns: 8 × 75mm; 6 × 25mm.
Design Similar in concept to the *Akitsu Maru* class, this vessel was in essence an amphibious assault ship with provision for deploying, but not recovering, JAAF aircraft in support of beach-head landings. Doors at the stern permitted the discharge via ramps of up to twelve 56ft or thirteen 46ft landing craft, and the fixed battery was a mix of single 3in and 25mm AA. A handling derrick was fitted aft, but it is uncertain whether a hangar and lift were installed. The original vessel from which the conversion was carried out was a standard 9,502grt M-type freighter.
Modifications Nil.
Service Notes Believed not to have been used in operational service, but employed as a transport post-war and subsequently reconfigured for her original cargo-carrying role.

Netherlands

The Royal Netherlands Navy promoted carrier aviation during the 1950s and 1960s, first with an ex-wartime escort carrier and subsequently with an ex-light fleet carrier. The latter operated in the strike role for a number of years, but later served in an ASW capacity until paying off.

GADILA CLASS

Ship	Builder	Launched	Commissioned
Gadila	Howaldtswerke	1 Dec 34	Mar 44
Macoma	Nederlandse Dok	31 Dec 35	May 44

Displacement: 16,000 tons / 16,256 tonnes (deep load).
Length: 463ft / 141.12m (pp); 481ft / 146.61m (oa); 450ft / 137.16m (fd).
Beam: 59ft 3in / 18.06m (hull); 60ft / 18.29m (fd).
Draught: 27ft 6in / 8.38m (mean).
Machinery: 8-cylinder MAN diesel engine; 1 shaft.
Performance: 4,000bhp; 12.75kts.
Aircraft: 4.
Guns: 1 × 4in; 2 × 40mm; 6 × 20mm.
Complement: 118.
Design Ex-8,000grt tanker merchant aircraft carriers (MAC-ships) of the British-operated *Rapana* class (qv) but manned by Dutch crews. *Gadila* was converted at Smith's Dock, Tyneside.
Modifications Believed none.
Service Notes *Gadila*: Atlantic escort duty during the last months of the Second World War. Reconverted post-war for the tanker role. Broken up at Hong Kong from mid 1958.
Macoma: Atlantic escort duty. Reconverted post-war. Scrapped at Hong Kong from mid 1958.

KAREL DOORMAN

Builder	Laid down	Launched	Commissioned
Swan Hunter	1942	20 May 43	1946

Displacement: 13,825 tons / 14,046 tonnes (standard); 16,980 tons / 17,252 tonnes (deep load).
Length: 498ft 3in / 151.87m (pp); 528ft 6in / 161.09m (oa); 495ft / 150.88m (fd).
Beam: 68ft / 20.73m (hull); 65ft / 19.81m (fd).

Left: *Macoma* with a pair of Swordfish; note the ASV radar fairing of the Mk III nearest the bows. (Royal Netherlands Navy)

Draught: 23ft 6in / 7.16m (mean); 25ft 8in / 7.82m (deep load).
Machinery: 5-cylinder Doxford diesel engines; 2 shafts.
Performance: 10,700bhp; 16kts.
Bunkerage: 1,655 tons / 1,681 tonnes.
Aircraft: 21.
Guns: 2×4in; 16×2pdr; 16×20mm.
Complement: 700.
Design The former British escort carrier *Nairana* (*Nairana* class, qv), transferred to the Royal Netherlands Navy in 1946.
Modifications Believed none.
Service Notes Served 1946–48. Reconverted to mercantile configuration as *Port Victor* in 1948.

Right: The first *Karel Doorman*, the former British escort carrier *Nairana*. Apparent in this view is the stub lattice mast abaft the island, carrying the low-angle surveillance Type 277 radar aerial; the complementary Type 293 'cheese' target-indicator is visible aloft, forward of the main search radar antenna (Type 281). It is not certain whether these systems were all present when the carrier was in Royal Navy service. (Royal Netherlands Navy)

KAREL DOORMAN

Builder	Laid down	Launched	Commissioned
Cammell Laird	3 Dec 42	30 Dec 43	28 May 48

Displacement: 15,900 tons / 16,154 tonnes (standard); 19,900 tons / 20,218 tonnes (deep load).
Length: 630ft / 192.02m (pp); 650ft / 198.12m (wl); 693ft 2in / 211.28m (oa); 685ft / 208.79m (fd).
Beam: 80ft / 24.38m (hull); 85ft / 25.91m (fd).
Draught: 21ft 6in / 6.55m (mean); 24ft 6in / 7.47m (deep load).
Machinery: Parsons geared turbines; 4 Admiralty 3-drum boilers; 2 shafts.
Performance: 40,000shp; 24kts.
Bunkerage: 3,000 tons / 3,048 tonnes.
Range: 12,000nm at 14kts.
Aircraft: 24.
Guns: 34×40mm.
Complement: 854.
Design The former British *Colossus*-class light fleet carrier *Venerable* (qv), purchased by the Royal Netherlands Navy in May 1948.
Modifications By 1950 *Karel Doorman* was operating Sea Furies and Fireflies, and aircraft complement was listed as nineteen although considerably more could be embarked. The crew figure given in the table excludes air personnel.

Between 1955 and 1958 the carrier was reconstructed to incorporate jet technology at the Wilton Fijenoord yard: the flight deck was extended by way of an 8° angled landing area (usable width now 105ft, maximum 112ft 6in), was strengthened, and had a steam catapult installed forward. A mirror landing sight was fitted, the lifts were stressed and the armament was renewed with 12×40mm. More obviously, the island superstructure was redesigned, with a lofty tripod-type lattice mast and a high, raked funnel. Dutch radar, including LW-01 air search, ZW-01 sea search, DA-01 target acquisition and VI-01 height-finder systems, was installed, and a typical embarked air group consisted of six Avenger ASW aircraft, six Sea Hawk fighter-bombers, four HSS-1N night ASW helicopters and two utility helicopters; from the mid 1960s the carrier operated in a pure ASW role, further helicopters and S-2 Trackers being taken on board at the expense of the Sea Hawks and Avengers.

Service Notes In service with the Dutch Navy until a boiler-room fire forced her withdrawal in 1968. Refitted and sold to the Argentine Navy as *25 de Mayo* (qv).

Below: The second *Karel Doorman* was the most radically altered ex-British light fleet carrier, her profile dominated after reconstruction by a reconfigured island topped with an extended funnel and new Dutch-built radar. She is shown here conducting flying operations, in about 1959. (Royal Netherlands Navy, by courtesy of Ian Sturton)

Right: *Karel Doorman* shows her redesigned flight deck and new steam catapult, February 1959. Two Avenger anti-submarine aircraft and two Sea Hawk strike fighters are visible on deck. (US Navy, by courtesy of A. D. Baker III)

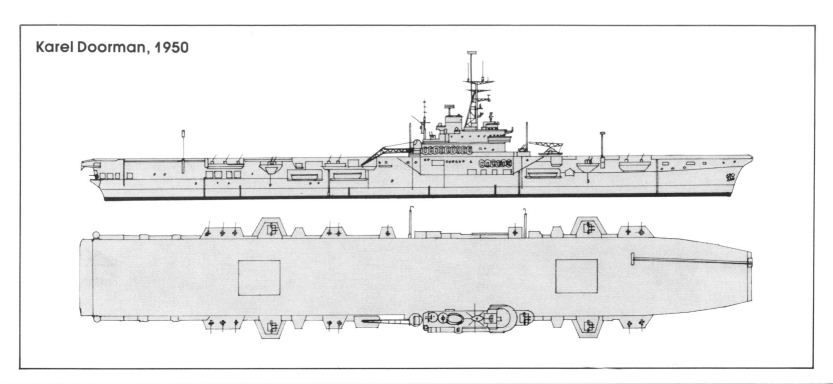

Karel Doorman, 1950

Soviet Union

The Soviet Union has never commissioned a fleet carrier, although with the postwar expansion of the Soviet Navy and following experience with the *Moskva*-class helicopter carriers and the carrier-like ASW *Kiev*s, it appears that the commissioning of the first of a number of large ships capable of operating conventional fixed-wing aircraft will not be long delayed.

ALMAZ

Laid down	Launched	Commissioned
1902	1903	1914

Displacement: 3,285 tons / 3,338 tonnes (standard).
Length: 365ft 9in / 111.48m (oa).
Beam: 43ft 6in / 13.26m (hull).
Draught: 17ft 6in / 5.33m (deep load).
Machinery: Vertical triple-expansion reciprocating engines; 2 shafts.
Performance: 7,500ihp; 19kts.
Bunkerage: 560 tons / 569 tonnes.
Aircraft: 4.
Guns: 7 × 4.7in; 4 × 3in.
Design Originally an armed yacht, the coal-burner *Almaz* was converted in 1914 to a seaplane carrier, generally two but occasionally four aircraft being stowed between main and mizzen masts and served by adjacent derricks.
Modifications Not known.
Service Notes Actively employed against the Turks in the Black Sea from May 1915, highlights being attacks on Igneada and Varna. Acquired by the French after the First World War.

Other Russian converted seaplane carriers to operate in the Black Sea during the war were *Alexander I* and *Nicolai I* (9,250 tons standard; 15kts; 6 × 4.7in, 6 × 3in; eight aircraft; renamed *Respublikanek* and *Aviator* respectively from 1917), while *Orlica* (3,800grt; 12kts; 8 × 3in; four aircraft) was used to effect against the Germans in the Baltic.

The Russian seaplane carrier division in the Black Sea was strengthened from the winter of 1917–18 with the arrival of the Roumanian ex-passenger ship conversions *Romania* (3,152grt; 18kts), *Regele Carol I* (2,369grt; 18kts; used also as a minelayer), *Dacia* (3,418grt; 18kts) and *Imperator Trayan* (3,418grt; 18kts), all of which were armed with four aircraft and a fixed battery of 4 × 6in and 4 × 3in guns.

KOMINTERN

Builder	Laid down	Launched
Nicolayev	1900	1902

Displacement: 6,200 tons / 6,299 tonnes (standard).
Length: 439ft 8in / 134m (oa).
Beam: 54ft 6in / 16.6m (hull).
Draught: 20ft 8in / 6.3m (mean).
Machinery: Vertical triple-expansion reciprocating engines; 10 Normand boilers; 2 shafts.
Performance: 10,000ihp; 12kts.
Design The *Bogatyr*-class protected cruiser *Komintern* (originally named *Kagul* and later *Pamiat Mercuriya*) was in used as a training ship in the early 1930s and her conversion to a Black Sea seaplane carrier was authorised at about that time. Work reportedly began with the removal of her boilers, but was soon abandoned because of the ship's generally poor condition.

Below: *Graf Zeppelin* might have provided the Soviet Union with its first genuine aircraft carrier, but following her takeover by the Russians at the end of the Second World War, and on passage to Leningrad, she foundered. This photograph was taken in the spring of 1947, at Swinemünde while the carrier, still incomplete, was in Soviet hands. (US Naval Historical Center)

MOSKVA CLASS

Ship	Builder	Laid down	Launched	Commissioned
Moskva	Nicolayev (S)	1962	1965	July 1967
Leningrad	Nicolayev (S)	1963	1966	1968

Displacement: 14,500 tons / 14,732 tonnes (standard); 18,000 tons / 18,288 tonnes (deep load).
Length: 625ft / 190.5m (wl); 645ft / 196.6m (oa); 295ft / 90m (fd).
Beam: 112ft / 34.14m (hull); 108ft / 33m (fd).
Draught: 24ft 11in / 7.6m (mean).

Machinery: Geared turbines; 4 water-tube boilers; 2 shafts.
Performance: 100,000shp; 30kts.
Bunkerage: 2,600 tons / 2,642 tonnes.
Range: 9,000nm at 18kts.
Aircraft: 18.

Above: *Leningrad* in the English Channel, 10 August 1981, accompanied by the frigate *Avenger*. (Ministry of Defence (Navy))

Guns: 4 × 57mm.
Torpedo tubes: 10 × 21in.
Missiles: 4 SA-N-3, 2 SUW N-1, 24 RBU 6000.
Complement: 800.

Design Believed to have been designed primarily as a counter to US Polaris submarines operating in the Eastern Mediterranean, the singularly distinctive

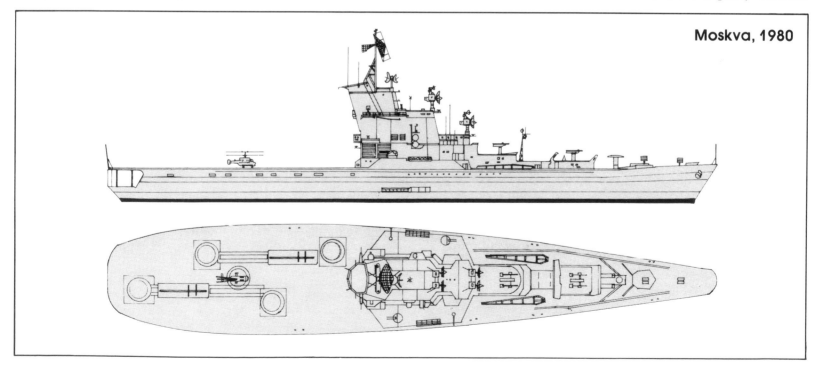

Moskva, 1980

*Moskva*s represent the first attempt by the Russians to build a significant air-capable ship. About half the length is given over to a very broad flight deck, the hull of the vessel being faired up to the edges and thus producing a unique 'teardrop' shape in plan view. Two lifts, each about 52ft × 15ft, are arranged *en échelon* and serve a total of four helicopter spots and a 220ft × 80ft hangar below with accommodation for eighteen Kaman Ka-25 ('Hormone') ASW helicopters. The towering superstructure amidships is dominated by an integral funnel and progresses in a series of 'steps' down to the forecastle carrying 'Top Sail' air surveillance and height-finding radar on a tall mast at the forward edge of the funnel, 'Head Net-C' search radar and two 'Head Light' and two 'Muff Cob' fire-control radars; two twin SA-N-3 launchers (AAW) and a twin SUW-N-1 launcher (ASW) are forward, with the two RBU 6000 ASW rocket-launchers at the bows. Hull-mounted sonar and VDS are fitted.

The ships have been criticised for their lack of an anti-surface capability, but it is probable that they are intended to deploy as centres of ASW hunting task groups, with the SSM function performed by escorts. **Modifications** The torpedo tubes have been removed since the ships first entered service.

Service Notes *Moskva*: Used in 1973 for VTOL (Yak-36 'Forger') trials when a temporary landing mat was installed aft on the flight deck. Operates in the Black Sea and Mediterranean.
Leningrad: Deployed to the Black Sea and Mediterranean. Engaged in mine-clearance duties in the Suez Canal, 1974.

Above: The *Moskva*s' missile battery is concentrated forward: one twin SUW-N-1 launcher for FRAS-1 and SS-N-14 anti-submarine missiles and, farther aft, a pair of twin SA-N-3 anti-aircraft ('Goblet') launchers; on and just abaft the cable deck are the two RBU 6000 ASW rocket-launchers. This is the name-ship, April 1970. (US Navy)

Right: *Kiev*, mid 1979. (US Navy)

KIEV CLASS

Ship	Builder	Laid down	Launched	Commissioned
Kiev	Nicolayev (S)	Sept 70	Dec 72	May 75
Minsk	Nicolayev (S)	Dec 72	Aug 75	Feb 78
Novorossisk	Nicolayev (S)	Sept 75	Dec 78	1982
Kharkov	Nicolayev (S)	Dec 78		

Displacement: 36,000 tons / 36,576 tonnes (standard); 42,000 tons / 42,672 tonnes (deep load).
Length: 898ft 11in / 274m (oa); 606ft 11in / 185m (fd).
Beam: 134ft 6in / 41m (hull); 157ft 6in / 48m (fd).
Draught: 32ft 10in / 10m (mean).
Machinery: Geared turbines; 4 shafts.
Performance: 180,000shp; 32kts.
Range: 13,000nm at 18kts.
Aircraft: 33.
Guns: 4 × 76mm; 8 × 30mm.
Torpedo tubes: 10 × 21in.
Missiles: 4 SA-N-3, 4 SA-N-4, 8 SS-N-12, 2 SUW-N-1, 24 RBU 6000.
Complement: 2,500.
Design Apart from some vague plans just prior to the Second World War, and the use to which the captured *Graf Zeppelin* was presumably intended to be put, the Soviet Union apparently never seriously entertained carrier aviation until the late 1950s when the designs for the *Moskva*s were first outlined. The latter were limited to the helicopter role, but in the late 1960s this idea was further developed into the first Soviet vessel to have a fixed-wing air group component.

Considerably larger than the *Moskva*s, the first of these new ships, *Kiev*, emerged as a curious hybrid with immense fixed-weapon power, but with an air capability that leaves some unanswered questions. A very beamy ship, with a massive combined island and uptake, she is armed in a similar manner to *Moskva* for what appears to be a primary ASW role, but has in addition two twin SA-N-4 launchers for what are presumably point-defence missiles. More significantly, four twin SS-N-12 launch tubes give the ship a long-range anti-surface function with mid-course missile (FRAS-1) guidance provided by a small number of Ka-25 'Hormone-B' helicopters. The radar suite is also based on that of *Moskva* except that a 'Top Steer' search set is installed in place of 'Head Net-C'. Two 'Owl Screech' (3in fire control) and two 'Pop Group' (SA-N-4 control) are carried, while four 'Bass Tilt' replace 'Muff Cob' for 30mm (as against 57mm) fire control: VDS and bow sonar are fitted.

The flight deck is angled out at 4½° from the fore-and-aft axis and features two principal lifts, 62ft × 33ft amidships and 62ft × 16ft 6in on the starboard side aft, and there is an elaborate trackway system running from the starboard after edge of the deck, outboard of the island and around the perimeter of the foredeck, presumably for the movement of ordnance. There is a long hangar, its width severely restricted by the mass of the boiler uptakes on the starboard side.

The air group, in addition to the 'Hormone-B' helicopters, consists of some 18 'Hormone-A' ASW helicopters and twelve Yak-36 'Forger' fixed-wing VTOL aircraft, the latter presumably for an air defence/air support role although markedly lacking the sophistication of contemporary land-based fighters. There are seven spots for helicopters plus a larger one aft for fixed-wing VTOL, though the apparent presence of heatproof tiles along the flight deck suggests a simultaneous launch and recovery capability. What is curious about the *Kiev*s is that they have a through flight deck, implying deployment of conventional take-off and landing (CTOL) aircraft; the Yak-36 certainly has this capability in addition to its VTOL mode, but the lack of arrester gear and catapults and the narrowness of the lifts seems to offer no prospect of operating more sophisticated, and hence by suggestion, larger aircraft. In this respect the cruiser-carrier concept as manifested by this class probably represents an 'ultimate' design.
Modifications Not known.
Service Notes *Kiev*: Assigned to the Soviet Northern Fleet.
Minsk: Pacific Fleet.
Novorossisk: Presumed destined for the Northern Fleet.

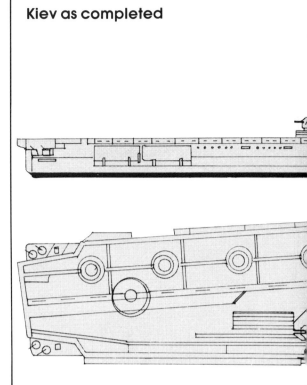

Kiev as completed

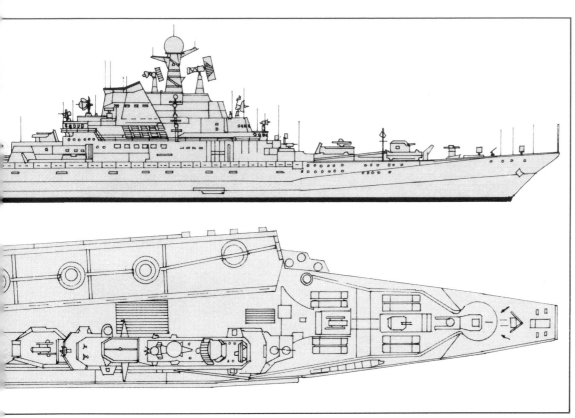

Top left: Although visually comparable to true aircraft carriers, the *Kiev*s are in reality anti-submarine cruisers, albeit with a significant air (and anti-surface) capability: in no sense can they be considered attack carriers. This is the name-ship, May 1978, with a dozen Ka-25s on the flight deck; that immediately abaft the island is sitting on one of the lift platforms (the other two lifts are obscured by the superstructure). (US Navy)

Below left: *Minsk* in February 1979. The cylinders on the forecastle deck are the ship's SS-N-12 launchers for anti-ship missiles. (Ministry of Defence (Navy))

Below right: The latest of the *Kiev*s to commission is *Novorossisk*, seen here in company with the British carrier *Illustrious*, 31 May 1983. One further ship of the class is understood to be completing. (Ministry of Defence (Navy))

Spain

Although experimenting as far back as 1917 (seaplane carrier *Dédalo*), Spain's first genuine aircraft carrier was not taken into service until the late 1960s. The replacement for this ship, built in Spain to a US design, is currently fitting out.

DÉDALO

Builder	Laid down	Launched	Commissioned
New York SB	13 Mar 42	4 Apr 43	30 Aug 67

Displacement: 13,000 tons / 13,208 tonnes (standard); 16,416 tons / 16,679 tonnes (deep load).
Length: 600ft / 182.88m (wl); 622ft 6in / 189.74m (oa); 544ft / 165.81m (fd).
Beam: 71ft 6in / 21.79m (hull); 73ft / 22.25m (fd).
Draught: 26ft / 7.92m (deep load).
Machinery: General Electric turbines; 4 Babcock & Wilcox boilers; 4 shafts.
Performance: 100,000shp; 30kts.
Bunkerage: 1,800 tons / 1,829 tonnes.

Range: 7,200nm at 15kts.
Aircraft: 20.
Guns: 26 × 40mm.
Complement: 1,112.

Design The ex-US light carrier *Cabot* (CVL-28, qv), lent to the Spanish Navy following a refit at Philadelphia in 1965–67 and purchased in December 1973. Prior to transfer the radar suite was upgraded: the SPS-6 air search set was retained, but other major systems were removed and a new fit of SPS-40 (air search), SPS-10 (surface search) and SPS-8 (height-finder) was added.

Modifications In the late 1970s SPS-52B (3-dimensional search) was officially listed. Since

Above: *Dédalo* in 1968, showing a modified island, upgraded radar systems and a reduced number of funnels since her days as the US Navy's CVL *Cabot*. (By courtesy of A. D. Baker III)

1976 between four and six AV-8A Matadors have been embarked on board the carrier in addition to the normal complement of 20 ASW helicopters. The defensive battery is unchanged from Second World War days, consisting of two quadruple and nine twin mountings. Displacement is currently (1983) given as 14,500 tons standard and 16,450 tons deep load.
Service Notes Scheduled to remain in front-line service until the commissioning of *Principe de Asturias*.

PRINCIPE DE ASTURIAS

Builder	Laid down	Launched
Bazan	8 Oct 79	22 May 82

Displacement: 15,000 tons / 15,240 tonnes (deep load).
Length: 640ft / 195.1m (oa); 575ft / 175.25m (fd).
Beam: 80ft / 24.4m (hull); 105ft / 32m (fd).
Draught: 21ft 8in / 6.60m (deep load).
Machinery: 2 General Electric LM2500 gas turbines; 1 shaft.
Performance: 40,000shp; 26kts.
Range: 7,500nm at 20kts.
Aircraft: 19.
Guns: 48 × 20mm.
Complement: 774.

Design Having negotiated considerable US assistance, both technical and financial, the Spanish Government ordered the PA11 (*Dédalo* replacement) ASW carrier on 29 June 1977. The design stems from the US Sea Control Ship study of early 1974, but has been considerably refined to include two lifts, one offset to starboard before the island and the second on the centreline at the after flight-deck edge, and a modified flight deck which, although technically axial, will have a take-off run for the ship's three or four fixed-wing V / STOL aircraft. It will be angled to starboard to afford deck parking on the starboard side aft, and will terminate in an integrally structured 'ski-jump' to enable the aircraft to launch with greater payloads. The island structure incorporates the uptakes and is placed well aft; serving as a command and control centre, it also carries the ship's only defensive battery, three 12-barrelled Meroka anti-missile guns, and the radar suite, which is listed as SPS-55 surface search, SPS-52C / D hemispheric search and SPN-35A CCA, plus fire control sets. The hangar will be able to accommodate fourteen SH-3 / LAMPS-type helicopters, plus the fixed-wing component, although the exact complement is yet to be defined and in practice will probably vary anyway. *Principe de Asturias*, scheduled for completion in 1985, is charged with the 'defence of territorial waters, protection of national maritime routes and enemy interception, offensive anti-submarine warfare, blockades and mining [and the], destruction of enemy forces'.

Below: *Principe de Asturias* in May 1982. (British Aerospace)

United States

The United States is currently the only nation whose navy operates a carrier fleet of any significance – indeed, in terms of carrier aviation, it has enjoyed an unchallenged superiority for the last 40 years. Individual feats of airmanship in taking off from and landing aboard ships were early US contributions to carrier development, and during the first World War US technology was responsible for the production of a reliable shipboard catapult. But it was not until the late 1920s, with the commissioning of *Lexington* and *Saratoga*, that the US Navy was in a position seriously to attend to the theory and practical projection of carrier warfare.

Although its contribution to carrier technology has historically been less significant than that provided by British constructors and engineers, there is no gainsaying the overwhelming influence exerted by the US Navy on the tactical and strategic operation of carriers. In a sense, the present US dominance can be traced back to *Lexington* and *Saratoga*: converted from massive battlecruiser hulls, they were capable of accommodating vast complements of aircraft and thus promoted such policies as maximum-strength air strikes and hence very fast flight-deck cycles.

Throughout the Second World War, the US Navy promoted the concept of the mass strike. Backed by huge industrial resources at home, which were able to furnish large numbers of ships and also the aircraft to fill them, the Navy, after some early setbacks, quickly moulded the fleet carrier into the most potent fighting ship yet devised, able to hit both land and sea targets at great range. The long reach of the US forces, defined during the 1941–45 Pacific War and continuing today as a result of the decision to maintain a worldwide naval presence, determined not only the need for generous aircraft accommodation but also that for sustained power projection at range and hence for generous fuel, ordnance and crew capacity. The adoption of nuclear power, first realised in *Enterprise* (CVAN-65), was a natural result of this doctrine, and great un-refuelled range has meant even greater stores capacity, which goes a good way towards explaining the size of current US carriers.

Despite its present virtual monopoly of carrier aviation, the US Navy has not enjoyed an entirely smooth ride in the development of its carrier force. Early postwar problems over responsibility for the strategic nuclear attack role led to the cancellation of the revolutionary *United States*, while during the 1970s the enormous cost of nuclear-powered carriers (about $2,000,000,000 apiece at that time) seriously threatened future building programmes and led to renewed clamours for smaller, conventionally powered vessels. Two postwar conflicts – Korea and Vietnam – have justified the wisdom of retaining carrier strike forces, at least in US eyes although it might be argued that in neither was there the sort of airborne or seaborne opposition that might be expected in a wider conflict.

Other themes of US carrier development have been noteworthy: the production of large numbers of escort carriers, serving as ASW and auxiliary strike carriers and as aircraft transports and replenishment ships during the Second World War; the postwar amphibious assault carrier, developed through CVHEs (ex-escort carriers) and converted *Essex*-class ships through to the current *Iwo Jima*s and *Tarawa*s; and the concern for ASW in the postwar years, prompted by the large Soviet submarine fleet and answered first by adapted escort carriers and then by converted *Essex*es, and finally integrated into the fleet carrier mission.

LANGLEY (CV-1)

Builder	Laid down	Launched	Commissioned
Mare Island	18 Oct 11	24 Aug 12	20 Mar 22

Displacement: 12,700 tons / 12,903 tonnes (standard).
Length: 519ft / 158.19m (wl); 542ft / 165.2m (oa); 534ft / 162.76m (fd).
Beam: 65ft 6in / 19.96m (hull); 64ft / 19.51m (fd).
Draught: 16ft 6in / 5.03m (mean); 22ft / 6.71m (deep load).
Machinery: General Electric turbo-electric drive; 3 Bureau boilers; 2 shafts.

Performance: 7,000shp; 14kts.
Bunkerage: 2,300 tons / 2,337 tonnes.
Aircraft: 34.
Guns: 4 × 5in.
Complement: 350.
Design The origins of the US Navy's first aircraft carrier lie in the decision by Congress, in July 1919, to authorise the conversion of the fleet collier *Jupiter* (AC-3) to a vessel capable of carrying, launching and recovering aircraft at sea. The value of the aeroplane as a fleet spotter had been appreciated since its introduction on board cruisers in 1916, but there is little

Above right: Langley about 1923, with *California* or *Tennessee* off the port quarter and two *New Mexico*-class battleships in the background. Note the flight-deck palisades, raised, and the centreline pole masts. Most of the VE-7s on deck have their engine cowlings covered, while what appears to be a TS-1 floatplane is carried in the working space below, under one of the gooseneck cranes. (US Navy, by courtesy of Norman Friedman)

Right: Langley in January 1925: a VE-7 lands amidst a flock of birds. A safety net is rigged aft, below flight-deck level, and the funnels are lowered. The calm waters and the fact that the carrier is making little way suggest a negligible wind-over-deck; however, the flight deck presents no obstacles for the pilot to be wary of. (US Navy, by courtesy of Ian Sturton)

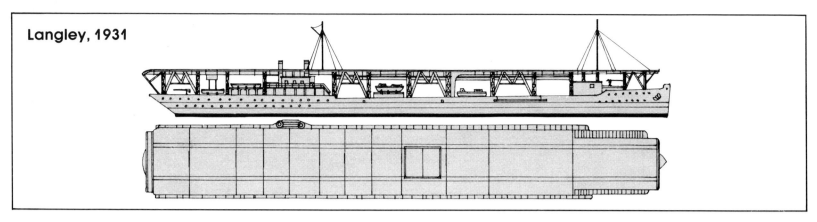

Langley, 1931

doubt that the major impetus towards the commissioning of a flush-decked carrier was borne out of US awareness of developments in the British Grand Fleet, with which US ships had served during the latter part of the First World War, particularly trials aboard *Argus* with the Sopwith Cuckoo torpedo-bomber at which US observers reportedly were present. *Argus* demonstrated the practicability of flying wheeled aircraft from a full-length flush deck, and the greater flexibility and versatility of this configuration over the 'semi-carriers' and seaplane carriers which had been to the forefront of shipboard aviation hitherto.

It was plainly desirable to bring a US project of similar concept to fruition as quickly as possible: the acquisition of a suitable existing hull would expedite the introduction into fleet service of such a vessel, and it would also keep expenditure to a minimum, an important factor in a vessel that could hardly be other than experimental. The two essential requirements were an uncomplicated superstructure which could be removed relatively easily, and a hull with sufficient usable internal volume for the stowage of aircraft, avgas (petrol) and munitions and for the installation of mechanical gear to bring the aircraft up to the flight deck. The fact that the boiler room uptakes discharged to port and starboard rather than via a centrally disposed funnel was also presumably influential.

The US Navy's fleet colliers met these requirements most satisfactorily, and had the added advantage that their future, with the introduction of oil-fired boilers in the fleet, was in some doubt in any case. The 19,360-ton *Jupiter*, originally commissioned in April 1913, was selected for conversion and in March 1920 was taken in hand at Norfolk Navy Yard. Four of the six holds were adapted to stow a total of 34 aircraft (or 55 maximum if disassembled), and that between each pair of these four was utilised as the lift well; the hold right forward became the avgas bunker, with a capacity of 578 tons.

The ship had no hangars in the true sense of the word: there was space on the main deck for maintenance, but the aircraft below were stored, as if so much cargo. Movement of machines was effected

in a somewhat cumbersome but evidently successful manner via two 3-ton cranes which travelled along a girder mounted on gantries over the main deck, lifted the aircraft in and out as required, and transported them to the electrically operated lift, below which was stowage for offensive stores, including 275 bombs and 24 torpedoes.

The machinery was unaltered: *Jupiter* was the first US Navy ship to have electric drive (Melville-McAlpine), in which the turbines powered a generator providing current to two electric motors which themselves were connected to the shafts. The generator governed the speed of the motors and provided the bridge both with a visual indication of the output at any given time and, more importantly, the means to control it, and hence the ship's speed, directly. The boiler uptakes were diverted to discharge to port only, with one hinged funnel sponsoned out adjacent to the boiler rooms.

Most of the after superstructure was removed, and a complex steel framework, utilising the support structure for the original coal booms, was erected over the main deck to carry a wood-planked flight deck running virtually the entire length of the ship; the bridge was retained forward, now below the flight deck. Two 35ft gooseneck cranes were fitted, port and starboard on the main deck, serving the lift and handling the floatplanes which were to form part of the ship's aircraft complement. Two removable pole masts were fitted along the flight deck centreline.

Jupiter was reclassified AV-1 and renamed *Langley* while undergoing conversion. Her standard complement consisted of twelve pursuit planes, twelve scouts

and ten torpedo-bombers, six of the latter being floatplanes, but in fact a wide variety of types was operated, particularly in the years immediately following her commissioning.

Arresting gear was provided in the form of both longitudinal wires – a similar system to that in vogue at the time on board British carriers – and transverse wires, the latter somewhat crude, consisting essentially of weighted cables intended to absorb only a small part of the forward energy of the landing aircraft. Two 60ft catapults were also installed, primarily for launching floatplanes, although trolley take-offs were also made with these types. Acceleration up to 50kts was achievable, depending on the particular aircraft involved.

Restrictions of space limited fixed armament to four single-mounted 5in / 51, sited one each side on the short forecastle and one on each quarter.

Modifications Shortly after commissioning, a second hinged funnel, duplicating the first, was added nearby on the port side, the exact circumstances surrounding its installation being obscure. Thereafter the ship was little modified for the next fifteen years, apart from adjustments to the flight-deck equipment, including the deletion of the longitudinal arrester wires, the renewal of the cross-deck system with more modern pendants, and the removal of the catapults. In 1937, however, with new carriers joining the fleet, it was decided to convert *Langley* to a seaplane tender. She was redesignated AV-3, and in order to embark the

Below: By 1938 *Langley* had been modified as a seaplane tender and redesignated AV-3. She is seen here in April 1939. (By courtesy of Ray Burt)

larger machines then in service, 250ft of the flight deck (*ie* the section from the lift well forward) was taken out, the bridgework modified and a handling derrick installed. Displacement fell to 11,050 tons normal; the 5in armament was unchanged.

Service Notes As the pioneer carrier in the US Navy, and indeed the only one for five years, *Langley* undertook a great deal of experimental work, not so much in the field of carrier operating tactics as in aircraft evaluation and flight-deck procedure. Although she took part in Fleet Problems and demonstrated the efficacy of carriers in naval engagements, her slow speed precluded her useful employment with the battle fleet; her trials had a significant bearing on US naval aircraft design, however, and she was also used in experimental techniques such as night landings and blind landings, and in cold-weather trials.

She was employed primarily as an aircraft transport after the outbreak of war, but her career was brief: attacked by Japanese bombers while bringing Curtiss P-40s to Java on 27 February 1942, she was hit five times and, listing badly, was finished off by 4in shells from her escorting destroyer *Whipple*.

Above: A view of the converted battlecruiser hull of *Lexington*, one day prior to launch. The white-helmeted figures by the sheds at the foot of the slipway are a telling indication of the size of the vessel. (US Navy)

LEXINGTON CLASS

Ship	Builder	Laid down	Launched	Commissioned
Lexington (CV-2)	Bethlehem	8 Jan 21	3 Oct 25	14 Dec 27
Saratoga (CV-3)	New York SB	25 Sept 20	7 Apr 25	16 Nov 27

Displacement: 38,500 tons / 39,116 tonnes (standard); 47,700 tons / 48,463 tonnes (deep load).
Length: 822ft / 250.55m (pp); 850ft / 259.08m (wl); 888ft / 270.66m (oa); 830ft / 252.98m (fd).
Beam: 104ft 7in / 31.88m (hull); 105ft 8in / 32.21m (fd).
Draught: 27ft 6in / 8.38m (mean); 32ft 6in / 9.91m (deep load).
Machinery: General Electric turbo-electric drive; 16 water-tube boilers; 4 shafts.
Performance: 180,000shp; 33.25kts.
Bunkerage: 5,400 tons / 5,486 tonnes.
Range: 10,000nm at 15kts.
Aircraft: 80.
Guns: 8 × 8in; 12 × 5in.
Complement: 2,122.

Design The origins of the first effective carriers in US Navy service lie, as in other navies, with the accelerated dreadnought building programmes of the First World War and the years immediately following; more specifically, they owed their existence to a class of six 35,000-ton (later 43,000-ton) battlecruisers laid down in 1920–21, the design for which typified the somewhat intoxicated thinking that was pervading naval circles the world over at that time. These vessels succumbed to the terms of the Washington Naval Disarmament Treaty of 1922, along with other, similar projects then under development in

Great Britain and Japan, but, as in these countries, capital ship hulls offered alternative opportunities.

Consideration for such employment was, in fact, well advanced, particularly in the United States, where the Navy was already much impressed with the capabilities and potential of shipboard aircraft: catapult-based scouts had been in regular use with cruiser squadrons, and the small carrier *Langley* was in service. Following with great interest the practical experience of the Royal Navy in conducting carrier operations – albeit somewhat experimental in nature – during the war, and benefiting from the secondment of the British constructor Stanley Goodall to the Bureau of Construction and Repair, who was thereby able to liaise very closely with his new colleagues in respect of British design thinking, the US Navy drew up plans for large, fast fleet carriers and quickly appreciated the possibilities inherent in the battlecruiser hulls when it became apparent that these, quite fortuitously, would remain incomplete.

The fundamental design characteristics of the *Lexington*-class battlecruisers did not differ too greatly from British (and hence Japanese) practice, except in terms of magnitude: typically slim in longitudinal hull form (length-to-beam ratio about 8.2:1); possessing a 9ft 4in deep armour belt 7in thick at the top, thinning to 5in at its lower edge and extending for approximately 62 per cent of the hull

length, 7in–5in bulkheads, and an armoured deck over the magazines composed of two layers of STS (Special Treatment Steel) totalling 2in in thickness; immensely powerful machinery to drive the hulls far beyond battle-line speeds (the *Lexington*s were to be the world's most powerful warships right up to the Second World War); and the heaviest and best protected guns (14in, later 16in) that could be accommodated. In short a battleship armament was to be carried on a hull with cruiser protection.

When the design was re-jigged to carrier configuration – the orders came in October (*Saratoga*) and November (*Lexington*) 1922 – the hull, together with its protection arrangements, remained virtually unchanged. On top of the hull was installed a massive hangar more than 450ft long, some 70ft wide and 21ft deep – the most voluminous accommodation known until the advent of the postwar 'super carriers'. Abaft the hangar was a 105ft-long maintenance shop, while below hangar deck level, aft, was a 120ft-long hold for disassembled aircraft. Including these dismantled machines, and allowing for the fact that a considerable number could be stowed slung from overhead girders, the total internal capacity of each carrier was about 80 first-generation (F6C, FB, OU, T3M) aircraft. This huge capacity was to prove invaluable in later years, even though the design team were not perhaps aware of this.

The boiler rooms were centrally disposed, eight on each side of the main machinery spaces; *Lexington* had Yarrow boilers, *Saratoga* White-Forster. Uptakes were trunked together, those on the port side being carried across the beam just beneath the hangar deck, to emerge through a single, massive funnel on the starboard side, 80ft high and a dramatic response to the vexing problem of smoke drift over the flight deck. Outboard of the boiler rooms were situated the main oil tanks. The capacity figure given in the table is for the initial usable bunkerage; the total volume of fuel would weigh some 6,500 tons, but 1,100 tons of this lay unused in port-side tanks to help counterbalance the considerable weight of the deck-edge superstructure on the starboard side.

The hull was plated up to the flight deck, belying subsequent US practice, and was pierced along its length for boat stowage. The bridge superstructure was separate from the funnel, but connected to it via a light catwalk at charthouse level. The flight deck, teak planked, featured two lifts, a large (30ft long × 60ft wide) unit adjacent to the bridge block with hinged flaps aft to accommodate long fuselages, and a smaller (30ft long × 36ft wide) lift in line with the after end of the funnel. A 155ft catapult was fitted forward.

The onboard armament, as completed, was as heavy as the Washington Treaty would permit. The tactical employment of the carriers envisaged them fending off attacking cruisers and torpedo-boats, especially in times of darkness and inclement weather. Eight 8in guns (Mk 14, 55-calibre) were mounted in twin turrets before and abaft the flight-deck superstructure. They were, predictably, of little use, and the whole approach to their installation was compromised: their position was the best possible in terms of reducing interference with hangar space, and the compact grouping allowed magazine arrangements and protection to be optimised; this same concentration, however, even though the turrets themselves had only splinter protection, contributed to the lateral imbalance noted earlier and, more importantly, restricted effective fire to starboard arcs only − elsewhere the blast damage inflicted by cross-decks fire would be intolerable. The 5in weapons were single-mounted Mk 19s and functioned as both anti-torpedo-boat and anti-air weapons, elevating to a maximum 85°. The 6pdrs were saluting guns. Consideration was given in the design stage to mounting torpedo tubes, but in the event none was fitted.

Modifications As with many pre-war vessels that fought in the Second World War, most of the alterations incorporated in aircraft carriers reflected new technology and combat experience, and concerned primarily the addition of radar and the enhancement of the fixed anti-aircraft batteries. However, a number of changes were effected before Pearl Harbor. In 1936, for example, 16 × 0.5in guns were fitted in four sponsons just below flight-deck level on each side of the bows and at the quarters, and a further eight

were added on the 8in turret roofs; elsewhere, *Lexington* was also fitted with a platform around the top of her funnel, carrying a further twelve such weapons.

In 1940 it was decided that the 8in turrets should be deleted and replaced with twin 5in (38-calibre) DPs, but it was not until 1942 that the old mountings were taken off; *Lexington* never did receive the new weapons, though her sister's were installed immediately. Meanwhile, *Lexington* was receiving 5 × 3in (50-calibre) guns, one on each sponson and one just forward of the funnel, but these were almost at once replaced with quad 1.1in machine-guns. In 1942 four more 1.1in mountings were sited on three of the former 8in barbettes, with three more around the funnel, while 18 × 20mm AA weapons were added on platforms outboard of the funnel and in the boat stowage recesses.

Saratoga had had all her 0.5in machine-guns replaced with 32 × 20mm by 1942, in which year her single 5in / 25s were deleted and 8 × 5in / 38 Mk 30 single mountings installed; 36 × 1.1in in quadruple mountings were also added. Subsequently 40mm and further 20mm guns were installed (some of the latter being replaced later with yet more 40mm), so that by 1945 she was carrying sixteen (reduced from 52) 20mm and 96 × 40mm, all but four of the latter in quadruple mountings.

Significant structural changes affected only *Saratoga*, although in 1941 both carriers had their flight decks widened forward. In 1942 *Saratoga*'s deck was extended in length to 900ft; at the same time her funnel was reduced in height by 14ft, her bridge remodelled and a pole mast fitted, and a prominent bulge was added to the starboard side of the hull to improve buoyancy, thus allowing her 1,100 tons of oil fuel ballast to be utilised and thereby increasing range to 12,500mm at 15kts.

In late 1941 both ships received CXAM-1 search radar; this was the only system ever installed in *Lexington*, but *Saratoga*'s set was replaced by SK later in the war. In early 1942 *Saratoga* received SC-1 (air search), SG-1 (surface search) and FD (fire control, fitted to her Mk 37 5in directors) sets; the funnel-mounted SC-1 was replaced by SC-3 later in the war, when a second SC-1 was also fitted. Her final suite included Mk 22 (FD auxiliary), SM height-finding radar and IFF systems, plus YE / YG radio beacons.

Other than the fitting of arrester wires forward, supplementing those aft and enabling machines to be landed from either direction, and the removal of the bow catapult (changes made to both ships in the mid 1930s), *Lexington*'s aircraft handling arrangements remained essentially unaltered throughout her life. In 1944 *Saratoga* had two new catapults installed, primarily to enable her to operate TBMs, and a new 45ft × 45ft lift, the after unit being removed and the flight deck plated over.

Changes in aircraft complements were more far-reaching: virtually the entire range of US biplane and

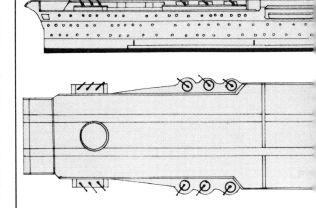

Lexington, 1938/39

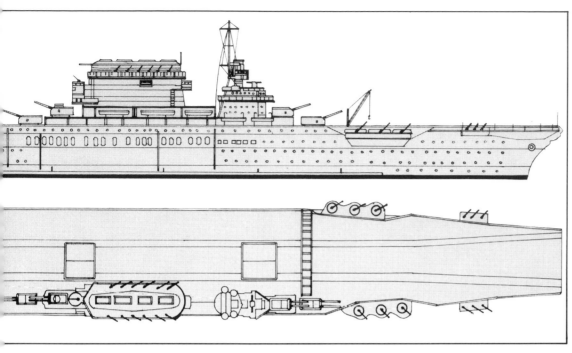

first-generation monoplane types were operated by *Lexington* and *Saratoga* during their careers, both fighter (FB, F6C, F2B, F3B, F4B, F11C, O2U, FF, SU, F2F, F3F, F2A, F4F) and attack (T3M, T4M, BM, BG, SBU, TBD, SBD) aircraft, sub-variants of a particular machine being embarked on occasions for merely a matter of months. Their very spaciousness allowed the carriers to adapt readily to the larger and more complex aircraft which came late in their careers: by 1945 *Saratoga* could still operate more than 70 TBMs and F6Fs, though not all could be internally stowed.

Service Notes *Lexington*: As the primary US carriers up to the Second World War – and the largest in the world until the commissioning of the *Midways* – both ships were responsible for formulating US naval air tactics (which would be put into serious practice later) and demonstrated throughout the 1930s the growing potency of airborne scouting, fleet

Below: *Saratoga*, about 1928. During the US Navy's prewar Fleet Problems, she and her sister ship were generally assigned to opposing forces, and for identification purposes *Saratoga* had a broad, black stripe painted down her funnel; this followed a number of unfortunate errors in the 1929 Problem. (US Navy, by courtesy of Norman Friedman)

defence and strike. One unusual, and celebrated, task which befell *Lexington* was during the winter of 1929–30, when her generators supplied the entire city of Tacoma, Washington, with power for a month after drought had caused the city's hydro-electric sources to fail.

The first weeks after Pearl Harbor were taken up by offensive patrols out of Hawaii, with skirmishes with the Japanese off Rabaul and New Guinea. *Lexington* returned to Pearl Harbor in late March 1942, departing for the same combat zone in mid April. On 8 May the carrier was struck by at least two torpedoes and two bombs from Japanese carrier aircraft operating from *Shokaku* and *Zuikaku*; fires were started, and near misses had strained her hull. Some two hours later she was rent by a serious explosion as aviation fuel ignited. Fresh fires were started, and when it became clear that the ship could not be saved she was deliberately sunk by five torpedoes from the US destroyer *Phelps*.

Saratoga: During patrols off Pearl Harbor in January 1942, *Saratoga* suffered a torpedo hit from the submarine *I-6* which caused insignificant damage. However, permanent repairs and major modifications (see above) were carried out at Puget Sound Navy Yard, Bremerton. She was more seriously damaged by a second hit (*I-26*) on 31 August of that year, with three boiler rooms flooded and the ship immobilised through shock. She was taken in tow to Tonga, patched up, and returned to Pearl Harbor for permanent repairs.

Most of 1943 was taken up by air strikes on land targets and Japanese shipping in the south-west Pacific; the first half of 1944 saw her operating with the British fleet in the Indian Ocean, and, following a three-month refit at Bremerton, she was used for pilot training until the end of the year.

February 1945 saw *Saratoga* in action with US forces once again, when she was severely crippled by hits from bombs and kamikazes off Iwo Jima. She managed to make Bremerton once more, however, where repairs were put in hand. The rest of the war was spent in further pilot training. After V-J Day she helped bring home US troops from the combat zone.

Seriously strained by war operations and encountering more and more problems working the heavier aircraft then in service, *Saratoga* was expended as a target in the atomic bomb tests at Bikini, 25 July 1946.

Above right: A late 1930s photograph of *Lexington*, showing some modifications to her original appearance: the 0.5in MG gallery below the funnel cap and the widened forward flight deck. (US Navy, by courtesy of Norman Friedman)

Centre right: *Saratoga* at Hobart, Tasmania, in March 1944. (Australian War Memorial)

Right: *Saratoga*, at Puget Sound. The striking camouflage (Measure 32, Design 11A) was unique to *Saratoga*, and she wore it from September 1944 (the date of this photograph) until 1945. (US Navy, by courtesy of Norman Friedman)

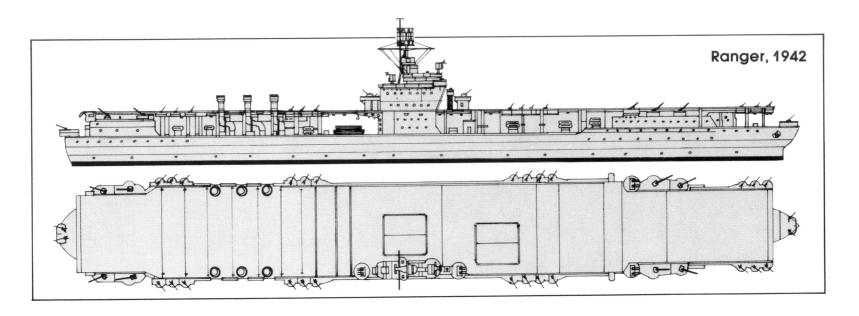

RANGER (CV-4)

Builder	Laid down	Launched	Commissioned
Newport News	26 Sept 31	25 Feb 33	4 July 34

Displacement: 14,000 tons / 14,224 tonnes (standard); 17,577 tons / 17,858 tonnes (deep load).
Length: 730ft / 222.5m (wl); 769ft / 234.39m (oa); 710ft / 216.41m (fd).
Beam: 80ft / 24.38m (hull); 87ft 6in / 26.67m (fd).
Draught: 19ft 8in / 5.99m (mean); 22ft 6in / 6.86m (deep load).
Machinery: Curtis / Parsons geared turbines; 6 Babcock & Wilcox boilers; 2 shafts.
Performance: 53,500shp; 29kts.
Bunkerage: 2,350 tons / 2,388 tonnes.
Range: 10,000nm at 15kts.
Aircraft: 76.
Guns: 8 × 5in.
Complement: 1,788.

Design The construction of new carriers after 1922 was dominated by the restrictive terms of the Washington Treaty. The governing factor was the upper limit placed on carrier fleets – in the US case, 135,000 tons. New carriers were limited to individual displacements of 27,000 tons, but this was of less importance than the overall tonnage, the direct effect of which was to encourage, at least in the US, the smallest practical vessel in order to allow the largest number of them. After the *Lexington*s (*Langley* was discounted), 69,000 tons were available for new construction, and it was confidently expected that five units could realistically be extracted from this figure.

In the design of *Ranger*, it was perhaps natural that constructors would look more to *Langley* than to the *Lexington*s as a basis from which to start, and the two

vessels thus shared some common features. The original scheme was for an entirely flush deck, with smoke discharging via six hinged funnels aft, disposed port and starboard; similarly, the flight deck was carried over the superstructure supported by light girder latticework. Unlike *Langley*, however, *Ranger*'s design was predicated almost exclusively on aviation requirements, which a converted vessel could never match: protection, fixed batteries, even speed and, as it proved, seakeeping qualities were sub-

Below: The first US Navy carrier designed and built as such was *Ranger*, seen here at Hunter's Point, San Francisco, March 1937. Note the 0.5in machine-guns sited along the flight-deck edge forward, and the twin saluting guns on the forecastle. The two 5in/25 weapons (just below flight-deck level, forward) are covered. (US Navy)

ordinate to the objective of embarking the maximum number of aircraft. These constraints are reflected in that whereas the mid 1930s *Saratoga* and *Lexington* showed about 450 tons per aircraft carried, *Ranger* needed only 180.

The experiences with previous carriers were evident in a number of *Ranger*'s characteristics. The boiler rooms were placed as far aft and as close together as possible, and abaft the machinery spaces, to minimise the trunking run of the uptakes while still permitting stern discharge, and to provide the maximum internal volume for aviation facilities, even at the price of increased vulnerability wherein one hit could deactivate the ship's entire propulsion system; and the two lifts were offset to starboard to enable landed aircraft to be moved forward quickly to the

bows to clear the flight deck aft for following machines. An island superstructure was added before completion when the desirability for improved command and control became apparent – an alteration which added a fair measure of topweight and took the ship rather beyond the originally specified displacement. The island was kept to minimum dimensions, not only so as to encroach as little as possible on the flight deck, but also perforce, since the optimum position amidships offered very restricted deck space, adjacent as it was to the lifts. Maximum flight-deck width was 109ft 6in.

The ship was unarmoured, and armament was restricted to single 5in / 25 AA, disposed one pair forward and one pair aft on each side, the forward pairs being split between forecastle (as in *Langley*) and deck-edge positions and the after four mountings being located just below flight-deck level.

Ranger's large air group consisted of 36 pursuit planes, 36 dive-bombers and four utility aircraft; there was no provision for torpedo-bombers. Despite this capacity, however, the ship proved a disappointment as a functioning aircraft carrier. In particular her small size and low power prevented her from operating with the larger fleet carriers and she showed poor seakeeping qualities in adverse conditions, being unable to launch her aircraft in even moderate swells.

Modifications An early modification was the relocation of the forecastle 5in guns to the sponsons carrying the other forward weapons, and in about 1935 two Mk 33 directors were added to the island for 5in fire control. By 1942, 16×1.1in machine-guns in quadruple mountings had been fitted, on pedestals before and abaft the island and just aft of the forward 5in mountings at the deck edge. Thereafter, additions were generally confined to wartime 40mm and 20mm mountings, CXAM-1 (1942), SC-2 (1944, replacing CXAM-1) and SK (1944, replacing SC-2) search radars and Mk 4 fire control radars (1942), as a result of which the ship's complement rose to about 2,000. In 1944 the flight deck was strengthened, a hydraulic catapult was fitted and, to save weight, all the 5in and 1.1in weapons and their directors were removed. Armament now consisted of six quadruple 40mm and 52 single 20mm, although by all the 40mms had been taken out.

Service Notes *Ranger*'s shortcomings as a fleet carrier led to her being used mainly in the Atlantic, where she was employed as a transport supplying aircraft for the Allied operations in North Africa and subsequently as an attack carrier in strikes against Vichy targets in that area. From 1943 she was attached to the British Home Fleet and used her SBDs against German shipping off Norway. Early in 1944 she was designated a training carrier, though still on occasion undertook aircraft transport duties. She was decommissioned on 18 October 1946 and sold for scrapping in January 1947.

YORKTOWN CLASS

Ship	Builder	Laid down	Launched	Commissioned
Yorktown (CV-5)	Newport News	21 May 34	4 Apr 36	30 Sept 37
Enterprise (CV-6)	Newport News	16 July 34	3 Oct 36	12 May 38
Hornet (CV-8)	Newport News	25 Sept 39	14 Dec 40	20 Oct 41

Displacement: 19,872 tons / 20,190 tonnes (standard); 25,500 tons / 25,908 tonnes (deep load).
Length: 770ft / 234.7m (wl); 809ft 6in / 246.74m (oa); 802ft / 244.45m (fd).
Beam: 83ft 3in / 25.37m (hull); 86ft / 26.21m (fd).
Draught: 21ft 6in / 6.55m (mean); 25ft 11in / 7.9m (deep load).
Machinery: Parsons geared turbines; 9 Babcock & Wilcox boilers; 4 shafts.
Performance: 120,000shp; 32.5kts.
Bunkerage: 4,360 tons / 4,430 tonnes.
Range: 12,000nm at 15kts.
Aircraft: 96.
Guns: 8×5in.
Complement: 1,890.

Design Even before *Ranger* was launched, the US Navy was having serious doubts about the wisdom of building five 'minimum' carriers in the total tonnage available, and recommendations that at least speed and protection be significantly improved resulted in the abandonment of the *Ranger* type and an optimum displacement figure of 20,000 tons. This would allow for a larger hull to accommodate the more powerful machinery required and for an even larger air group to be operated. Only two such vessels could be managed within the Washington limitations, however, although a third, smaller carrier could use up the balance.

Nevertheless, the *Yorktown* design had much in common with *Ranger* and at first showed a completely flush deck with folding funnels; it was considered, however, that such an arrangement would be incompatible with the high sea speed demanded of the design, owing to excessive smoke discharge and the consequent problems posed to landing aircraft, so an island arrangement was settled upon. The hangars were again built up as a light superstructure rather than as an integral part of the hull, with their sides closed off by rolling shutters to enable supplies to be readily loaded and offloaded and to permit aircraft to run up their engines before being taken to the flight deck; the design was to have other benefits, especially with regard to the natural dispersal of petrol vapour, as discussed in the introductory chapters. The

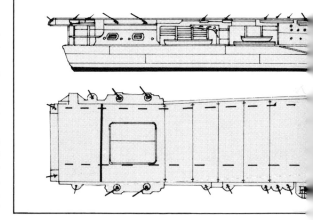

Yorktown, 1942

increased hull volume and the decision to incorporate an island structure permitted a more conventional and less cramped machinery arrangement than in *Ranger*, with the nine boilers disposed amidships and the machinery itself aft. The main uptakes were routed below the hangar deck.

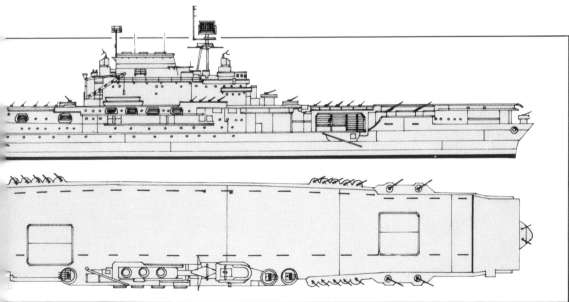

The extra displacement available permitted a 2½in–4in waterline belt, 4in bulkheads and a 1½in armoured deck over machinery and magazines, but did not allow armoured hangars or flight deck as had been tentatively proposed at one stage. Subdivision was more extensive than in previous US carriers.

The *Yorktown*s showed an improved disposition of lifts, with three units (four were at one time mooted) each capable of handling 15,000lb. The flight deck was of 6in wood planks, and arrester gear was provided both aft (nine wires) and forward (four) in keeping with the US Navy requirement for over-the-bows landings with the ship full astern. Two hydraulic catapults were installed on the flight deck forward, but for the first time a further unit, launching athwartships in opposite directions, was located on the forward hangar deck, an interesting parallel with the Royal and Japanese Navies' capability of launching aircraft from auxiliary positions without interfering with flight deck operations. The flight deck itself was asymmetric in outline: although the lift amidships was located to starboard of the centreline, it was found necessary to widen the flight deck along the port side at this point to enable landed aircraft to be brought forward with the necessary clearance.

The theoretical aircraft complement given in the table was made up of eighteen fighters (F2F), 36 torpedo-bombers (TBD), 37 dive-bombers (BT, SBC) and five general-purpose aircraft, but in practice there were rarely more than 80 machines on board because of overcrowding. The fixed battery consisted of the

new 5in / 38 dual-purpose mounting first introduced in *Farragut*-class destroyers (DD-348) whose design predated that of the *Yorktown*s by about a year.

Hornet differed in detail from her two sister ships; her construction was not envisaged when the designs were drawn up and she was produced as an emergency measure. The Washington Treaty had lapsed, the first London Treaty (1930) had terminated, and the second London Treaty (1936) placed no restrictions concerning total permissible tonnage; with the threat of war in Europe and uncertain developments in the Far East, Congress authorised the expansion of the carrier fleet in May 1937 and funds were appropriated for 40,000 tons of additional ships. The designs for the *Essex* class were then being formulated, but to save time a repeat *Yorktown* was ordered. The flight deck of the new carrier was apparently somewhat wider (maximum 114ft as against 109ft); it was also reportedly a little longer, although this is difficult to confirm from the available evidence.

Hornet had an additional short-range battery upon commissioning, consisting of 16 × 1.1in machine-guns and 24 single-mounted 0.5in. The 1.1in, quadruple-mounted, two before the island and one abaft, with the fourth set sponsored out to starboard further aft, were designed into the class though the

weapons themselves were not available until well after *Yorktown* and *Enterprise* had been commissioned. As a result of these modifications, *Hornet* displaced some 200 tons more and drew an additional 6in at standard displacement. She also differed in island detail, carrying two Mk 37 5in directors instead of the Mk 33s in her sisters.

Modifications All three carriers were fitted with CXAM search radar in 1941–42, apparently the only sets fitted to *Yorktown* and *Hornet* before each was lost. *Enterprise* had CXAM-1 and SC-2 by the end of 1943, and by 1945 these had been replaced by an updated suite of SK, SC-2 and SP, together with fire control sets Mk 4.

By 1942 both *Enterprise* and *Yorktown* had received their 16 × 1.1in machine-guns and several 20mm, *Yorktown* additionally carrying sixteen single 0.5in AA. *Hornet* had received 30 × 20mm by the time she was lost, and *Enterprise*'s AA was progressively augmented throughout the war so that by 1945 she was showing eleven quadruple 40mm, eight twin 20mm and sixteen single 20mm. Her flight deck was reportedly lengthened in 1943, when she was also given bulges to improve her stability and buoyancy against the considerable added topweight brought about by the build-up of modifications.

Service Notes *Yorktown*: Peacetime deployments

Above: *Hornet* (CV-8) in mid 1941. On completion her 5in/38 gun positions had protective plating (unlike those in *Enterprise* and *Yorktown*), but the weapons had apparently not yet been fitted when this photograph was taken. (US Navy)

Right: The three elements of *Yorktown*'s 1942 fixed battery can be seen here: two of her 20mms at the bows; a 5in/38 trained outboard off the flight-deck edge; and an elevated quadruple 1.1in mounting (a second, not easy to make out, is abaft and above it) before the island. The photograph was taken at Pearl Harbor, during repairs after Coral Sea and prior to Midway, where the carrier was to be lost. (US Navy)

took *Yorktown* to the East Coast, and she was at Norfolk Navy Yard at the time of Pearl Harbor. She transferred to the Pacific immediately on the outbreak of war, and during early 1942 operated off New Guinea, attacking Japanese shipping and shore installations. Joined by the carrier *Lexington* in May, she struck at the Japanese carrier *Shoho* in the Coral Sea, her aircraft helping to sink the enemy vessel and also damaging the fleet carrier *Shokaku*. *Yorktown* herself was damaged and had to be temporarily patched up at Pearl Harbor.

In company with *Enterprise* and *Hornet* she deployed once more to the battle zone at Midway and on 4 June launched a successful strike against the Japanese carrier *Soryu*, which was left ablaze. *Yorktown* herself was hit by two waves of attackers,

however, suffering three bomb hits in the first and two torpedo hits in the second which crippled her. She was taken in tow, but two days later was hit by more torpedoes from *I-168*. She sank next day.

Enterprise took part in the Midway battle, but her TBD torpedo-bombers suffered considerable losses; however, her SBD dive-bombers helped account for *Akagi*, *Kaga* and *Hiryu*. Off Guadalcanal in August 1942 she suffered several hits from Japanese bombers, but was repaired at Pearl in time for Santa Cruz in October. Hit again during that action, and repaired again, she returned to sink the battleship *Hiei* and several smaller units in the following month.

The remainder of the war, after a big refit during the second half of 1943, was taken up in strikes against Japanese targets on the Pacific islands, and against significant enemy vessels such as the battleships *Fuso* and *Musashi*. A kamikaze hit in May 1945, which blew out the forward lift, put her in dock until after hostilities had ended. She was repaired, but she decommissioned on 17 February 1947 and was placed in reserve, being redesignated an ASW carrier (CVS-6) in July 1953. She never saw operational service again, and despite strenuous efforts to preserve her as a memorial she was sold for scrapping on 1 July 1958.

Hornet lasted in service barely more than a year, but will be best remembered for the celebrated 'Doolittle Raid' in April 1942. All her air group was stowed below and aircraft which she was hardly designed to operate – 16 Army B-25 Mitchell medium bombers – were ranged on deck for an attack on the Japanese mainland which caused little material damage, but was magnificent propaganda.

Hornet participated at Midway, but was sunk at Santa Cruz on 27 October 1942, after taking four bomb and sixteen torpedo hits, from both Japanese and US vessels (after the latter had failed in an attempt to take her in tow).

Below: *Hornet* at Pearl Harbor in 1942, probably in late April just after the 'Tokyo Raid'. Note the 20mm guns along the after flight deck, just in silhouette. (US Navy)

Bottom: The open-type hangars of the *Yorktown*s are obvious in this May 1942 photograph of *Enterprise* at Pearl Harbor. The half-ton antenna of her CXAM system, the earliest US production search (warning) radar, is visible on the foremast. (US Navy)

WASP (CV-7)

Builder	Laid down	Launched	Commissioned
Bethlehem	1 Apr 36	4 Apr 39	25 Apr 40

Displacement: 14,700 tons / 14,935 tonnes (standard); 18,500 tons / 18,796 tonnes (deep load).
Length: 688ft / 209.7m (wl); 741ft 3in / 225.93m (oa); 727ft 6in / 221.74m (fd).
Beam: 80ft 9in / 24.61m (hull); 93ft / 28.35m (fd).
Draught: 20ft / 6.1m (mean); 24ft 6in / 7.47m (deep load).
Machinery: Parsons geared turbines; 6 Yarrow boilers; 2 shafts.
Performance: 70,000shp; 29.5kts.
Bunkerage: 2,400 tons / 2,438 tonnes.

Range: 12,000nm at 15kts.
Aircraft: 84.
Guns: 8 × 5in.
Complement: 1,889.

Design More than any other carrier, *Wasp* was a product of the Washington Treaty: had it not been for that agreement there is no doubt that she would never have been built. With the laying down of *Yorktown* and *Enterprise*, 15,000 tons only was available to bring the US carrier fleet up to its maximum permissible size, and the General Board had little option but to 'squeeze' *Wasp*'s design as much as practicable, incorporating as many of the *Yorktown*s' features as possible. The result was a somewhat unsuccessful ship, showing shortcomings which would prove fatal.

As in *Ranger*, much was sacrificed in order to extract the maximum air capability from the design: hence low-power machinery was installed, in order to save space, and although provision for armour protection was made in the design it was not incorporated when the carrier commissioned –

Below: *Wasp* was the first US carrier to have a deck-edge lift, albeit a somewhat basic design, comprising essentially a hinged girder. In this early 1942 photograph it is just visible, lowered, casting its shadow across the hull, forward. The aircraft on the flight deck appear to be F4Fs and SB2Us. (US Navy)

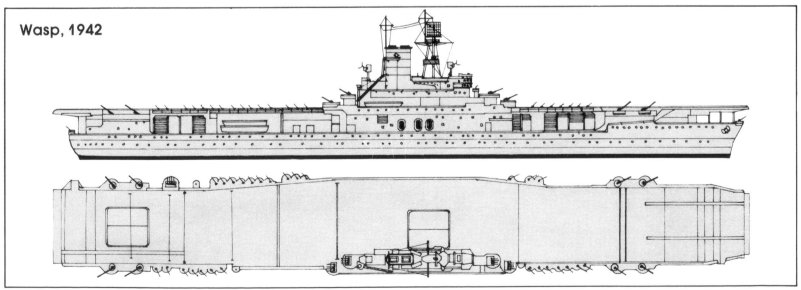

Wasp, 1942

Above: *Wasp* spent most of her brief wartime career in the Atlantic, but in June 1942 departed Norfolk Navy Yard (where this photograph was taken) for the Pacific. The structure angled abaft the island is a handling crane, a feature also of the *Yorktown*s. Note the row of 20mm positions along the flight-deck edge. (US Navy, by courtesy of Norman Friedman)

indeed, there is some doubt as to whether it was subsequently added, as had been the intention. Most significantly, there was a complete absence of effective anti-torpedo protection.

US designers had studied the possibility of fitting separate flying-off decks to carriers in the 1930s, presumably following the pattern established by British and Japanese carriers, but in *Wasp*'s case a pair of hangar-deck catapults were installed, one forward and one aft, launching athwartships following the system introduced in the *Yorktown*s; two further units were installed on the flight deck forward. One novelty, highlighting the stability problems associated with the adoption of island superstructures atop the flight deck, was the asymmetric hull form, which was widened to port to compensate the additional weight on the starboard side, enabling the total bunker capacity to be used and providing additional internal volume at the same time.

The boiler rooms were situated between the forward and aft machinery spaces, which lessened the risk of one hit stopping the ship completely.

Topside, arrester wires were installed to enable landings to be conducted from either end of the flight deck, but a further step in the evolution of aircraft lift location was the installation of the third unit in the form of a movable girder at the edge of the flight deck. The latter was carried, as in *Ranger* and the *Yorktown*s, on a substructure built up over the main deck and thus did not contribute to the strength of the ship. Below, the 500ft × 75ft hangar, with a working height of 17ft 2in, was open-sided though it could be closed off by shutters in bad weather.

Wasp's air group initially numbered one squadron each of fighters and dive-bombers and two of scout-bombers; there was no provision for torpedo stowage (*cf Ranger*), and in fact she did not operate torpedo-bombers until VT-7 (TBF) embarked in August 1942, a few weeks before her loss. The fixed armament consisted of single 38-calibre open mountings, disposed as in *Yorktown*.

Modifications Alterations to *Wasp* were confined chiefly to enhancing her AA armament, improving splinter protection and installing radar. By 1941 16 × 1.1in machine-guns in quadruple mounts had

been installed around the island and at the deck edge further aft on the starboard side, together with 16 × 0.5in AA; by mid 1942, however, the ineffectual 0.5in weapons had been replaced by 20 × 20mm, and reportedly the first US Navy installation of the quadruple 40mm had been made aboard her. By this time she was also fitted with CXAM-1 search and Mk 4 (Mk 33 directors) fire control radar. Splinter shields had been added around the 5in positions, and the forward pairs of 5in had additionally been enclosed in protective gunhouses. Her complement rose to 2,167, of whom 779 formed the air group.

Service Notes With the Atlantic Fleet in 1941, *Wasp* assisted significantly in the relief of Malta in March–May 1942, transporting approximately 100 Spitfire fighters in two passages from Britain for the defence of that island. She returned to Norfolk Navy Yard, then departed in June 1942 for the Pacific. Attacks against Japanese positions around Guadalcanal were carried out, but on 15 September she was struck by three torpedoes fired from the submarine *I-19* which caused serious fires and explosions through ruptured avgas lines. She was abandoned, and her end was hastened by torpedoes from the US destroyer *Lansdowne*.

LONG ISLAND (CVE-1)

Builder	Launched	Commissioned
Sun	11 Jan 40	2 June 41

Displacement: 7,886 tons / 8,012 tonnes (standard);
14,050 tons / 14,275 tonnes (deep load).
Length: 465ft / 141.73m (wl); 492ft / 149.96m (oa);
360ft / 109.73m (fd).
Beam: 69ft 6in / 21.18m (hull); 78ft / 23.77m (fd).
Draught: 25ft 6in / 7.77m (mean).
Machinery: 7-cylinder Sulzer diesel engine; 1 shaft.
Performance: 8,500bhp; 16kts.
Bunkerage: 1,429 tons / 1,452 tonnes.
Aircraft: 16.
Guns: 1×4in; 2×3in; 4×0.5in.
Complement: 970.

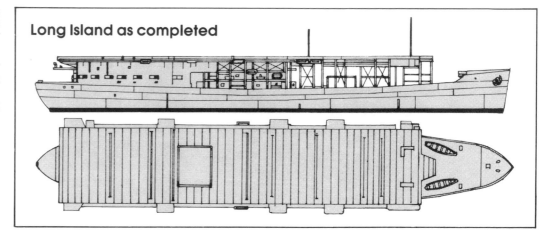

Long Island as completed

Above: This broadside view of the prototype US escort carrier, *Long Island*, makes plain the ship's mercantile origins. She is seen in early 1944, after her flight deck had been extended forward some 60ft. (US Navy, by courtesy of Norman Friedman)

Design Since the early 1930s there had been considerable US interest concerning the provision of small carriers capable of transporting aircraft, either to replenish fleet carriers or, more importantly, to move Army aircraft from the USA to overseas bases. Under the Washington Treaty the tonnage allowance would clearly best be used for the building of front-line units, and – significantly, as it turned out – the agreement did not concern itself with aircraft carriers which might be considered auxiliary vessels, in other words might appear superficially to resemble aircraft carriers but were not used exclusively as such; further, it was not concerned with ships capable of carrying aircraft but those which displaced less than 10,000 tons.

One project courted in the United States throughout much of the interwar period was some type of cruiser-carrier, a ship of cruiser proportions, limited by Treaty to 10,000 tons, but capable of handling a useful air group via its extended flight deck aft; it would retain 6in or 8in guns in sufficient numbers to justify its classification as a cruiser, but would be a means of getting more aircraft to sea outside the limits of Washington. The project was never brought to fruition, but it illustrates the anxieties of the time.

The conclusive impetus towards providing additional flight decks for the US Navy stemmed principally from growing concern in the late 1930s about Japanese ambitions in the Pacific; through a realisation that the new *Essex*-class carriers were some way off and that more aircraft at sea were desperately needed to fill the gap; and finally from the British request to supply such vessels cheaply and with immediacy under Lend-Lease for convoy protection. Incidentally, the supposed influence of *Audacity* is doubtful since the first US auxiliary carrier was commissioned more than three months before that vessel was brought into action.

The acquisition of a number of merchantmen from the Moore-Macormick Line was finalised in the spring of 1941, and the *Mormacmail*, a C3 cargo vessel, was taken in hand for immediate conversion to an auxiliary aircraft carrier (AVG-1), a Presidential stipulation being that work be concluded within three months; other hulls purchased were destined for Royal Navy service, although one of these would be retained by the US Navy.

Mormacmail was diesel-powered, which tended to reduce the problem of providing elaborate smoke discharge facilities, but had a limited sea speed, deemed acceptable, however, in view of the intended role. A hangar, enclosed aft for approximately 120ft, was served by a single centreline lift. The hull was unarmoured, and there was provision for 100,000 US gallons of aviation fuel. A wood-planked flight deck, extending for about 70 per cent of the ship's length, left the forecastle clear, and a navigating bridge was installed forward, just below the flight-deck edge. Two single 3in / 50 guns were set forward on the forecastle, with a single 4in aft on the quarter-deck; 21 aircraft were originally envisaged (SOC, F2A), but only sixteen were embarked on completion, although capacity was considerably enhanced in *Long Island*'s primary task as a transport.

Modifications After only a few months of service, *Long Island* was refitted at Mare Island with a longer (420ft) flight deck to enable her aircraft to operate more effectively; this was extended forward, and the bridge was abandoned in favour of two positions sponsored out port and starboard at the deck edge. At first, defensive armament was increased by $5 \times$ 20mm, but by 1944 the 4in weapon had been replaced by a single 3in / 50 and numerous additional twin 20mms had been installed along the deck edge; a new catapult was added to take the stress of heavier aircraft coming into service on board fleet carriers, for which *Long Island* served as a ferry. A radar mast, carrying an SC antenna (replaced by SC-2 by 1944), was fitted after the ship had been in commission for about a year.

Service Notes During the Second World War, *Long Island* was used almost exclusively as a transport and training carrier. She was redesignated ACV-1 in 1942, and CVE-1 in July 1943. Withdrawn from service in March 1946, she reverted to merchant configuration as the *Nelly* in 1949 and was renamed *Seven Seas* in 1953. She was hulked at Rotterdam in 1966.

CHARGER (CVE-30)

Builder	Launched	Commissioned
Sun	1 Mar 41	3 Mar 42

Displacement: 11,800 tons / 11,989 tonnes (standard); 15,126 tons / 15,368 tonnes (deep load).
Length: 465ft / 141.73m (pp); 465 / 141.73m (wl); 492ft / 149.96m (oa); 440ft / 134.11m (fd).
Beam: 69ft 6in / 21.18m (hull); 78ft / 23.77m (fd).
Draught: 21ft 6in / 6.55m (mean); 25ft 2in / 7.67m (deep load).
Machinery: 6-cylinder Doxford diesel engine; 1 shaft.
Performance: 8,500bhp; 17kts.
Bunkerage: 3,200 tons / 3,251 tonnes.
Aircraft: 36.
Guns: 3 × 4in; 10 × 20mm.
Complement: 856.

Design One of the six vessels earmarked in late 1941 for conversion to an auxiliary carrier was the diesel-powered *Rio de la Plata*, another C3 cargo ship from the Moore-Macormick Line and closely similar to *Mormacmail*. Incomplete when acquired, the ship, to be renamed *Charger*, emerged in somewhat different form from *Long Island*: in particular, a longer (190ft) hangar, 16ft high, was added to the hull, and a full-length flight deck was fitted from the first. The single lift (42ft × 32ft) was retained.

More conspicuously, a simple box island was placed off the starboard deck edge, supported by a narrow sponson, well forward to keep the maximum unobstructed flight-deck length for landing-on and to assist navigation. There was no funnel, diesel exhaust being vented via small ducts on each side of the flight deck amidships. Over-the-bows arrested landings were catered for, complementing the conventional system aft.

As in *Long Island*, considerable amounts of fuel could be accommodated, including up to 90,000 US gallons of aviation fuel, which suggests roles other than that of a pure transport; British naval officers were to frown upon the petrol stowage arrangements, blaming the loss of one of *Charger*'s sister ships on over-zealous US bunkerage at the expense of safety.

The armament indicated in the table was that first fitted, as the ship was originally completed to RN requirements.

Modifications Upon entry into US service, *Charger* showed a revised armament of 1 × 5in / 51 on the quarterdeck and 2 × 3in / 50 on the forecastle, the smaller weapons in protective 'tubs' sponsoned out over, and faired into, the hull. At least ten single 20mms were present by the end of the war, fewer than in other escort carriers, but explicable in that the ship was held for pilot training.

Service Notes Designated BAVG-4 for the Royal Navy, *Charger* was completed as such in mid 1941, but by October had been taken back by the US Navy, to be retained as a 'school' for Fleet Air Arm trainees. In January 1942 she was redesignated AVG-30, in August 1942 ACV-30, and in July 1943 CVE-30. She was not used in combat and was decommissioned in March 1946, stricken and sold. Converted back to a merchant ship from 1947, she was renamed *Fairsea* in 1949.

SANGAMON CLASS

Ship	Builder	Laid down	Launched	Commissioned
Sangamon (CVE-26)	Federal	13 Mar 39	4 Nov 39	25 Aug 42
Suwannee (CVE-27)	Federal		4 Mar 39	24 Sept 42
Chenango (CVE-28)	Sun		1 April 39	19 Sept 42
Santee (CVE-29)	Sun		4 Mar 39	24 Aug 42

Displacement: 10,500 tons / 10,668 tonnes (standard); 23,875 tons / 24,257 tonnes (deep load).
Length: 525ft / 160.02m (wl); 553ft / 168.55m (oa); 495ft / 150.88m (fd).
Beam: 75ft / 22.86m (hull); 75ft 6in / 23.01m (fd).
Draught: 30ft 7in / 9.32m (deep load).
Machinery: Allis-Chalmers geared turbines; 4 Babcock & Wilcox boilers; 2 shafts.
Performance: 13,500shp; 18kts.
Bunkerage: 4,780 tons / 4,856 tonnes.
Range: 24,000nm at 15kts.
Aircraft: 30.
Guns: 2 × 5in; 8 × 40mm; 12 × 20mm.
Complement: 1,080.

Design With the supply of convertible C3 hulls exhausted, the US Navy cast about for alternative hulls that might serve as a basis for aircraft transport construction, and selected four of its ex-merchant

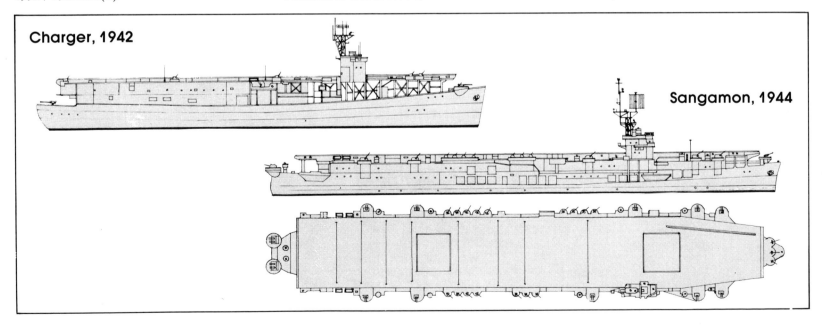

Charger, 1942

Sangamon, 1944

T3-type tankers (oilers) purchased as such for use in the service during 1940–41. It is perhaps an indication of the clamour for further sea-going flight decks that these ships were chosen: their configuration was relatively adaptable, but their value to the Fleet was already high.

The four vessels were converted in 1942 along similar lines to the *Bogues*, but there were important differences, resulting from their different origins: their hulls could accommodate a longer hangar (albeit still handicapped by the sheer forward and aft) and a longer flight deck, while their dual-shaft turbines and increased power output improved manoeuvrability and gave a useful increase in speed. The machinery spaces and boiler rooms were situated right aft, permitting short trunking to the four small funnels disposed in pairs to port and starboard.

The unarmoured hull was plated up to flight-deck level along the hangar sides, but featured openings amidships for ventilation and to permit the vessels to function still as oilers (which, on occasion, they were to do). The general flight-deck layout followed that of the *Bogues*, with two lifts of similar dimensions and capacity; a single catapult was installed forward, on the port side. The island, with its lattice mast (SC radar) also resembled that of the *Bogues*.

The armament was schemed somewhat differently, being located on the forecastle (three single 20mm), on the quarters (two single 5in / 51), right aft, in sponsons (two twin 40mm) and along the flight-deck edge (two twin 40mm sponsoned out forward, and the remaining 20mm). Designed for thirty aircraft, it was found that 36 could be adequately embarked (two full squadrons, initially one F4F and one SBD / TBF).

Conversion work was undertaken at Newport News (*Sangamon* and *Suwannee*), Norfolk Navy Yard (*Santee*) and Bethlehem, Staten Island (*Chenango*).

Modifications SC radar was modified to SC-2

Top left: Charger in January 1944, showing a very basic radar fit: the 15ft × 4ft 6in SC-2 air-search mattress and the smaller SG surface-search antenna below it; at the masthead is the YE aircraft homing beacon. (US Navy)

Bottom left: The Sangamons were among the first US escort carriers to commission. Their design was generally more successful than that of the C-3 conversions, mainly because of their larger size and twin-shaft machinery. This is the name-ship, early in her career: her AA armament would soon be considerably up-graded. (US Navy, by courtesy of A. D. Baker III)

Top right: The Royal Navy needed escort carriers primarily for convoy protection duties in the Atlantic; by comparison, few US CVEs were so employed. One was *Santee*, which is seen here serving as an Atlantic ASW carrier in June 1943. (US Navy)

Bottom right: A view of *Chenango* in 1942–43, showing the pair of twin 40mms tub-mounted right at the stern and, further forward and below the overhanging flight deck, one of the two 5in/51s. (US Navy)

(*Sangamon*, 1943) and to SK (*Santee*, *Suwannee*) by 1945; *Chenango* carried SC and SG throughout the war. Defensive armament was upgraded, the final standard battery including ten twin and two quadruple 40mm and 27 single 20mm. A second catapult was added, forward, in 1944.

Service Notes *Sangamon* was completed as *Esso Trenton*, but designated AO-28 and renamed on take-over by the US Navy; on conversion to carrier configuration she was redesignated AVG-26, then in July 1943 CVE-26. Her conversion was completed for her to take part in Operation 'Torch', the Allied landings in North Africa in October 1942, but she spent the rest of her wartime career in the Pacific, as a transport, as an attack carrier, and in the training role. Three times damaged in action (bombs and a kamikaze hit late in 1944 and a further kamikaze strike in April 1945), she was stricken from the Navy List soon after the war's end, because of the extensive repairs needed, and broken up from 1948.

Suwannee: Originally named *Markay*, *Suwannee* (AO-33, then AVG-27) served with *Sangamon*,

Santee and *Chenango* in the North African landings, deploying subsequently (CVE from July 1943) in the Pacific, where she was hit by bombs in October 1944 and again seriously damaged in May 1945 as the result of an internal explosion, the exact circumstances surrounding which are unclear. She decommissioned in 1946 (redesignated CVHE from June 1955), to be stricken in March 1959 and broken up three years later.

Chenango: The *Esso New Orleans* was commissioned into the US Navy as *Chenango* (AO-31; AVG-28 on completion as a carrier), taking part in 'Torch' and, from 1943, operating in the Pacific. She was redesignated a CVE in mid 1943, and her subsequent career followed closely that of her sister-ship *Suwannee*.

Santee: Ex-*Esso Seakay*, then AO-29 and from January 1942 AVG-29, *Santee* spent much of her

BOGUE CLASS

Ship	Builder	Laid down	Launched	Commissioned
Bogue (CVE-9)	Seattle-Tacoma		15 Jan 42	26 Sept 42
Card (CVE-11)	Seattle-Tacoma		21 Feb 42	8 Nov 42
Copahee (CVE-12)	Seattle-Tacoma		21 Oct 41	15 June 42
Core (CVE-13)	Seattle-Tacoma		15 May 42	10 Dec 42
Nassau (CVE-16)	Seattle-Tacoma		4 Apr 42	20 Aug 42
Altamaha (CVE-18)	Seattle-Tacoma		22 May 42	15 Sept 42
Barnes (CVE-20)	Seattle-Tacoma		22 May 42	20 Feb 43
Block Island (CVE-21)	Seattle-Tacoma		6 June 42	8 Mar 43
Breton (CVE-23)	Seattle-Tacoma		27 June 42	12 Apr 43
Croatan (CVE-25)	Seattle-Tacoma		3 Aug 42	28 Apr 43
Prince William (CVE-31)	Seattle-Tacoma	18 May 42	23 Aug 42	9 Apr 43

Displacement: 8,390 tons / 8,524 tonnes (standard); 13,980 tons / 14,112 tonnes (deep load).
Length: 465ft / 141.73m (wl); 496ft / 151.18m (oa); 440ft / 134.11m (fd).
Beam: 69ft 6in / 21.18m (hull); 82ft / 24.99m (fd).
Draught: 23ft 3in / 7.09m (mean); 26ft / 7.92m (deep load).
Machinery: Allis-Chalmers geared turbine; 2 Foster Wheeler boilers; 1 shaft.

Performance: 8,500shp; 18kts.
Bunkerage: 2,400 tons / 2,438 tonnes.
Range: 26,300nm at 15kts.
Aircraft: 28.
Guns: 2 × 5in; 10 × 20mm.
Complement: 890.

Design Experience with *Long Island* and *Charger*, and increasing pressure from Great Britain to supply further escort carriers, led the US Government to

authorise the conversion of more C3-type merchantmen at the end of 1941, just after Pearl Harbor. Twenty hulls were available, and the opportunity was taken to revise the design slightly in the light of experience with the first two AVGs.

The immediate requirement − and a recognition of the combat potential of the vessels − was for an increased air group and better facilities for handling it. Accordingly, the hangar (18ft high) was extended and enclosed at the sides over its entire length, to be served by two lifts, one at each end, instead of one unit amidships; each lift could accept a 6½-ton load. The wood-planked flight deck was slightly larger than in *Charger*, and had a catapult, stressed for a 3-ton aircraft, at its forward end. An island with a distinctive lattice mast was added forward of amidships on the starboard side; the funnel discharged further aft.

The most significant change from *Charger*, however, was the adoption of geared turbine machinery; this gave a higher maximum speed, but reduced range somewhat, a characteristic emphasised by the lesser fuel bunkerage. About 100,000 US gallons of petrol could be stowed.

Externally, a number of sponsons for an improved defensive battery were added to the hull: single 5in / 38s were installed at the stern, with 20mms on the forecastle and along the deck edge; early units apparently commissioned with some of their sponsons empty, awaiting receipt of twin 40mms, of which four were initially installed. It is believed that all were completed with SC and SG radar.

The improved aircraft facilities permitted a significant increase in combat complement, the original standard carriage being sixteen fighters and twelve

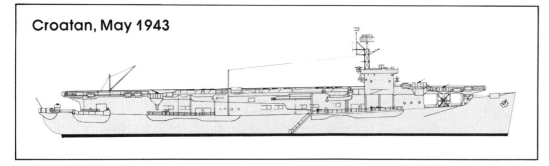

Croatan, May 1943

early deployment in the Atlantic, taking part in 'Torch', carrying out ASW sweeps and ferrying aircraft to Europe. From early 1944 she operated in the Pacific, acting as a transport, resupply and occasional combat carrier, and sustaining torpedo damage at Samar in October 1944. Repaired, she rejoined the Fleet in the spring of 1945. She was placed in reserve in October 1946, her subsequent fate being as for *Suwannee* and *Chenango*.

torpedo-bombers. When functioning as transports, up to about 100 aircraft could be stowed, about one-third of them in the hangar and the rest topside.

Copahee, *Nassau*, *Altamaha* and *Prince William* were completed at Puget Sound Navy Yard.

Modifications Wartime refits saw SC replaced by SK radar and the fixed AA batteries strengthened: up to 28 single 20mms and ten twin 40mms were fitted along the flight-deck edge, on the forecastle and on hull sponsons at main deck level by the war's end.

In 1942, all this class, in common with other ships of the same type, were redesignated ACV, and on 15 July 1943 they were again reclassified, as CVE. In the late 1950s *Card*, *Core*, *Breton* and *Croatan* were

modified for use as aircraft transports: their islands were strengthened, their funnels raised and their armament deleted. The aircraft they ferried, principally USAF types for combat in the South-East Asian theatre, could not land on or take off, and so heavy handling cranes were installed on the flight deck. *Croatan* served under NASA tenancy for a brief period, having various experimental antennae rigged.

Service Notes *Bogue*: Ex-*Steel Advocate*, *Bogue* served principally in the Atlantic on ASW and transport duties until after VE-Day. She was placed in reserve at the end of 1946, was redesignated CVHE (helicopter escort carrier) in June 1955, and was scrapped in Japan from December 1960.

Card: Atlantic ASW and transport duties occupied *Card* until the spring of 1945, when she was used for pilot training and was subsequently transferred to the Pacific. Decommissioned in May 1946, and redesignated CVHE-11 in June 1955, she was reactivated as CVU-11 on 1 July 1958 for transporting aircraft in the Pacific; in 1959 she was again redesignated, this time AKV-40. During the Vietnam War she struck a mine at Saigon in May 1964 while acting as a transport, but was raised and repaired. She was finally stricken in early 1970 and broken up for scrap the following year.

Copahee: Ex-*Steel Architect*, *Copahee* was employed solely as a transport in the Pacific theatre, except for a short period as a combat carrier in late 1942. Decommissioned in July 1946, and redesignated CVHE in June 1955, she was sold and broken up for scrap in the early 1960s.

Core: Another *Bogue* used mainly in the Atlantic during the Second World War for ASW and transport, *Core* was deactivated in October 1946 but, after redesignation as a CVHE in 1955, was reactivated on 1 July 1958 as CVU-13 for transport duties under MSTS (Maritime Sea Transportation Service).

△3 ▽4

△1 ▽2

Reclassified ten months later as AKV-41 (aircraft ferry), she was stricken and scrapped in the early 1970s.

Nassau was used primarily for transporting combat aircraft in the Pacific during the war, resupplying island bases and fleet units. She was deactivated in October 1946, but although redesignated an escort helicopter carrier (CVHE) in 1955 she never again commissioned and was sold for scrap in 1961.

Altamaha saw service as an ASW carrier in the Pacific theatre during the war in addition to her usual ferrying and transport duties. She was deactivated in

September 1946 and scrapped as CVHE-18 from 1961.

Barnes: Employed exclusively in the Pacific throughout her career, mainly as a ferry, *Barnes* was deactivated in August 1946, redesignated CVHE-20 in July 1955 and AKV-38 in 1959, but sold for scrapping in mid 1960.

Block Island: The only *Bogue*-class carrier to be lost in combat, *Block Island* was torpedoed and sunk by *U-549* in May 1944, having spent her brief career as a transport and ASW carrier in the Atlantic.

Breton's only active service was in the Pacific as an

aircraft transport, first during the war and then from the late 1950s under MSTS auspices as CVU-23 (1958) and then AKV-42 (1959 on). She was first decommissioned in August 1946, and reclassified before reactivation as CVHE-23 (1955). Stricken in October 1970, she was broken up from 1972.

Croatan: Another of the Atlantic escort carriers, *Croatan* served both as a transport and, from 1944, as an ASW 'hunter-killer' unit. She was decommissioned in May 1946; reclassified as a CVHE in 1955 and reactivated in June 1958 for MSTS service (CVU-25 from July that year), she was again

1: *Card* under way. Note that the flight decks of these carriers are completely unobstructed: even the island is sponsored out from the hull. (US National Archives)

2: An early 1943 photograph of *Core*. The camouflage demarcation line of the Measure 22 paint scheme, parallel to the waterline, contrasts with the sheer of the hangar deck, indicated by the attitude of the lower hull sponsons. The problems caused by the sloping ends of the hangar deck can be imagined. (US Navy)

3: Although the *Bogue*s were used extensively in the ASW role, they were also employed as transports; indeed, unlike the Royal Navy, which saw escort carriers primarily as offensive warships, the US Navy ranked them as equally if not more valuable as ferries. Here *Barnes* shows a deck load of USAAC P-38s (their wings removed to maximise numbers) and P-47Ds en route to the Western Pacific in January 1943. (US Navy)

4: Emphasising the ferry mission once more, the CVE *Altamaha* departs for the combat zone with a deck load of P-51 fighters, July 1943. The carrier's wind-break is erected at the forward edge of the flight deck. (US Navy)

5: The *Bogue*s featured two lifts, one at each end of the hangar, as shown in this May 1943 view of *Breton*. Note, too, the single flight-deck catapult, to port. The 40mm positions can be identified by their 'ribbed' tubs; the 20mms are higher up, just below the flight-deck edge. The medium (5in) guns are located on the quarters, as in the *Sangamon*s; however, those installed here appear to be 51-calibre weapons rather than the 38-calibre intended for the class. (US Navy)

6: Throughout 1943, SK air search antennae began to replace the smaller SC series systems on board escort carriers, increasing radar range by a quarter to one-third. It is shown here aboard *Block Island*, October 1943. The smaller system at its top edge is IFF (Identification Friend or Foe), not a radar as such but an interrogator compatible with the beacons installed in aircraft. Perhaps the escort carrier's most telling weapon is in fact visible in this photograph: the pole mast forward of the island is topped with HF/DF (high-frequency direction-finder, or 'huff-duff'), which enabled ASW to be effectively prosecuted since the carriers could pick up and establish the bearings of U-boat radio communications. (US Navy)

7: *Croatan* was employed as a 'hunter-killer' ASW carrier during 1944, armed with TBM strike aircraft and FM fighters. Escort carriers were probably more responsible than any other agency in defeating the submarine menace during the Second World War. (US Navy)

8: *Nassau*, April 1944, shows a derrick fitted near the after lift to enable her to load and offload aircraft and equipment for the war zone. Army aircraft were generally unable to take off from escort carrier decks, while land facilities for disembarking aircraft at Pacific destinations were often primitive and sometimes non-existent. (US Navy)

redesignated, as AKV-43, in 1959. She served as an experimental platform for NASA for six months from October 1964, but after a further spell under MSTS command she was finally decommissioned in 1970 and scrapped the following year.

Prince William operated as a transport in the Pacific until mid 1944, whence she took up training and transport duties in the Atlantic. A return to the Pacific in June 1945 was followed by a long spell in the reserve fleet from August 1946 (reclassified CVHE in 1955) until she was stricken and scrapped in the early 1960s.

5△

6△

7△ 8▽

WOLVERINE (IX-64)

Builder	Launched	Commissioned
Detroit	9 Nov 12	12 Aug 42

Displacement: 7,200 tons / 7,315 tonnes (standard).
Length: 484ft 6in / 147.68m (wl); 500ft / 152.4m (oa).
Beam: 58ft 3in / 17.75m (hull); 98ft / 29.87m (fd).
Draught: 15ft 6in / 4.72m (mean).
Machinery: Inclined compound engines; 4 cylindrical boilers; 2 paddles.
Performance: 8,000ihp; 16kts.
Aircraft: Nil.
Guns: Nil.
Complement: 270.
Design The incompatible needs to commit Navy carriers to combat yet provide water-borne flight decks for pilot training led to the decision in late 1941 to convert a pair of vessels for the latter purposes.

Left: The bizarre but invaluable *Wolverine* takes shape, summer 1942. At left is the *Greater Buffalo*: her superstructure will soon be razed and a flight deck fitted in order to provide a second training carrier for the US Navy, *Sable*. (US Navy)

ESSEX CLASS

Ship	Builder	Laid down	Launched	Commissioned
Essex (CV-9)	Newport News	28 Apr 41	31 July 42	31 Dec 42
Yorktown (CV-10)	Newport News	1 Dec 41	21 Jan 43	15 Apr 43
Intrepid (CV-11)	Newport News	1 Dec 41	26 Apr 43	16 Aug 43
Hornet (CV-12)	Newport News	3 Aug 42	30 Aug 43	29 Nov 43
Franklin (CV-13)	Newport News	7 Dec 42	14 Oct 43	31 Jan 44
Ticonderoga (CV-14)	Newport News	1 Feb 43	7 Feb 44	8 May 44
Randolph (CV-15)	Newport News	10 May 43	29 June 44	9 Oct 44
Lexington (CV-16)	Bethlehem	15 Sept 41	26 Sept 42	17 Feb 43
Bunker Hill (CV-17)	Bethlehem	15 Sept 41	7 Dec 42	25 May 43
Wasp (CV-18)	Bethlehem	18 Mar 42	17 Aug 43	24 Nov 43
Hancock (CV-19)	Bethlehem	26 Jan 43	24 Jan 44	15 Apr 44
Bennington (CV-20)	Newport News	15 Dec 42	26 Feb 44	6 Aug 44
Boxer (CV-21)	Newport News	13 Sept 43	14 Dec 44	16 Apr 45
Bon Homme Richard (CV-31)	New York	1 Feb 43	29 Apr 44	26 Nov 44
Leyte (CV-32)	Newport News	21 Feb 44	23 Aug 45	11 Apr 46
Kearsarge (CV-33)	New York	1 Mar 44	5 May 45	2 Mar 46
Oriskany (CV-34)	New York	1 May 44	13 Oct 45	25 Sept 50
Antietam (CV-36)	Philadelphia	15 Mar 43	20 Aug 44	28 Jan 45
Princeton (CV-37)	Philadelphia	14 Sept 43	8 July 45	18 Nov 45
Shangri-La (CV-38)	Norfolk	15 Jan 43	24 Feb 44	15 Sept 44
Lake Champlain (CV-39)	Norfolk	15 Mar 43	2 Nov 44	3 June 45
Tarawa (CV-40)	Norfolk	1 Mar 44	12 May 45	8 Dec 45
Valley Forge (CV-45)	Philadelphia	7 Sept 44	18 Nov 45	3 Nov 46
Philippine Sea (CV-47)	Bethlehem	19 Aug 44	5 Sept 45	11 May 46

Displacement: 27,200 tons / 27,635 tonnes (standard); 34,880 tons / 35,438 tonnes (deep load).
Length: 820ft / 249.94m (wl); 872ft / 265.79m (oa); 860ft / 262.13m (fd).
Beam: 93ft / 28.35m (hull); 96ft / 29.26m (fd).
Draught: 23ft / 7.01m (mean); 27ft 6in / 8.38m (deep load).
Machinery: Westinghouse geared turbines; 8 Babcock & Wilcox boilers; 4 shafts.
Performance: 150,000shp; 32.7kts.
Bunkerage: 6,330 tons / 6,431 tonnes.
Range: 15,000nm at 15kts.

Yorktown, 1945

Aircraft: 91.
Guns: 12 × 5in; 32 × 40mm; 46 × 20mm.
Complement: 2,682.
Design Less than half the 40,000 tons voted by Congress in May 1937 for the construction of new carriers was taken up by *Hornet*, and although the

With U-boat activity off the East Coast and naval developments somewhat unpredictable off the West Coast, using the Great Lakes seemed an ideal move. Furthermore, coal-burning Lakes paddle-steamers seemed large and adaptable enough to form the basis for extemporary modification.

The first, the excursion steamer *Seeandbee*, was taken in hand at Buffalo, New York, early in 1942. The superstructure was completely removed, and a wooden flight deck, overhanging bow, stern and sides by a considerable margin and tapering sharply towards its forward end, was fitted. No hangar structure was built up (thus no lifts were fitted), and consequently effective freeboard was minimal. A small island, mainly to route up the four funnels and provide realistic flight-deck conditions rather than for any complex command facilities, was built out over the vast starboard paddlebox sponson, and a basic 8-wire arrester system was installed. There were no catapults; indeed, there was no fixed aircraft complement, trainee pilots operating from nearby land bases and using the flight deck for 'circuits and

bumps'. The ship, named *Wolverine* (IX-64) on commissioning, was unarmed, unarmoured and had no radar.

Modifications Apparently no modifications were made to *Wolverine* throughout her career.

Service Notes Sold post-war and scrapped from 1947.

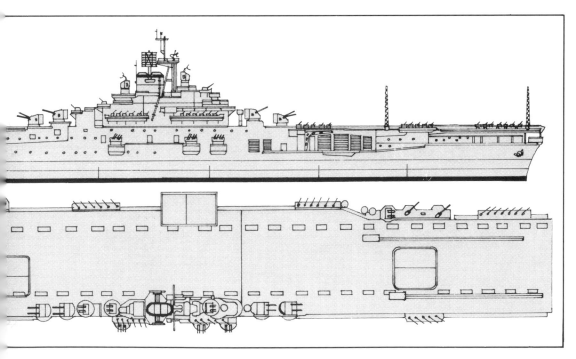

second ship could have an additional few hundred tons of displacement it was clear that in general terms the designs of the two ships would not be far apart. This proved to be true when the preliminary schemes were drawn up, but the General Board had requested a 10 per cent increase in aircraft capacity and rather more substantial protection than was worked into *Hornet*. The result was a foretaste of the explosive growth in carrier size that would take place post-war: the extra aircraft (two rather than one squadron of fighters were requested) required not only a larger flight deck, but also a larger hull, in order to stow the increased aviation fuel (240,000 US gallons, compared to 178,000) and munitions. The increased armour, giving a 4in–2½in belt, 3in–2in bulkheads, a 1½in main deck and, for the first time, an armoured (3in) hangar deck, would cost an additional 100 tons. To maintain the required speed these additions would in their turn necessitate more powerful machinery which, despite the fitting of more efficient high-pressure boilers, would still demand 500 tons more than *Hornet*. It was plain that nothing much could be achieved by way of improvement by adhering to the original tonnage specifications and, encouraged by the lapsing of all treaty regulations, they were quickly swept away: the CV-9 design progressed through six stages, the final modification showing a 28 per cent increase in displacement over the first.

Thus although the *Essex* design had its roots in that of the *Yorktown*s, it was considerably enlarged in terms of both displacement and dimensions; moreover, it showed a number of significant improvements from the point of view of aircraft operation. The main fixed armament was strengthened, eight of the weapons being mounted in twin gunhouses disposed before and abaft the island and the remaining four in unshielded positions along the port-side deck edge. Not only did this relocation provide improved sky arcs for the 5in / 38s, but it minimised the narrowing of the flight deck demanded by side-mounted weapons and thereby gave more space for aircraft movement. An amidships deck-edge lift, capable of being folded upwards to facilitate the ships' transit through the Panama Canal, was standard equipment, and new, improved catapults were installed. The latter were the subject of much discussion whilst the *Essex* design was being formulated, proponents of hangar-deck and flight-deck gear each stressing the respective advantages. The design settled on two flight-deck and one hangar-deck unit, but topweight then ruled out one of the flight-deck catapults; production problems led to some ships (for example, *Essex*) completing with only the hangar-deck gear, and finally the latter was deleted in favour of two catapults topside, as shown on ships commissioning after early 1944.

The boilers and machinery spaces were disposed *en échelon*, a pattern which would become standard for subsequent US carriers and one which gave optimum protection against an underwater hit amidships. Anti-torpedo protection was enhanced over the *Yorktowns* in any case, and was designed to withstand a 500lb charge, while superior subdivision within the hull was to stand the class in good stead during their Pacific campaigns.

The original armament called for, besides the 5in dual-purpose mounts, 24 × 1.1in machine-guns in quadruple mounts, but these were withdrawn before the first carrier was completed and replaced by varying dispositions of the new 40mms: early units carried eight quadruple mounts, disposed four on the island, two by the deck-edge 5in mounts, one at the stern and one on the forecastle. This last was overhung by the flight deck and thus commanded poor arcs of fire, and it was apparently for this reason that *Ticonderoga*, *Randolph*, *Hancock*, *Boxer*, *Antietam*, *Shangri-La*, *Lake Champlain* and the members of the class completed post-war were fitted with a lengthened bow, which carried two quadruple 40mm mounts side by side forward of the flight deck overhang, and increased overall length to 888ft.

The optimum aircraft complement indicated in the table, originally numbering 36 fighters, 37 dive-bombers and eighteen torpedo planes, was easily achieved even under wartime conditions and, indeed, *Essex*-class carriers frequently operated more than 100 machines in combat. The carriers proved especially adaptable to the rising weights and dimensions of new aircraft, as will be shown in a moment.

Two ships laid down during the Second World War but not completed were: *Reprisal* (CV-35) at New York Navy Yard on 1 July 1944 and *Iwo Jima* (CV-46) on 29 January 1945 at Philadelphia Navy Yard; the former was used as a target post-war and the latter was broken up. Additionally, six units (CV-50 to -55) were authorised, but never begun. *Oriskany*

Far right: The second *Essex*-class carrier to complete was *Lexington*, seen here in early 1943. The original single quadruple 40mm mounting is seen offset at the stern; a new sponson arrangement would later allow two mountings to be sited here. Forward, there is provision for two flight-deck catapults, although only one is as yet fitted. (US Navy, by courtesy of Norman Friedman)

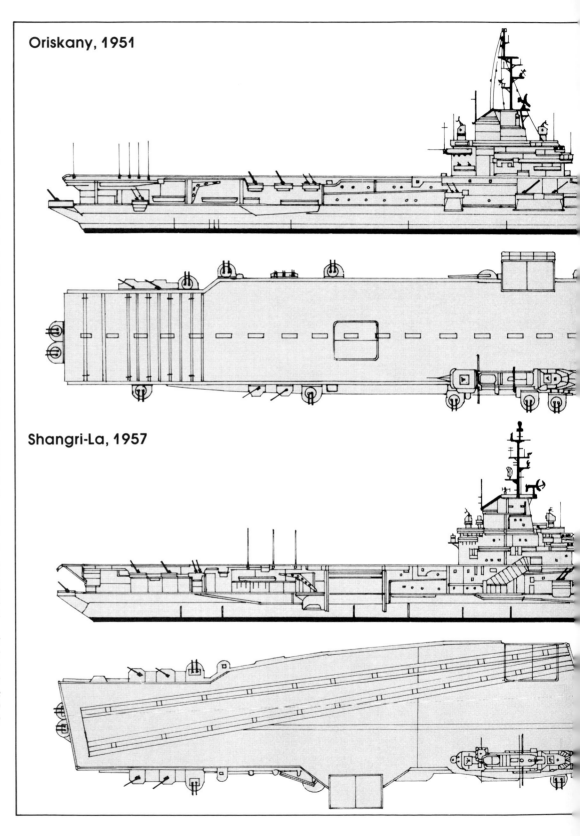

Oriskany, 1951

Shangri-La, 1957

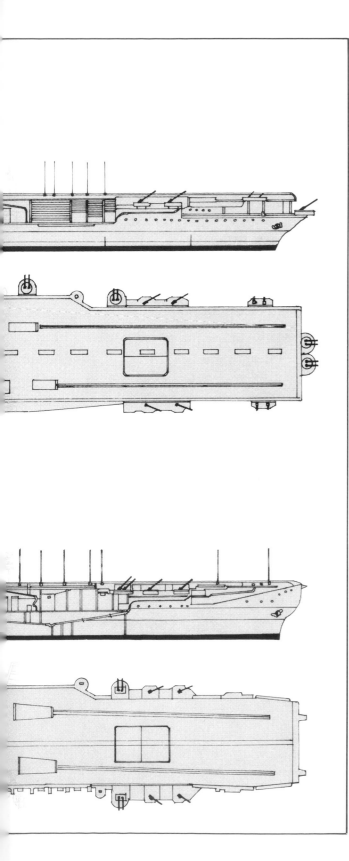

(CV-34) was completed post-war to a much modified (SCB-27A) design, with no flight-deck-mounted 5in guns, an extra four single 5in, fourteen twin 3in / 50s and no 40mms. The island was reconfigured, new lifts capable of handling 40,000lb aircraft (30,000lb for the deck-edge lift) were installed, 210ft H8 catapults replaced the H4s of the original design, and the flight deck itself was strengthened so that it could accept much heavier aircraft. In addition, there was much rearrangement within the hull, mainly to accommodate fuel for jet aircraft and increased ordnance and ammunition. The net effect was to increase standard displacement to 30,800 tons (39,800 tons deep load), with the result that the ship had to be bulged to retain buoyancy, thereby increasing below-water beam.

Modifications The modifications worked into *Essex*-class carriers were many and complex. During the war the additions were confined mainly to the usual upgrading of the anti-aircraft armament, wherein up to eighteen quadruple 40mm were finally carried, most of the additional guns being sited at hangar-deck level; 20mm batteries varied enormously from ship to ship, with up to about 60 barrels in twin or single mountings (or both), positioned principally along the edge of the flight deck and sponsored out on narrow platforms on the starboard side of the bridge block. Radar suites were exchanged as circumstances permitted: most of the early vessels had their original SK search sets updated with the 17ft SK-2 antenna, with which later vessels were fitted on commissioning, and most by the end of the war had SC-2 and either SP or SM. Several of the early ships' Mk 4 fire control radars were replaced by Mk 12 / 22, fitted as standard on those entering service from 1944 on.

More far-reaching modifications were effected in *Essex*-class carriers post-war, however, and it is a tribute to their design that – to a point – they proved adaptable to the demands of the jet age throughout the 1960s and beyond. To be sure, there were problems. Aircraft development moved so fast that one modernisation programme quickly became overtaken by the need for further modifications. Two of

Top: Early *Essex*-class carriers were characterised by their short bows, as seen in this October 1944 photograph of *Yorktown*. The distinctive camouflage is Measure 32, Design 10A, the latter carried by three of her sister ships at various times. The hangar catapult, visible in the wartime photograph of *Intrepid* shown elsewhere, has been removed. (US Navy)

Centre: The ill-fated *Franklin*, just prior to commissioning in the spring of 1944. The camouflage is Measure 32, to Design 3A; the starboard side of the ship was, unusually, finished to a different design, 6A. (US Navy, by courtesy of Norman Friedman)

Right: F4Us, F6Fs and, aft, SB2Cs ranged on board *Essex*, May 1945. The flight-deck galleries are lined with single 20mms, although by this time the shortcomings of the weapon in respect to stopping power were widely appreciated. The disposition of 5in mountings – eight in twin turrets before and abaft the island and single guns below the port-side deck-edge – is evident here. (US Navy)

the class, *Franklin* and *Bunker Hill*, were not retained post-war, and *Boxer*, *Leyte*, *Princeton*, *Tarawa*, *Valley Forge* and *Philippine Sea* did not receive major reconstruction.

The first programme, SCB-27A, has already been referred to in connection with *Oriskany*, and *Essex*, *Yorktown*, *Hornet*, *Randolph*, *Wasp*, *Bennington*, *Kearsarge* and *Lake Champlain* were refitted to this standard, short-bow vessels having to have their stems lengthened as in the other ships. SPS-6 search radar replaced the wartime sets, and SPS-8 height-finding radar was added, as was a CCA (Carrier-Controlled Approach) system. A new, tall mast allowed the radar suite to be arranged in the most convenient manner.

The refits were underway in 1948, but by the time the first pair (*Essex* and *Wasp*) had been recommissioned it had become apparent that further alterations were required: even heavier aircraft were in prospect, demanding stronger lifts and arrester gear, while the advent of the steam catapult provided an opportune substitute for the advanced powder catapult which had been earmarked for use but which had proved problematic. These modifications were incorporated into the SCB-27A programme to become SCB-27C, which also involved the allocation of a percentage of the ships' oil fuel for aviation use – mixed with petrol it would provide jet fuel, thus increasing the number of sorties its air group could fly, albeit at some cost in the ships' range. SCB-27C was scheduled for *Intrepid*, *Ticonderoga* and *Hancock*, and was applied in 1951–54.

The advent of the angled deck, however, had a revolutionary effect on carrier design, and came at a time when the *Essex* modernisation programme was in full swing. Accordingly, three ships, *Lexington*, *Bon Homme Richard* and *Shangri-La*, scheduled to receive SCB-27C reconstructions, were modified instead to SCB-125 standards, which involved primarily the reconfiguration of the flight deck to incorporate the angled landing area and the enclosure of the bows ('hurricane' bow) to improve weatherliness. In addition, the island was altered to

Top: *Intrepid*, another 'short-hull' *Essex*, at Norfolk, 25 November 1943. Note the absence of 40mm sponsons along the hull amidships: these were fitted as part of the general up-grading of carrier AA armament, in *Intrepid*'s case in the summer of 1944. (US Navy, by courtesy of Norman Friedman)

Centre: Not often evident in photographs of *Essex*-class carriers is the system of plating which made up the construction of the hull; however, favourable angles of sun and camera have thrown it into sharp relief on this occasion. The subject is *Bunker Hill*, January 1945. Note the large sponson carrying a pair of quad 40mms occupying the position taken in earlier ships of the class by the hangar-deck catapult; *Bunker Hill* was one *Essex* never to receive this equipment. (US Navy)

Left: *Princeton* at sea in May 1946, her deck-edge lift lowered. The deck-edge lift gave extra room not only on flight decks – it released valuable hangar space too. (US Navy)

Above: The SCB-27A programme was the first of the *Essex* rebuilds, initiated primarily to enable the carriers to operate the new generation of jet aircraft during the immediate postwar years. Some of the changes are evident in this September 1952 view of *Lake Champlain*, a 'long hull' *Essex*: the remodelled island superstructure and single heavy radar mast; and the twin 3in/50 bow mountings. Note the folded deck-edge lift. (US Navy, by courtesy of Norman Friedman)

Below: SCB-27A also saw the removal of the flight-deck twin 5in/38s, but the addition of four single 5in on the starboard side, mirroring those already disposed to port; considerably more powerful catapults, with longer tracks; and a new 'ready room' for flying crew deep within the ships, connected to the flight deck via an enclosed escalator below the island. *Kearsarge* displays these modifications in an April 1952 photograph. (US Navy, by courtesy of A. D. Baker III)

give improved control facilities, arrester gear was strengthened and the number of wires reduced, and a larger forward lift was installed, and there were a number of other improvements. The three carriers first affected by SCB-125 were out of dock by late 1955, by which time all the SCB-27C-refitted ships, all but *Lake Champlain* of the SCB-27A carriers, and also *Oriskany*, were undergoing conversion to similar standards. The other *Essex*-class carrier retained postwar, *Antietam*, was fitted with an angled deck (1952), but this was considered an experimental installation.

An important point about SCB-125 was that it effectively divided the reconstructed carriers into two distinct groups: only *Oriskany* was fitted with steam catapults under the programme, which meant that those ships earlier reconstructed under SCB-27A retained their hydraulic gear and therefore were unsuitable for employment as attack carriers. Thus they were redesignated anti-submarine carriers under the FRAM (Fleet Rehabilitation and Modernisation) 11 programme in the early 1960s. This refit, designated SCB-144, provided them with a sonar dome under the bows (as a result of which the hawsepipes and anchors had to be moved forward to the stem) and the appropriate command facilities. They could carry about 45 aircraft, generally S-2 Trackers and helicopters. Three of the unreconstructed ships, *Boxer*, *Princeton* and *Valley Forge*, were recommissioned in 1959–61 as amphibious assault ships (LPH-4, -5 and -8), concurrent with the building of the *Iwo Jimas* (qv).

The reconstruction programmes inevitably gave rise to considerable increases in weights: in 1962, for example, *Shangri-La* displaced about 33,100 tons standard and 43,000 tons deep load, length overall had extended to 894ft 4in, and deep load draught to 31ft. Extreme width was 192ft and ship's complement more than 3,000. To help save weight, the 3in/50 battery was progressively reduced so that by the ends of their careers most ships had only their 4 × 5in/38 singles. Many were fitted to operate the Regulus I missile in the mid 1950s.

Six *Essex*-class carriers are currently (1983) retained by the US Navy: *Hornet*, *Bennington* and *Shangri-La* (CVS), *Oriskany* (CV), *Bon Homme Richard* (CVA) and *Lexington*, the last the only one in commission (as a training carrier, CVT). It was suggested in 1983 that one or more of these vessels might be reactivated as an attack carrier, albeit of restricted effectiveness; however, this is now considered unlikely.

Service Notes *Essex*: During operations against Luzon in November 1944, *Essex* suffered a kamikaze hit on the port-side deck edge, forward of the midships lift, but her capabilities were little impaired. Her aircraft helped damage the battleship *Nagato* and sank the carrier *Kaiyo* and a number of destroyers in the last days of the war.

Decommissioned on 9 January 1947 and placed in reserve, she was refitted under SCB-27A from 1

September 1948 to 5 September 1951, recommissioning with F2H, F8F and AD aircraft. She took part in two Korean deployments and was redesignated CVA-9 in October 1952. SCB-125 lasted from July 1955 to March 1956, but, unable to operate the new fast (F8U) and heavy (A3D) aircraft, she was designated an ASW carrier (CVS) in the spring of 1960, operating S2Fs and HSSs. FRAM II occupied *Essex* for six months from March 1962. She was decommissioned on 30 July 1969, stricken from the Navy List in July 1973, and scrapped.

Yorktown was originally named *Bon Homme Richard*, but was rechristened to perpetuate the name of the sunken CV-5. She operated in the Pacific throughout her wartime career, refitting at Puget Sound Navy Yard August–October 1944. In March 1945 she was hit by a bomb, but suffered no serious damage. Her most newsworthy exploit of the war was the part her TBF torpedo-bombers played in the destruction of the battleship *Yamato*.

Decommissioned together with the bulk of the early *Essex*-class carriers in January 1947, she was reconstructed under SCB-27A from May 1951 until December 1952, having been redesignated CVA-10 while in dock; she went to Korea, but was too late for combat. SCB-125 lasted from March to October 1955, and she was redesignated CVS-10 in September 1957. She covered attack carrier operations off Vietnam in the 1960s.

Although scheduled for FRAM II in 1966 she was not modernised again, and decommissioned in the summer of 1970, to be preserved as a museum from 1975 at Charleston Harbor, South Carolina.

Intrepid suffered considerably during the Pacific campaign: her steering gear was put out of action by a Japanese aerial torpedo (February 1944) and a hit by a kamikaze (October 1944) caused slight damage. A pair of kamikazes (November 1944) caused serious fires and a cessation of flight-deck operations. A near miss by a further kamikaze (March 1945) started fires and, finally, she was crippled by yet another kamikaze (April 1945) which caused fires in the hangar and her temporary withdrawal from service. It was indeed fortunate that what US carriers lacked in protection they made up for in weight of numbers, both of aircraft per ship and of ships themselves. *Intrepid* was repaired from May to July 1945 and returned to combat in time to carry out a number of strikes before the war ended. She was decommissioned in early 1947 and placed in reserve.

SCB-27C lasted from February 1952 to June 1954, the ship having been redesignated CVA meanwhile, and SCB-125 from September 1956 to April 1957. *Intrepid* was redesignated CVS-11 on 31 March 1962, embarking S2Fs, AD-5Ws and HSS-2 helicopters; FRAM II modernisation was effected from April to October 1965. After three tours of duty off Vietnam, 1966–68, she was decommissioned in March 1974 and is now preserved as a museum at New York.

Hornet: Originally *Kearsarge*, *Hornet* was renamed a few months after her keel was laid, to honour CV-7, lost at Santa Cruz. She helped sink the battleship *Yamato*, and the only major damage sustained during the war was that caused by a typhoon in June 1945 when, like *Bennington*, she suffered a buckled forward flight deck, an experience which led ultimately to the so-called 'hurricane bow' fitted in post-war *Essex*-class reconstructions.

She decommissioned in January 1947, but was reactivated for SCB-27A in March 1951, the refit lasting until recommissioning as CVA-12 in September 1953. SCB-125 started in January 1956 and was completed that summer, and in July 1958 she was redesignated CVS. FRAM II took from June 1964 to February 1965, after which the carrier deployed to South-East Asia for ASW patrols.

Hornet was decommissioned and placed in reserve at Puget Sound in June 1970, where she currently (1983) remains.

Franklin was the only *Essex* carrier that came close to being lost during the war, indeed, the seriousness of the damage she suffered was the reason why she was never modernised post-war. In March 1945 she was hit by two 250kg bombs which penetrated the flight deck and exploded in the hangar where armed TBMs, SB2Cs, F6Fs and F4Us were being readied for a strike, causing fires and explosions and putting her completely out of action. Superb damage control saved the ship and she managed to make Pearl Harbor. She was repaired, deactivated in February 1947, redesignated CVA-13 in October 1952, CVS-13 in August 1953 and finally an aircraft transport (AVT-8) in May 1959, but she was never recommissioned and went for scrap in July 1966.

Ticonderoga: Reportedly exchanging names with *Hancock* (CV-19) before launching, *Ticonderoga* sailed to the Pacific combat zone in October 1944 and launched her first strikes in the following month. She was seriously damaged by a kamikaze hit in January 1945, which caused serious fires in the hangar and another hit an hour later damaged the island. The fires were controlled by skilful manoeuvring against the effects of the wind and by deliberately flooding the ship to give a list to port. She was repaired by the end of April and returned to attack Japanese homeland ports, her aircraft assisting in the sinking of the battleships *Haruna*, *Ise* and *Hyuga* and the carrier *Kaiyo*.

She was taken out of service in January 1947. Following a short commission, she was docked at New York Navy Yard on 1 April 1952 for SCB-27C, which was completed in summer 1954. *Ticonderoga* recommissioned as CVA-14. She was used for carrier compatability trials of the A4D and F4D in September 1955, and was taken in hand for SCB-125 from August 1956 to April 1957.

She was refitted and given bridle catchers in 1962 and was deployed to the Far East the following year, where in the famous 'Maddox Incident' her F-8s sank or damaged a number of North Vietnamese patrol boats and initiated major US involvement in the Vietnam War. She conducted a large number of strikes throughout the war, being refitted as an ASW support carrier (CVS-14) from October 1969 to summer 1970. She was decommissioned for the last time on 17 October 1973, stricken in November, and sold for breaking up on 15 August 1974.

Randolph was another *Essex* carrier to suffer a kamikaze hit, this time while at anchor in Ulithi Atoll, a staging post and forward supplies base for Pacific operations, on 11 March 1945. The damage was quickly repaired and the carrier returned to Japanese waters, her air groups striking at the mainland and assisting in the sinking of *Nagato* and *Hyuga*.

She was used post-war for training, but was placed in reserve in June 1947. SCB-27A followed in January 1952–July 1953 (redesignated CVA-15), and SCB-125 in August 1955–January 1956; she conducted the first Regulus I firing from an Atlantic Fleet carrier early that year. Redesignated CVS-15, she underwent SCB-144 (FRAM II) modernisation during the winter of 1960–61. Decommissioned on 13 February 1969, she was stricken on 15 June 1973.

Lexington: CV-16 was laid down as *Cabot*, but shortly before launching the ship was renamed to commemorate CV-2. Her steering gear was jammed by an aerial torpedo in December 1943, but despite some flooding, makeshift emergency gear enabled the carrier to make Puget Sound Navy Yard for repairs. Back in action by March 1944, *Lexington* took part in the Marianas 'Turkey Shoot', when her F6Fs accounted for 45 enemy aircraft. Further assaults against Japanese-held islands were followed in October 1944 by attacks with *Essex* against the carriers *Zuikaku*, *Zuiho* and *Chitose*, all of which were sunk. The following month a kamikaze hit damaged her island.

Lexington was deactivated on 23 April 1947, redesignated CVA-16 on 1 October 1952 and taken out for SCB-27C, extended to SCB-125, on 1 September 1953. Recommissioned on 15 August 1955, she was redesignated CVS on 1 October 1962; she succeeded *Antietam* as the US Navy's training carrier in that year, and on 1 July 1969 was again reclassified, as CVT-16, and then in July 1978 as AVT-16. She is still in commission in her training role, though she is unarmed and has no permanent air group.

Bunker Hill: Together with *Franklin*, *Bunker Hill* sustained more critical damage than any other *Essex*-class carrier during the Second World War: two kamikaze hits on 11 May 1945, one striking the after flight deck, destroying parked aircraft and buckling the after lift, and the other crashing nearer the island, caused severe fires throughout the ship requiring extensive repairs. She was ready for combat once more by July 1945 but saw no further action.

Decommissioned in January 1947, she was re-classified as an auxiliary aircraft transport (AVT-9) in May 1952, but remained out of commission. She was stricken from the Navy List in November 1966, though was used for experimental work by the Naval Electronics Laboratory at San Diego from 1965 until removed for scrapping in July 1973.

Wasp: Laid down as *Oriskany*, but renamed on 13 November 1942 in memory of CV-7, *Wasp*'s only war damage was that caused by a bomb which broke through the flight deck and detonated in the hangar, her air capability, however, not being seriously impaired. She was placed in reserve in February 1947 and underwent SCB-27A from September 1948 until September 1951. SCB-125 followed (April–December 1955).

Wasp was redesignated CVS-18 on 1 November 1956 and she took part in the blockade of Cuba in November 1962. FRAM II occupied the second half of 1967, and she was finally decommissioned on 1 July 1972, arriving at Kearny for breaking up in the summer of 1973.

Hancock: Laid down, it appears, as *Ticonderoga*, *Hancock* played a very active part in the Pacific campaign. Two set-backs were: an avgas explosion coinciding with a returning TBM (January 1945), in an incident which has never been satisfactorily explained; and a kamikaze strike in April of the same year which damaged the port-side catapult and aircraft spotted on deck. Neither event necessitated the carrier returning to port.

Hancock was decommissioned on 9 May 1947; SCB-27C (July 1951–March 1954) included the first US installation of steam catapults (C11), the first launch being made in June 1954 with an S2F, the carrier by now designated CVA-19. SCB-125

1: *Essex*, her SCB-27A almost complete, in the spring of 1951. The raked funnel cap helped to ensure that corrosive gases from the ship's boilers were kept away from the complex network of radar antennae surmounting the island. (US Navy, by courtesy of A. D. Baker III)

2: SCB-27C encompassed the modifications required under SCB-27A but went further: the most obvious external changes, as seen in this view of *Hancock* (March 1954), were the installation of a pair of steam catapults forward and the addition of a deck-edge lift on the starboard side. Not evident in this photograph are other -27C features: stronger lifts and arrester gear; improved internal fuel stowage arrangements; and, significantly, standardised stowage for nuclear weapons. (US Navy, by courtesy of A. D. Baker III)

3: SCB-125 saw further improvements to the island structure, a reduced AA battery and, more obviously, the fitting of an angled flight deck and the enclosure of the open *Essex* bows in an attempt to improve seakeeping. The last characteristic is evident in this photograph of *Bennington*, at San Francisco late in 1957. (US Navy, by courtesy of A. D. Baker III)

4: *Kearsarge* in January 1957, following SCB-125. The row of portholes across the flight-deck round-down are a back-up conning position. Very few 3in/50s are retained; one pair can be detected at hangar-deck level, beneath the island. (US Navy, by courtesy of A. D. Baker III)

△1

△2

△3 ▽4

followed in April–November 1956, and *Hancock* continued in service as an attack carrier, operating for lengthy periods off Vietnam in the late 1960s and early 1970s. She was decommissioned on 30 January 1976 and stricken the next day, the ship having been redesignated CV-19 once again in 1975.

Bennington's Pacific career included the final strikes against *Yamato*, 7 April 1945, and typhoon damage (similar to that which befell *Hornet*), June 1945, although despite the latter disaster she was able to continue limited air operations. She was deactivated at Norfolk Navy Yard on 8 November 1946, but emerged for SCB-27A in October 1950, recommissioning as CVA-20 on 13 November 1952. A serious catapult explosion resulting in more than 100 casualties took her to New York Navy Yard in June 1954, whereupon she was given her SCB-125 reconstruction, completed by March 1955.

The first US Navy mirror-sight landing was made on board *Bennington* on 22 August 1955 with an FJ-3 Fury, which was also that aircraft's first deck landing. The first half of 1959 saw the carrier undergoing a refit to CVS standards, FRAM II following in September 1962–May 1963. She was decommissioned on 15 January 1970 and placed in reserve at Puget Sound Navy Yard, where she currently (1983) remains.

Boxer sailed for the Pacific in September 1945, too late to see action in the war, but the carrier remained in commission throughout the late 1940s and served in the Korean conflict, being damaged in an avgas explosion in August 1952 which brought serious fires in the hangar but did not put the ship out of action. During four tours of duty off Korea, *Boxer* was redesignated CVA-21, and she was again reclassified, as a CVS, in November 1955. A third redesignation came in January 1959 when the carrier became an amphibious assault ship, LPH-4, with Marine Corps HR2S and HUS helicopters. She saw action off Vietnam during a short tour in early 1966.

Boxer was one of the four *Essex*-class carriers never to be reconstructed, and with the commissioning of the *Iwo Jima*-class assault ships her capabilities were of reduced value. She was stricken in December 1969 and broken up two years later.

Top right: Later carriers rebuilt to SCB-125 showed a variation in the configuration of the 'hurricane' bow which gave a smoother profile and displaced the 'knuckle' previously evident just above hangar-deck level. This is *Randolph* during a fleet review, 12 June 1957; ranged in perfect alignment are North American FJs (forward), McDonnell F2Hs and Douglas ADs (aft) and three North American AJs. An unmodified *Essex*-class carrier provides a contrast astern. (US Navy, by courtesy of A. D. Baker III)

Right: By 1961, when this photograph was taken, *Antietam* was being employed as a training carrier by the US Navy, which accounts for the T2J Buckeyes visible on board. The bow weapon sponsons are vacant and the 5in deck-edge positions shrouded; the twin 5in turrets before and abaft the island are also out of commission. (US Navy)

Bon Homme Richard arrived off Okinawa in time to participate in the final attacks on Japan, but was deactivated some eighteen months later on 9 January 1947. She recommissioned for the Korean conflict (in her original state) in January 1951, operating F4Us, F9Fs and ADs. As CVA-31, her SCB-27C, extended to -125, lasted from May 1953 until September 1955. She deployed to Vietnam on numerous occasions from 1964 to 1970. Deactivated in July 1971, she is still in existence, awaiting possible reactivation as a limited attack carrier.

Leyte: Ex-*Crown Point*, but renamed prior to launching, *Leyte* was completed almost a year after the end of the Second World War and was one of the few *Essex* carriers never to undergo an SCB modernisation. She operated off Korea 1950–51, and in August 1953 was reclassified as a CVS, conversion occupying three months from October that year. She decommissioned on 15 May 1959 and was placed in reserve as AVT-10; she was stricken ten years later and scrapped.

Kearsarge was in commission until 16 June 1950, when she underwent SCB-27A, undocking in February 1952 prior to deployment in the Far East, where she carried out sorties in the Korean conflict. Redesignated CVA-33 in October 1952, the ship was converted under SCB-125 from July 1956 until February 1957. She was classed as a CVS from 1 October 1958, and was decommissioned in February 1970 and placed in the Reserve Fleet. She was sold for breaking up on 18 January 1974.

Oriskany: As described earlier, work on *Oriskany* was suspended after she was launched pending decisions on the SCB-27 programmes, and she was completed to SCB-27A standards. In October 1952, as CVA-34, she arrived in Korean waters for a six-month tour of duty.

Oriskany was the final *Essex*-class carrier to undergo SCB-125 and differed from other -27A vessels in receiving steam catapults during this refit, which latter lasted from January 1957 to March 1959 and was reportedly assigned the code SCB-125A. Her air group flew sorties in the Vietnam conflict during the 1960s, and she was seriously damaged when fire swept the hangar deck in October 1966, apparently caused by one of her flare lockers igniting. As CV-34 (from 1 July 1975), she was stricken in September 1976 and is still (1983) laid up at Puget Sound.

Antietam: Too late for active service in the war, *Antietam* nevertheless deployed to the Far East in late 1945, but was placed in reserve on 21 June 1949, only to be recommissioned on 17 January 1951 for service off Korea, sailing for that theatre in September. She returned in April 1952, and five months later was taken in hand at New York Navy Yard for the installation of a 10.5° angled deck, a prototypical conversion, as it were, for SCB-125: she did not receive any of the actual SCB modifications during her career. Emerging in April 1953 as

CV-36, she conducted exhaustive tests with the new landing deck configuration, and was reclassified again, this time to CVS-36, in August 1953. She continued in front-line service until May 1963, her last six years being spent as a training carrier. She was stricken on 1 May 1973 and sold for breaking up on 19 December of that year.

Princeton: Originally named *Valley Forge*, but rechristened to commemorate the light fleet carrier of the same name lost in October 1944, *Princeton* was on her first commission from November 1945 to June 1949, when she was placed in reserve. In August of the following year, however, she was the first deactivated *Essex* to be recommissioned, for close-support operations over Korea, where she undertook three tours. She was redesignated CVA-37 in October 1952, and CVS-37 in November 1953, and within two months she was in dock for conversion work to bring her up to ASW carrier standards.

Scheduled for decommissioning in early 1959, she was instead reclassified as an amphibious assault ship, LPH-5, her conversion lasting from March to May and undertaken at Long Beach. FRAM II occupied *Princeton* from December 1960 until June 1961, and in September 1964 the carrier deployed to Vietnam on several tours until the end of 1968. She was decommissioned for the last time on 30 January 1970 and broken up in September 1973.

Shangri-La: Following shake-down, *Shangri-La* was involved in experimental flight-deck operations with USAAC aircraft off the East Coast of the United States, deploying to the Pacific in February 1945. The next two months were spent conducting air group training, followed by entry into the combat zone off Japan and strikes against enemy targets. She took part in the 'Operation Crossroads' atomic tests at Bikini in early 1946, launching surveillance drones; she was decommissioned in November 1947.

Redesignated CVA-38 on 1 October 1952, she was taken in hand for SCB-27C/-125 at Puget Sound, recommissioning in January 1955. She was redesignated again, as CVS-38, in June 1969, but never operated as an ASW vessel, being employed as a limited attack carrier off Vietnam for a period in 1970. She was decommissioned on 30 July 1971, but remains in reserve, laid up at Philadelphia.

Lake Champlain: Another of the *Essex*-class vessels just too late to see service in the war, *Lake Champlain* was first deactivated less than a year after commissioning, in March 1946. SCB-27A took from August 1950 to 19 September 1952, and the carrier deployed to Korea, launching strikes during the last six weeks of the conflict until July 1953. Like other *Essex*-class ships, she was redesignated CVA in October 1952, and on 1 August 1957 she was reclassified again, as CVS-39. She decommissioned for the last time on 19 May 1966, was stricken on 1 December 1969, and was scrapped at Kearny in 1972.

Tarawa: CV-40 commissioned as a training carrier, a role which lasted until 1 October 1948. In reserve from June 1949 at New York, she was reactivated in February 1951, again serving as a training carrier, but then as an attack carrier, CVA. Conversion to an ASW vessel took place from January to May 1955, and as CVS-40 she continued operational training until the late 1950s, when she resumed her ASW duties with the fleet. She was placed in reserve in May 1960, being redesignated an auxiliary aircraft transport, AVT-12, twelve months later. She was sold for scrapping on 3 October 1968.

Valley Forge: The last *Essex* to be launched, *Valley Forge* continued in service after her completion during the late 1940s, and was the first US carrier on station off Korea, soon after the outbreak of hostilities in June 1950. Four tours of duty, broken by a refit at Puget Sound (April–December 1951) and reclassification to CVA-45 in late 1952, were followed by modification during the latter part of 1953 for ASW operations, and the ship was redesignated CVS-45 on 12 November that year. From March until July 1961 she was again in dock for modifications, this time to amphibious assault ship configuration, and as LPH-8 she deployed to Vietnam in mid 1965 and was involved in an operational capacity in that theatre throughout the late 1960s. She was decommissioned on 15 January 1970, and subsequently broken up.

Philippine Sea: The fifth *Essex* carrier never to be modernised, *Philippine Sea* was also one of the first of the class to be stricken from the post-war fleet. Two tours of duty off Korea from the summer of 1950 until the ceasefire in July 1953, during which she was reclassified as a CVA, were followed by further reclassification, in late 1955, as an anti-submarine carrier (CVS). The ship was modified to modern CVS standards by January 1956. *Philippine Sea* was redesignated again on 15 May 1959, this time as AVT-11, but she was stricken from the Navy List on 1 December 1969 and sold for breaking up.

Right top: Valley Forge as an LPH, April 1966; the only guns evident are Nos. 2 and 3 twin 5in/38s. (US Navy)

Right centre: Boxer was employed as an amphibious assault carrier for several years. This photograph of 5 December 1966 shows the eighteen deck spots and a similar number of H-34 (HSS) Seahorse helicopters. In contrast with *Valley Forge*, she retains all four twin 5in mountings. (US Navy)

Far right, top: Hornet in 1966. The two big radar antennae visible are the dish of the SPS-30 height-finder and (left) the SPS-43A long-range search 'mattress'. (US Navy)

Right: Shangri-La in 1970. Her principal weapons are her A-4 light attack aircraft; the interceptor function is borne by F-8 Crusaders and AEW by E-1 Tracers. Also evident are the UH-2C plane guard/rescue helicopter and a single Skywarrior, which by this time was in use as a tanker (KA-3B) or ECM/tanker (EKA-3B) aircraft. (US Navy)

Far right: Oriskany, seen here during the early 1970s, has been proposed for reactivation as a light strike carrier (A-4Ms) for deployment during the 1980s, but costs appear to have ruled out the project. (US Navy)

INDEPENDENCE CLASS

Ship	Builder	Laid down	Launched	Commissioned
Independence (CVL-22)	New York SB	1 May 41	22 Aug 42	1 Jan 43
Princeton (CVL-23)	New York SB	2 June 41	18 Oct 42	25 Feb 43
Belleau Wood (CVL-24)	New York SB	11 Aug 41	6 Dec 42	31 Mar 43
Cowpens (CVL-25)	New York SB	17 Dec 41	17 Jan 43	28 May 43
Monterey (CVL-26)	New York SB	29 Dec 41	28 Feb 43	17 June 43
Langley (CVL-27)	New York SB	11 Apr 42	22 May 43	31 Aug 43
Cabot (CVL-28)	New York SB	13 Mar 42	4 Apr 43	24 July 43
Bataan (CVL-29)	New York SB	31 Aug 42	1 Aug 43	17 Nov 43
San Jacinto (CVL-30)	New York SB	16 Oct 42	26 Sept 43	15 Dec 43

Displacement: 10,662 tons / 10,833 tonnes (standard); 14,750 tons / 14,986 tonnes (deep load).
Length: 600ft / 182.88m (wl); 622ft 6in / 189.74m (oa); 544ft / 165.81m (fd).
Beam: 71ft 6in / 21.79 m (hull); 73ft / 22.25m (fd).
Draught: 21ft / 6.4m (mean); 24ft 3in / 7.39m (deep load).
Machinery: General Electric turbines; 4 Babcock & Wilcox boilers; 4 shafts.
Performance: 100,000shp; 31kts.
Bunkerage: 2,633 tons / 2,765 tonnes.
Range: 13,000nm at 15kts.
Aircraft: 30.
Guns: 2 × 5in; 16 × 40mm; 10 × 20mm.
Complement: 1,569.

Design With the prospect of conflict in the Pacific and the gap in new carrier construction between the commissioning of *Hornet* (late 1941) and the second batch of *Essex*-class ships (envisaged as late 1943 / early 1944), the US President pressed for an emergency programme of carrier building, pointing to the fact that a large number of cruisers (*Cleveland* class) whose hulls might support a viable air group, were then on the ways.

The General Board, whose responsibility it was to predict future naval needs and draw up ship require-ments accordingly, were somewhat less than enamoured with this intervention, and outlined the difficulties inherent in adapting light cruiser hulls to carry aircraft. The narrow beam of the hulls would constrict hangar space, the more so if the boiler uptakes were to be routed to starboard and ducted through an island, as in the *Yorktown*s and *Essex*es; further, an island might reduce the effective width of the flight deck, already minimised by the size of the hull. There were more difficulties forward: the curve to the bows meant that any forward lift would have to be placed a considerable distance from the stem, if it were to handle larger aircraft, while a flight deck extended to the bows could not be adequately sup-ported; still further, the pronounced sheer of the cruiser forecastle deck would preclude that area assuming the role of a hangar deck.

The result was that a compromise allowed the conversions to proceed. A truncated flight deck was accepted; the advantages of an island conning position outweighed its effect on flight-deck area (though it was made very small, of similar design to that adopted for escort carriers, and placed outboard of the hull structure), stability being maintained by bulging the hull; and a short (320ft × 57ft 9in) hangar, keeping lifts well towards amidships, was built on to the hull,

there being no real option without major redesign, which would defeat the object of undertaking the pro-gramme in the first place.

The original cruiser machinery was unchanged, but to save space the uptakes were routed individually through the superstructure below the flight deck and kept as far as possible away from the latter by being supported on lattice framing outboard of the hull. The *Cleveland*-class protection, a 5½in belt thinning to 1½in and enclosed by 5in bulkheads with, across the top, a 2in armoured deck, was also retained, but the bulges caused modifications to the belt armour, which was removed altogether from early vessels to expedite delivery of the carriers to the fleet.

The flight deck, wood planked and unarmoured, had two (one in the original design) H2 catapults forward and eight arrester wires aft. The armament as given in the table only affected *Independence* herself: subsequent ships deleted the 5in guns at bows and stern and substituted quadruple 40mm instead; similarly, further 40mms were installed on later vessels in the class.

The air group originally was to have consisted of 45 aircraft, then 30, comprising three squadrons, one VF (F6F), one VT (TBM) and one VB (SBD), but with normal strength halved in the case of the last two and reduced by one-third for the fighters; operating as transports in the latter stages of the Pacific campaign, however, the class were able to stow about 40 aircraft below and an additional 60–70 on the flight deck, the numbers depending, as always, on type. The standard search radar fit for each vessel consisted of SK and SC-2, carried on a pole mast on the island.

All the class, originally designated CVs, had their cruiser names changed before commissioning: CVL-22 was formerly *Amsterdam* (CL-59), CVL-23 was *Tallahassee* (CL-61), CVL-24 was *New Haven*

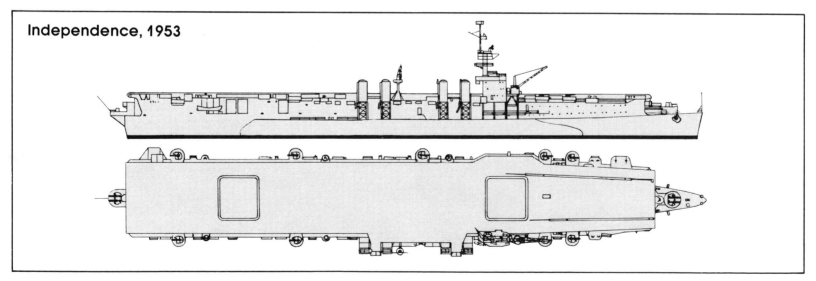

Independence, 1953

(CL-76), CVL-25 was *Huntington* (CL-77), CVL-26 was *Dayton* (CL-78), CVL-27 *Fargo* (CL-85), CVL-28 *Wilmington* (CL-79), CVL-29 *Buffalo* (CL-99) and CVL-30 *Newark* (CL-100), CVL-27 and CVL-30 being first renamed *Crown Point* and *Reprisal* respectively.

The *Independence*s were undoubtedly cramped compared to the fleet carriers in service during the Second World War, but they had the virtue of high speed; they also represented a design which had already been taken to its limit, however, and therefore did not lend themselves to the changing requirements of carrier aviation post-war.

Modifications Wartime modifications were restricted to upgrading the close-range armament (by 1945 all the class had 26 to 28 × 40mm, in twin and quadruple mountings, mostly at the expense of some 20mms), and radar (SK-2, SP and / or SPS-2 being substituted for SK / SC-2 on some ships, and Mk 28 fire control radar for the 40mm battery being added).

Post-war, those ships retained on strength by the US Navy were little altered, being seen as fighter-only carriers (a complement of 48 per unit of the new F8F point-defence fighter was specified) which would operate in consort with other, better-equipped units.

Service Notes *Independence*: Damaged by a Japanese aerial torpedo off Tarawa in November 1943, *Independence* was out of action for the first half of 1944 for repairs; thereafter, strikes and patrols occupied her until September 1945. She was used in the atomic tests at Bikini in the summer of 1946; relatively undamaged, she was formally decommissioned in August of that year and used as a weapons trials ship until February 1951, when she was sunk as a target.

Princeton: Following a year of combat in the Pacific, *Princeton* was hit by a 250kg bomb just abaft amidships during landing-on operations, 24 October 1944; the bomb penetrated the flight deck and detonated in the hangar, setting off fires which spread

Top: The cruiser-hulled CVLs (this is *Belleau Wood*, April 1943, shortly after commissioning) were seen as a stopgap development to provide the US Navy with additional flight decks at sea before the commissioning of the first of the *Essex*es; in the event, the name-ship of the class of big fleet carriers was completed first. Some measure of anti-surface defence was at first envisaged; one of the 5in weapons was to have occupied the platform just below the forward round-down, but *Belleau Wood* shows a quadruple 40mm already installed in lieu. (US Navy, by courtesy of Norman Friedman)

Above: The four funnels of the *Independence*s are clearly evident in this May 1943 view of *Monterey*; note how they are canted well away from the flight deck, both to reduce problems of visibility during air operations and to minimise the corrosive effects of the gases upon aircraft parked on the flight deck. (US Navy)

out of control. Her own fire-fighting gear was put out of action and she was dependent upon ships coming alongside, but munitions explosions within the hangar and magazines left her beyond salvage and she was scuttled by torpedoes from the light cruiser *Reno*.

Belleau Wood's air group was responsible for the sinking of the Japanese carrier *Hiyo* during her Pacific operations in June 1944. She was hit by a kamikaze in October 1944, repairs requiring three months. Decommissioned on 23 January 1947, she was lent to France as *Bois Belleau* (*qv*) until

Top: The narrowness of the CVL hulls dictated that the forward lift be positioned much farther aft than was ideal, and hangar length was in consequence restricted; its outline is apparent in this July 1943 photograph of *Cowpens*. The SK air-search radar located before the third funnel complemented the SC-2 above the island; one insured against the failure of the other. The other antennae visible are the small SG scanner for surface and low-level air search and the inevitable YE homing beacon at the masthead. (US Navy, by courtesy of Norman Friedman)

Centre: Another photograph of *Cowpens*, taken on the same day as the previous view and demonstrating, if nothing else, the difficulties inherent in establishing colour schemes from black and white pictures. The variations in the US national insignia as applied to the TBFs and SBDs on deck reflect the directive that from July 1943 white rectangles be added and the whole design outlined in red. Note the particularly diminutive markings applied to one of the Dauntlesses right aft. (US Navy, by courtesy of Norman Friedman)

Left: *San Jacinto*, at speed early in 1944, shows the markedly fine lines of the CVLs. The single catapult is visible before the windscreen; a second would soon be allocated to each ship of the class. (US Navy)

September 1960, when she was returned, formally stricken, and sold for scrap.

Cowpens: CVL-25 was damaged in December 1944 in the same typhoon which struck *Hornet* and *Bennington*, but was quickly repaired. After the war she was deactivated in January 1947, and on 16 May 1959 was redesignated an auxiliary aircraft transport, AVT-1. She never recommissioned, however, and was stricken in November 1959 and sold for breaking up, the latter completed by late 1961.

Monterey: Damaged in the notorious typhoon off the Philippines in December 1944, *Monterey* had to return to the West Coast for repairs: aircraft stowed in the hangar were flung about and several fires broke out. The last four months of the war saw her back in action in the Pacific. She decommissioned on 11 February 1947, but was one of the few *Independence*s to be taken on strength post-war by the US Navy: reactivated on 15 September 1950, she was employed as a training carrier based at Pensacola until being placed in reserve once again in 1955. She was redesignated AVT-2 in May 1959, but was finally stricken in June 1970 and sold for scrapping.

Langley: In combat in the Pacific throughout 1944 and until May 1945, when she started a six-month refit, *Langley* was decommissioned in January 1947 and transferred to France as the *Lafayette* (*qv*) in January 1951; returning in March 1963, she was immediately stricken and sold for breaking up.

Cabot: The only US wartime ex-*Cleveland* CVL still (1983) in service – as the Spanish carrier *Dédalo* (*qv*) – *Cabot* was twice hit by kamikazes and once by bombs during the war; damage, although fairly serious on each occasion, did not warrant her withdrawal for extended periods, however. Decommissioned on 11 February 1947, she was reactivated in October 1948 for air-crew training, but was back in reserve by January 1955. Reclassified AVT-3 in May 1959, she was lent to the Spanish Navy in August 1967 and bought outright in 1972.

Bataan: Escaping unscathed from some eighteen months of war service, *Bataan* was placed in reserve in May 1947, but was reactivated to participate in the Korean War in mid 1950, the only *Independence* to be used as an attack carrier in the post-war US Navy. Two tours of duty saw her engaged in air strikes

Top: An overhead view of *Bataan*, March 1944, shows the disposition of the AA defences: a quadruple 40mm is mounted at the bows and on the stern, and twin 40mms are carried in the large circular tubs along the flight-deck edge; 20mms occupy the remaining platforms. Note how the flight deck broadens abreast the forward lift, to allow aircraft to be moved around it. (US Navy, by courtesy of Norman Friedman)

Centre: On this occasion, 7 October 1944, *Bataan* has a deck-load of PV Venturas although three F6Fs intrude. As did the CVEs, the *Independence*s frequently acted as transports during the Pacific War. (US Navy)

Right: *Monterey* with other units of the US Fleet at Ulithi late in 1944. (US Navy)

against land targets; by early 1954, however, she was back in reserve, being redesignated AVT-4 in May 1959. In September 1959 she was stricken from service altogether, and was sold the following year and broken up.

San Jacinto: Fully engaged in the drive towards the Japanese mainland during the latter part of the Second World War, *San Jacinto* emerged without significant damage to be deactivated in January 1947. She remained in reserve until stricken and sold in June 1970, having been redesignated AVT-5 in 1959. She was scrapped soon after her sale.

Above: *Langley*, in company with other ships, returns from a strike, December 1944. The heavy crane before the island, characteristic of the *Independence*s, was required to serve the hangar deck via the lift; unlike fleet carriers, the CVLs did not have open sides. The carrier accompanying *Langley* is *Ticonderoga*. (US Navy, by courtesy of Norman Friedman)

Right: A postwar photograph of *Monterey*. Her forward AA guns have protective 'cocoons' over them; more interestingly, half her boilers are inactive, witness the capped funnels. (US Navy, by courtesy of Norman Friedman)

SABLE (IX-81)

Builder	Launched	Commissioned
American	27 Oct 23	8 Mar 43

Displacement: 8,000 tons / 8,144 tonnes (standard).
Length: 519ft / 158.19m (wl); 535ft / 163.07m (oa).
Beam: 58ft / 17.68m (hull); 90ft / 27.43m (fd).
Draught: 15ft 6in / 4.72m (mean).
Machinery: Inclined compound engines; 4 cylindrical boilers; 2 paddles.
Performance: 10,500ihp; 18kts.
Aircraft: Nil.
Guns: Nil.

Complement: 300.

Design Soon after *Wolverine*'s completion, conversion work was commenced at the same yard and followed generally similar lines, but a steel flight deck was fitted and the island was of rather different configuration, squared-off forward and with a covered bridge, a more substantial mast, and a pair of raked funnels. *Sable*'s original name was *Greater Buffalo*.

Modifications By late in the war *Sable* was showing a pair of outriggers for parked aircraft forward of the island; it appears, also, that YE and YG homing beacons were installed at the masthead.

Service Notes Not retained after the war, and scrapped from 1948.

Below: The second Lakes paddle-steamer to be converted as a training carrier was *Sable*, seen here in June 1945. The configuration generally resembled that of *Wolverine*, but a steel flight deck was fitted. (See photograph on page 220.) (US Navy)

Bottom: Crewmen gather as an F3F hits the safety barrier having overshot *Sable*'s arrester wires. A crowded deck park, fortunately, does not have to be contended with; the two training carriers had no air complement of their own. (US Navy, by courtesy of Norman Friedman)

CASABLANCA CLASS

Ship	Builder	Laid down	Launched	Commissioned
Casablanca (CVE-55)	Kaiser	3 Nov 42	5 Apr 43	8 July 43
Liscombe Bay (CVE-56)	Kaiser	9 Dec 42	19 Apr 43	7 Aug 43
Anzio (CVE-57)	Kaiser	12 Dec 42	1 May 43	27 Aug 43
Corregidor (CVE-58)	Kaiser	17 Dec 42	12 May 43	31 Aug 43
Mission Bay (CVE-59)	Kaiser	28 Dec 42	26 May 43	13 Sept 43
Guadalcanal (CVE-60)	Kaiser	5 Jan 43	5 June 43	25 Sept 43
Manila Bay (CVE-61)	Kaiser	15 Jan 43	10 July 43	5 Oct 43
Natoma Bay (CVE-62)	Kaiser	17 Jan 43	20 July 43	14 Oct 43
St Lo (CVE-63)	Kaiser	23 Jan 43	17 Aug 43	23 Oct 43
Tripoli (CVE-64)	Kaiser	1 Feb 43	2 Sept 43	31 Oct 43
Wake Island (CVE-65)	Kaiser	6 Feb 43	15 Sept 43	7 Nov 43
White Plains (CVE-66)	Kaiser	11 Feb 43	27 Sept 43	15 Nov 43
Solomons (CVE-67)	Kaiser	19 Mar 43	6 Oct 43	21 Nov 43
Kalinin Bay (CVE-68)	Kaiser	26 Apr 43	15 Oct 43	27 Nov 43
Kasaan Bay (CVE-69)	Kaiser	11 May 43	24 Oct 43	4 Dec 43
Fanshaw Bay (CVE-70)	Kaiser	18 May 43	1 Nov 43	9 Dec 43
Kitkun Bay (CVE-71)	Kaiser	31 May 43	8 Nov 43	15 Dec 43
Tulagi (CVE-72)	Kaiser	7 June 43	15 Nov 43	21 Dec 43
Gambier Bay (CVE-73)	Kaiser	10 July 43	22 Nov 43	28 Dec 43
Nehenta Bay (CVE-74)	Kaiser	20 July 43	28 Nov 43	3 Jan 44
Hoggatt Bay (CVE-75)	Kaiser	17 Aug 43	4 Dec 43	11 Jan 44
Kadashan Bay (CVE-76)	Kaiser	2 Sept 43	11 Dec 43	18 Jan 44
Marcus Island (CVE-77)	Kaiser	15 Sept 43	16 Dec 43	26 Jan 44
Savo Island (CVE-78)	Kaiser	27 Sept 43	22 Dec 43	3 Feb 44
Ommaney Bay (CVE-79)	Kaiser	6 Oct 43	29 Dec 43	11 Feb 44
Petrof Bay (CVE-80)	Kaiser	15 Oct 43	5 Jan 44	18 Feb 44
Rudyerd Bay (CVE-81)	Kaiser	24 Oct 43	12 Jan 44	25 Feb 44
Saginaw Bay (CVE-82)	Kaiser	1 Nov 43	19 Jan 44	2 Mar 44
Sargent Bay (CVE-83)	Kaiser	8 Nov 43	31 Jan 44	9 Mar 44
Shamrock Bay (CVE-84)	Kaiser	15 Nov 43	4 Feb 44	15 Mar 44
Shipley Bay (CVE-85)	Kaiser	22 Nov 43	12 Feb 44	21 Mar 44
Sitkoh Bay (CVE-86)	Kaiser	23 Nov 43	19 Feb 44	28 Mar 44
Steamer Bay (CVE-87)	Kaiser	2 Dec 43	26 Feb 44	4 Apr 44
Cape Esperance (CVE-88)	Kaiser	11 Dec 43	3 Mar 44	9 Apr 44
Takanis Bay (CVE-89)	Kaiser	16 Dec 43	10 Mar 44	15 Apr 44
Thetis Bay (CVE-90)	Kaiser	22 Dec 43	16 Mar 44	21 Apr 44
Makassar Strait (CVE-91)	Kaiser	29 Dec 43	22 Mar 44	29 Apr 44
Windham Bay (CVE-92)	Kaiser	5 Jan 44	29 Mar 44	3 May 44
Makin Island (CVE-93)	Kaiser	12 Jan 44	5 Apr 44	9 May 44
Lunga Point (CVE-94)	Kaiser	19 Jan 44	11 Apr 44	14 May 44
Bismarck Sea (CVE-95)	Kaiser	31 Jan 44	17 Apr 44	20 May 44
Salamaua (CVE-96)	Kaiser	4 Feb 44	22 Apr 44	26 May 44
Hollandia (CVE-97)	Kaiser	12 Feb 44	28 Apr 44	1 June 44
Kwajalein (CVE-98)	Kaiser	19 Feb 44	4 May 44	7 June 44
Admiralty Islands (CVE-99)	Kaiser	26 Feb 44	10 May 44	13 June 44
Bougainville (CVE-100)	Kaiser	3 Mar 44	16 May 44	18 June 44
Matanikau (CVE-101)	Kaiser	10 Mar 44	22 May 44	24 June 44
Attu (CVE-102)	Kaiser	16 Mar 44	27 May 44	30 June 44
Roi (CVE-103)	Kaiser	22 Mar 44	2 June 44	6 July 44
Munda (CVE-104)	Kaiser	29 Mar 44	8 June 44	8 July 44

Displacement: 8,200 tons / 8,331 tonnes (standard); 10,900 tons / 11,074 tonnes (deep load).
Length: 490ft / 149.35m (wl); 512ft 3in / 156.13m (oa); 475ft / 144.78m (fd).
Beam: 65ft 2in / 19.82m (hull); 85ft / 25.91m (fd).
Draught: 20ft 9in / 6.32m (mean).

Machinery: Skinner Uniflow reciprocating engines; 4 boilers; 2 shafts.
Performance: 9,000ihp; 19kts.
Bunkerage: 2,200 tons / 2,235 tonnes.
Range: 10,200nm at 15kts.
Aircraft: 28.

Guns: 1 × 5in; 8 × 40mm; 12 × 20mm.
Complement: 860.

Design With the United States totally in the grip of a prolonged war with Japan and the pattern of Pacific naval campaigns being well established, the requirement for yet further aircraft transports was plain to see. Britain's need of additional escort carriers to fight the Atlantic U-boat war was also great, and indeed it was in the US interest to ensure that these would be made available.

Speedy entry into service was the driving consideration, and in 1942 Henry J. Kaiser proposed to the US Government a scheme for the mass-production of such vessels, using the S4 special naval hull, which was already being used for the merchantmen his company was building. A rigorous construction schedule was presented, and the US authorities had no hesitation in responding positively to the ideas: fifty vessels were to be built at one yard, all within twelve months. In the event, the Navy decided against transferring any of the ships to the Royal Navy, diverting later batches of *Bogue*s instead.

The *Casablanca*s were marginally smaller than the *Bogue*s and, with a similar air group, proved somewhat cramped. The hulls had markedly less sheer, which improved mobility on the hangar deck and manifested itself externally in that the sponsons were virtually parallel to the waterline. A transom stern was a feature of the design, enabling only one single 5in / 38 to be mounted aft.

Flight deck and island configuration closely followed that adopted for the *Bogue*s, but the class differed fundamentally in being fitted with triple-expansion reciprocating engines, driving two screws; speed was increased somewhat, but range fell off. Water-tube boilers (Babcock & Wilcox, Foster Wheeler or Combustion Engineering) were fitted. Petrol stowage was 100,000 US gallons.

The original standard close-range armament consisted of twin 40mms and single 20mms, and all ships were fitted with SC air search (or its developed successors SC-2, SK or SK-2) and SG surface search radars, plus the standard carrier YE homing beacon at the masthead. The designed aircraft complement numbered nine fighters (F4F) and either nine torpedo-bombers (TBF) and nine dive-bombers (SBD) or eighteen torpedo-bombers.

Modifications By the end of the war most units had an augmented AA armament, with eight twin 40mm mountings and thirty 20mms, disposed in 'tubs' just below flight-deck level. Radar suites remained essentially unchanged although many early ships had their SC sets upgraded to SC-2 or SK (requiring essentially the substitution of a new, IFF-bearing improved antenna). *Salamaua* had a zenith search facility (SG-6) by 1945.

Post-war, six *Casablanca*s were reactivated for various duties: four, *Corregidor*, *Sitkoh Bay*, *Cape*

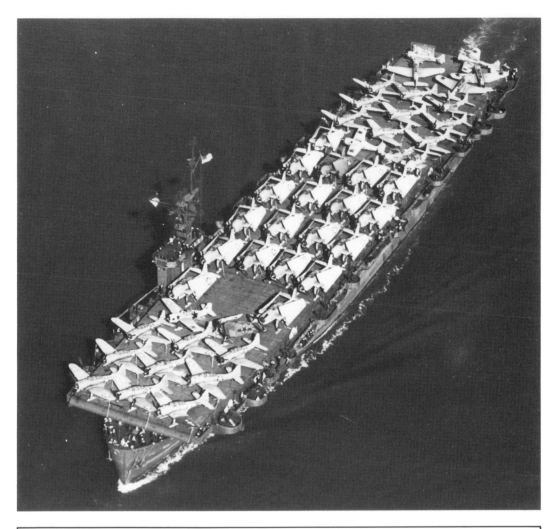

Esperance and *Windham Bay*, were assigned MSTS duties as aircraft transports from 1950, to and from the Korean War zone; *Tripoli* was also recommissioned under MSTS, but for transporting aircraft to Europe. All were fundamentally unmodified from their Second World War configuration, although much of the battery was non-operational.

The sixth ship, *Thetis Bay*, was the subject of a major conversion at San Francisco Navy Yard from June 1955 until July 1956. The flight deck was shortened; the catapult and arrester gear were taken out; the forward lift was sealed; a new lift was installed right aft, open at its after end; and a small ammunition lift was added in a trunked casing on the port side aft. She emerged as a helicopter assault ship (CVHA), with a much modified island, new radar (SPS-10, SPS-12) and enlarged 40mm sponsons at the forward deck edge. Displacing (1960 figures) 8,000 tons standard and 11,000 tons deep load, and with an overall length of 501ft and an extreme width of 108ft, she could carry 15−20 helicopters and 1,600 troops, her ship's complement rising to 930.

Service Notes *Casablanca*: Originally named *Ameer* (AVG-55) for the Royal Navy, but retained by the US Navy (ACV-55 20 August 1942), renamed *Alazon Bay* (January 1943) and finally *Casablanca* (April 1943). CVE-55 from 15 July 1943, she was employed on transport and training duties in the Pacific during the war. Deactivated on 29 August 1946, and stricken from service in March 1959, she was scrapped in 1961.

Liscombe Bay: First designated ACV-56, but classified CVE from 15 July 1943. Her Pacific career was terminated after only a few weeks of operational service by a torpedo fired from the Japanese submarine *I-175* off the Gilbert Islands, were she sank on 24 November 1943.

Anzio entered service as *Coral Sea* (CVE-57), having first been known as *Alikula Bay* (ACV-57); her final name was adopted in September 1944 to release the name *Coral Sea* for the fleet carrier CVB-43, laid down two months previously. She operated principally in the ASW role (Pacific) from late 1944 onwards. Placed in reserve in August 1946, she was redesignated CVHE (helicopter escort carrier) in July 1958, was stricken in March 1959 and was scrapped the following year.

Corregidor: Part of the batch of *Casablanca*s destined for the Royal Navy, ACV-58 was retained by the US Navy, changing her name from *Anguilla Bay* to *Corregidor* in April 1943; the CVE designation came into effect in July 1943. Her service during the war included transport, training, attack and ASW. Placed in reserve in July 1946, she was reactivated as an auxiliary transport under MSTS auspices after the

Thetis Bay, 1956

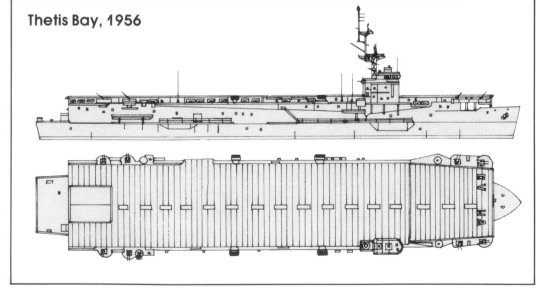

△1

△4

△2 ▽3

△5

△6 ▽7

outbreak of the Korean War, May 1951. She continued to function in auxiliary duties until finally decommissioned in September 1958. She was deleted the following month and broken up from 1960.

Mission Bay: ACV-59 was originally named *Atheling*, but was rechristened a few days after launch. CVE from July 1943, she spent most of her active service in the Atlantic theatre as an ASW and convoy escort carrier, although she had one transport deployment to India in early 1944. *Mission Bay* was engaged in transport duties post-war, but was placed in reserve in February 1947. Designated CVU-59 from 12 June 1955, she was deleted in September 1958, sold in April 1959 and broken up from January 1960.

Guadalcanal: Ex-*Astrolabe Bay* (ACV-60), but renamed in April 1943 and redesignated CVE three months later, *Guadalcanal* was another Atlantic escort and ASW carrier, her career highlighted by the capture of *U-505* in May 1944. She was decommissioned into reserve in July 1946 and reclassified CVU in June 1955; stricken from service in May 1958, she was sold and scrapped with *Mission Bay* in 1959–60.

Manila Bay: Ex-*Bucareli Bay* (ACV-61), but renamed *Manila Bay* in April 1943; she was reclassified CVE in July 1943. She operated in the transport and attack roles in the Pacific during 1943–45 and was struck by a kamikaze in January 1945 which damaged her island and forced her return to the USA. She was repaired within three months. In reserve from August 1946, she was deleted as CVU-61 in May 1958, sold in September 1959 and broken up from February 1960.

Natoma Bay: Built originally for the Royal Navy, but held back for US service, *Natoma Bay* (ACV-62, CVE from July 1943) operated in the Pacific for the first half of 1944, mainly as a transport, but subsequently spent two months training pilots off the West Coast; returned to the combat zone in October 1944,

she supported the advance to Japan until a kamikaze hit in June 1945 effectively put her out of action for the remainder of the war. She was placed in reserve in May 1946, redesignated CVU in May 1958, and was sold and scrapped in 1959–60.

St Lo: The escort carrier *St Lo* was another vessel to undergo a succession of name changes, and was one of the few of her type to be lost in action. She was originally named *Chapin Bay* (ACV-63), but was rechristened *Midway* prior to launching; however, to free this name for the new fleet carrier CVB-41, she became *St Lo* (CVE) in September 1944. An active Pacific career in the transport and support role culminated in her being the first victim of the Japanese kamikaze tactic: hit by a Zero which spilled fuel and set off fires and explosions across the hangar deck at Leyte, 25 October 1944, she sank within half an hour.

Tripoli: The former *Didrickson Bay* (ACV-64), but renamed in November 1943 just after completion, *Tripoli* had her commissioning delayed through an accidental explosion while undergoing last-minute modifications prior to service entry. Most of her career (throughout 1944) was spent undertaking ASW (one U-boat sunk, August) and convoy escort missions, but from early 1945 she operated in the Pacific in transport and training roles. Placed in reserve in May 1946, she was reactivated for MSTS transport duties in January 1952, finally being stricken in November 1958. CVE from July 1943 and CVU from June 1955, she was sold in 1959 and broken up from 1960.

Wake Island was originally named *Dolomi Bay* (ACV-65), but was renamed in April 1943 after her keel had been laid, and reclassified CVE that July. She had a varied career, operating both in the Atlantic (one U-boat sunk, June 1944) and in the Pacific, in a multitude of roles, as a combat vessel and as a transport and training carrier. She was struck by a pair of kamikazes in April 1945 during the assault on Okinawa and retired temporarily for repairs. She was stricken in April 1946, but her condition did not warrant her retention in the 'mothball fleet', and she was scrapped the following year.

White Plains: Laid down as ACV-66 *Elbour Bay*, this carrier was commissioned under her new name and CVE designation. Following work-up, she was employed as a transport, training and combat carrier in the Pacific, and was seriously damaged by a kamikaze hit in the same wave that sank *St Lo* and struck *Kitkun Bay*, October 1944. Following repairs, *White Plains* was used purely in the transport role. She was, however, retained post-war (deactivated July 1946); reclassified CVU-66 on 12 June 1955, she was deleted in June 1958 and broken up at Baltimore during 1959.

Solomons: Originally scheduled for Royal Navy Service (HMS *Emperor*), ACV-67 was instead retained by the US Navy as *Nassuk Bay*, being redesignated CVE in July 1943 and renamed

Solomons on 6 November of that year. She undertook one voyage as a transport in the Pacific, but from February 1944 operated in the Atlantic as an ASW and transport carrier. She was deactivated and stricken in mid 1946, and scrapped in 1947.

Kalinin Bay: ACV-68 (CVE from July 1943) served exclusively in the Pacific during the war. She was part of TU-77.4.4 which was so badly mauled off Samar during the Leyte campaign, October 1944, and suffered considerable damage through a kamikaze hit and also from gunfire. Following repairs, she was used mainly as an aircraft transport. Deleted from service in May 1946, she was sold at the end of the year and broken up.

Kasaan Bay: ACV-69 was reclassified CVE in July 1943, and following commissioning deployed to Pearl Harbor as a transport. However, the remainder of 1944 was spent in the Mediterranean, where she undertook a variety of roles, including support during the Allied landings in southern France. She transferred to the Pacific in early 1945. After the war, she was placed in reserve, being redesignated CVHE in June 1955. She was struck off the Navy List in March 1959, sold to a German concern in February 1960 and broken up at Hamburg.

Fanshaw Bay: (ACV-70; CVE from July 1943) was employed in the Pacific throughout her active career, being struck and damaged by Japanese bombs in the summer of 1944 and hit by shells during the mêlée off Samar that October. She was back in action by March the following year. Placed in reserve post-war, she was redesignated CVHE in 1955 and disposed of and scrapped in 1959.

Kitkun Bay: Another escort carrier employed only in the Pacific, ACV-71 (CVE from July 1943) was used as a transport and training ship for the first few months of 1944, but joined combat that summer. She was damaged in a kamikaze attack off Samar, October 1944, and was subsequently engaged in transport duties. She was not retained post-war, being stricken in May 1946 and broken up in 1947.

Tulagi: ACV-72's original name was *Fortezela Bay*, but following reclassification as a CVE she was renamed *Tulagi* in November 1944. She served both in the Atlantic (spring 1944–September 1944) and in the Pacific (early 1944 and from October 1944), mainly as a transport and ASW hunter-killer, although she was present at the Allied invasion of southern France (August 1944) and at Okinawa (March–June 1945). Decommissioned in April 1946, she was immediately deleted, and was scrapped the following year.

Gambier Bay: Another escort carrier war loss, ACV / CVE-73 served for some eight months in the Pacific in a variety of roles, but was caught by Japanese forces off Samar, 25 October 1944, and was sunk by gunfire from the Japanese cruisers *Chokai*, *Hagura* and *Noshiro*.

Nehenta Bay: Part of the Royal Navy's proposed batch of *Casablanca*s, *Nehenta Bay*, the first escort carrier to be laid down with a CVE designation, was in the event retained by the US Navy, serving in the Pacific theatre for the duration of her career. She was seriously damaged by hurricanes in the winter of 1944–45. Deactivated in May 1946, she was redesignated CVU in mid 1955 and then AKV (aircraft ferry) in May 1959; she saw no further service, however, being sold for scrapping in 1960.

Hoggatt Bay: While operating in the Pacific, *Hoggatt Bay* was damaged by an explosion during the Luzon campaign, January 1945. Following repairs, she was present during the Okinawa assaults and the final occupation of Japan. She decommissioned in July 1946 and remained in reserve, being reclassified CVHE (1955) and AKV (1959) before being disposed of for breaking up in September 1959.

Kadashan Bay: Employed during active service in the Pacific, *Kadashan Bay* performed the usual variety of transport, support and attack duties during the war. She was another of the kamikaze victims at Lingayen Gulf (invasion of Luzon, January 1945) and was obliged to retire to the USA for repairs. Upon completion of the latter she was confined to transporting replenishment aircraft. Decommissioned in June 1946, she was reclassified as a CVU in June 1955 and as AKV-26 in May 1959, but was stricken and scrapped in 1959–60.

Marcus Island: The former *Kanalku Bay* (renamed in November 1943) was confined chiefly to the transport role during the war, but was present at Leyte and took part in the action off Samar. She escaped damage on that occasion, but suffered in the hurricane which hit the Third Fleet off the Philippines in December 1944. Employed mainly as a transport during the ensuing months, *Marcus Island* was decommissioned on 12 December 1946; she was redesignated CVHE-77 in June 1955 and AKV-27 in May 1959, but was deleted and sold for scrapping in 1959–60.

Savo Island was first named *Kaita Bay*, but her name was changed some weeks prior to launching. She was present at the Samar action in October 1944 and was hit by a kamikaze early the following year; otherwise, she acted mainly as an aircraft transport. She was decommissioned in December 1946, becoming CVHE-78 in June 1955 and being reclassified as AKV-28 in May 1959. She was sold in September 1959 and scrapped at Hong Kong from mid 1960.

Ommaney Bay: Following training and transport tasks for much of 1944, *Ommaney Bay* escaped unscathed at Samar, but suffered crippling damage from a kamikaze attack en route for Lingayen Gulf several weeks later in early January 1945, in the same action which left *Manila Bay* (CVE-61) damaged. Beyond salvage, she was sunk by torpedoes fired from the destroyer *Burns* (DD-588).

Petrof Bay: First employed as an aircraft transport, *Petrof Bay* sailed for Guadalcanal in the summer of 1944 and subsequently participated in the Leyte, Iwo Jima and Okinawa campaigns. She was decommis-

sioned in July 1946, but remained in the reserve fleet for a further twelve years (CVU-80 from mid-1955) before being stricken and sold in 1958 and broken up the following year.

Rudyerd Bay: Another carrier employed only infrequently as a combat unit and principally as a transport during the war, *Rudyerd Bay* was relegated to the reserve fleet in June 1946, was reclassified as a CVU in June 1955 and as AKV-29 in May 1959, and was stricken and sold for scrapping in 1959–60.

Saginaw Bay: As with many of the 'jeep' carriers, CVE-82 was employed mainly in unglamorous but vital support roles during her period of active service from April 1944. She was deactivated and placed in reserve in June 1946, surviving as CVHE-82 from 1955 until disposed of and scrapped in 1959–60.

Sargent Bay acted as a Pacific support carrier for much of her wartime career. She sustained some damage in a collision with a US destroyer early in 1945, but went on to assist in the Iwo Jima and Okinawa campaigns. She decommissioned in mid 1946, was designated a utility carrier (CVU) in June 1955, and was sold and scrapped in the Netherlands in 1959.

Shamrock Bay: CVE-84 saw service in the Atlantic, ferrying aircraft to North Africa during the autumn of 1944, but joined the US forces in the Pacific late that year and took part in the two major US escort carrier combat missions from February 1945, the assaults on Iwo Jima and Okinawa. She was placed in reserve in

July 1946 and, reclassified CVU in 1955, was sold and scrapped in Hong Kong in late 1959.

Shipley Bay was engaged mainly in transport duties and training operations throughout her career, acting as a combat carrier only on rare occasions. She was decommissioned along with the bulk of the *Casablancas* in mid 1946; designated CVU from June 1955, she went for scrap in 1959 and was broken up during 1961.

△1

△2

△3 ▽4

△5

△6

△7 ▽8

Sitkoh Bay: Having worked as a resupply and replenishment ship for much of her wartime service, *Sitkoh Bay*, deactivated late in 1946, was recommissioned as an MSTS transport in the summer of 1950 to assist in supplying aircraft for the Korean War. She was placed in reserve once again in July 1954, and was finally stricken as AKV-30 in 1960 and scrapped the next year.

Steamer Bay: Transport missions for much of the latter half of 1944 were followed by more active service during the first months of 1945, and *Steamer Bay* participated in actions around Lingayen Gulf, Iwo Jima and Okinawa. She sustained damage on two occasions: in April 1945 she collided with the US destroyer *Hale* and in June that year an aircraft landing accident forced her temporary withdrawal from the combat zone. She went into reserve early in 1947, and although designated CVHE in mid 1955 was never again commissioned, being sold and scrapped in 1959.

Cape Esperance was one of the four *Casablanca*-class carriers reactivated post-war for MSTS service in the Korean War zone. During the Second World War she had operated purely as an aircraft transport in the Pacific. She was originally to have been known as *Tananek Bay*, but her name was changed before work on her began. First decommissioning was in August 1946, CVU redesignation came in June 1955, second deactivation in January 1959, and sale for scrap in March 1959. She was broken up in Japan in 1961.

Takanis Bay: Used for ferrying and training during

the war, *Takanis Bay* was taken out of service in May 1946, reclassified CVU in mid 1955, AKV-31 in May 1959, and stricken, sold and scrapped in 1959–60.

Thetis Bay: Without doubt the most gainfully employed *Casablanca*-class vessel in the post-war years, *Thetis Bay* was converted in 1955–56 as the US Navy's first amphibious assault ship, commissioning as a CVHA on 20 July 1956. She subsequently deployed both to the Pacific and the Atlantic and experience with her paved the way for the *Essex*-class conversions and, ultimately, the design of the *Iwo Jima*s and *Tarawa*s of the 1960s and 1970s. During the war she had been employed mainly as a transport in the Pacific. She was in the reserve fleet from August 1946 until her conversion, and was redesignated LPH-6 in May 1959. Her sale to the Spanish Navy was reportedly considered after final deactivation in March 1964, but in the event the light carrier *Cabot* was subsequently transferred. *Thetis Bay* was broken up in 1966.

Makassar Strait: At first scheduled to receive the name *Ulitka Bay*, CVE-91 was renamed before construction was implemented and operated almost exclusively as an aircraft transport in the Pacific during 1944–45, although she did take part in the assault on Okinawa in the spring of 1945. Placed in reserve in mid 1946, *Makassar Strait* met an eventful fate, being brought out to serve as an experimental target for Tartar and Terrier missiles, testing their efficacy as ship-to-ship weapons rather than their designed anti-aircraft capabilities. She sank following a series of such tests in 1961–62.

Windham Bay: Training and transport occupied *Windham Bay* for most of her wartime career, during which she was caught in a typhoon (June 1945) and had to return to dock for repairs. Withdrawn from service early in 1947, she was acquired for transport duties under MSTS direction in the autumn of 1951; redesignated CVU in mid 1955, she was stricken in 1959 and sold for scrapping in 1961.

Makin Island: The name *Woodcliff Bay* was originally allocated for CVE-93, but the ship was renamed prior to being laid down. She had an active wartime career, participating in the US advance on the Japanese homeland from late 1944 (Lingayen, Iwo Jima, Okinawa). Deactivated in April 1946 and placed in reserve, she was sold and scrapped the following year.

Lunga Point: Employed in the Pacific from the summer of 1944, *Lunga Point* (ex-*Alazon Bay*) was struck by a kamikaze during operations off Iwo Jima, February 1945, which did not, however, force her withdrawal. She participated in the landings on Okinawa. She saw no further active service following her decommissioning in late October 1946: although redesignated CVU in June 1955 and AKV-32 in May 1959, she was sold in 1960 and scrapped in Japan from November of that year.

Bismarck Sea: At the time of her launch, CVE-95

was named *Alikula Bay*, but in May 1944 she took the name *Bismarck Sea*. She was a victim of kamikaze attack off Iwo Jima in February 1945, hit by two aircraft in the same strike that put the fleet carrier *Saratoga* out of action. She sank within a few hours, on the 21st.

Salamaua: Allocated the name *Anguilla Bay* before her keel was laid, but almost immediately renamed, *Salamaua* served as a transport, ASW and strike carrier during her wartime Pacific career. Twice sustaining damage during the course of her duties – once as a result of a kamikaze hit (off the Philippines, January 1945) and once during a hurricane (the same that afflicted *Hornet* and *Bennington*, Okinawa, 5 June 1945) – she was stricken soon after the end of the war and broken up in 1947.

Hollandia: Originally named *Astrolabe Bay*, *Hollandia* was rechristened by the time she commissioned and was employed throughout late 1944 and 1945 purely as a training / transport carrier. On 17 January 1947 she was deactivated and placed in reserve, and she was stricken, sold and scrapped in 1960, having received the new designations CVU-97 in mid 1955 and AKV-33 in May 1959.

Kwajalein was tentatively named *Bucareli Bay* until a few days before her launch. She was used as a transport back-up for the US Pacific forces for the duration of her career, spending two months out of service early in 1945 as a result of hurricane damage sustained off the Philippines. Placed in reserve upon decommissioning in August 1946, she was reclassified CVU in June 1955 and AKV-34 in 1959, being sold for scrapping the following year.

Admiralty Islands: The escort carrier *Chapin Bay* (a name also allocated to CVE-63 at one time) was renamed *Admiralty Islands* prior to launching. She was utilised in the transport role for much of her early career, but took part in the Iwo Jima and Okinawa campaigns. In the reserve fleet from April 1946 for only a fortnight, she was straightaway sold for breaking up.

Bougainville: The second *Casablanca* to be originally named *Didrickson Bay*, *Bougainville* was another member of the class to be renamed just before launch. Employed, like many of her sister-ships, on transport missions during the latter half of 1944, assisting in the build up of the final assault on Japanese-held islands, she saw more action during 1945 as the invasions of Iwo Jima and Okinawa got underway. She was a victim of the typhoon on 5 June. She remained in the reserve fleet from November 1946 until her sale for scrapping in 1960, being redesignated CVU (June 1955) and AKV-35 (May 1959) before she was stricken.

Matanikau: CVE-101 was laid down as *Dolomi Bay*, but changed her name before being launched. During the war she was employed principally as a transport in the Pacific. Following deactivation in October 1946, she was held in reserve (CVHE 1955, AKV-36 1959) until stricken, sold and scrapped in 1960–61.

1: *Shipley Bay* in the Marshall Islands, May 1944, with a deck load of replacement aircraft. (US Navy)

2: *Lunga Point* prepares to accept a TBM as a second passes overhead. Note the raised safety barrier just abaft the island. (US Navy)

3: *Ommaney Bay* with lifts lowered, July 1944. Note the additional width of the after lift, enabling non-folding aircraft such as the F4F-4 to be brought up from and taken down to the hangar deck. (US Navy)

4: The HF/DF aerial on the starboard side forward betrays the ASW role of this *Casablanca*: *Mission Bay*, summer 1944. (US Navy)

5: *Guadalcanal* in September 1944. Note the 'feathered' effect of the camouflage bands, a style also seen for a while on the escort carrier *Solomons* and the French battleship *Richelieu* after her US refit. (US Navy)

6: *Bismarck Sea* taking it green, June 1944. These conditions were frequently the lot of ASW escort carriers. (US Navy)

7: *Takanis Bay* in August 1944. (US Navy)

8: A July 1944 photograph of *Matanikau*. In this and some other photographs of *Casablanca*s reproduced on these pages it can be seen that the SK air search 'mattress' is not fitted and in its place is SK-2, a 'dish' aerial developed with the object of concentrating the energy of the radar beam into a single, and thus more powerful, lobe. (US Navy)

Attu: Used exclusively, it is believed, as a transport carrier during the war, *Attu* (ex-*Elbour Bay*) sustained damage in the June hurricane off Okinawa and was not retained in reserve post-war. She was stricken a month after decommissioning in June 1946 and by 1950 had been scrapped.

Roi: Formerly *Alava Bay*, but commissioned as *Roi*, CVE-103 acted as a supply and replenishment carrier during her twelve months of active war service. She was placed for disposal immediately upon decommissioning in May 1946 and was broken up the following year.

Munda: The last of the *Casablanca*s was originally to have been named *Tonowek Bay*, but in common with many of her sisters the provisional 'Bay' series nomenclature was abandoned in favour of recent Pacific actions. Apparently never employed as an attack carrier, *Munda* operated in the support role until the Japanese surrender, going into reserve in September 1946. She survived into the 1950s, but was one of the first *Casablanca*s to be disposed of, being stricken in September 1958 (as CVU-104), sold in 1960 and subsequently scrapped.

Left, top: *Makin Island*, early 1945. (US Navy)

Left, centre: By October 1945 *Casablanca* was still fitted with SC-2 radar, considerably smaller in size than the SK which characterised most of the ships of her class at this time. (US Navy)

Left, below: *Wake Island*, May 1945. (US Navy)

Right, top: An interesting arrangement of radar antennae is seen in this late-war photograph of *Salamaua*: in an effort to solve the problem of enemy aircraft attacking directly from overhead, i.e. undetected by conventional air-search radars, a zenith system was developed to provide coverage across the complete sky arc. The two antennae of the SG-6 zenith search system can be seen. YE is, again, at the masthead. (US Navy)

Right, centre: A photograph of *Hollandia* dated, rather improbably, January 1951: by this time she had been deactivated and, in any case, was unlikely to have been wearing camouflage. (US Navy)

Right, below: One of a handful of *Casablanca*-class carriers reactivated postwar for transportation tasks during the Korean War, *Cape Esperance* is seen here with F-84s, F-86s, T-6s, F-80s, F6Fs and liaison aircraft aboard, en route for the combat zone. Note the single 5in gun aft, characteristic of the *Casablanca*s. (US Navy)

Far right, top: A further assortment of machines bound for Korea, this time aboard *Sitkoh Bay*. The Navy Invaders (amidships) were not used by that service as attack aircraft but as target tugs, designated JD. (US Navy)

Far right, centre: *Windham Bay* was also reactivated for Korean War duty. Note that, as in other photographs of this period, the *Casablanca*s had their after 40mm mountings 'cocooned'; note also the vacant 20mm positions. (US Navy)

Far right, below: *Thetis Bay*, modified as a helicopter assault carrier (LPH-6) and showing her cut-down after flight deck and the prominent ammunition trunk on the port side aft. (US Navy)

COMMENCEMENT BAY CLASS

Ship	Builder	Laid down	Launched	Commissioned
Commencement Bay (CVE-105)	Todd-Pacific	23 Sept 43	9 May 44	27 Nov 44
Block Island (CVE-106)	Todd-Pacific	25 Oct 43	10 June 44	30 Dec 44
Gilbert Islands (CVE-107)	Todd-Pacific	29 Nov 43	20 July 44	5 Feb 45
Kula Gulf (CVE-108)	Todd-Pacific	16 Dec 43	15 Aug 44	12 May 45
Cape Gloucester (CVE-109)	Todd-Pacific	10 Jan 44	12 Sept 44	5 Mar 45
Salerno Bay (CVE-110)	Todd-Pacific	7 Feb 44	26 Sept 44	19 May 45
Vella Gulf (CVE-111)	Todd-Pacific	7 Mar 44	19 Oct 44	9 Apr 45
Siboney (CVE-112)	Todd-Pacific	1 Apr 44	9 Nov 44	14 May 45
Puget Sound (CVE-113)	Todd-Pacific	12 May 44	30 Nov 44	18 June 45
Rendova (CVE-114)	Todd-Pacific	15 June 44	28 Dec 44	22 Oct 45
Bairoko (CVE-115)	Todd-Pacific	25 July 44	25 Jan 45	16 July 45
Badoeng Strait (CVE-116)	Todd-Pacific	18 Aug 44	15 Feb 45	14 Nov 45
Saidor (CVE-117)	Todd-Pacific	29 Sept 44	17 Mar 45	4 Sept 45
Sicily (CVE-118)	Todd-Pacific	23 Oct 44	14 Apr 45	27 Feb 46
Point Cruz (CVE-119)	Todd-Pacific	4 Dec 44	18 May 45	16 Oct 45
Mindoro (CVE-120)	Todd-Pacific	2 Jan 45	27 June 45	4 Dec 45
Rabaul (CVE-121)	Todd-Pacific	29 Jan 45	14 July 45	
Palau (CVE-122)	Todd-Pacific	19 Feb 45	6 Aug 45	15 Jan 46
Tinian (CVE-123)	Todd Pacific	20 Mar 45	5 Sept 45	

Displacement: 18,908 tons / 19,211 tonnes (standard); 21,397 tons / 21,739 tonnes (deep load).
Length: 525ft / 160.02m (wl); 557ft 1in / 169.80m (oa); 495ft / 150.88m (fd).
Beam: 75ft / 22.86m (hull); 80ft / 24.38m (fd).
Draught: 27ft 11in / 8.51m (deep load).
Machinery: Allis-Chalmers geared turbines; 4 Combustion Engineering boilers; 2 shafts.
Performance: 16,000shp; 19kts.

Bunkerage: 3,134 tons / 3,184 tonnes.
Aircraft: 33.
Guns: 2 × 5in; 36 × 40mm; 20 × 20mm.
Complement: 1,066.

Design The final expression of the US escort carrier, the *Commencement Bay* class were, again, adapted merchant hulls, but had greater Navy involvement in their design than previous such ships. The *Bogue*-based carrier was somewhat handicapped by its small

size, and so an oiler hull was once more selected; the new class had much in common with the four *Sangamon*s, sharing their huge bunkerage (more than 12,000 tons as oilers, as which they might continue to function if the need arose) and hence their quite phenomenal range.

Early batches were all to be built at the renamed Seattle-Tacoma yard, but of a projected 35 ships only nineteen were actually completed, eight postwar; four (*Bastogne, Eniwetok, Lingayen* and *Okinawa*, CVE-124 – CVE-127) were laid down but not launched; and twelve (CVE-128 – CVE-139) were projected only, the last eight being assigned to the Kaiser yard at Vancouver.

The hull form and general layout followed closely those of the *Sangamon*s, but there were some important differences, particularly a switch to *en échelon* machinery and boiler rooms. The stern was slightly fuller, and the hull sides were sponsored out at hangar-deck level to accept eight additional twin 40mm mountings. Three quadruple 40mms were carried, one on the forecastle and two in tubs right aft, with additional twin 40mms to port and starboard, forward of the island. Single 20mms were carried at flight-deck level, along the edge. The single 5in / 38s were mounted on the quarters.

Flight-deck facilities were developed from those offered by the earlier oiler conversions: the after lift still had to be located well forward, to clear the machinery spaces right aft, but two catapults rather

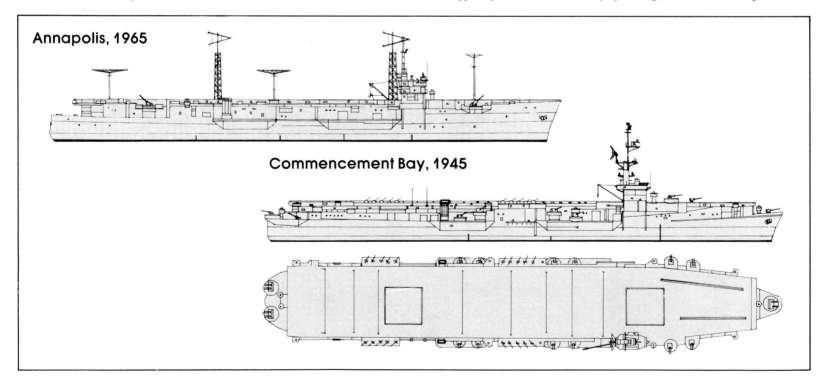

Annapolis, 1965

Commencement Bay, 1945

Gilbert Islands: This carrier was first allocated the name *St Andrews Bay*, but was renamed whilst under construction. She participated in the Okinawa campaign and remained in the Pacific until December 1945, being decommissioned into the reserve fleet five months later. She was reactivated in September 1951 because of the Korean War and assisted in the transportation of aircraft to the combat zone. She was decommissioned again at the beginning of 1955 and was for disposal in June 1961, only to be selected for conversion to a Major Communications Relay Ship (AGMR-1) before the end of that year. During conversion, she was renamed *Annapolis*, and she recommissioned as such in March 1964. She continued in that role until the end of 1969, having been deployed to Vietnam for a period from 1965. She was stricken in October 1976.

Kula Gulf (ex-*Vermillion Bay*) operated in the Pacific for the last few weeks of the war, but had been deactivated by July 1946. She emerged again in 1950, being employed in transport and training duties during the Korean War. From mid 1953 she operated as an ASW carrier in the Atlantic until committed to the reserve fleet once more in December 1955. Brought out for MSTS ferrying purposes in June 1965 (AKV-8), she was used during the Vietnam War as an aircraft transport. She was finally stricken in September 1970 and broken up the following year.

Cape Gloucester: Originally to have been named *Willapa Bay*, *Cape Gloucester* deployed to the north-west Pacific in July 1945, in time to see combat. She was placed in reserve in November 1946, redesignated CVHE in June 1955, reclassified AKV-9 in May 1959, stricken in the summer of 1960 and immediately had the order revoked, and stricken for a second time in April 1971.

Salerno Bay: CVE-110, originally to have been named *Winjah Bay*, was used for air-crew training post-war, before being deactivated in October 1947. She was recommissioned as an ASW carrier in 1951, remaining in front-line service until early 1954. Reclassified AKV-10 in May 1959, she was struck off and sold in late 1961 and scrapped the following year in Spain.

Vella Gulf: Ex-*Totem Bay* (renamed while under construction), *Vella Gulf* was completed in time to see service during the war, but was employed principally as a training carrier, a task she continued for some months after hostilities had ceased. In reserve from August 1946, she was to have followed *Gilbert Islands* as a conversion to AGMR configuration, but *Saipan* was completed in her stead. She had

than one (improved H4C type) were installed. The island was similar in general appearance to earlier classes, but carried a strengthened mast with, as standard, SK-2 (SP in some later units) and SG radar.

Modifications Twelve *Commencement Bay*s were retained in the active list after the Second World War or reactivated subsequently and the class formed the basis of the US Navy's post-war anti-submarine fleet. By the early 1950s the radar suite was SPS-6 and SPS-4 (or SP), the wartime SG being generally retained. Some (for example *Badoeng Strait*, *Mindoro*) had their bridges extended and covered; others (*eg Point Cruz*) had them extensively remodelled, with an extra enclosed platform built up. Many had their 5in / 38s and quadruple 40mm bow mountings deleted, and 20mms were generally removed. *Kula Gulf* was taken over by MSTS in the mid 1960s and had a heavy crane added behind the island, and, reportedly, her forward lift was replaced with a larger unit.

Gilbert Islands was extensively modified in the early 1960s as a Major Communications Relay Ship (AGMR) and renamed *Annapolis*. The armament was stripped, four twin 3in / 50 mountings were added forward and aft, just below flight-deck level, the catapults were removed, and the forecastle was enclosed, the bows and hangar sides being completely plated up to flight-deck level. Five antenna masts were

erected along the flight-deck centreline. Internally, the hangar was converted to house the various transmitters, receivers and other equipment; SPS-10 was carried for the ship's own use.

Service Notes *Commencement Bay*: The lead ship of the *Commencement Bay* class, originally named *St Joseph Bay*, was, like many of her successors, employed purely in an auxiliary role during her short wartime career, in her case functioning mainly as an air-crew training vessel in the Eastern Pacific. Decommissioned into reserve in late November 1946, she was redesignated a helicopter escort carrier (CVHE) in June 1955 and AKV-37 in May 1959, being stricken from the Navy list on 1 April 1971.

Block Island: CVE-106, laid down as *Sunset Bay* but renamed prior to launch, deployed to the Pacific early in 1945. She decommissioned in May 1946, but continued in use as a floating school-ship at Annapolis until 1950. In April 1951 she recommissioned for service in the Atlantic, but was returned to reserve by autumn 1954. A proposal to convert her to a helicopter-carrying amphibious assault ship was not taken up, even though she received the designation LPH-1 in December 1957 (reverting to CVE in 1959). As AKV-38, she was sold in late 1959 and broken up in Japan the following year.

△1

△4

△2 ▽3

△5 ▽6

7△

8△

9△ 10▽

been reclassified as CVHE-108 in mid 1955 and again as AKV-11 in May 1959, and was finally stricken from the Navy List in December 1970.

Siboney: CVE-112, ex-*Frosty Bay*, had completed working up in time to deploy to the Pacific before VJ-Day, and continued in service until first decommissioning at the end of 1947. Reactivated for a short spell of transport duty during 1948, she was returned to reserve in early 1949. *Siboney* was in front-line service again by 1951, however, as an ASW carrier like several of her sister ships, operating in the Atlantic and Mediterranean. She was back in reserve again by mid 1956, being subsequently redesignated AKV-12. She was deleted in June 1970 and scrapped the following year.

Puget Sound: Ex-*Hobart Bay*, *Puget Sound* had a very brief operational career, commissioning just before the end of the Pacific War and decommissioning in October 1946; she survived in the reserve fleet (CVHE July 1955, AKV-13 May 1959) until being deleted in mid 1960 and sold and scrapped in 1962.

Rendova's original name was *Mosser Bay* (changed prior to keel-laying). Commissioned some weeks after the end of the war, *Rendova* saw considerable service

1: Unlike the *Bogue*s and *Casablanca*s, the *Commencement Bay*s were retained on the US Navy active list postwar. This is *Gilbert Islands*, May 1946. (US Navy)

2: *Bairoko* just before the end of the Second World War. SK-2 air-search radar was the standard initial fit for *Commencement Bay*-class carriers. Note the rounded stern, contrasting with the transom of the earlier *Casablanca*s and carrying two quad 40mm sponsons; visible forward of the port-side sponson is the muzzle of one of the pair of 5in/38s. (US Navy)

3: *Point Cruz* with reconfigured island: an additional platform carries SP height-finding radar for fighter control. (US Navy)

4: *Sicily* on transport duties at the time of the Korean War. (US Navy)

5: A March 1945 view of *Cape Gloucester* in Measure 22 camouflage.

6: *Commencement Bay*-class escort carriers were fitted with two catapults, and that on the port side was the more powerful, longer-tracked H4; in order to clear the forward lift, the H4 was angled away from the centreline, as can just be seen in this photograph of *Vella Gulf*, August 1945. (US Navy)

7: *Puget Sound* immediately after her completion. (US Navy)

8: *Salerno Bay*, 29 May 1946. (US Navy)

9: *Sicily* again, this time in April 1949. The chevron-type deck markings are believed to be associated with airship ('blimp') trials. (US Navy)

10: A Goodyear K-type patrol blimp leaves *Mindoro*, 28 April 1950. Non-rigid airships were used by the US Navy during the Second World War for anti-submarine patrol more widely than is generally supposed, and experiments continued throughout the postwar decade. (US Navy)

UNITED STATES 251

Top left: During the immediate postwar years the helicopter showed much promise as a vehicle which might be effectively employed in beachhead assault, and prior to the conversion of the *Casablanca*-class carrier *Thetis Bay* (see above), trials were conducted aboard the *Commencement Bay*-class *Palau*. The latter is shown, June 1950, with Piasecki HRPs ('Flying Bananas') aboard. (US Navy)

Centre left: In the postwar US Navy, the major role of the *Commencement Bay*s was as stop-gap ASW carriers; they were the forerunners of the *Essex*-class CVS conversions. This is *Siboney*, with anti-submarine Avengers on her flight deck; the aircraft to port of the forward lift is the TBM-3W variant, which carried ASW radar in a prominent ventral dome. (US Navy)

Below left: *Rendova* was one of two *Commencement Bay*s to operate as a Marine strike carrier during the Korean conflict. F4Us are seen on deck, and the new SPS-6 air-search antenna can be seen on the island, abaft the mast. (US Navy)

Right: *Mindoro* operating with Marine Corps HRS troop-carrying helicopters, October 1953. This particularly crisp photograph shows clearly the new-style flight-deck markings evident aboard US carriers at this time. (US Navy)

in the post-war US Navy, deploying to the Indian and Pacific Oceans and functioning as a training carrier, a transport, a support carrier (including Korean War service) and an ASW carrier. She was in reserve during 1950, for much of 1953 and again from mid 1955, being reclassified as a CVHE in the summer of 1955 and as AKV-14 in May 1959. She was stricken and scrapped in 1971.

Bairoko: Ex-*Portage Bay*. Following a short spell in the reserve fleet (April–September 1950), *Bairoko* was engaged in active service during the Korean War, suffering some damage as a result of an on-board explosion in May 1951. She took part in H-bomb tests at Eniwetok during 1954 and was returned to reserve the following year. She was redesignated AKV-15 in May 1959, stricken in April 1960 and scrapped at Hong Kong during 1961.

Badoeng Strait: Originally to have been named *San Alberto Bay*, *Badoeng Strait*, following reactivation in January 1947 after seven months in reserve, was the principal US Navy trials ships for ASW tactics during the late 1940s and early 1950s. Her career included a long period of service operating as an ASW carrier during the Korean conflict. She was decommissioned in May 1957; reclassified as an aircraft ferry (AKV-16) in May 1959, she was stricken late in 1970 and subsequently scrapped.

Saidor: In a brief service career lasting barely 21 months, *Saidor*'s principal contribution was her service as a headquarters ship for photographic processing during the Bikini atomic tests in the summer of 1946. She was placed in reserve in September 1947, reclassified CVHE in June 1955, reclassified again as AKV-17 in the spring of 1959, and sold and scrapped in 1970–71. She had been allocated the name *Saltery Bay* prior to keel-laying.

Sicily: CVE-118, originally named *Sandy Bay*, remained in service throughout the late 1940s and undertook several tours of duty off Korea, 1950–52,

mainly in an ASW capacity. She was deactivated in July 1954 and placed in reserve; in mid 1960 (as AKV-18), *Sicily* was stricken and sold, to be broken up the following year.

Point Cruz, together with *Kula Gulf* (CVE-108) was the last *Commencement Bay*-class carrier to be employed on active service, being used as a transport (AKV-19) during the Vietnam conflict from 1965 to 1970, under the MSTS system. Her original name was *Trocadero Bay* (changed before laying down), and following pilot training duties in the immediate post-war months and a period in the reserve fleet from June 1947 until July 1951, she was one of the group of *Commencement Bay*s that formed the principal US

ASW carrier force during the early 1950s. She saw service during the Korean War, 1953. *Point Cruz* was struck off the Navy List and broken up in 1970–71.

Mindoro was in continuous active service from February 1946 until mid 1955, initially for air-crew training but for the most part as a component of the US ASW carrier force in the Atlantic. She was reclassified as AKV-20 while in reserve, and was disposed of in 1959–60.

Rabaul: Not commissioned into the US Navy, *Rabaul* was completed on 30 August 1946 but immediately placed in reserve, where she remained, through redesignation as CVHE in 1955 and

AKV-21 in 1959, until being stricken in September 1971. She was broken up the following year.

Palau was employed somewhat sporadically during her career, operating mainly in the Atlantic, both with the Sixth Fleet and as a transport. She decommissioned formally in mid 1954, and was sold and broken up (as AKV-22) in 1960.

Tinian: The last *Commencement Bay* carrier to be completed (30 July 1946), *Tinian*, however, never actually commissioned for service: like *Rabaul*, she was placed in reserve upon completion and remained there until being stricken in June 1970, despite redesignation to CVHE in June 1955 and AKV-23 on 7 May 1959. She was scrapped in 1971.

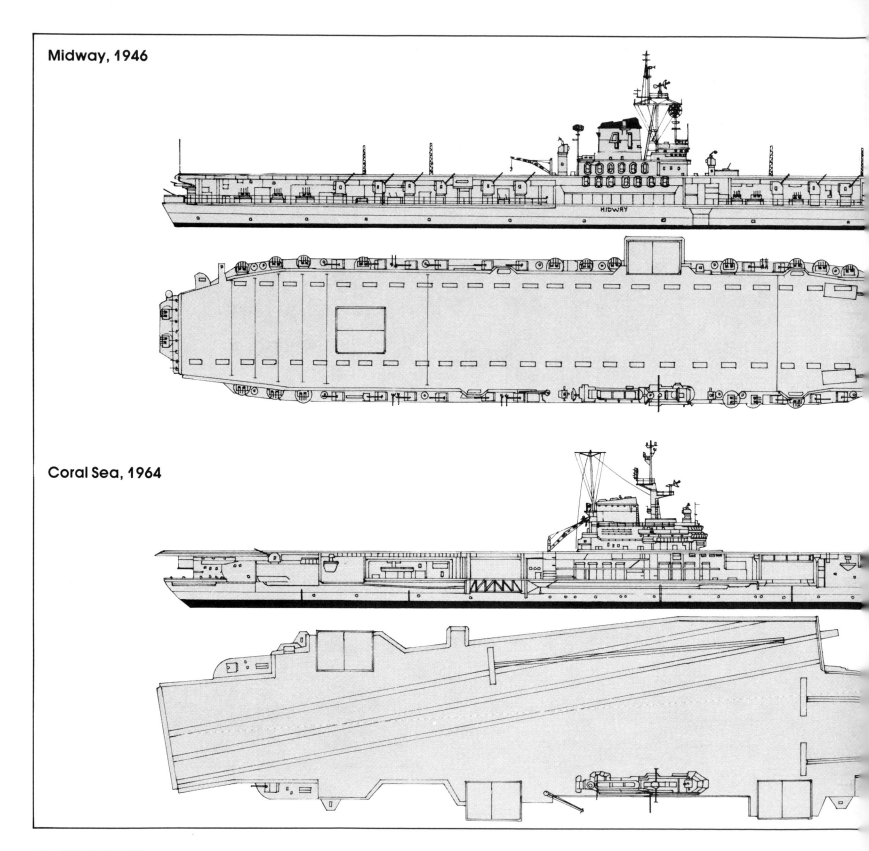

Midway, 1946

Coral Sea, 1964

MIDWAY CLASS

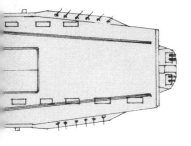

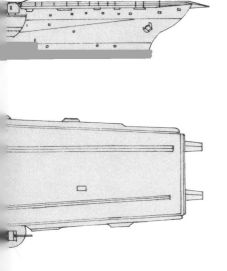

Ship	Builder	Laid down	Launched	Commissioned
Midway (CVB-41)	Newport News	27 Oct 43	20 Mar 45	10 Sept 45
Franklin D. Roosevelt (CVB-42)	New York	1 Dec 43	29 Apr 45	27 Oct 45
Coral Sea (CVB-43)	Newport News	10 July 44	2 Apr 46	1 Oct 47

Displacement: 47,387 tons / 48,145 tonnes (standard); 59,901 tons / 60,858 tonnes (deep load).
Length: 900ft / 274.32m (wl); 968ft / 295.05m (oa); 932ft / 284.07m (fd).
Beam: 113ft / 34.44m (hull); 113ft / 34.44m (fd).
Draught: 32ft 9in / 9.98m (mean); 34ft 6in / 10.52m (deep load).
Machinery: Geared turbines; 12 Babcock & Wilcox boilers; 4 shafts.
Performance: 212,000shp; 33kts.
Bunkerage: 10,000 tons / 10,160 tonnes.
Range: 15,000nm at 15kts.
Aircraft: 137.
Guns: 18 × 5in; 84 × 40mm; 68 × 20mm.
Complement: 2,510.

Design The three *Midway*s represent a major watershed in US fleet carrier design in that they proved to be the ultimate development of the built-up hangar and flight deck concept, yet by introducing armour protection above hangar-deck level on an extensive scale, thereby ensuring a massive increase in size over the *Essex*es, pointedly drew attention to its limitations. Plans for their construction were approved in the summer of 1942, the General Board

apparently having been much impressed with the performance of the British carriers *Illustrious* and *Formidable*, which in early 1941 had taken 500kg and 1,000kg bomb hits but had survived thanks to their armoured hangars; the experiences of US carriers a year later in the Pacific were to be more unfortunate. In a sense, too, the *Midway*s were a product of the Washington Treaty, despite that agreement having lapsed some years before they were laid down, since the original requirement for armour protection stemmed from the desire to immunise the ships against 8in cruiser fire, the heaviest available from such ships for the foreseeable future and the heaviest permitted under Washington.

The specification of armouring the new carriers to such an extent was the basis for their increased size:

Below: The *Midway*s were the first US carriers to have armoured flight decks, but the last in which the flight decks were built up over the hull rather than as an integral part of it; as completed, they also retained the open bow of the *Essex*es, occupied in this photograph of *Midway* on 20 October 1945 by two quadruple 40mm mountings. The practice of painting the ship's name on the hull amidships did not last. (US National Archives, by courtesy of A. D. Baker III)

an 8in waterline belt (7in on the starboard side, to
help balance the weight of the island), 6.3in
bulkheads, 2in above the belt up to hangar-deck level,
a 2in main deck, a 2in armoured hangar deck and a
3.5in flight deck would consume 4,000 extra tons on
an *Essex* and give an unacceptable drop in speed, and
so the spiral was initiated. More speed required more
power, which in turn required a larger hull and still
more armour to protect the longer spaces occupied by
the vitals: the compromise was halted at 45,000 tons
standard displacement.

Aircraft capacity in the *Midways* was entirely
incidental to the requirement for superior protection,
and it was in a way a by-product of the design that the
supportable air group for each ship saw a virtual 50
per cent rise compared to the *Essex*-class carriers, the
figure quoted in the table numbering 73 F6Fs and
F4Us and 64 SB2Cs. Avgas bunkerage was about
350,000 US gallons, and air-crew added about 1,600
to the complement figure shown.

The machinery was arranged *en échelon* and was
virtually identical with that earmarked for the
abortive *Montana*-class battleships. *Franklin D.
Roosevelt* had General Electric turbines, and the
other two ships Westinghouse. The machinery spaces
were subdivided to contain flooding in the event of an
underwater hit, again on a par with the *Montanas*.

Top left: *Franklin D. Roosevelt*, in January 1951, shows the beginnings of the progressive reduction of the fixed armament which characterised the careers of the three *Midways*: gone are her two aftermost 5in mountings, as are her 40mms, although in place of the latter are the new twin 3in/50 weapons. Present on the flight deck are Grumman Panthers, symbolic of the new jet age — which was to have far-reaching consequences on carrier design. (US Navy, by courtesy of A. D. Baker III)

Centre left: *Roosevelt* in March 1954, awaiting SCB-110. The two identical radar aerials on pole masts before and abaft the funnel are SPS-6B, an air-search system widely used in the US Navy during the 1950s. (US Navy, by courtesy of A. D. Baker III)

Below left: The SCB-110 programme brought the *Midways* into the jet age, much as the SCB-27 and SCB-125 refits did for the *Essex*-class carriers. Among the modifications most apparent in this late 1957 photograph of *Midway* are the new angled deck and the new deck-edge lift on the starboard side, abaft the island, entailing further sacrifices in the 5in battery. Also visible are the tracks for the new steam catapults, two forward and one in the waist (angled deck) position. (US Navy, by courtesy of A. D. Baker III)

much as in the *Essex* carriers, with an amidships deck-edge lift to port, though rather larger. Arrester gear consisted of sixteen wires, arranged exclusively aft.

The *Midways* were originally to have numbered six, but one, CVB-44, part of the original order approved in 1942, was cancelled on 11 November 1943 and two projected units, CVB-56 and -57, were cancelled in March 1945; all would have been built at Newport News.

Modifications In 1947–48 the *Midways* had to have their flight decks stressed in order to receive the heavy AJ bomber; at the same time, $20 \times 3in / 50$ in twin mounts were added to *Coral Sea* and replaced the 40mms in her two sister ships, which had four of the single 5in removed in part-compensation. By the early 1950s, all three vessels were fitted to operate Regulus I.

In the middle and late 1950s all three ships were reconstructed in a programme (SCB-110) which paralleled that specified for the *Essex*-class carriers. *Franklin D. Roosevelt* and *Midway* had their flight decks modified to incorporate an angled landing area and had their flight-deck gear replaced to accept heavier and larger aircraft: three C11 steam catapults were installed, stronger arrester gear was introduced and the lifts were reconfigured, that aft being replaced by a deck-edge lift on the starboard side and that forward being considerably enlarged. Additionally, the open bow was sealed and the island extended, a new mast (tapered pole in *Roosevelt*, lattice in *Midway*) being installed to carry the improved electronics, which now consisted of SPS-12, SPS-8A and SC-2 (*Roosevelt*) and SPS-43, SPS-12 and SPS-8A (*Midway*), replacing the wartime and post-war sets the ships were carrying. Internally, the avgas capacity was considerably enhanced. To allow for this additional weight, the belt armour was removed and the 5in armament reduced. Even so, displacement rose, so that *Roosevelt* showed 51,000 tons standard,

The hangar was built up over the main (strength) deck and although protected by the armoured flight deck above was itself unarmoured against air attack; however, it was considered that by arranging the fixed battery the full length of the hull, at hangar-deck level, the mountings themselves would act as protection for the vulnerable open sides, although the taking on of provisions and stores, readily accomplished hitherto via the shuttered openings to the hangar, would not be so conveniently achieved. The armament consisted of 18 single-mounted 5in / 54

dual-purpose weapons (twins were considered, but rejected on the grounds that they would occupy too much space, to the detriment of flight deck area), although *Coral Sea* was completed with only fourteen; the 40mm guns were in quadruple mountings, but it is doubtful whether the entire complement of 20mms, indicated in the table, was ever fitted — *Coral Sea* had only about 28 on commissioning and, moreover, had no 40mms at all.

The armoured flight deck featured two hydraulic catapults forward and three lifts, the latter disposed

63,400 tons deep load; draught 16ft deep load; and maximum flight-deck width 174ft. Armament now amounted to 10×5in / 54 and 22×3in / 50, while aircraft capacity fell to about 80 (F8U, F3H, A3D, A4D, AD).

Coral Sea was modernised somewhat later (SCB-110A) and somewhat more extensively: the forward centreline lift was taken out completely and a new

unit was added on the starboard deck edge, forward of the island, another new lift being added on the port side right aft to avoid interference with the landing deck, together with a third on the starboard side, as in *Midway.* Mk 7 arrester gear was added, and three C11 catapults were fitted, one located at the forward end of the landing deck. Bulges were added to the hull to increase buoyancy (beam underwater increased to 121ft), and the armour belt was removed. The island was modified, and a tubular pole mast fitted, carrying SPS-12, SPS-37 and SPS-8A main radars. To pay for this extra weight, the fixed battery was dramatically reduced, all the 3in / 50s being removed and only 6×5in / 54 remaining.

A further modernisation (SCB-101.66) was put in hand for *Midway* in the late 1960s: the flight deck was further extended, giving overall dimensions of 979ft (including bridle catchers) $\times$ 238ft, *ie* about 4 acres; new lifts capable of handling 100,000lb each (75,000lb in *Coral Sea*) were installed, before and abaft the island on the starboard side and aft, to port; C13 catapults (two only, forward) were fitted; and stronger arrester gear was added. Already down to 4×5in guns, *Midway* emerged from the refit with only three (her 3in had been removed by 1961), but retained her SPS-43 and SPS-30 radar, the latter having been substituted for SPS-12 / SPS-8A about 1963.

Mirror landing facilities were added to *Franklin D. Roosevelt* in late 1960, but the cost of SCB-101 precluded similar work being undertaken on her, and the ship was given a scaled-down second

modernisation in 1968, involving principally the deletion of her centreline lift forward and the installation of a third deck-edge lift before the island. Electronics now consisted of SPS-43 and SPS-30, together with the standard Mk 25 radar for the 5in / 54s, fitted to all the *Midway*s in the early 1950s. The fixed battery, however, was now down to 4×5in guns, all the 3in having been taken out as with *Midway* and *Coral Sea.*

Subsequent refits upgraded the radar systems of *Midway* and *Coral Sea*, so that in 1980 the suite consisted of SPS-10, SPS-30, SPS-43, SPS-48C (*Midway* only) and SPS-58 / 65 main radars, and SPN-6 and -10 navigation radars. Three Close-In Weapon Systems (Mk 15, Phalanx, 20mm) were fitted in 1980–81, and *Midway* received BPDMS (Mk 25 Sea Sparrow) and the attendant Mk 115 control systems in 1979.

Service Notes *Midway*: Test-firings of captured German V-2 rockets were made aboard *Midway* in September 1947 ('Operation Sandy'), and with Regulus I subsequently. The carrier was redesignated CV-41 on 1 October 1952 and decommissioned on 15 May 1955 for SCB-110, completed 30 September 1957. She saw action off Vietnam from April to November 1965 and on 15 February 1966 docked at Hunter's Point for SCB-101.66. Since October 1973 she has been based at Yokosuka, Japan, designated CV-41 from July 1975. Pacific Fleet.

Franklin D. Roosevelt: Reclassified CVA-42 from October 1952, *Franklin D. Roosevelt* decommissioned on 23 April 1954 for SCB-110, which was

completed almost exactly two years later. She under-took a short tour of duty off Vietnam in late 1966, and in July 1968 she received her second modernisation. She was redesignated CV-42 on 1 July 1975, but, the least capable of the *Midway*s, was stricken in late 1977 and broken up from April 1978. Atlantic Fleet.

Coral Sea was the first carrier to test-land an AJ Savage, the US Navy's nuclear bomber, in August 1950. She was redesignated CVA-43 from October 1952, and after a short refit in September 1955–February 1956 she docked for SCB-110A in April 1957 at Puget Sound. Recommissioned on 26 January 1960, she was the first carrier to operate the new F4H Phantom, when test-landings were carried out in the autumn of that year. *Coral Sea* was heavily involved in the Vietnam War, from February 1965 onwards. In 1977 she was employed mainly as a training carrier, but from 1979 has been used as a back-up attack carrier, while more modern successors are undergoing refit. Plans to use her as a permanent training carrier, in place of *Lexington* (AVT-16), have now been shelved, and she will be retained as a full CV through the 1980s. A short refit in 1978–79 improved her air group facilities, but she cannot handle F-14s, which limits her value at present. Pacific Fleet.

SAIPAN CLASS

Ship	Builder	Laid down	Launched	Commissioned
Saipan (CVL-48)	New York SB	10 July 44	8 July 45	14 July 46
Wright (CVL-49)	New York SB	21 Aug 44	1 Sept 45	9 Feb 47

Displacement: 14,500 tons / 14,732 tonnes
(standard); 18,750 tons / 19,050 tonnes (deep load).
Length: 664ft / 202.39m (wl); 683ft 7in / 208.36m
(oa); 600ft / 182.88m (fd).
Beam: 76ft 8in / 23.37m (hull); 80ft / 24.38m (fd).
Draught: 24ft 6in / 7.47m (mean); 27ft / 8.23m
(deep load).
Machinery: General Electric geared turbines;
4 Babcock & Wilcox boilers; 4 shafts.
Performance: 120,000shp; 33kts.
Bunkerage: 2,500 tons / 2,540 tonnes.
Range: 10,000nm at 15kts.
Aircraft: 48.
Guns: 40 × 40mm; 32 × 20mm.
Complement: 1,553.

Design As the Pacific War developed, carrier task
group operating patterns began rapidly to emerge,
and it was common practice for one light carrier to
combine tactically with two fleet carriers; with nine

Left: Bearing a resemblance to the CVLs of the *Independence*
class, the two *Saipan*s were somewhat different, owing much
to the *Baltimore*-class cruisers rather than to the *Cleveland*s.
They were, for example, larger than the other CVLs, and had
better internal safety arrangements. This is *Saipan* in the
spring of 1948. (US Navy)

Below left: *Wright* in the early 1950s, with Grumman AF
ASW aircraft on deck, recognisable immediately by their
curiously cranked main undercarriage legs. The aftermost
funnel appears to be sealed, as indeed does *Saipan*'s in the
previous photograph. (US Navy, by courtesy of Norman
Friedman)

CVLs in commission by early 1944, it was anticipated that a loss rate of two such ships per annum
might be incurred. Accordingly, the General Board
pressed for additional units to be laid down as replacement vessels.

The *Independence* design, however, generally
satisfactory in concept as it appeared to be, was somewhat tight for space, and an alternative needed to be
sought: while building programmes were so stretched
as to preclude conversions of existing or projected
ships, a suitable design might be utilised to expedite
delivery to the fleet. A cruiser hull was the obvious
choice, and the *Baltimore*-class form seemed to offer
potential. Even so, it was discovered, after the first
two ships had been ordered as such, that modifications would have to be made.

In order to save weight the 6in waterline belt was
much reduced, but to improve stability the beam was
increased by 6ft. The hangar was built up over the
forecastle deck, similar in general arrangement to that
of the earlier CVLs. *Baltimore* machinery was
retained, with four boiler rooms discharging via two
pairs of funnels canted out amidships, to starboard,
much as in *Independence*. Vitals were protected by a
3in main deck, above a 2in lower deck, as in the
*Baltimore*s.

The flight deck, stressed for 9-ton aircraft, was also
similar in layout, though longer and with more widely
spaced lifts, to port of which the deck broadened to
permit roomy aircraft movement forward. A heavy

crane, serving the forward lift, was fitted to starboard,
and at the forward end were fitted a pair of H2C
catapults, staggered (rather than diverging, as in
contemporary escort carriers) to permit two aircraft to
be readied for launch simultaneously.

The island was an adaptation of the *Commencement Bay* installation, with a heavy, plated mast; a
second mast was located at the deck edge further aft,
amidst the uptakes.

The armament as completed showed two quadruple
40mms on the forecastle, with a further pair at the
stern and a single quad mounting at the starboard
flight-deck edge, aft; eight twin 40mms were disposed
along each edge of the flight deck.

The initial radar fit was SP fighter-control and SK-2
(*Saipan*) and SR-2 (*Wright*) air search; both also
carried Mk 29 fire control sets for the 40mm guns.
The designed air group consisted of twelve torpedo-
bombers (TBM) and two full squadrons of fighters
(F6F, F4U).

Modifications By 1950 *Wright* had received SC-2
and SPS-6 in place of SR-2 and *Saipan* SPS-6 instead
of SK-2 air search radars, and both ships had had their
foremost funnels deleted. The 20mm battery had
been removed and the 40mm reduced by the mid
1950s. Each carrier was the subject of a major
conversion in the early 1960s.

The drive behind these conversions was the
perceived desirability to provide the US Government
with mobile command and control headquarters in
the event of a knock-out missile attack on Washington
(National Emergency Command Post Afloat programme); work on *Wright* was authorised under
FY62 and conversion of *Saipan* in FY63.

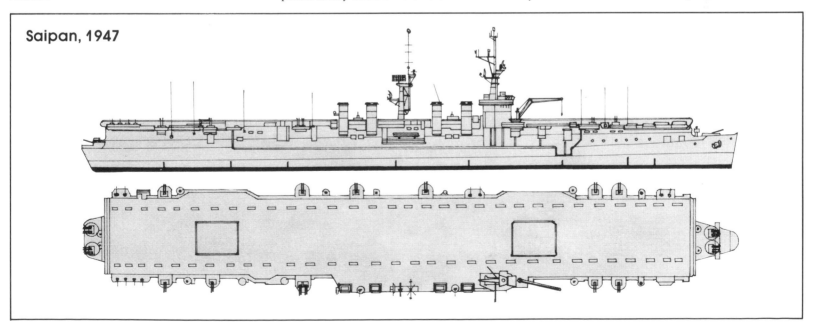

Saipan, 1947

As it happened, only the former was refitted according to the original scheme. Her hangar was gutted to accept the extensive communications equipment necessary; two tall fibreglass masts were erected along the flight-deck centreline carrying antennae for long-range, tropospheric-scatter signalling, with three somewhat shorter masts on the port-side deck edge. Various other antennae were rigged, the ship retaining SPS-6B on her stub second mast (replaced by a heightened mast carrying a steerable scatter dish in mid 1965). The catapults were removed, but the after flight deck was left clear, enabling helicopters to operate. Only four twin 40mms were kept on board.

Saipan's refit, in fact, saw her emerge as a Major Communications Relay Ship; her appearance was not dissimilar to *Wright*'s, but she lacked the internal degree of sophistication demanded by Presidential occupancy. Her original second mast was struck, and she carried four 3in / 50 twin mountings forward and aft, at the flight-deck edge. She was renamed *Arlington* upon conversion. Full-load displacement rose to 19,600 tons and draught deepened to 28ft. Three helicopters were accommodated, as in *Wright*.

Service Notes *Saipan*: The first eight months of *Saipan*'s career were spent training pilots. From late December 1947 she was part of the Operational Development Force based at Norfolk, Virginia, which was formed to gather experience in the deployment of jet aircraft aboard carriers; in May 1948 she embarked the first operational squadron of carrier-based US Navy jet fighters (FH-1). The early 1950s were taken up principally with training duties, and the ship was placed in reserve on 30 October 1957. Redesignated AVT-6 in May 1959, she was moved into dock for conversion to a command ship (designated CC-3) in 1963 but emerged in 1966 as AGMR-2, *Arlington*. She saw service during the Vietnam conflict as a communications headquarters from 1967, but was deactivated in January 1970 and subsequently scrapped.

Wright: Training of pilots and reservists occupied *Wright* during her early service years, and from June 1952 she operated with Atlantic ASW hunter-killer forces, resuming training late that year. Following participation in the 'Wigwam' nuclear tests in the Pacific, spring 1955, she was officially deactivated in March 1956. Redesignated AVT-7 in May 1959, she was taken in hand in March 1962 for conversion to a command ship, being recommissioned on 11 May 1963 as CC-2. She functioned in this capacity until May 1970, when she was deactivated for a second time.

Above right: A magnificent photograph of *Arlington* (ex-*Saipan*) as she appeared in August 1966 as a Major Communications Relay Ship. Half her 3in/50 battery is clearly visible, just forward of the former flight deck. (US Navy, by courtesy of A. D. Baker III)

Right: *Wright* as converted to a command ship, with her SPS-6B now replaced by a scatter dish (dark-painted mast). The photograph is dated November 1968. (US Navy)

UNITED STATES (CVA-58)

Builder	Laid down
Newport News	14 Apr 49

Displacement: 66,850 tons / 67,920 tonnes
(standard); 78,500 tons / 79,756 tonnes (deep load).
Length: 1,030ft / 313.94m (wl); 1,090ft / 332.23m
(oa); 1,025ft / 312.42m (fd).
Beam: 130ft / 39.52m (hull); 190ft / 57.91m (fd).
Draught: 34ft 6in / 10.52m (deep load).
Machinery: Geared turbines; 8 boilers; 4 shafts.
Performance: 280,000shp; 33kts.
Bunkerage: 11,505 tons / 11,689 tonnes.
Range: 12,000nm at 10kts.
Aircraft: 72.
Guns: 8 × 5in; 12 × 3in; 20 × 20mm.
Complement: 4,127.

Design The design of *United States*, although not
followed through, was to have a profound influence
on the character of post-war US attack carriers, and
indeed major elements of current construction can be
traced back to it. Though possessing some common
features with the preceding *Midway*s, notably in the
arrangement of the machinery and in the fact that it
was to be armoured against air attack, CVA-58 was in
reality a totally new concept in aircraft carriers,
founded entirely on the advent of the atomic bomb
and the desire of the US Navy to be equipped with the
means to deliver it.

Early atomic bombs were heavy affairs, and
required large aircraft to carry them; in addition, the
aircraft themselves would need to stow large amounts
of fuel in order to give them the range to strike deep

into enemy territory, the latter predicted as being the
vast land area of the Soviet Union, given the post-war
political situation. The outcome was a 45-ton
aeroplane, which in turn required a very large flight
deck from which to operate: there would be no 'one-
way ticket', as in the 'Doolittle Raid' of April 1942.

The configuration and size of the aircraft had much
more of an effect on the design of the ship, however:
not only did the flight deck have to be of sufficient size
to fly it off and land it again, it had also to permit the
maximum number of aircraft (the Bureau of
Aeronautics wanted 24) to be carried permanently on
it – originally there was to have been no hangar,
again, because of the aircraft's dimensions.
Furthermore, the carrier was to be completely flush-
decked, to permit maximum flight-deck capacity, the
boiler gases being vented to port and starboard via
faired sponsons.

For the first time in a US carrier, the flight deck,
showing 3in armour, was to be the lateral strength
member of the hull – a feature forced on a somewhat
reluctant design team owing to the sheer size of the
hull and its consequent need to withstand severe
bending moments. Design modifications prior to keel-
laying provided for a 28ft-high hangar in order to
accommodate the new bomber, and the complement
of aircraft was cut to permit operation of escort
fighters (F2H), which latter were originally to be
flown off escorting *Essex*es; the figure of 72 given in
the table corresponds to the maximum number of
aircraft that could be carried – in this instance 54
F2Hs and eighteen projected 25-ton bombers, an

alternative to the heavier machines. The forerunner
of the angled deck could be seen in the flight-deck
layout, although this was not to be a landing area as
evolved from the 1950s: for maximum take-off
capability, the *United States* was to be furnished with
four powder-type catapults, two at the bows and one
each port and starboard, canted outwards to clear
those aircraft deploying forward. Four deck-edge lifts,
two to starboard, one to port and one right aft, would
bring aircraft up for strike operations.

The gun battery, consisting of 5in / 54 in single
mountings, was to be installed forward and aft, just
below flight-deck level, with additional 3in twins on
the forecastle and at the stern. The problem of
conning a flush-decked ship was solved by sponsoring
out control positions from the sides, forward, while
that of providing high platforms for search radar
aerials was solved by not having any, the escorting
ships (without which CVA-58 would never operate)
taking care of all major electronics.

It appears that four carriers of this type were
envisaged, but, mainly because of stiff opposition from
the USAF to the whole concept of a strategic attack
capability being placed in Navy hands, the
programme ended with the cancellation of *United
States* only nine days after the keel was laid; with it, of
course, died the 45-ton bomber.

Below: The rather startling lines of the *United States*,
captured in an artist's impression. Note especially the
completely flush deck, the four widely-spaced catapults and
the four deck-edge lifts. (US National Archives)

FORRESTAL CLASS

Ship	Builder	Laid down	Launched	Commissioned
Forrestal (CVA-59)	Newport News	14 July 52	11 Dec 54	1 Oct 55
Saratoga (CVA-60)	New York	16 Dec 52	8 Oct 55	14 Apr 56
Ranger (CVA-61)	Newport News	2 Aug 54	29 Sept 56	10 Aug 57
Independence (CVA-62)	New York	1 July 55	6 June 58	3 Apr 59

Displacement: 60,000 tons / 61,637 tonnes (standard); 78,000 tons / 79,248 tonnes (deep load).
Length: 990ft / 301.75m (wl); 1,039ft / 315.77m (oa); 1,015 ft / 309.37m (fd).
Beam: 129ft 6in / 39.47m (hull); 240ft / 73.15m (fd).
Draught: 37ft / 11.28m (deep load).
Machinery: Geared turbines; 8 Babcock & Wilcox boilers; 4 shafts.
Performance: 260,000shp; 33kts.
Bunkerage: 7,800 tons / 7,925 tonnes.
Range: 12,000nm at 20kts.
Aircraft: 90.
Guns: 8 × 5in.
Complement: 4,142.
Design The cancellation of CVA-58 was a bitter pill for the US Navy to swallow, but it did not have long to wait before the question of providing a US seaborne nuclear strike capability once more came under scrutiny. Navy protagonists in Congress would not permit the concept to be abandoned, and there were hints that were the Navy to reduce the size of the ships it had in mind the project might succeed.

There were, however, arguments available in favour of a large carrier: jet aircraft, whose future as the only realistic fast combat types was by 1950 assured, required considerably more fuel than their piston-engined predecessors and thus demanded more fuel bunkerage per aircraft if the same number were to be embarked without affecting their capabilities. Jets also required a larger flight deck (owing to their higher speeds), irrespective of their size, and there was no reason why a mixed conventional / nuclear mission could not be accommodated in a single hull.

The new attack aircraft in prospect was the Douglas A3D, the design of which had been ready at about the time CVA-58 was cancelled. Contracts for the new bomber were awarded immediately, and although the A3D would be capable of operating effectively from the *Midway*s, deployment aboard *Essex*-class carriers would be marginal.

Uncertainties within Congress were dissolved with the outbreak of the Korean War in June 1950, and the design of the new carrier was authorised a few

Right: Developed during the revolutionary period of postwar carrier design, the *Forrestal*s were the subject of several re-thinks from the time they were originally conceived. They finally emerged fully capable of coping with the demands of the new jet age, however, with steam catapults, angled decks and sufficient bunkerage for the fuel-thirsty first-generation jet aircraft. This is *Ranger*, just prior to commissioning. Four catapults were installed, but in this photograph the inboard waist unit is masked by the flight-deck markings. (US Navy, by courtesy of A. D. Baker III)

Below right: *Saratoga* in June 1957. Her starboard forward 5in guns are visible but, as in the *Midway*s, the gun battery of the *Forrestal*s was progressively reduced in service. (US Navy, by courtesy of A. D. Baker III)

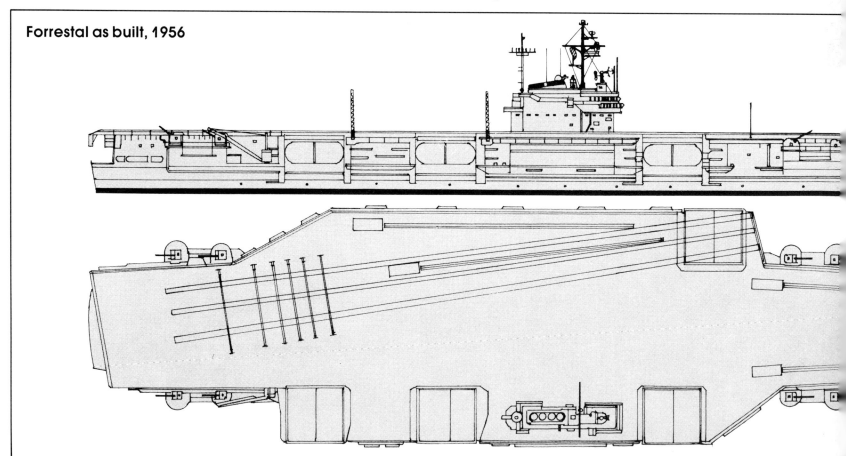

Forrestal as built, 1956

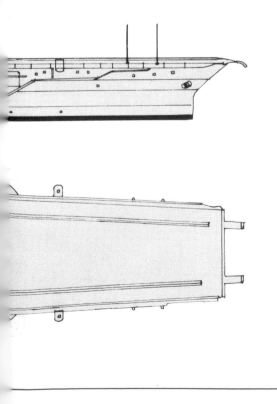

months later: funds were appropriated for FY52, envisaging five sister carriers, one per fiscal year, to follow; and *Forrestal* was ordered in July 1951.

The design of the carrier was closely associated with the evolving A3D. Hangar height was 25ft (virtually a 50 per cent increase over the *Midway*s), and accommodation for some 1,800 tons of ordnance and 750,000 US gallons of aviation fuel was provided. Lifts capable of handling the 75,000lb weight of the aircraft and its 74ft 6in × 49ft folded measurements were installed (deck-edge lifts were selected for their non-interference with flight-deck operations and with flight-deck structural strength). Furthermore, a flush deck with no island, again as in *United States*, would provide for simultaneous launching and obviate the problem of smoke drift. Command and control still posed difficulties, however, sponsoned-out bridges presenting restricted fields of view (and no view of the flight deck) and telescopic positions providing no facilities at all when they might most be needed.

That particular problem, and others besides, was solved by the coming of the angled deck, introduced just at the time *Forrestal* was building; hence an island, with all its advantages, as well as an 8° deck, could be incorporated as a design modification, the cost increase being acceptable and the delay in construction apparently being minimal. Type C7 steam catapults also became available during building, and these were fitted in place of the originally selected power units.

For the first time in a completed US carrier the flight deck was built as an integral member of the hull structure. The reasoning which determined this – otherwise insufficient longitudinal strength – also influenced the fact that it needed to be of 3in steel, although to what extent this was a protective measure (*ie* comprised armour plate) is uncertain. For the first time also, therefore, the major-calibre gun platforms had to be sponsoned out externally from the hull, each side forward and each side aft, the guns themselves being single 5in / 54 Mk 42s. Overall flight-deck width as redesigned was 252ft.

The original aircraft complement numbered three fighter (F9F, F2H), two attack (AD, A4D) and one heavy attack (A3D) squadrons, eight special types (SAR helicopters, PR and AEW) making up the number quoted in the table. On completion radar

Top right: This photograph of *Independence*, the last of the quartet of *Forrestal*s, was taken on 2 March 1959, just prior to her commissioning. The massive hull-mounted sponsons needed to support the 5in battery and, in particular, the overhang of the angled deck can be seen. (US Navy, by courtesy of A. D. Baker III)

Right: *Saratoga* shows her new Mk 25 8-cell Sea Sparrow box launchers, one forward on the starboard side and the second aft, to port. The four catapult tracks are clearly visible, one of them with its blast screen erected. Just discernible in this October 1975 photograph is the open-type stern, which distinguished the first two ships of the class. (US Navy)

consisted of SPS-12 and SPS-8A though *Independence*, the last of the class, was able to receive SPS-37 and had -8B instead of -8A.

At first the class was to have numbered six ships, but the last two were reconfigured as 'Improved *Forrestals*'; in fact, the 3½-year gap between completion of CVA-59 and CVA-62 permitted several design modifications to be worked in each succeeding vessel, so that each differed in detail; for example, *Saratoga* measured 1,046ft overall and *Ranger* and *Independence* 1,047ft (because of their different bridle arresters), while the last pair featured enclosed sterns. In addition, slightly more powerful machinery (280,000shp, giving 33.5kts) was fitted to *Forrestal*'s three sister ships.

Modifications Neither the *Forrestals* nor subsequent US carriers have undergone structural alteration as significant as that affecting the *Midways* and *Essexes*, although during the 1980s all four *Forrestals* will be taken in hand for SLEP (Service Life Extension Program), during which the ships will be completely overhauled and have three Phalanx CIWS installed. Modifications have been made since their first commissioning, however, these being concerned principally with the progressive substitution of more advanced electronics and changes to the AA defence battery.

In order to improve seakeeping qualities, the forward 5in guns were deleted from all the class in the early 1960s, all but *Ranger* having the associated sponsons taken out as well. *Forrestal*'s after 5in battery was seriously damaged in the fire which broke out aboard in 1967; during repairs the following year a single Sea Sparrow launcher (BPDMS Mk 25) was fitted in the starboard side forward, the missile battery being augmented with an extra Mk 25 on the port quarter in 1976. The remaining guns were removed from *Independence* in 1973, from *Saratoga* in 1974 and from *Ranger* in 1975 (first pair) and 1977 (second pair); two Mk 25 BPDMS were installed aboard *Independence* and *Saratoga* in lieu of the guns, and three Mk 29 BPDMS (NATO Sea Sparrow) in *Ranger*, *Independence* having her two Mk 25s subsequently replaced by three Mk 29s. *Forrestal* and *Saratoga* operated Regulus for a brief period in the 1950s.

By the early 1960s the class were showing SPS-43A, SPS-12 and SPS-8A / 8B radar, SPS-30 replacing -12 and -8A / 8B by the end of the decade. SPS-58

Top left: By 1974 *Independence* was showing several subtle changes, including the removal of her gun armament and the installation of two Mk 25 (Sea Sparrow) box launchers, one of which is visible here, on the after sponson. The large 'mattress' is SPS-43A air search radar, typically fitted to fleet carriers from the mid 1960s; the dome below houses carrier-controlled approach (CCA) radar. (US Navy)

Left: *Ranger* in 1975 had only two 5in mountings, one of which is visible. Note that the landing-deck centreline marking is continued down the stern of the carrier, to assist approaching pilots. (US Navy)

was installed with the BPDMS fit, and SPS-48 (3-D) and -49 (2-D) search radars now equip all, *Saratoga*'s being the last installation, during her SLEP refit of 1980–83.

The *Forrestal*s, the first two originally designated CVB, were reclassified from CVA to CV in the early 1970s. SLEP will enable the class to remain in front-line service until the end of the century.

Service Notes *Forrestal*: A disaster of major proportions overtook *Forrestal* while she was about to launch a strike off Vietnam in July 1967, apparently caused by the ignition of leaking fuel from an A-4. The flames destroyed armed aircraft waiting aft, and explosions wrecked a large portion of the flight deck. Damage was considerable, but the carrier survived; whether a ship of smaller dimensions would have done so is open to speculation. SLEP is scheduled for *Forrestal* for 1983–85. Atlantic Fleet.

Saratoga: A fire and a collision in the early part of 1961 did little damage. *Saratoga* was the first carrier to operate the A-6, and she carried out CV Concept evaluation for the US Navy in 1970. She took part in Vietnam operations for a short period in 1972. SLEP modernisation lasted from 1980 until 1983. Atlantic Fleet.

Ranger was involved off Vietnam during 1964 and again from 1968. She was the first carrier to operate the A-7, and will be the last of the class to undergo SLEP, in 1987–89. Pacific Fleet.

Independence was deployed to Vietnam for a short period in early 1965. She will be refitted under SLEP in 1985–87. Atlantic Fleet.

Right: The Improved *Forrestal*s (*Kitty Hawk* is seen, shortly before commissioning) were broadly similar to their predecessors, but a major redesign of the flight deck resulted in the provision of two lifts before the island on the starboard side; their positions can be seen here. (US Navy, by courtesy of A. D. Baker III)

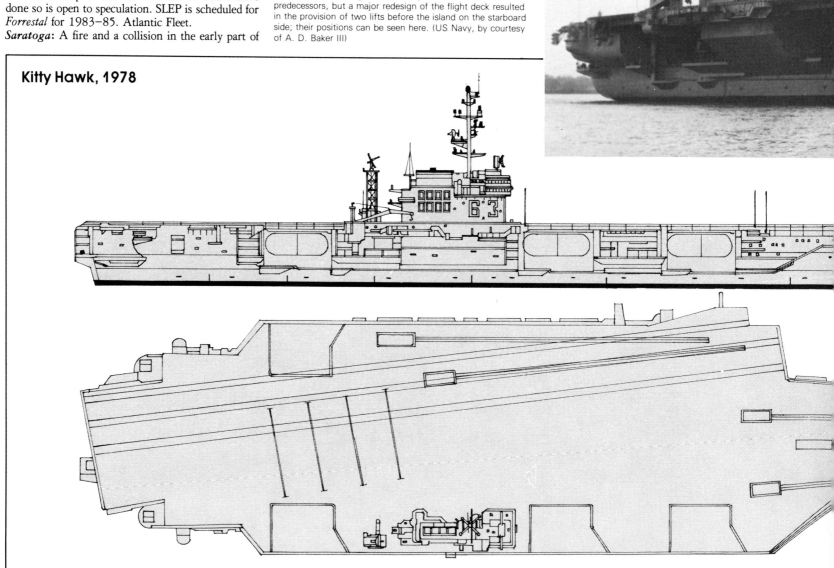

Kitty Hawk, 1978

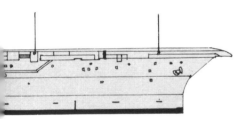

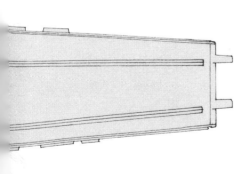

IMPROVED FORRESTAL CLASS

Ship	Builder	Laid down	Launched	Commissioned
Kitty Hawk (CVA-63)	New York SB	27 Dec 56	21 May 60	9 June 61
Constellation (CVA-64)	New York	14 Sept 57	8 Oct 60	19 Jan 62
America (CVA-66)	Newport News	9 Jan 61	1 Feb 64	23 Jan 65
John F. Kennedy (CVA-67)	Newport News	22 Oct 64	27 May 67	7 Sept 68

Displacement: 60,100 tons / 61,062 tonnes (standard); 78,250 tons / 79,502 tonnes (deep load).
Length: 990ft / 301.75m (wl); 1,062ft 5in / 323.83m (oa); 1,040ft / 316.99m (fd).
Beam: 129ft 4in / 39.42m (hull); 252ft / 76.81m (fd).
Draught: 35ft / 10.67m (deep load).
Machinery: Geared turbines; 8 Babcock & Wilcox boilers; 4 shafts.
Performance: 280,000shp; 33kts.
Bunkerage: 7,800 tons / 7,925 tonnes.
Range: 12,000nm at 20kts.
Aircraft: 87.
Guns: Nil.
Missiles: 4 Terrier.
Complement: 4,500.

Design More than at any other time during their short history, carriers in the 1950s were under pressure from advancing technology, not so much from the point of view of marine engineering (the nuclear revolution, although far-reaching, did not materially affect the general configuration of carriers), but rather because of the dramatic developments in the speed and — tasked with ever more demanding missions — size of the aircraft they were being called upon to embark. Indeed, strides were so rapid that had the *Forrestal*s been completed to their original design, obsolescence would have been immediately apparent, given the four years it took to build them; accordingly, the feature of modern carrier construction (and, for that matter, that of other types of warship) is to adapt the design as building proceeds, in the light of new technology and, on occasion, new strategies. The fifth and sixth *Forrestal*s (*Kitty Hawk* and *Constellation*) were sufficiently different from their erstwhile sister-ships to warrant a new class.

Most obviously, the gun armament was dispensed with altogether. At first, no defensive battery at all was considered since the carriers were envisaged as operating in Second World War-type task forces whose defence would be undertaken by screening ships and escorts. The sheer volume taken up by task force area defence missiles (launchers, reloads, guidance systems), however, together with the desire

to deploy the maximum number of such missiles within the task force, meant that the weapons were best placed aboard ships that could most readily cope – in other words, the carriers. Thus *Kitty Hawk* was quickly fitted with four Terrier Mk 10 launchers, a twin on each quarter, and the two following carriers received similar installations prior to commissioning; two further launchers, to have occupied sponsons forward, were not fitted. The lifts were redistributed, that on the port side being moved aft, away from the landing deck, and the second deck-edge lift on the starboard side changing places with the island, making it more accessible to the forward (C13) catapults. Less obviously, the flight deck was slightly enlarged.

Internally, the Improved *Forrestal*s showed much in common with their immediate predecessors: the machinery was arranged in a compromise 'unit system', with turbines and boilers sharing spaces, close together to concentrate the uptakes, but separated by auxiliary rooms to lessen the effect of a single damaging hit. Aviation fuel stowage, at 1,900,000 US gallons, was increased, but ordnance capacity, 1,800 tons, was comparable. The data given in the table are for *Kitty Hawk*; other ships differ. For example, *Constellation* is 1,072ft × 260ft extreme dimensions; while *America*, shorter at 1,047ft overall, displaces slightly more than the figures given. Maximum flight-deck width in all but *Constellation* is 252ft. *America* is fitted with a slimmer funnel and has SQS-23 sonar, above-water evidence showing in her stem hawsepipes.

John F. Kennedy differs so much from the other three as to constitute a separate sub-class, and was the subject of some political controversy before she was laid down. There was some discussion even before

Kitty Hawk had her keel laid as to whether the Improved *Forrestal*s should be nuclear powered, but in the event it seemed unwise to commit elements of the main US seaborne strike force to an as yet relatively untried powerplant. By the time *John F. Kennedy* was being funded, however, *Enterprise* (CVAN-65) had been in commission for some time and had already proved the advantages of nuclear power (most evidently increased range, but also from the point of view of aircraft operation and survivability – see introductory chapters), and the Navy requested that CVA-67 be similarly fitted. The US Government, in particular Secretary of Defense McNamara, looked to the cost of *Enterprise* and rejected the Navy line, a decision which caused much wrangling within Congress and much unhappiness within the Navy itself. *John F. Kennedy* was therefore based on the conventionally powered *Kitty Hawk*.

Nevertheless, she showed some external differences: the forward contours of the landing deck were remodelled, and the funnel was angled outwards

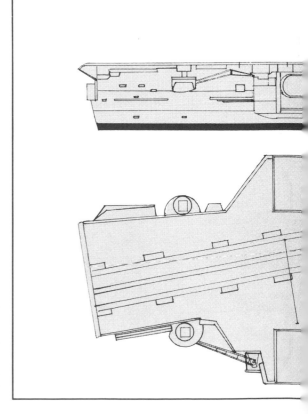

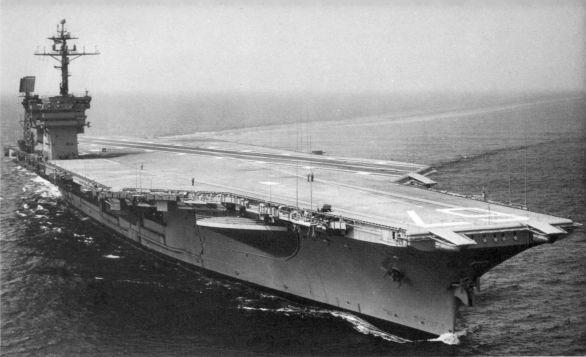

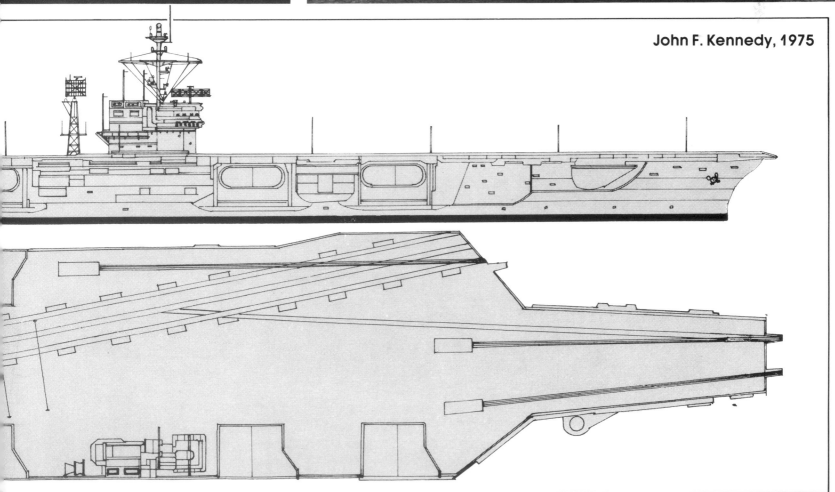

John F. Kennedy, 1975

to vent exhaust gases away from the flight deck (some problems had been encountered with the earlier carriers, apparently with the corrosive effects of the gases rather than with problems of visibility affecting pilots landing on). *Kennedy*'s armament also differed: she was originally scheduled to receive a Tartar battery (preferred over Terrier mainly because of its semi-active guidance system and hence more compact shipboard back-up requirement), but these were never installed, more because of changing concepts in US task force defence tactics than economic considerations. Instead, three 8-tube Sea Sparrow (BPDMS Mk 25) box launchers were installed, one on each quarter and one forward, on a starboard sponson.

John F. Kennedy, because of her modified design, displaces 61,000 tons standard and 82,000 tons deep load. Length overall is 1,052ft and deep load draught 36ft. She has Westinghouse turbines and Foster Wheeler boilers. Her stem anchor suggests that she carries sonar, although reportedly none is fitted.

Modifications The three Terrier-equipped ships have now had three (two in *Kitty Hawk*) point defence Sea Sparrow missile-launchers (BPDMS Mk 29) installed instead of Terrier, together with their guidance systems (Mk 91). Three 20mm Phalanx CIWS have been fitted in *Kennedy*, *America* and *Constellation*, and will be added to *Kitty Hawk*.

Left: *Kitty Hawk* (March 1978) displays her air complement: A-7 and A-6 attack aircraft; two S-3 ASW aircraft; E-2 early warning aircraft; F-14 fighters; SH-3 anti-submarine helicopters; a pair of EA-6 counter-measures aircraft right aft; two Skywarrior electronics/tanker aircraft; and a single RA-5C reconnaissance aircraft. (US Navy)

Below: One identification feature of *Kennedy* is her angled funnel, canted outboard of the island in the manner of some of the Japanese fleet carriers of the Second World War. Note also the separate radar mast, topped by SPS-48 radar, and the Sea Sparrow launchers forward and aft. (US Navy)

Above: *Constellation*, her Terrier battery removed and awaiting Sea Sparrow. The inboard surfaces of the island are painted black, presumably to disguise exhaust stains. (US Navy)

Right: *Kitty Hawk* about the same time as the photograph opposite, though now joined by a pair of CH-46 helicopters and refuelling an attendant *Adams*-class destroyer. (US Navy)

Radars have undergone updating: all except *Kennedy* retain their original SPS-43, but additional fits have progressed from the SPS-39 / SPS-12 first shown to the SPS-30 / SPS-52 now carried. *Kennedy* originally had SPS-43 and -48; SPS-58 was added about 1976, and SPS-49 is now also carried.

Service Notes *Kitty Hawk*: A machinery room fire during the carrier's first tour off Vietnam in December 1965 was quickly controlled, and her deployment continued. She was redesignated CV-63 on 29 April 1973. Pacific Fleet.

Constellation: A serious fire while fitting out delayed *Constellation*'s completion. The carrier took part in offensive operations off Vietnam from 1961 until the mid 1970s, being redesignated CV-64 in June 1975. Pacific Fleet.

America launched combat missions during three tours of duty off Vietnam, 1968–73. She was redesignated CV-66 in June 1975. Atlantic Fleet.

John F. Kennedy: Redesignated CV-67 on 1 December 1974, *Kennedy* sustained slight damage as a result of arson while refitting at Norfolk Navy Yard in April 1979. Atlantic Fleet.

IWO JIMA CLASS

Ship	Builder	Laid down	Launched	Commissioned
Iwo Jima (LPH-2)	Puget Sound	13 Feb 59	17 Sept 60	30 Oct 61
Okinawa (LPH-3)	Philadelphia	1 Apr 60	19 Aug 61	13 Apr 62
Guadalcanal (LPH-7)	Philadelphia	1 Sept 61	1 Aug 62	25 Jan 63
Guam (LPH-9)	Philadelphia	15 Nov 62	22 Aug 64	16 Jan 65
Tripoli (LPH-10)	Ingalls	15 June 64	31 July 75	6 Aug 66
New Orleans (LPH-11)	Philadelphia	1 Mar 66	3 Feb 68	16 Nov 68
Inchon (LPH-12)	Ingalls	8 Apr 68	24 May 69	20 June 70

Displacement: 17,000 tons / 17,272 tonnes (standard); 18,350 tons / 18,644 tonnes (deep load).
Length: 592ft / 180.44m (oa).
Beam: 84ft / 25.6m (hull); 105ft / 32m (fd).
Draught: 25ft / 7.62m (mean); 26ft 7in / 8.1m (deep load).
Machinery: Geared turbine; 4 boilers; 1 shaft.
Performance: 22,000shp; 20kts.

Aircraft: 20.
Guns: 8 × 3in.
Complement: 900.

Design Following experience with the ex-escort carrier *Thetis Bay* (qv), the US Marine Corps was quickly convinced of the advantages of possessing ships capable of moving troops and equipment quickly and in large numbers to assault beaches by air (Vertical Envelopment concept); three *Essex*-class carriers (qv) were modified to provide this capability as an interim measure, but in the meantime the decision had been taken to build a new class of purpose-designed vessels.

With assault force speeds of around 20kts, there was no particular need at the time to provide high-powered machinery; the main requirements were simplicity of construction (for fast delivery) and maximum enclosed volume (to house not only the necessary number of troops, but also the extensive command facilities required to direct amphibious operations). Hence the hull was similar to that of a merchantman, and was fitted with a 230ft-long hangar, 20ft high, to stow and service helicopters. Machinery was simple in the extreme: one Westinghouse (*Tripoli* De Laval, *Inchon* General

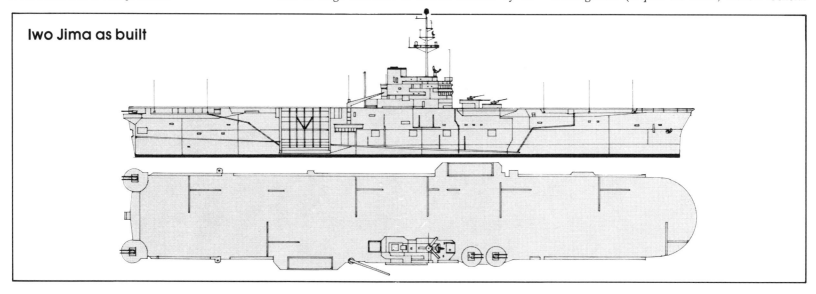

Iwo Jima as built

Electric) steam turbine feeding off four Combustion Engineering (*Guam* Babcock & Wilcox) boilers and driving a single propeller.

A full-length flight deck was fitted, with seven spots for helicopter operations, the deck being connected to the hangar via two 50ft × 42ft lifts, one to port forward of amidships and the other abaft the island, which were situated at the deck edge and could fold upwards when lowered to enclose the hangar. The hull was otherwise plated up to flight-deck level. The large island enclosed the command facilities and the funnel trunking, and was fitted with a tall pole mast for the main radar (SPS-10, SPS-40, marshalling) and communications equipment.

The designed armament of four twin 3in / 50s was disposed forward of the island and at the stern, and accommodation was provided for 2,000 troops plus 20 CH-37 (or 30 UH-34) helicopters.

Modifications From 1970 each ship was rearmed to accommodate two Mk 25 BPDMS (Sea Sparrow) systems and their directors: *Okinawa* had one 8-cell launcher fitted in 1970 and a second in 1973; *Inchon* and *Tripoli* received both in 1972, *New Orleans* and *Iwo Jima* in 1973, and the remaining pair in 1974. These systems replaced the forward 3in mounting before the island and that on the port quarter. Complement had now fallen to 609.

In 1971–72 *Guam* was modified to Interim Sea Control Ship configuration, testing the efficacy of operating AV-8A V / STOL aircraft with a view to producing a new, small aircraft carrier. The concept was abandoned in 1974, but AV-8s are still deployed at times aboard all ships of the class.

Service Notes *Iwo Jima*: Deployed to the Vietnam theatre from 1963. Atlantic Fleet.

Okinawa: Took part in operations in Vietnam from March 1967. Recovery ship for the Apollo VI space project. Pacific Fleet.

Guadalcanal: Gemini X recovery ship, July 1966. Atlantic Fleet.

Guam: Deployed to the Caribbean 1965–66 (Amphibious Ready Squadron). Sea Control Ship test vessel 1967–74. Invasion of Grenada, October 1983. Atlantic Fleet.

Tripoli: Vietnam theatre from 1967 (conducted first all-boat landing from an LPH, September 1967). Operation 'Endsweep' mid 1973 (mine clearance from North Vietnamese waters). Pacific Fleet.

New Orleans: Pacific Fleet.

Inchon: Atlantic Fleet.

Left: Not strictly aircraft carriers, the *Iwo Jima*s are nevertheless air-dedicated ships; indeed, the major criticism levelled at the class is that they were designed without any facilities to operate landing craft, which thereby closed an option for getting troops ashore in weather unfavourable for flying. This is *Okinawa* in mid 1962, showing the original armament of four twin 3in/50 mountings. (US Navy)

Right: *Guadalcanal* shows a newly resurfaced flight deck, May 1977, the markings contrasting with the circular helicopter spots of earlier years. (US Navy)

Above: *Tripoli* shows some modifications, July 1973: only one of the after 3in mountings is retained and only one before the island (not visible from this angle); the others have been replaced by Sea Sparrow launchers. (US Navy)

Below: *New Orleans* about to depart for mine-clearance off Vietnam in February 1973, the task to be undertaken by the six CH-53 helicopters specially embarked for the purpose. Note the two enclosed forward 3in mountings. (US Navy)

ENTERPRISE (CVAN-65)

Builder	Laid down	Launched	Commissioned
Newport News	4 Feb 58	24 Sept 60	25 Nov 61

Displacement: 75,700 tons / 76,911 tonnes (standard); 89,600 tons / 91,034 tonnes (deep load).
Length: 1,040ft / 316.99m (wl); 1,123ft / 243.29m (oa); 1,100ft / 335.28m (fd).
Beam: 133ft / 40.54m (hull); 252ft / 76.81m (fd).
Draught: 36ft / 10.97m (deep load).
Machinery: 4 Westinghouse geared steam turbines; 8 Westinghouse A2W reactors; 4 shafts.
Performance: 280,000shp; 35kts.
Range: 400,000nm at 20kts.
Aircraft: 99.
Guns: Nil.
Complement: 5,500.

Design Several years of vacillation as to whether to provide future US carriers with nuclear propulsion ended in 1956 when CVAN-65 was authorised under the FY58 programme. Nuclear-powered carriers had been suggested as far back as 1949, but the infancy of atomic science and doubts about the cost of installing such plants aboard so large a vessel delayed the project; in the event, the move away from conventional oil-fired boilers proved eminently justified in terms of ship design and operating flexibility, albeit at a high economic price, a fact which has contributed significantly to the one overriding issue in United States carrier philosophy throughout the

last 25 years – the desirability or otherwise of the 'super carrier'.

Studies for nuclear-powered *Forrestal*s were continued alongside the building of that class, and thus when CVAN-65 was given the go-ahead the existing hull form and structure of the Improved *Forrestal*s were used as a basis. The essential difference, the use of reactors instead of boilers to drive the turbines, did not conveniently release a vast internal volume, however, since the oil bunkerage had to be retained to serve as anti-torpedo protection. The somewhat bulky reactors, eight of which, requiring 32 heat-exchangers, occupied a greater proportion of the hull than the conventional *Forrestal* plant, and the requirement to carry the amount of aircraft fuel (2,750,000 US gallons) and munitions (2,500 tons) necessary to sustain the air group for a period more consistent with the range of the ship, drove up the size dramatically.

The 4½-acre flight-deck layout showed little difference from that schemed for the Improved *Forrestal*s, with four deck-edge lifts and four steam catapults (C13 Mod 0). Maximum flight-deck width was 257ft, and a Mk 7 arrester system was installed. The one significant difference topside concerned the island: its location no longer determined by machinery requirements, it could theoretically have been sited anywhere, but for obvious reasons it occupied much the same position as in earlier carriers; however, since there was no funnel, it did

consume less flight-deck area than the island of a conventional carrier (a point emphasised by its slender pedestal), and this enabled the after starboard lift to be brought slightly further forward.

A characteristic of the island in its original configuration was its four SPS-32 search and four SPS-33 tracking (pencil-beam) radar antennae, fixed arrays in the form of huge panels on each side, set as low as possible because of their considerable weight, but high enough to clear tailfins of aircraft on deck. This system was fitted also only to the cruiser *Long Beach*; it was grossly expensive and evidently not an unqualified success (its size and complexity reportedly produce insurmountable maintenance difficulties), since it has now been removed.

The spiralling cost of CVAN-65, ultimately showing a 70 per cent increase over the contemporary *Constellation*, was apparently the reason why the ship was not given any form of fixed defensive battery, at least not at first. Two twin Terrier Mk 10 systems, as in *Kitty Hawk*, were a part of the design, but the ship completed without them. Her original complement totalled 4,600, but in commission the figure approximated to that given in the table. *Enterprise*'s designed air group numbered five attack squadrons (one A3D, one AD, three A4D), two fighter squadrons (F8U, F4H), plus nine other miscellaneous types.

Modifications An SPS-12 search radar set was added to the after starboard edge of the island shortly after

Enterprise commissioned, and in 1967 2 × 8-tube Sea Sparrow launchers (BPDMS Mk 25) were added, one each side aft; the latter have now (1983) been replaced by three Mk 57 Sea Sparrow launchers and supplemented by three 20mm Phalanx (CIWS Mk 15) systems. In her 1979–81 refit, the ship had SPS-10 and SPS-58 / 65 radars added for her new Sea Sparrow defence, and the island was rebuilt, deleting the SPS-32 / 33 arrays and the ECM 'dome' above and installing SPS-48C / 49 instead.

First refuelling took place in early 1965 after about 200,000 miles, and another set of cores was installed in 1969–71, after a further 300,000 miles. These were replaced in the 1979–81 refit. With the entry into service of the F-14 (refit 1974), aircraft complement fell and now averages 84.

Service Notes The obvious and pointed demonstration of the Navy view about how its future carrier fleet should be composed, a round-the-world cruise in company with other, similarly powered US ships (1963), proved the technological viability of nuclear

carriers, but did not immediately have the desired political effect. The advantages of nuclear propulsion were less flamboyantly but more decisively shown during the carrier's sustained operations off Vietnam in several tours from late 1965 on. A fire off Hawaii in January 1969 after a rocket explosion laid waste the after end of the flight deck required extensive repairs, the ship recommissioning in May that year. *Enterprise* was redesignated CVN-65 on 1 July 1975. Atlantic Fleet until 1965, then Pacific Fleet.

Left: During the mid 1970s the US Navy reclassified its carriers in the light of the 'CV Concept', which embraced an ASW capability on a single flight deck rather than aboard specialised ASW carriers. Representative of this development are the eight S-3 anti-submarine aircraft, wings folded, just before the island aboard *Enterprise* as she enters Hobart, Tasmania in October 1976. (US Navy)

Right: A February 1982 photograph of *Enterprise* showing a return to more conventional radars following a big refit. Also visible, on the port quarter, is one of the Sea Sparrow box launchers and, on the extreme quarter, lower, one of her CIWS Mk 15 systems. (US Navy)

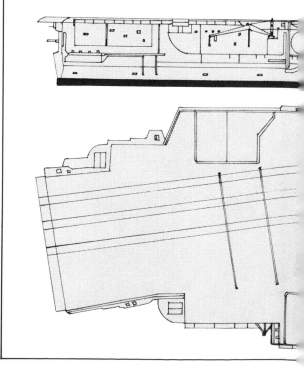

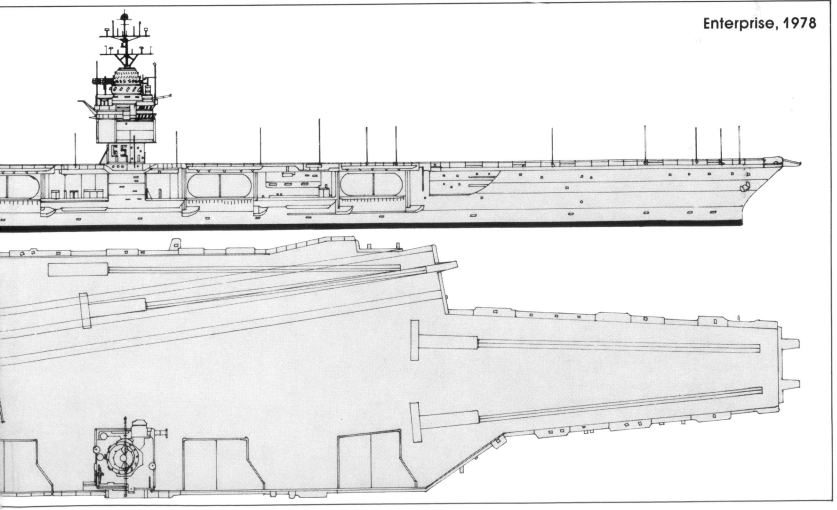

Enterprise, 1978

NIMITZ CLASS

Ship	Builder	Laid down	Launched	Commissioned
Nimitz (CVN-68)	Newport News	22 June 68	13 May 72	3 May 75
Dwight D. Eisenhower (CVN-69)	Newport News	15 Aug 70	11 Oct 75	18 Oct 77
Carl Vinson (CVN-70)	Newport News	11 Oct 75	18 Mar 80	13 Mar 82
Theodore Roosevelt (CVN-71)	Newport News	31 Oct 81		

Displacement: 81,600 tons / 82,906 tonnes
(standard); 93,400 tons / 94,894 tonnes (deep load).
Length: 1,040ft / 316.99m (wl); 1,092ft / 332.84m
(oa); 1,070ft / 326.14m (fd).
Beam: 134ft / 40.84m (hull); 252ft / 76.81m (fd).
Draught: 37ft / 11.28m (deep load).
Machinery: General Electric geared turbines;
2 Westinghouse A4W reactors; 4 shafts.
Performance: 280,000shp; 33kts.
Range: 1,000,000nm at 20kts.
Aircraft: 89.
Guns: Nil.
Missiles: 24 Sea Sparrow.
Complement: 6,400.

Design Current indications are that the *Nimitz* class will eventually number six vessels, CVN-68 – CVN-73; however, this grouping together is somewhat misleading, since the time-gaps between the completion dates of each unit offer considerable scope for improvement and modification. In the case of *Carl Vinson*, the changes have been quite detectable; in that of *Theodore Roosevelt*, they will, reportedly, be significant, although their precise nature is as yet unrevealed.

In a sense, *Nimitz* herself is a developed *John F. Kennedy* with a nuclear powerplant; comparisons with *Enterprise* are perhaps less valid. The increased displacement over CVA-67 is largely a result of greater flight-deck (hence overall) length, greater (25ft 6in) hangar height and, reputedly, more extensive armouring. The machinery is less space-consuming than in *Enterprise*, with only two (albeit individually larger) reactors, widely spaced amidships, giving an increased available volume for aviation fuel, 280,000 US gallons, and ordnance, 2,600 tons, the spacing reducing the chance of a single crippling hit which in *Enterprise* was deterred by sheer numbers of units. Despite the apparent spaciousness, maximum aviation capability, with aircraft complement marginally bigger and back-up facilities (spares, etc.) considerably so, is extracted from the design, enlarged sponsons being built up to provide additional work space: with more than 6,000 crew, *Nimitz* is in reality quite cramped.

The flight-deck layout is essentially that of *Kennedy*, with four deck-edge lifts and four catapults disposed in similar manner; the island is also similar in general appearance, though of course lacks the

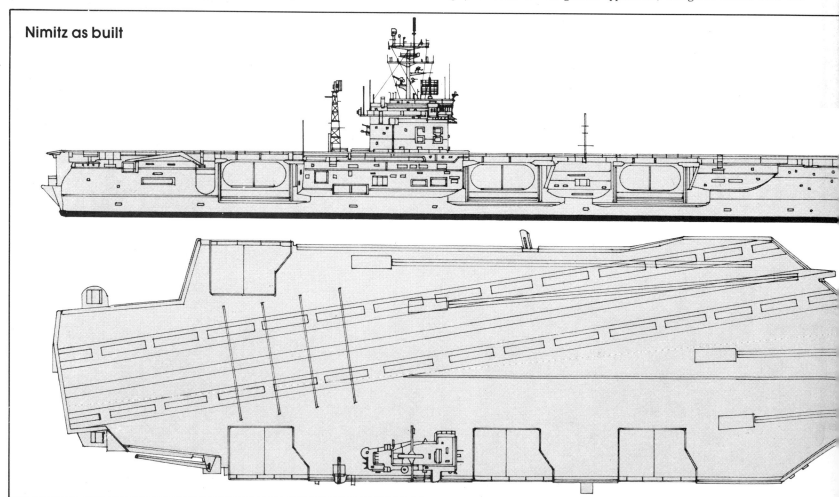

Nimitz as built

funnel uptake; and a detached lattice radar mast is positioned aft, moving the after lift on the starboard side back once more as compared to *Enterprise*. The radar fit itself consists of SPS-43A and -48 air search and SPS-10F surface search; it has been suggested that CVN-71 may complete with the new RCA SPY-1A system, with, presumably, a dramatic effect on the appearance of the island.

The fixed battery consists of three 8-cell Mk 25 BPDMS, although *Carl Vinson* completed with Mk 29 and four Mk 15 CIWS (Phalanx) 20mm mountings. The original standard air group numbered two fighter and three attack squadrons, plus 31 other (tanker, ECM, ASW, reconnaissance) types; almost half the crew complement is taken up by the air wing, an interesting contrast with pre-Second World War practice when the ratio of air-crew to aircraft embarked was in the region of 10 to 1.

The first two ships were reclassified from CVAN to CVN on 1 July 1975. In October 1983 it was reported that CVN-72 and -73 are to be named *Abraham Lincoln* and *George Washington* respectively.

Modifications *Nimitz* and *Dwight D. Eisenhower* have had their Mk 25 Sea Sparrow launchers replaced by Mk 29 and are having three Mk 15 CIWS fitted.
Service Notes *Nimitz*: Atlantic Fleet.
Dwight D. Eisenhower: Atlantic Fleet.
Carl Vinson: Atlantic Fleet.

Top: *Eisenhower* on trials, August 1977. The length of the catapults, which are clearly visible here, is a major factor in determining the size of current carriers; the catapults in turn are a response to the ever-increasing weights and speeds of modern combat aircraft. (Newport News Shipbuilding and Dry Dock Co.)

Above: The most recent fleet carrier to join the US Navy is *Carl Vinson*, seen here in January 1982. Despite attempts to stem the growth in size of carriers, even to revert to smaller designs, the *Nimitz*es appear to represent the minimum permissible for fleet requirements. (US Navy)

Left: Unlike *Enterprise, Nimitz* was armed from the start with a missile battery: two of the three systems can be made out in this January 1975 view. The huge hull sponsons not only support the overhanging flight deck but also house work-shops, etc., servicing the hangar. (US Navy)

Right: An overhead view of *Eisenhower* shows clearly how small are the islands of modern fleet carriers in relation to the rest of the ship. Note that while landing-on is taking place only the bow catapults can be used, although three can be occupied. (US Navy)

Below left: The Mk 25 Sea Sparrow launcher was an adaptation of a standard ASROC box married to a 3in/50 mounting, but the Mk 29 (NATO Sea Sparrow) was rather different in configuration, as can be seen in this photograph of *Vinson*; the missile itself is derived from the air-launched Sparrow carried by fighter aircraft. Four Phalanx systems are fitted to the carrier. (US Navy)

Below right: The *Tarawa*s have a fire support capability, provided by three 5in/54 guns, two of which are evident in this photograph of the name-ship, early 1976. Although similar in concept, the *Tarawa*s are considerably larger than the *Iwo Jima*s. (US Navy)

TARAWA CLASS

Ship	Builder	Laid down	Launched	Commissioned
Tarawa (LHA-1)	Ingalls	15 Nov 71	1 Dec 73	29 May 75
Saipan (LHA-2)	Ingalls	21 July 72	18 July 74	15 Oct 77
Belleau Wood (LHA-3)	Ingalls	5 Mar 73	11 Apr 77	23 Sept 78
Nassau (LHA-4)	Ingalls	13 Aug 73	21 Jan 78	28 July 79
Peleliu (LHA-5)	Ingalls	12 Nov 76	25 Nov 78	3 May 80

Displacement: 39,300 tons / 39,929 tonnes (deep load).
Length: 778ft / 237.13m (wl); 820ft / 249.94m (oa).
Beam: 106ft / 32.31m (hull).

Draught: 27ft 6in / 8.38m (deep load).
Machinery: Westinghouse geared turbines; 2 Combustion Engineering boilers; 2 shafts.
Performance: 140,000shp; 24kts.

Range: 8,500nm at 20kts.
Aircraft: 25.
Guns: 3×5in; 6×20mm.
Missiles: 16 Sea Sparrow.
Complement: 902 (exclusive of troops)

Design The effectiveness of the *Iwo Jima*s in providing a seaborne assault capability was quickly grasped, but the design had some limitations: in particular, the ships' small size and the fact that they could initiate essentially *airborne* operations prevented them from moving anything other than

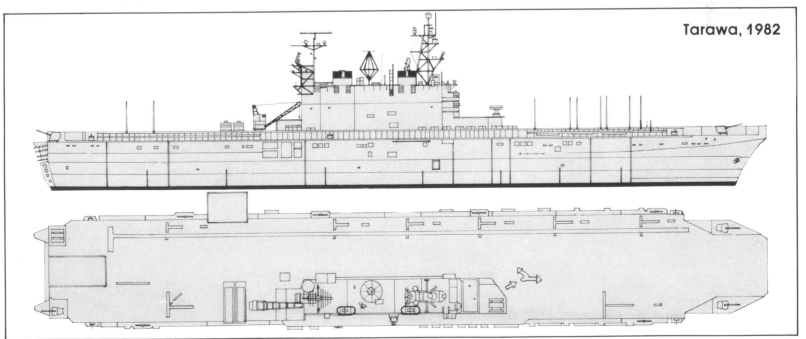

Tarawa, 1982

light equipment. Accordingly, there existed a requirement for a ship which could land heavy armour, vehicles, artillery, etc., to back up the battalion of troops it might carry.

In an attempt to hold down costs, a class of nine such ships were ordered from a single yard, under the Total Package Procurement system; however, LHA-6 to -9 were cancelled as a result of cost overruns.

The *Tarawa*s were based on the *Iwo Jima* concept but, because of their increased capabilities, emerged as significantly larger and somewhat different vessels. Externally there were some marked similarities: the slab-sided hull (for maximum capacity) supported a full-length, 118ft wide flight deck and a huge island for command and control (Integrated Tactical Amphibious Warfare Data System, or ITAWDS). Internally, however, the hangar (265ft long, 78ft wide, 20ft high) was built over a floodable dock with a stern gate from which landing craft could deploy; vehicles would be stowed forward, and further craft (LCM-6) would be stowed on the flight deck, abaft the island and handled by a large crane. Two deck-edge lifts, one on the port side and one on the centreline aft, would bring up the helicopters and equipment.

The machinery was very much more powerful than the *Iwo Jima*s', and a bow-thruster was fitted to aid manoeuvring when docking the landing craft; however, speed increased only marginally, and the much-discussed Rapid Deployment Force concept, in which these vessels, it is assumed, would have a major role to play, is somewhat handicapped as a result.

The ships have a genuine fire-support capability, with three single 5in / 54s, a pair forward and one aft on the starboard side; two Mk 25 BPDMS are also installed for point defence, one before the island and one on the port quarter. The helicopter complement generally consists of a CH-53 / CH-46 mix, and AV-8s can be carried. There is accommodation for 1,800 troops. The radar suite is more extensive than in the *Iwo Jima*s, consisting of SPS-10F surface search, SPS-40B lightweight air search and SPS-52B 3-D air search, and SPG-50 for fire control, plus the Mk 115 tracker / illuminator for Sea Sparrow.

Modifications Two CIWS Mk 15 (Phalanx) 20mm systems are scheduled for fitting in each ship.

Service Notes *Tarawa*: Pacific Fleet.
Saipan: Atlantic Fleet.
Belleau Wood: Pacific Fleet.
Nassau: Atlantic Fleet.
Pelileu: Pacific Fleet.

Top left: The transom stern of the *Tarawa* design (*Saipan* is shown, October 1977), reflects the floodable docking well for the four LCUs; above, on deck, are seen the two LCMs, handled via the adjacent crane. The large dome abaft the island conceals the CCA radar. (US Navy)

Left: The box-like *Tarawa* hull-form is well conveyed in this September 1980 view of *Saipan*. In addition to the CH-46 helicopter forward, AV-8As and OV-10s are visible on deck, although these are not operated from LHAs on a permanent basis. (US Navy)

Bibliography

Unpublished sources

Rimell, R. *Zeppelin!* (to be published in 1984 by Conway Maritime Press, London and Canada's Wings Inc)

Ships' Covers, National Maritime Museum, London: HM aircraft carriers *Argus, Courageous, Eagle, Furious, Glorious, Hermes, Illustrious* and *Implacable*

Published sources

Anderson, R. M. and Baker III, A. D. 'Lex and Sara'. *Warship International*, No. 4, 1977

Beaver, P. *The British Aircraft Carrier*. Patrick Stephens, Cambridge, 1982

Bonds, R. (ed) *The Balance of Military Power*. Salamander Books, London, 1981; St. Martin's Press, New York, 1981

Breyer, S. *Battleships of the World, 1905-70*. Conway Maritime Press, London, 1980; originally *Schlachtschiffe und Schlachtkreuzer, 1905-70*, published by J. F. Lehmanns Verlag, Munich, 1970

Brown, D. K. 'The Development of the British Escort Carrier', from *Warship 25*, Conway Maritime Press, 1983; Naval Institute Press, Annapolis

Brown, J. D. *Carrier Operations in World War II*. 2 vols. Ian Allan, London, 1968 and 1974

— 'HMS Ark Royal', from *Warship 2*, Conway Maritime Press, London, 1977; Naval Institute Press, Annapolis

Conway's All the World's Fighting Ships, 1922-46 (ed Roger Chesneau). Conway Maritime Press, London, 1981; Naval Institute Press, Annapolis, 1981

Conway's All the World's Fighting Ships, 1947-82 Part 1 (ed Robert Gardiner). Conway Maritime Press, London, 1983; Naval Institute Press, Annapolis, 1983

Dousset, F. *Les Porte-Avions Français*. Éditions de la Cité, Paris, 1978

Dull, P. S. *A Battle History of the Imperial Japanese Navy*. Naval Institute Press, Annapolis, 1978

Friedman, N. *Carrier Air Power*. Conway Maritime Press, London, 1981; Naval Institute Press, Annapolis, 1981

— *Naval Radar*. Conway Maritime Press, London, 1981; Naval Institute Press, Annapolis, 1981

— 'SCB-27: The Essex Class Reconstructions', from *Warship 18*, Conway Maritime Press, London, 1981; Naval Institute Press, Annapolis

— *US Aircraft Carriers*. Arms and Armour Press, London, 1983; Naval Institute Press, Annapolis, 1983

— *US Naval Weapons*. Conway Maritime Press, London, 1983; Naval Institute Press, Annapolis, 1983

—, Lott, A. S. and Sumrall, R. *Ships' Data 7-USS Yorktown (CV10)*. Leeward Publications, Annapolis, 1977

Jane's Fighting Ships, various editions

Jentschura, H., Jung, D. and Mickel, P. *Warships of the Imperial Japanese Navy, 1869-1945*. Arms and Armour Press, London, 1977; Naval Institute Press, Annapolis, 1977

Layman, R. D. 'Furious and the Tondern Raid', from *Warship International*, No. 4, 1973

Lengerer, H. 'Akagi and Kaga', from *Warship* Nos 22-24, Conway Maritime Press, 1982; Naval Institute Press, Annapolis

Marder, A. J. *From the Dardanelles to Oran*. Oxford University Press, London and New York, 1974

— *From the Dreadnought to Scapa Flow*. 5 vols. Oxford University Press, London and New York, 1961-70

Mitchell, A. 'The Development of Radar in the Royal Navy', from *Warship* Nos 13, 14, 17, 20, Conway Maritime Press, 1980-81; Naval Institute Press, Annapolis

Polmar, N. *Aircraft Carriers*. Macdonald, London, 1969; Doubleday, New York, 1969

— *Guide to the Soviet Navy*. Arms and Armour Press, London, 1983; Naval Institute Press, Annapolis, 1983

Poolman, K. *Escort Carrier*. Ian Allan, London, 1972

Preston, A. *Aircraft Carriers*. Hamlyn, London, 1979

Roberts, J. *The Aircraft Carrier Intrepid*. Conway Maritime Press, London, 1982; Naval Institute Press, Annapolis, 1982

Swanborough, G. and Bowers, P. M. *United States Navy Aircraft since 1911*. Putnam, London, 1968; Naval Institute Press, Annapolis, 1976

Terzibaschitsch, S. *Aircraft Carriers of the US Navy*. Conway Maritime Press, London, 1980; Naval Institute Press, Annapolis, 1980

— *Escort Carriers of the US Navy*. Conway Maritime Press, London, 1981; Naval Institute Press, Annapolis, 1981

Thetford, O. *British Naval Aircraft since 1912*. Putnam, London, 1962; Rowman, Totowa, New Jersey, 1962

Till, G. *Air Power and the Royal Navy, 1914-45*. Jane's Publishing Co, London and New York, 1979

US Naval Historical Center *Dictionary of American Naval Fighting Ships*, vols I-VII

Wallin, H. N. *Pearl Harbor: Why, How, Fleet Salvage and Final Appraisal*. US Navy History Division, 1968

Zimm, A. D. 'The USN's Flight Deck Cruiser', from *Warship International*, No. 3, 1979

Index

LIST OF ABBREVIATIONS*

AAW Anti-Aircraft Warfare
ACV Auxiliary Aircraft Carrier (US)
AEW Airborne Early Warning
AGMR Major Communications Relay Ship (US)
AIO Action Information Organisation
AKV Aircraft Ferry (US)
AMC Armed Merchant Cruiser
ASR Air-sea Rescue
ASW Anti-Submarine Warfare
AV Seaplane Tender (US)
AVG Aircraft Escort Vessel (US)
AVT Auxiliary Aircraft Transport (US)
BAVG British Aircraft Escort Vessel (US)
BPDMS Basic Point-Defence Missile System
CAM Catapult-Armed Merchant (Ship)
CAP Combat Air Patrol
CC Command Ship (US)/Battlecruiser (US)
CCA Carrier-Controlled Approach
CIC Combat Information Centre
CIWS Close-In Weapon System
CL Light Cruiser (US)
CTOL Conventional Take-Off and Landing
CV Aircraft Carrier (US)
CVA Attack Aircraft Carrier (US)
CVAN Nuclear-powered Attack Aircraft Carrier (US)
CVB Heavy Aircraft Carrier (US)
CVE Escort Aircraft Carrier (US)

CVHE Helicopter Escort Aircraft Carrier (US)
CVL Light Aircraft Carrier (US)
CVN Nuclear-powered Aircraft Carrier (US)
CVS Support (Anti-submarine) Aircraft Carrier (US)
CVU Utility Aircraft Carrier (US)
DLCO Deck Landing Control Officer
DP Dual-Purpose (gun)
ECM Electronic Countermeasures
FAA Fleet Air Arm
FRAM Fleet Rehabilitation and Modernisation (Program) (US)
HA High-angle
HF/DF High-frequency direction-finding
ITAWDS Integrated Tactical Amphibious Warfare Data System
LAMPS Light Airborne Multi-Purpose System (US)
LHA Multi-purpose Amphibious Assault Ship (US)
LPH Amphibious Assault Ship (US)
LSO Landing Signal Officer (US)
MAC Merchant Aircraft Carrier
MSTS Maritime Sea Transportation Service (US)
NECPA National Emergency Command Post Afloat (US)
PA Porte-Avions (Fr.)
PH Porte-Hélicoptères (Fr.)
RNAS Royal Naval Air Service (or Station)

TARPS Tactical Airborne Reconnaissance Pod System (US)
TBR Torpedo-Bomber-Reconnaissance (aircraft)
TSR Torpedo-Spotter-Reconnaissance (aircraft)
SAM Surface-to-Air Missile
SAP Semi-armour-piercing
SAR Search And Rescue
SLBM Submarine-Launched Ballistic Missile
SLEP Service Life Extension Program (US)
SSM Surface-to-Surface Missile
STO Short Take-Off
STOVL Short Take-Off and Vertical Landing
STS Special Treatment Steel
VB Bomber Squadron (US)
VDS Variable-Depth Sonar
VF Fighter Squadron (US)
V/STOL Vertical/Short Take-Off and Landing
VT Torpedo-bomber Squadron (US)
WOD Wind-over-deck
W/T Wireless telegraphy

*In these abbreviations, 'V' signifies 'heavier than air' in US terminology.